Strategies for Declining Businesses

Strategies for Declining Businesses

Kathryn Rudie Harrigan
University of Texas
at Dallas

LexingtonBooks
D.C. Heath and Company
Lexington, Massachusetts
Toronto

65945

Library of Congress Cataloging in Publication Data

Harrigan, Kathryn Rudie
    Strategies for declining businesses.

    Bibliography: p.
    Includes index.
    1. Industrial management. 2. United States—Industries. I. Title. II. Title:
Declining businesses.
HD38.H348   658.4'062   79-48032
ISBN 0-669-03641-2

Second printing, December 1980.

Published simultaneously in Canada.

Printed in the United States of America.

International Standard Book Number: 0-669-03641-2

Library of Congress Catalog Card Number: 79-48032

Contents

List of Figures
and Tables

Foreword

For three decades following World War II, economic growth occupied center stage. In truth, it became quite common to rank national economies, even economic systems, according to the annual growth rate of their real Gross National Product. Through the economic and business literature of the 1950s, the German "Miracle" became the shorthand definition for that country's abnormally high economic growth rate bordering on 8 percent per year, a record to be eclipsed in the 1960s by Japan's phenomenal growth rate of 11 percent.

Not surprisingly, business firms also began to use growth as a measure of success. Annual reports and annual board meetings began by comparing this year's sales with those of a year ago. Investment in capital equipment was guided by industry growth patterns and whole firms were acquired in order to gain footholds in growth industries. Professor William Baumol of Princeton University, in his *Business Behavior Value and Growth*, called for a restatement of the conventional theory of the firm to accommodate the new emphasis on growth. With ever-increasing economic activity assumed to be the norm, little or no analysis was directed toward the problems of business decline.

Kathryn Harrigan's impressive study of strategies for declining businesses goes far toward remedying this deficiency in the literature of business analysis. Her focus is on those factors that influence the strategies chosen by firms confronting declining industries. Her analysis is guided by two key hypotheses. First, the environmental features of declining industries differ; hence, company strategies for dealing with declining demand will differ. In her adopted terminology, endgames—strategies to cope with decline—will differ according to the variations in those factors making up the industrial environment. Second, even when the environmental factors are held constant, there may be no unique strategy for effectively dealing with a declining industry; that is, several business strategies might be appropriate for dealing with declining demand in a given industry environment.

Harrigan tests her hypotheses with empirical data obtained through extensive field work and questionnaire returns covering sixty firms in seven industries. The data tend to confirm those hypotheses. Of particular interest, she finds that within each industry environment, at least one firm managed to pursue a reasonably successful endgame strategy. Careful analysis of these particular strategies provides extremely useful insights into what might eventually turn out to be the critical ingredients of a generalized endgame optimizing model.

Business managers and students of business strategy will find Harrigan's analysis especially useful. It is refreshingly original in that it deals with an area of business management heretofore neglected. Further, economists and business analysts will welcome her findings as unusually timely and applicable to a business phenomenon of growing importance. If present trends offer a reasonably reliable clue to the future, the pace of economic growth in the industrialized countries is clearly on the decline. A logical consequence is that business firms will confront endgame situations much more frequently in the future than they have in the high-growth decades of the recent past. This book will greatly help business management to deal effectively with such situations. The distinctive merits of Harrigan's study in this regard were recognized in 1979 when it won the General Electric Award for Outstanding Research in the field of strategic planning, awarded jointly by the General Electric Company and the Planning Division of the Academy of Management.

Jesse W. Markham
Charles Edward Wilson Professor of
Business Administration
Harvard University

Acknowledgments

Funding for travel related to this research project was made possible by a grant from the Division of Research, Graduate School of Business Administration, Harvard University. The Board of Research, Babson College, supported preparation of the manuscript.

I would like to thank Jesse Markham, Norm Berg, and Michael E. Porter, all of Harvard Business School, for their assistance and support in this undertaking. Their ideas and criticisms helped me to clarify my own understanding of the subject of declining businesses. Michael Porter, in particular, suffered through many fragmented iterations of the manuscript and patiently guided my research.

I wish to acknowledge the skills of Sally Markham of Harvard University; of Jan Manter, Brenda Lumsden, and Victoria DelBono of Babson College; and of Linda Chianese and Wilma Oakes of The University of Texas at Dallas, all of whom prepared drafts of the manuscript. S. Prakash Sethi, the Center for Research in Business and Social Policy, and the Office of Sponsored Projects, all of The University of Texas at Dallas, also supported the final preparation of the manuscript.

Finally, I wish to acknowledge Rick Harrigan, without whose support this project would not have been completed when it was.

Strategies for Declining Businesses

1

The Problem of Declining Demand

What strategies are best for businesses in decline? Declining industries were once growth industries, but today demand for their products has been shrinking absolutely for a prolonged period. Which strategy alternatives should firms in such businesses consider? Because the resale market for a business's assets usually shrinks as industry demand declines, the most frequent strategy recommendation for this problem has been a "harvesting" procedure of reducing investment levels to generate higher cash flows from the business, followed by ultimate divestiture. Under which conditions might a firm be well advised to increase its investment in its declining business instead?

This study explores the complex competitive challenge of declining demand for the products of a firm's line of business. It investigates the nature of the determinants of a declining industry's environment (hereinafter called "the endgame environment") and the attributes of strategy alternatives appropriate for responding to industry decline, given the characteristics of that particular declining business environment. The study also considers how firms might choose among the strategy alternatives identified, seeks to match firms in different endgame environments with feasible strategies for coping with the problem of substantially declining demand, and suggests how to predict which strategies competitors might pursue.

Businesses operating within an endgame environment frequently face great uncertainty regarding the duration of expected demand for their products. Unlike the product revitalization problem (which has been explored elsewhere in "product life cycle"-oriented studies), demand for products within an endgame environment is expected, at best, to plateau at a substantially reduced level. At worst, demand for such products is expected to dwindle to a level which no longer justifies continued production or merchandising of the products by any former manufacturers.

The endgame challenge differs from that of revitalization in the following way. Analysis of the product revitalization problem proceeds from a perception that temporarily flagging demand for a product might be reestablished by finding new markets or new uses for the product in question. Analysis of the endgame problem proceeds from the basic problem of coping with substantially less demand for the products of such a business and possibly of prolonged industry-wide excess capacity where there is little hope for reestablishing consumption at its formerly high levels. It is the

1

problem of determining which firms should remove portions of their productive capacity from an obsolete industry and when their exits should occur. The study concentrates upon "product forms," which means that, although generic demand continued, it was satisfied increasingly by substitute product forms which were considered technologically, economically, or culturally superior to the products of businesses within large, diversified firms or of an entire firm in a single-business context.

Strategic Questions Concerning the Endgame

As competitors in these twilight industries recognize the coming demise of their investments, they ask important questions concerning their futures, such as: How can I maximize the opportunities presented by market decline? Does it pay for me to stay in this business and dominate it? Which rivals seem best suited to remain in this industry? When should I exit? Which exit barriers will be the most devastating to me in attempting to escape?[1] Which strengths will be most important to me for remaining in endgame? If I do stay invested, how should I compete?

The "product life cycle" literature which has discussed product decline has proposed strategies which treat all declining industries as if they behaved homogeneously in their decline. These studies seem to imply that all industries can offer equally rewarding (or unrewarding) opportunities within the endgame environment.[2] At their worst, they assume that the experiences of all firms within the same declining business environment will be similar.

Strategy research has not devoted much attention to the problems of declining industries. The literature discussing "harvesting" strategies[3] has suggested largely the same strategy for all declining industries and for most firms within them. These generalized treatments of the strategic problem of decline have ignored the differences between firms' corporate-wide strategic requirements and their internal corporate attributes. These treatments have also assumed that firms will respond to decline in the same ways.

Observation suggests that this is not true. All firms do not act alike in coping with declining businesses, nor should they. Similarly, industries which have differed throughout earlier phases of development do not shed their dissimilarities in decline. Most importantly there are several ways firms have coped with the challenge of endgame. A firm is not limited to harvesting, and may not want to harvest at all. Given a firm's strengths, its broader strategic needs, and the structural traits of its particular industry, some strategic alternatives for coping with endgame will be better suited to it than others. An objective of this study is to suggest a matching of appropriate strategies with the varying conditions of endgame.

Characteristics of a Declining Business

The product life cycle (PLC) literature has depicted business "decline" in terms of generalized truisms (which was necessary because it tried to aggregate industry behavior). It has suggested, for example, that market decline is usually accompanied by (1) reductions in the number of competitors; (2) narrower product offerings; (3) the abandonment of small customers and market segments; and (4) a reduction in competitors' promotional and developmental expenditures. The PLC literature has assumed that products have a limited life. During the decline phase it has suggested that all profit will disappear because competitors will use price reductions as a basis for competition. Advertising expenditures will be cut back. Research and development (R&D) investments will be eliminated. Product lines will be pruned and will revert to commoditylike (simple) differences among competitors' products.[4]

One of the principal uses of the product life cycle literature has been as a guide for analyzing trends in industry environments. But, to that end, it is flawed because its description of declining industries has been a homogeneous one. In decline, the PLC literature suggests that the market shrinks as buyer loyalties disappear and the cross-elasticity of demand grows higher. The degree of product differentiation is reduced. Prices fall closer to their costs. Marginally sized plants are shut down. Raw materials become less available. Transportation and distribution costs increase. Competitive structure, it suggests, will evolve (after the second shakeout) into an oligopoly.

The PLC's portrayal of competition in a declining industry, although accurate for some scenarios, does not consider industries where the behaviors of competitors have differed. It relies upon the behaviors of firms in a declining industry to be similar, assuming all competitors will interpret the advent of endgame in the same way and will, therefore, respond similarly. For example, the differences in the structural characteristics of endgame environments have been oversimplified. Distinctions have not been made among declining demands within different types of businesses which (1) serve different types of customers; (2) operate with different types of technologies; (3) use different ways of marketing their declining products; or (4) execute different types of competitive responses to declining demand and to other firms' actions.

According to the PLC's analysis, pressures to reduce costs become increasingly strong because of the growing price competition said to be endemic to declining industries. Excess capacity (due largely to plants which competitors will not close down) exacerbates those pressures to reduce prices.[5] If prices cannot be reduced because of rising labor costs or raw materials costs, then firms' gross margins will be smaller, or so the PLC literature has suggested.

This forecast is also oversimplified. There will be differences in the cash flow traits and profitability potentials of different declining industries. Within them all firms' prices and profit margins will not decline proportionately as demand declines because firms possess differing cost structures. Moreover, the prices of some firms' products will increase significantly, instead of declining. Differences in the product offerings and in the markets served will correspond to differences in the potential returns on investment available within various industries during their decline.

There has been little agreement among the authors who have written about the decline of business demand concerning the characteristics of the customers which remain in the market. This is a virtue in the PLC literature because, indeed, cusotmers in endgame do differ. Unfortuantely, the distinctions which the PLC literature has drawn regarding customers have not been very useful for strategy formulation. Previous discussions have not focused on the important differences among customer groups. Smallwood has suggested, for example, that these remaining customers are laggards or have specialized needs. Patton said that they are sophisticated and would see no differences among various competitors' product offerings in a declining industry.[6] Michael has suggested these customers are somewhat undesirable: old in age, conservative in nature, unreceptive to changes, and generally laggards in the diffusion process.[7] Some of these distinctions among customers in different declining markets could be important in analyzing the likely success of strategies which might be appropriate for particular firms to pursue. By overlooking these relevant differences among groups of customers, a firm could suboptimize in its endgame performance. It could be overlooking potentially rewarding strategy options within some industries by not serving these specialized pockets of demand.

Although some PLC treatments of declining businesses have recognized that there are exceptions to these cursory descriptions of industries, conclusions regarding these differences which would be useful for strategy formulation have been sparse. They have not gone far enough. For example, some declining products have been said to be exempt from the supposed "facts" of the life cycle's industry description because (1) they possessed patent protection; (2) they were in an industry where competitors were not inclined to compete vigorously for the shrinking patronage of their customers; (3) they have been advertised heavily to perpetuate the value of their brand names; or (4) a single producer holds the dominant share of the market which is declining.[8] Yet, despite these potentially useful descriptive distinctions, few alternative theories of strategy formulation which utilize the reasons for declining demand or these exceptions have been developed. Subsequent treatments of the product life cycle still have suggested that firms in a declining market would be able to serve primarily replacement markets, regardless of the reasons for product decline.[9]

Reasons for Product or Business Decline

The PLC literature has suggested that the primary reasons for product decline are (1) technological obsolescence; (2) competitors have advertised more heavily or have introduced a competitive product; (3) fashions or cultural values are changing; (4) the product is no longer needed; or (5) the product is "sick." Useful distinctions among these reasons for product decline and their relevance for strategy formulation have not been made in many discussions of the life cycle theory. They could have been applied to the analysis. They would have been useful distinctions, Levitt noted, because certain types of business declines could preclude the use of some strategy alternatives.[10]

Characteristics of the Strategies Suggested for Declining Industries

In the product life cycle literature, the strategy options suggested for declining demand have also been oversimplified. Where the process of demand has been assumed to be relentless, few strategic alternatives have been offered for managers.[11] The "divestiture" strategy advocates have argued that products whose primary demand has been replaced by technological substitutes are obsolete and could be divested soon.[12] The least efficient rivals, it has been suggested, will be forced to exit relatively early through competition, if not through choice.[13] Since excessive managerial time may be devoted to hopelessly declining businesses, divestiture has been a frequently recommended strategy for minimizing the unremunerative uses of managerial resources.[14] A framework which could be used in assessing which declining businesses are indeed "hopeless" has been lacking, however.

The advocates of the harvesting strategy have sometimes avoided making distinctions between low-growth and declining businesses by lumping them together in discussions of the problem of low-growth industries. There have been a few, infrequent studies which have at least acknowledged that there is a difference between these problems. Most of these treatments have come from the business press, not from scholarly journals.

Although a few of the treatments of the harvest strategy have acknowledged that the likelihood of success for a particular strategy will be a function of the firm's position and strengths prior to the execution of a harvesting strategy,[15] the distinctions they have drawn have usually been reduced to measures of market share. Indeed, market share has been the basis for several strategy formulation frameworks which purport to treat the problem of business decline as a part of industry evolution. But in the case of an analysis of declining demand, a framework which could identify which industries offered the greatest promise of benefits for having a sizable market share in decline would be more useful than a framework which compared generalized strategies for small market share companies with those appropriate for larger ones.

Kotler recommended harvesting a product if it would soon be obsolete or if management had a replacement ready. This prognosis ignored market considerations (for example, how substantial would demand likely continue to be for this product in the future?) and strategic considerations (is the declining product a part of a full-line or interrelated product offering?). Indeed, the only businesses Kotler has implied a "maintenance" strategy would suit are "strong cash cows."[16]

Several discussions of the product life cycle have recommended "revitalization" or "recycling" strategies as being an appropriate response to the problem of declining demand.[17] There has been some empirical evidence in scholarly journals (based upon simulations and studies of catalogs of manufacturers) substantiating the existence of the recycling pattern found in studying the sales patterns of some firms' products.[18] However, in many cases these were studies at the "brand" level, not at the "product form" level. Individual managers can often do little to halt the industry-wide decline for an entire form of products.[19] Hence these types of studies do not suggest how a particular manager should respond to declining demand.

Michael's discussion of the "product petrification" phase more closely approached what would be needed in order to match strategy alternatives with particular declining industries' traits. But it does not go far enough. Michael built a theory based on empirical study which suggested that a harvesting strategy would be generally appropriate where (1) the rate of decline of sales volume was not increasing and where (2) demand was somewhat price-inelastic due to high brand or product loyalty.[20] Closer analysis reveals that Talley's book about product management and Wasson's prescription regarding appropriate strategies at each stage of the life cycle were also advocating harvesting strategies, although they did not define the environmental conditions where such strategies for decline would be most successful. Fox identified some of the relevant structural determinants of endgame strategy formulation in his summary article about product management and the life cycle, but he did not match strategies to these factors. He only enumerated them.[21]

Thus, the major problem with previous treatments of strategies for declining businesses has been that there have not been any scholarly (or popularized) attempts to sort out the factors which influence the strategic choices managers will face. Cursory treatments of the environment of declining demand have been included as parts of studies of the product life cycle theory, but little, if any, analytical attention has actually been devoted to this problem. Popular business periodicals have contained the most informative articles about the endgame problem.

Where there have been discussions of the problem of declining demand, the shortcoming of these treatments has been that they looked at only one pattern of declining product or industry demand; they espoused only one strategy alternative for coping with declining demand. A simplified view of this problem is scarcely adequate for decision-makers' needs, however, because differences in the industry structures, the reasons for decline and expectations regarding future demand, and many other characteristics previously overlooked are too important to the development of an appropriate strategy for this environment to be ignored.

The Research Problem

Given these weaknesses in prior treatments of the problem of formulating strategies for environments of declining demand, there is a need for a study which distinguishes among the traits of declining business environments and which advances what is known about these strategic environments. There is a need for a study which probes beyond the single reason for decline, hence single strategy-type of treatment of endgame. Some empirical studies have suggested that the decline phase of a product class could conceivably last as long as the other combined phases of products' existences.[22] Were this an accurate observation for the phenomenon of declining industry-wide sales of a product class, the inadequacies of previous statements of this strategic problem would be magnified since they have assumed that an endgame is relatively short and bereft of interesting problems.

What is needed is a study of declining industries which recognizes that there are variations in environmental factors which may provide a key to competing successfully within an environment of declining demand. This study compares competition over the twilight years of several declining businesses, and contrasts the performance of firms within the same industry who managed different strategies which were each intended to maximize the value of their respective participations in endgame. The study also considers the reasons why other firms divested these businesses when challenged by product or market decline and seeks to develop a framework for analyzing the problem of strategy formulation in declining industries. To that end, such a framework is proposed in the following chapter, where generic strategy alternatives which might be appropriate for coping with the types of declining demand firms face are developed. The reasons for the decline of businesses and the importance of these reasons for strategy formulation are also amplified in that chapter.

The factors which should be considered in developing appropriate strategies for firms within environments of declining demand are traits concerning demand characteristics, the structural characteristics of the economic environment, and traits which pertain to the aspirations and qualities of the firm itself. These factors are

1. reasons for declining demand and the uncertainty surrounding decline;
2. industry structural traits;
3. corporate-wide strategic needs, exogenous to the endgame; and
4. possession of internal corporate strengths appropriate for the competition of the particular industry in question.

The validity of the framework which will be posited in the next chapter is tested using a hybrid research methodology that compared the experiences of many firms within several declining industries. The types of questions this study seeks to explore require testing of the relationships between strategies and environments where firms would execute these strategies. The prescriptions of previous discussions which have treated the strategy formulation problem of declining industries are, in fact, largely untested. That may mean, also, that little is known about how different firms have responded to the same problem. The methodology used to test the validity of the strategy alternatives proposed for endgame has incorporated the strategy formulation problem at this individual firm level.

The study's research methodology is positioned between the single-site observation and the canvassing of hundreds of firms which have weathered an endgame. In order to test the several classes of variables which are hypothesized to be important for endgame strategy formulation, several observations within several declining industries were necessary. Therefore, a type of cross-sectional field study design was developed to incorporate the differences among products, industry structural traits, and firms which could affect endgame strategy formulation, the details of which are explained in another chapter. Briefly, the problem of formulating appropriate strategies for declining businesses was explored using field studies which included (1) firms in declining industries (including those firms which had divested declining business units and the spun-off businesses); (2) their customers and suppliers; and (3) representatives of their trade associations. A combination of library research and quantitative analysis was employed to substantiate the findings of that study.

An Overview of the Endgame Strategic Study

Chapter 2 models the interactions among firms, their strategies, their environments, and the nature of declining demand for their products. Briefly, the range of different strategies which are appropriate is seen to derive from whether pockets of demand for the declining products will remain viable and whether customers will remain loyal for the products of a particular firm. The timing of a firm's exit is seen to be influenced by the industry's economic exit barriers as well as the firm's strategic exit barriers and expectations concerning future demand. The decaying of a resale market for firms' partially depreciated assets will impede exit. Other competing internal corporate needs for working capital or other assets will expedite firms' exit from the endgame.

Chapter 3 describes the study's research methodology. Sources of data are identified, the presentation of the data is explained, the type of data processing to be employed is described, and a summary of how the data will be used is presented.

Briefly, each industry study details the variables which are identified in the framework presented in chapter 2. The strategies of competitors within each sample industry are tracked and compared. The history of the endgame strategies and individual firm's performances within the endgame are then analyzed (using the framework developed in chapter 2). These analyses are collected and compared in a subsequent chapter which abstracts the common patterns of endgame behavior across the several industries studied, investigates their variances, and extrapolates meaningful changes likely to occur in industry endgames in the future. The implications of the study's finding are presented in a separate, concluding chapter.

Notes

1. For a discussion of the managerial implications of barriers to exit, see Michael E. Porter, "Please Note Location of Nearest Exit: Exit Barriers and Strategic and Organization Planning," *California Management Review* 19: no. 2 (Winter 1976):21-33.

2. See, for example, Donald K. Clifford, "Leverage in the Product Life Cycle," *Dun's Review and Modern Industry*, May 1965, pp. 62-67; or Walter J. Talley, Jr., "Profiting from the Declining Product," *Business Horizons* 7 (Spring 1964):77-84; C.F. Rasseveiler, "Product Strategy and Future Profits," *Research Review*, April 1961, pp. 1-8.

3. "Harvest" refers to the practice of using cash flows generated from mature businesses to subsidize the start-up cash consumption needs of new or growing businesses contained within the corporate "portfolio." For additional information, see Bruce D. Henderson, "The Experience Curve-Reviewed," *Careers and the MBA-75*, March 19, 1972; Patrick Conley, "Experience Curves as a Planning Tool," in *Corporate Strategy and Product Innovation* ed. Robert R. Rothberg (New York: The Free Press, 1976), pp. 307-318; Boston Consulting Group, *Perspectives on Experience*

(Boston: Boston Consulting Group, 1968). See also Philip Kotler, "Harvesting Strategies for Weak Products," *Business Horizons*, August 1978, pp. 15-22.

4. Thomas Staudt, Donald Taylor, and Donald Bowersox, *A Management Introduction to Marketing* (Englewood Cliffs, N.J.: Prentice-Hall, Inc., 1976); Philip Kotler, *Marketing Management: Analysis, Planning and Control* (Englewood Cliffs, N.J.: Prentice-Hall, Inc., 1972), chapter 12; Richard T. Hise, *Product/Service Strategy* (New York: Petrocelli-Charter, 1977); Joel Dean, "Pricing Policies for New Products," *Harvard Business Review*, November 1950, pp. 45-53; Chester R. Wasson, *Dynamic Competitive Strategy and Product Life Cycles* (St. Charles, Ill.: Challenge Books, 1974), p. 210; see also Theodore Levitt, "Exploit the Product Life Cycle," *Harvard Business Review*, November-December 1965, pp. 81-94.

5. E. Jerome McCarthy, *Basic Marketing: A Managerial Approach* (Homewood, Ill.: Richard D. Irwin, Inc.); Arch Patton, "Top Management's Stake in the Product Life Cycle," *Management Review*, June 1959, pp. 9-14, 67-79.

6. John E. Smallwood, "The Product Life Cycle: A Key to Strategic Marketing Planning," *MSU Business Topics* 21 (Winter 1973):29-35; Patton, "Top Management's Stake," p. 13.

7. George C. Michael, "Product Petrification: A New Stage in the Life Cycle Theory," *California Management Review*, Fall 1971, pp. 88-91.

8. Patton, "Top Management's Stake," p. 68.

9. David T. Kollat, Roger D. Blackwell, and James F. Robeson, *Strategic Marketing* (New York: Holt, Rinehart and Winston, Inc., 1972), p. 211; Albert Wesley Frey, *Marketing Handbook* (New York: Ronald Press, 1964), chapter 5.

10. Levitt, "Exploit," p. 87.

11. David J. Luck and Arthur E. Prell, *Market Strategy* (Englewood Cliffs, N.J.: Prentice-Hall, Inc., 1968), pp. 187-188; Walter J. Talley, *The Profitable Product* (Englewood Cliffs, N.J.: Prentice-Hall, Inc., 1965); for a different viewpoint, see John B. Matthews, Robert D. Buzzell, Theodore Levitt, and Ronald E. Frank, *Marketing: An Introductory Analysis* (New York: McGraw-Hill Book Company, 1964), p. 193; see also Levitt, "Exploit," p. 87; Wasson, *Dynamic*, pp. 6, 70; Kollat et al., *Strategic*, p. 211; David J. Luck, *Product Policy and Strategy* (Englewood Cliffs, N.J.: Prentice-Hall, 1977), chapter 7; and Kotler, "Harvesting Strategies," pp. 15-22.

12. Wasson, *Dynamic*, pp. 6, 70; Philip Marvin, *Product Planning Simplified* (New York: American Management Association, 1972); Donald K. Clifford, "Managing the Product Life Cycle," in *Corporate Strategy*, ed. Rothberg, pp. 61-68; Luck and Press, *Market Strategy*, pp. 187-188; Arthur Brettauer, "Strategy for Divestments," *Harvard Business Review*,

March-April 1967, pp. 116-124; Robert H. Hayes, "New Emphasis on Divestment Opportunities," *Harvard Business Review*, July-August 1972, pp. 55-64; Philip Kotler, "Phasing Out Weak Products," *Harvard Business Review*, March-April 1965, pp. 107-118.

13. R.S. Alexander, "The Death and Burial of Sick Products," *Journal of Marketing*, April 1964, pp. 1-7; Michael L. Johnson, "Pruning Products to Pad Profits," *Industry Week*, May 31, 1976, pp. 37-40; see also Theodore Levitt, *The Marketing Mode* (New York: McGraw-Hill, 1969), p. 32.

14. George F. MacKenzie, "Product Life Cycle Makes ROI Analysis Relevant, Can Tell You When to Run the Ads," *Industrial Marketing*, June 1971, p. 100; David J. Luck, *Product Policy and Strategy* (Englewood Cliffs, N.J.: Prentice-Hall, Inc., 1977), chapter 7, p. 75; Leonard Vignola, Jr., *Strategic Divestment* (New York: American Management Association, 1974); Jon G. Udell, *Successful Marketing Strategies* (Madison, Wisconsin: Mimir, 1972).

15. See, for example, Donald K. Clifford, Jr., "Managing the Product Life Cycle," in *The Arts of Top Management: A McKinsey Anthology* ed. Roland Mann (New York: McGraw-Hill Book Company, 1971), pp. 216-226. Compare this with Robert D. Buzzell, Bradley T. Gale, and Ralph G.M. Sultan, "Market Share—A Key to Profitability," *Harvard Business Review*, January-February 1975; Sidney Schoeffler, Robert D. Buzzell, and D.F. Heany, "Impact of Strategic Planning on Profit Performance," *Harvard Business Review*, March-April 1974; Bernard Catry and Michel Chevalier, "Market Share Strategy and the Product Life Cycle," *Journal of Marketing*, October 1974, p. 29ff.

16. Kotler, "Harvesting," p. 16.

17. Nariman K. Dhalla and Sonia Yuspeh, "Forget the Product Life Cycle Concept!" *Harvard Business Review*, January-February 1976, pp. 102-112; Levitt, "Exploit," p. 87; Clifford, "Leverage," pp. 62-67; and Tally, "Profiting," pp. 77-84.

18. Rolando Polli and Victor Cook, "Validity of the Product Life Cycle," *Journal of Business* 42 (October 1969):385-400; William E. Cox, Jr., "Product Life Cycles as Marketing Models," *Journal of Business*, 40 (October 1967):375-384.

19. Ben M. Enis, Raymond LaGarce, and Arthur E. Prell, "Extending the Product Life Cycle," *Business Horizons*, June 1977, pp. 46-56.

20. Michael, "Product Petrification," p. 89.

21. Harold W. Fox, "A Framework for Functional Coordination," *Atlanta Economic Review* 23: no.6 (1973):8-11.

22. Polli and Cook, "Validity," pp. 385-400; Cox, "Product," pp. 375-384.

The Endgame Strategy Model: The Conceptual Framework

What are the alternatives for a firm facing endgame? There may be several strategies appropriate for firms facing an environment of significantly declining demand. Some of these strategies can be risky, however, because their execution could require reinvestment (for example, seizing market share, rather than surrendering it, requires cash). In order to retain one's position or execute one's maneuvers in endgame, special attentions from the firm's financial and production managers may be required. Investments in marketing programs or research and development may be necessary. These expenditures constitute one of the major risks of endgame: a firm could plow back its earnings and the value of these reinvestments could become "locked in" (that is, successful extrication of the investment may become impossible).

The Objectives of Endgame

If the firm stays invested, it seeks to be successful in recovering profits from the endgame. If a rewarding performance does not seem to be forthcoming, it might choose to exit, instead. In formulating a strategy for the environment of declining demand, the firm might use the economic abandonment value calculation to plan the timing of its exit so that (1) the discounted cash flows it could obtain by exiting (the assets' salvage values) equal or exceed (2) the expected value of net cash flows (valued before taxes and corporate overhead burden) which could be earned with these assets through continued competition. The relevant discount rate for valuing operating incomes would be the firm's opportunity cost of funds, determined by the alternative returns available from other uses of the endgame resources.

Because the market for undepreciated endgame business assets is dynamic and could deteriorate rapidly, the firm may seek to retain maximum strategic flexibility in order to dispose of its endgame investment easily when the realizable market valuation of its assets approaches this unstable criterion rate. The firm will likely be concerned about the shrinking resale value of its assets since this determines the investment value which could be salvaged at various times from endgame. The firm may find that it possesses value in its endgame assets (its plants or equipment) if they are relatively flexible, that is, if they can be used to manufacture other products. The firm may be able to recover some of the value of its past investments in brand names which could still generate some buyer demand, or in the value of its long-term customer contracts, its useful, proprietary technologies, or its other intangible assets. Many of these assets could be marketable to the right buyer if exit from endgame became necessary.

However, holding these assets is not riskless. Although the firm reinvests with the explicit expectation of being able to retrieve the value of the investment later through (1) sales of assets, (2) cash flows generated from the investment, or (3) benefits conferred upon other products in the firm's strategic portfolio, there is no guarantee that this value can be recovered. The endgame strategies which are sketched below should be considered against the backdrop of this precarious asset disposal problem.

What Are the Alternatives?

The strategies which observation suggests could be appropriate for a particular firm in endgame vary along a continuum by (1) the relative market share the firm seeks to attain and also by (2) the relative degree of asset commitment (or reinvestment) needed to maintain a particular strategic position. The strategies requiring reinvestment are particularly risky in volatile endgame environments. Firms undertake these risks to attain high expected returns. Although the risk of losing one's investment could deter new expenditures in endgame, evidence from these studies of endgame suggests that, under some circumstances, the risk of making them may be acceptable. Some firms which have undertaken this risk in the past have attained high returns. If other conditions within a particular industry setting seem to be "favorable" (as defined below), strategies calling for a continuing presence, including some reinvestment, could be advantageous for some competitors.

The degree of reinvestment which a firm is willing to undertake will be determined by its expectations concerning (1) the rate at which demand for its products will decline, and (2) which market segments will encounter deteriorating demand earliest. Logically, it may be suggested that there are five generic strategies for coping with declining demand. Each strategy will represent differing degrees of optimism regarding the duration of demand for a firm's products and differing amounts of reinvestments of assets into (or disinvestments from) the business. The variation in firms' expectations regarding demand characteristics will also suggest different expectations competitors will hold regarding the likely recovery of asset values and cash flows over the endgame. These strategies are:

Increase the Investment (seek dominance).

Hold Investment Level.

Shrink Selectively.

Milk the Investment.

Divest Now.

These strategies are explained below.

Increase the Investment

"Increase the Investment" means reinvesting in the endgame industry to attain market dominance. Cash flows into the endgame business in a maneuver which is intended to take advantage of a declining market situation to *achieve market leadership*. It means that the firm is willing to make a commitment to remain in the industry and to protect its long-range strategic positioning. It may mean making expenditures to ensure that the endgame environment (discussed below) does not become highly volatile. Although the firms which reinvested in such a business would expect to recover the value of their assets, they would be less likely to worry about short-term recovery because this investment posture connotes an expectation that higher rents will be attainable by the last firms in the industry.

A firm which pursued a strategy of "Increase the Investment" might acquire exiting competitors (or help competitors to exit sooner). The firm might seek to dominate its industry by investing in marketing campaigns or using other expansionary tactics in following this strategy. The firm might also exert price-cutting pressure upon its higher-cost competitors in the short run to rationalize the industry.

It would be expected that "Increase the Investment" would be a strategy option because there are likely to be pockets of demand which endure within some endgames. Firms which either already serve these markets or reposition themselves to serve these markets may find it necessary to undertake investments of the nature which have been described in order to obtain or to maintain a profitable and advantageous position in the endgame.

Hold Investment Level

"Hold Investment Level" means that some reinvestments are made in the declining industry to enable a firm to compete by continuing to use the same tactics it had formerly employed or to wait until some uncertainties regarding competitors are resolved. This is, in essence, a strategy of defensive reinvestment. It means that the firm has made a commitment to the industry to maintain the earnings power of its original investment. (The intent of this strategy differs, however. This is not a strategy of seeking and retaining dominance. It is a holding pattern.)

If a firm were to follow the "Hold Investment Level" strategy, it would be expected that the firm might match competitors' price changes and marketing expenditures, and would make maintenance investments in its plants to compensate for losses of operating efficiency. It would not make substantial reductions in the width of its product line nor would it shut down plants used to produce the declining product. It would be expected that "Hold Investment Level" would be a strategy which would be appropriate when (1) the firm was serving a market of loyal customers whose demand was unlikely to deteriorate; (2) when a firm possessed competitive strengths; (3) when the declining business was relatively important to the firm, and when the firm believed that there were good reasons why it wished to continue to compete, yet wished to avoid potential conflict with another deeply committed rival; and (4) where one of the firm's significant competitors had communicated a credible threat that it too intended to dominate the endgame industry. Then the endgaming firm might prefer to hold its market share level, rather than strive to attain dominance as well. Of, if the industry structural environment were not so encouraging for successful strategy implementation, but the firm was already heavily invested in it (and wished to protect this investment because the firm possessed a strong market position), it would be expected that it might prefer to hold its market share level by making maintenance reinvestments only. Also, if the firm could not ascertain with certainty how rapidly or in which market segments demand was shrinking most rapidly, it might prefer to delay until it could resolve its uncertainty by holding its market position and investment level, for the short term. In hesitating, however, the firm could conceivably lose some advantages by not better realigning itself strategically. Losses of this nature would depend upon competitive movements by the other firms in endgame.

Shrink Selectively

"Shrink Selectively" is a repositioning strategy. It means retrieving the value of investments in some parts of the market while reinvesting in other parts, if necessary. The object of the "Shrink Selectively" strategy is to get to the profitable market segments first and to create loyalties among the customers in these enduring pockets of demand. Because some niches of industry demand will continue to be profitable while demand for other uses shrivels, the firm's objective is to capture the desirable niches.

In order to pursue a strategy of "Shrink Selectively" a firm must perceive which downstream industries are *least* likely to convert to newer technologies or products and it must reposition itself to exploit the expected demand for the endgame products of these customers (perhaps by raising entry barriers around these niches before the other endgame customers have perceived these changes in the market).[1] It would be expected that a firm which chooses a "Shrink Selectively" strategy has some internal competitive advantages which it hopes to preserve. Although the firm may represent a small share of the market, its investment could be a major part of the firm's own assets (for example, it could be a single business firm). Thus, it may prefer to retain some part of its former markets by shrinking (exiting from other markets) rather than discarding entirely the advantages it had built up through years of competition.

In the strategies explained above—increasing the investment, holding the investment level, and selective shrinking—it has been assumed that acceptable returns are being earned on the endgame investments or that there is a credible likelihood that, by making these investments, acceptable returns could be enjoyed. Also, these are business strategies which it is expected are likely to be preferred where the firm's company-wide strategy calls for its continued presence in the industry—due to strategic barriers to exit, for example. Thus, it would be expected that firms would pursue relatively aggressive strategies to protect their commitments to the endgame where the competitors believed that they could enjoy the greatest rewards from continuing to compete and perhaps become the last surviving firm in their respective industry.

If an acceptable return on assets cannot be earned by remaining invested in the endgame business, a company may wish to exit. However, if the market for its relatively undepreciated endgame assets is depressed, yielding a return below what it could expect to earn by continuing its endgame, the firm may be forced to continue to compete until it has recovered more of the value of its investment through operations (and depreciation). In such cases, the firm may be relatively ill-equipped to compete as a lowest cost competitor (due to inefficient operating cost structures) and yet the firm may be locked into competition in the industry for an indeterminate time. In such situations, it would be expected that the firm may wish to "Milk the Investment," thus avoiding further investments in endgame.

Milk the Investment

"Milk the Investment" means retrieving the value of earlier investments. Cash flows out, not in. This is the "harvest" strategy.[2] It means that, although participation in the industry still yields attractive cash flows, the firm has made a commitment to depart from the industry as soon as (1) the salvage value of its assets equals the expected value of cash flows generated or (2) some other corporate criterion has been fulfilled. Thus, "Milk the Investment" connotes a draining of resources and cash without regard for long-run positioning.

Even the "Milk the Investment" strategy carries a risk that it may not be executed as desired. If uncontrollable external events force firms to shut down early, they will not be able to extract all of the "milk" they have invested in such businesses. The objectives of "Milking the Investment" are (1) to increase return on investment by surrendering market share, or (2) to funnel as much cash as possible into other projects as quickly as possible. Firms who intend to milk their investment need to keep these objectives in mind in order to execute this strategy because both suppliers and customers may exert pressures to keep the firm invested, even when it wants to exit.

Divest Now

"Divest" means "get out now." The objective of this strategy is one of prudent timing. As the earning power of the endgame business is shrinking, sell it before the asset values shrink too much. "Divest" could be a sale of business assets or an abandonment decision. It means selling the endgame business's assets to competitors, if necessary, or simply junking them in order to avoid sustaining chronic losses and to release committed cash (working capital) to other uses.

Different alternatives will yield differing payouts when executed in different industries. If the net cash receipts from other endgame strategies are no longer adequate when compared with the firm's opportunity cost of capital, divestiture from endgame is an appropriate option when other, more acceptable uses for the firm's physical and other resources exist.

Timing is a major concern in this strategy. Effective execution of the divestiture (or shutdown) strategy requires the endgaming firm to maintain a flexible asset position (one which will be relatively easy to liquidate) or a realistic assessment of the salvage value of its assets. Flexibility is the firm's critical consideration here because the skill with which a divestiture strategy is executed amid a rapidly deteriorating resale market can ultimately determine the profitability of a firm's endgaming venture.

Should the firm exit early? If competitors are acting in a manner which severely changes the expected earnings of the firm in operations or the expected future marketability of the firm's endgame assets, it would be expected that this strategy may be preferred. Timing is important in endgame if the firm desires to recover the value of its investment, particularly where the industry's structural traits constrain the variety of endgame strategies which might be feasible options. The objective of an early divestment strategy would be to recover upon exiting a substantial proportion of cash, equivalent to the expected cash flows of continued operations. Early exit is a strategy which would be motivated where there was a severe risk that other strategies—including "Milk the Investment"—were not expected to yield acceptable performances. If the firm can assess with reasonable certainty that the more promising traits in the industry have been eroded, it may be advantageous to "cash in" on its investment early.

Measurement of Firms' Performances in Endgame. It would be expected that firms which performed well in an endgame environment and exited could do so without (1) incurring significant losses and (2) without creating significant disruptions to their other business activities upon exit. It would be expected that firms which performed well in an endgame environment and which remained invested in the declining business would have done so while (1) earning above-average long-term profits in this business, and (2) while facing few doubts about their abilities to continue to prosper or to execute a satisfactory, nondisruptive exit in the future.

By contrast, it would be expected that firms which performed poorly in an endgame environment and exited would have suffered (1) substantial losses upon exiting and (2) considerable disruptions to their remaining business operations in doing so. It would be expected that firms which performed poorly in an endgame environment and which remained invested in the declining business at the time of the study (1) would have lost money repeatedly on the endgame business's operations and (2) were expected to be forced out of the endgame by losses or other forces.

In choosing the strategies which would be expected to be most appropriate for coping with significant declining demand, this study also considered that some firms which performed poorly in endgame were unable to execute an immediate exit. This fact exacerbated the poor performances suffered by other firms in those firms' industries. If competitors could foresee that a rival was locked in by such exit barriers, one would expect that they would have adapted their strategies for endgame accordingly by protecting themselves, perhaps by reducing the extent of their investments themselves to reduce their future potential losses.

It will be noted that the endgame strategies mentioned above offer a significant contrast to the PLC's homogeneous prescriptions. Incorporating the differences among competitors and endgame industries provides alternative strategies which are richer and more complex than a program of harvesting would suggest. Several strategies for endgame do exist and should be considered because the nature of firms' operating environments and other strategic variables differ. What are these variables which should be used in determining optimal endgame strategies? How do they affect the firms' strategy alternatives?

The Firm's Choice of Endgame Strategies

It would be expected that firms would pursue different strategies in end-game because (1) they pursue differing business-unit missions within their corporate-wide strategies; (2) they possess differing competitive strengths; and (3) the industry structural traits encountered in different endgames limit or facilitate the success of the various strategy options. Also, firms each perceive the ramifications of industry structural changes, the likelihood of resuscitated demand, or the implications of competitive events within the endgame industry differently because of the dissimilar strategic investments each firm may have made there in the past.

Differing perceptions will lead to differing strategic responses to decline. A firm will be more likely to respond to declining demand by favoring its historical tactics than by acting as the economics of the situation might dictate. For example, a firm which was a single-business competitor might be less willing to acknowledge that its total market was shrinking and might be more likely to continue to refurbish its plants and to invest in R&D than would a firm which was widely diversified. Thus, firms' expectations concerning the nature of decline will constitute a major determinant of the hospitality of the industry for continued competition because it will determine who tries to remain in the endgame.

The Endgame Determinant Variables

Firms will pursue different strategies in an environment of declining demand because:

1. There are different reasons for declining demand which will affect how long demand will endure, how slowly it will decline, and how large remaining pockets of demand (if any) will be. (As was explained above, firms' perceptions will differ regarding these factors and these differences will themselves influence which strategic choices they deem appropriate.)
2. Firms pursue differing business-unit missions within their corporate-wide strategies, hence the strategic needs of a corporation, exogenous to the endgame industry, could influence a firm's strategic decisions regarding endgame.
3. Firms possess differing combinations of competitive strengths and have used differing ways of competing, prior to the decline of demand. Based

upon these part investments in assets and strategic postures, some firms may be better suited to pursue certain strategies than are their rivals. They will be in a more favorable position to continue to compete.

4. The industry structural traits that determine the nature of industry evolution over endgame could limit or facilitate the likelihood of success for different strategy options. Hence, the nature of an industry's traits could increase the relative riskiness of continued investment in some endgames.

The framework outlined below assumes that the internal and external variables presented in table 2-1 should be considered in determining an endgame strategy for a particular firm. The presence of certain types of industry or corporate traits could make the recovery of a firm's asset values difficult, and it would be expected that an industry would be "unfavorable" in this study if its structural traits made the likelihood of executing the more aggressive endgame strategies successfully poor or unlikely, or if they made exit difficult and continued performance unrewarding. The influence of these industry traits upon endgame competition and

Table 2-1
Variables That Influence Endgame Strategy Formulation

Market (Demand) Characteristics

Reasons for declining demand
Rate at which demand is declining
Presence of pockets of petrified demand
Firms' expectations concerning demand

Industry Structural Traits

Product characteristics
Buyer characteristics
Supplier characteristics
Economic exit barrier characteristics
Factors influencing the volatility of competition

Needs of the Firm Exogenous to Endgame Industry

External strategic influences
Image maintenance goals
The "single-business" firm
Short-term reporting goals
Vertical integration constraints
Other strategic exit barriers

The Firm's Internal Strengths Relative to Rivals in the Industry

Financial advantages
Marketing and selling skills
Product design and engineering skills
Production advantages
Firms' perceptions of the reality of declining demand

performance is explained below. The influence of corporate attributes upon endgame strategy formulations, given these industry traits, is discussed in the following section.

Demand Characteristics and Endgame

All other factors held constant, the most important market characteristic which could determine the relative promise of industries' profitability would be the existence of pockets of enduring customer demand. Whether such demand endures is determined by the reasons for declining demand. Whether pockets could exist is determined by the inherent differentiability of the product.

It would be expected that the presence of pockets of demand would enhance the likelihood that firms which repositioned themselves correctly early could enjoy relative "staying power" within a declining industry and avoid "head-to-head" competition on the basis of price alone. Different pockets of demand will decline at different speeds, and therefore analysis of the nature of demand could suggest which niches will be most enduring.

Competitors' expectations regarding the duration of customers' demand for declining products in the future will greatly influence firms' competitive behavior within their respective endgames. Other factors held constant, it would be expected that if there is great confusion among competitors regarding the rate at which demand will decline and which pockets of demand will deteriorate most rapidly, if there is uncertainty (or disagreement) regarding the likelihood of revitalized demand for the product, or if demand is deteriorating slowly, then the declining industry environment would be more chaotic because firms would be less likely to shut down excess capacity or to exit in an orderly fashion. Then excess industry capacity could exacerbate price warfare.

If there is relative certainty regarding the rate at which demand will decline, firms can formulate their strategies in light of their relative strengths or their strategic needs. If there is mutual recognition regarding where demand will deteriorate most rapidly, it would be expected that, other things being equal, exits should be more orderly.

An important determinant of profitable demand characteristics is whether there is an enduring pocket of demand for the declining product. The endgame will be more promising if demand remains strong in some market segments after other customers' demand has abated. The nature of customer demand—whether it is for original equipment manufacturers (OEMs) or replacement consumption or both—will determine the price sensitivity of customers.

If the endgame product is sold to markets which may be slow to adopt substitute products, due to high "switching costs" or other reasons, it would be expected that the endgame industry will be more favorable than an industry where substitution is easy.

If downstream customers still use the endgame product for original equipment purposes, they may be more desirable customers because their demand for the product will not be as badly eroded until they discontinue the product. Even then, replacements for the endgame product may be needed well into the future. Therefore, if the endgaming firm believes that some customers' needs for the endgame product will endure, it may desire to position itself to serve that expected demand. If an endgame product is sold only as a replacement product in a market that experiences high switching costs, it would be expected that demand for the endgame product will be determined by the speed with which the technology used by the endgame product's markets is replaced. This condition would constitute a favorable endgame environment if the technology is replaced slowly.

An analysis of the nature of the declining demand may suggest (1) whether geographically remote or low-volume distribution outlets (the costlier customer groups) should be abandoned, and (2) whether too many models and too many market segments are being served. An analysis of which market segments will remain will suggest which particular customer market segments might be most remunerative to serve in endgame. This knowledge could direct a firm in shrinking to serve the most profitable pockets of demand while abandoning those customers which will be less profitable or more troublesome to serve in the future.

If firms can correctly forecast the speed with which demand for a product will decline, they will be in more advantageous positions to make the appropriate investments in their declining business units which would allow them to be the lowest-cost producers or to reposition themselves to serve those pockets of demand where consumption of the product will decline more slowly, if they assess that it would be desirable to do so. Therefore, it would be expected that the uncertainties (or certainties) of firms regarding where and how rapidly demand will decline would be important factors in forecasting the endgame's characteristics because of the influence these uncertainties could have upon competitors' hopes regarding demand for their products in the future and hence upon how competitors will try to compete there.

Reasons for Declining Demand

The PLC literature is unclear concerning the causes of decline. It appears to ascribe homogeneous causation to all declining industries. As has been suggested above, some variations in the reasons for declining demand have been identified in previous studies, but they have not been used to improve the analysis of this strategic problem.

The reasons for declining demand in a particular industry will have implications for the nature of competition in that endgame. It would be expected that if demand is declining due to technological change, the likelihood of successful revitalization will be lower than if demand declined for demographic reasons. Revitalization of demand would be most likely in a fashion-motivated decline (however, the waves of fashion demand may have more widely spaced peaks and troughs than the waves of demographic changes).

Endgames induced by technological change—by factors which have created substitute products (such as old-style commercial airplane propellers replaced by jet-propelled engines) or which have lessened the need for the endgame product (as in ironing boards and hand-held irons in a "permanent press" era)—could leave pockets of price-insensitive residual demand by users who would convert to new technologies slowly, or not at all. It would be expected that such an environment would be favorable because all competitors could recognize the technological obsolescence which had occurred and could phase out their productive capacity in an orderly fashion until the price-sensitive demand of the remaining loyal customers could be satisfied by the output of one company.

It would be expected that endgames created by demographic changes, such as a decline in the number of buyers (due to falling birth rates or other reasons for the mortality of customers), would be less likely to create price sensitivity as would the substitutes which would become available in an endgame created by technological changes. There would simply be fewer customers in an endgame due to demography, and it would be necessary to recover more dollars of profitable sales per buyer to perform at an acceptable level in such an environment.

If an endgame is created because a major customer industry (or occasionally a major supplier industry) has changed its technology—making it less compatible with the endgame business's products—or if the customer is suffering declining demand itself (as in millinery blocks, steam locomotives, or passenger train cars), the interrelatedness of the endgame firm's fortunes with those of the downstream industry could make successful endgaming more expensive because the firm may be obliged to keep its customers healthy in order to continue to sell its own products. Although (as will be explained below) not being vertically integrated in this case might afford the endgame business manager greater strategic flexibility, it would also be expected that it could multiply the number of uncontrollable factors he or she must monitor if the firm's continuing presence in endgame is to be viable.

In summary, the reasons for declining demand will suggest whether there is a high likelihood of revitalization of demand. The rate at which demand is declining will suggest the timing associated with maneuvers intended for use in a particular market segment (and hence will suggest which strategy alternatives are feasible during the time when demand is expected to endure).

The presence of pockets of petrified demand will offer at least one firm a justification for remaining in the endgame. If there is relative certainty among the competitors within a market regarding the rate and extent of the obsolescence of the endgame product, it would be expected that an orderly pattern of plant shutdowns would be executed in a manner that resulted in no major write-offs on their retirements.

Industry Structural Traits

The industry structural traits which determine the overall nature of competition in endgame and thereby the relative likelihood for success of the various generic strategy alternatives are (1) product traits, (2) buyer structure, (3) supplier structure, (4) economic exit barriers, and (5) the volatility of competition. Depending upon these traits, endgames can offer differing profit opportunities for firms invested in them.

Product Traits

If a product is differentiated, higher prices can be justified for certain product attributes, and different market niches preferring various product attributes are likely to exist. Endgame products may possess actual physical differences or perceived differences which have been created through firms' marketing activities. The longer products have been sold to customers, (1) the less proprietary the production process is likely to be, (2) the more like a "commodity" the products will tend to become, and (3) the greater the potential expense that would be expected to be required to continue to "differentiate" the product in the minds of its customers. Product differentiability is important for endgame strategy formulation because it represents a potential basis for carving out a niche of loyal customers. Other factors held constant, where a product has developed commodity traits—where the product is well understood by customers and several firms carry standard models of the product in their lines—it is expected that it will be more difficult to justify receiving a premium price for the endgame product. But where there are physical or perceived differences in product offerings which satisfy the preferences of existing customer groups, these differences could constitute loyal "niches" of customers which only a few firms (or only one firm) may have invested in serving. Other factors held constant, it is expected that the more intrinsic product differentiation which is possible, the greater the likelihood that customers might value more highly those products and services which have been produced for their needs and preferences and might be willing to pay a slightly higher price for them.

The way in which the endgame product is marketed can also suggest (1) to what extent the product is differentiable and (2) how important the downstream industries are in differentiating the endgame product to ultimate consumers (hence, how much bargaining power they could possess over the endgame firms). The way in which a product has been marketed can also suggest how costly continued competition in the industry is likely to be. If the endgame product *is* differentiable, then advertising, product and packaging improvements, and other promotional expenditures may be necessary in order to retain the advantages of product differentiation and to compete effectively. This will increase the stakes of endgame.

It would be expected that if the endgame product has been sold through channels where attributes other than its price have been emphasized as selling points to customers, then the product can be differentiated and the industry will be more favorable for prolonged participation than if the markets where the endgame product is sold used price discounting or other appeals which tended to erode a product's distinctiveness. When a product competes on the basis of price within the endgame, the differentiability of the product is substantially reduced. It loses its potential to be distinctive.

If an endgame product has been differentiated through patents, brand name identification, or good service records in the past, the firm may benefit by continuing to invest in the relative competitive advantages of these intangible assets. However, if the endgame product is indeed becoming "commoditylike," it would be expected that further investments in product differentiation activities may be futile.

Where a declining product is not differentiable—where there are no loyal customer niches—it would be expected that the lowest-cost competitors would enjoy the greatest relative staying power. If a product were to lose its perceived differences and relative desirability, this would be tantamount to destroying firms' differentiated customer niches. But reinvestments made in trying to preserve the differentiation of products which are developing commoditylike traits tend to be among the most costly and least desirable types of reinvestment requirements. (High required reinvestments, it is expected, will tend to precipitate firms' exits.) Therefore, it would be expected that one of the major determinants of how many types of strategies will be feasible in an endgame would be the differentiability of the endgame product. It would be expected that relatively undifferentiated endgame products would justify the existence of only a few firms unless price competition were an important part of endgame behavior. But if there were customer groups whose needs were substantially unalike, then several firms (each pursuing different strategies for endgame) could coexist.

Buyer Behavior[3]

Other factors held constant, downstream customer industries which exercise their bargaining power over endgaming firms will (1) reduce the profitability of the declining product for its producers and (2) possibly keep prices depressed (if the ultimate consumers are price sensitive). If a substantial proporiton of the value-adding product differentiation activity has been performed by the downstream industries in the past (for example, if the endgame product is complex, and demonstrations, explanations, or technical servicing have been necessary in order for the ultimate consumer to utilize the endgame products), customer industries which have provided these services will possess some bargaining power over the endgame firms. Where, by contrast, the differentiated image of an endgame product is largely the result of the endgaming firm's own efforts, it will have more bargaining power, although customers who control scarce shelf space may still be able to extract rents from the endgaming firm.

Analysis of the number and size distribution of the customers of an endgame firm will suggest what degree of bargaining power a particular downstream firm may possess over the endgame competitor. If a large portion of the sales volume of the endgame products of a particular firm are purchased by one or a few customers, those customers will become more important to the endgame competitor as total demand for its product decreases.

Customers will differ in their "intrinsic bargaining power"[4] and in their propensity to exercise it. If buyers are (1) sensitive to price or (2) know that they constitute a substantial portion of an endgaming firm's sales volume, these buyers might try to pressure the firm into making price concessions or into making reinvestments in the endgame industry for the customer's benefits which the endgaming firm would rather avoid. Therefore, it would be expected that the presence of a few powerful customers who used their influence over the firm in the past would increase the costliness for that firm of continuing to operate in the endgame if these customers chose to exercise their bargaining power over the firm to extract higher margins for distributing its products in a price-sensitive endgame market.

The familiarity of customers with the endgame product will suggest what degree of relative bargaining power the endgaming firms will possess over downstream user firms. Where the endgame product has been standardized (it will seem to be more like a commodity), the customer firms will better understand the bundle of attributes they are purchasing. Therefore, customer firms may seek price reductions by expressing an unwillingness to pay premium prices for a particular firm's "branded" commodity. But if the endgaming firm *has* established a strong brand or corporate image in the minds of its customers and if the endgaming firm's product still seems to be differentiated to these customers, the endgaming firm may wish to adapt its marketing tactics for the product to exploit whatever market advantages remain.

If demand for customers' products is also declining, these customers will become more price-sensitive when purchasing raw materials and components from the endgaming firms because they may no longer be able to pass on higher costs to their customers as successfully as before. It would be expected that price-sensitive ultimate customers would limit the ability of the endgame firm (and of its intermediate customers, the distribution companies, grocers, retailers, and so on) to raise its prices.

Supplier Behavior

Other factors held constant, it would be expected that where the endgame industry represents a substantial proportion of supplier firms' sales, suppliers will assist the firms which are experiencing declining demand if they possess the appropriate strengths to do so. If sales of the endgame product are important to supplier firms, their help in developing (1) higher quality, (2) faster delivery and turn-around times, or (3) other distinguishing attributes could be rewarding where the endgame product can indeed be differentiated.

If the endgaming firms are important to the upstream firms, it would be expected that an endgaming firm's suppliers may have invested working capital in it or they may have committed themselves to their customer's endgame through long-term contracts. (The objective of such contracts would be to give their customer a competitive advantage which would enable it to remain viable in its endgame for the ultimate welfare of the upstream industry.)

Endgaming firms could enjoy competitive advantages over their rivals if they possessed favorable, long-term raw materials contracts which gave them lower operating costs or access to superior raw materials. In other cases, endgaming firms may have invested in R&D to develop special inputs for their suppliers to use in preparing the appropriate raw materials for them.

Both examples imply that it may be to the mutual benefit of supplier firms to help their customers in the endgame. From these examples it also follows that an indifferent supplier group (or one which faces more attractive sales prospects elsewhere) could exacerbate the profitability problems of endgaming firms. If a large portion of the raw materials used to produce the endgame products is provided by such suppliers, those firms will become more important to the endgame competitors as other suppliers cease to supply the endgame firms. If suppliers know that they constitute a substantial portion of an endgaming firm's raw materials, these suppliers might try to raise their prices. Thus, the presence of powerful suppliers could increase the costliness of continuing to operate in the endgame, particularly if it is difficult or uneconomic for the endgame firm to backward-integrate.

Economic Exit Barriers[5]

Other factors held constant, it would be expected that the presence of high economic exit barriers would deter firms' timely exits and result in high opportunity costs being incurred. Economic exit barriers represent factors which will influence a firm to operate its assets even where it earns a subnormal rate of return on them. They can be the costs associated with eliminating a plant or the lack of a resale market for the plant and assets. Their effect is to keep excess capacity which should have been retired operating instead. In endgame, where there may be too little demand to sustain the presence of several firms, this problem can become particularly severe. The economic calculations used to analyze whether to discontinue investments which are not earning acceptable returns could advise retaining these businesses where the assets are relatively new and undepreciated until their value has been recovered in operations (through depreciation).

The economic valuation regarding whether a particular investment should be retained (the abandonment value calculation) compares the (discounted) expected value of continued, future operations (as the numerator) with the expected salvage or sale value available upon exit (as the denominator). If the disposal value of an asset will be low (due to the technological factors explained below), the calculation of whether to remain invested will yield a ratio which is greater than one (which would advise continued operations).

The factors which influence the "height" of economic exit barriers are predominantly characteristics which relate to the product's manufacturing technology: (1) capital intensity, (2) asset specifity, (3) age of the assets (the extent to which their value has been depreciated), and (4) technological or operating reinvestment requirements. If the expenditures for other types of investments—advertising, R&D, or plant improvements—were not expensed, they too could constitute economic exit barriers.

Economic exit barriers are important because they may deter the firm's timely exit from an industry where it may be suffering losses. Where the value of a firm's fixed and working capital investments will be difficult to retrieve it would be expected that high economic exit barriers would lock a firm into prolonged competition at unattractive returns in the declining business. Other things held constant, it would be expected that where exit barriers were high, competition will be more volatile among the "trapped" participants because their cost structures would encourage them to use price-cutting in order to fill their plants.

Asset Specificity

Although economies are often obtained by purchasing highly specialized assets, the specialized nature of such machinery or plants may make them more difficult for the firm to sell later if it desires to exit from a declining business. (This may be a part of the generalized flexible assets versus the specialized, low labor costs technology trade-off.) The use of specialized assets will increase the height of exit barriers.

A distinction must be made here between truly inflexible assets which have no other economic uses outside of the endgame business, and assets which *could* be used to manufacture other products if managerial resistance could be overcome. (This latter type of resistance could be a strategic or managerial exit barrier which will be discussed below.)

If an active resale market for highly specialized assets used in an endgame business existed, then asset specificity would not constitute a high exit barrier. In some declining industries, a firm may be able to sell used, specialized capital equipment which purchasers customize for other uses for more than its book value since good used equipment might be more desirable for other firms to purchase than new, untried machinery. If a firm's capital assets are truly unique to the endgame business, there will be no resale market or other way (other than salvaging the value of the metals in the equipment) to retrieve its value.

Capital Intensity

Other factors held constant, it would be expected that the presence of capital-intensive competitors will increase the likelihood that price competition may be used in endgame. Firms which operate large, capital-intensive plants may enjoy scale economies when they are fully utilized, but they will also likely have higher break-even volumes to attain to do so. A high break-even goal makes fluctuations in industry demand difficult for a large firm to weather in regular operations and makes fluctuating demand particularly disastrous for firms in endgame. Where there is less total demand for the declining product, pressures to cut prices to fill these plants will be strong. Thus, being large in a capital-intensive technology may not necessarily be to a firm's advantage in endgame, where the volumes demanded will be lower.

Technological Reinvestment Requirements

Other factors held constant, it would be expected that required reinvestments in a declining business will raise the height of exit barriers and may encourage firms to exit from the endgame. The effect of technologies which require sizable annual reinvestments (for maintenance or technological revisions) from previous years' earnings is to reduce the amount of cash which could be extracted from the business unit. Most endgame businesses are being sustained with a recognition that their continued operations will be finite. Hence, corporations are seeking to channel cash out of their endgame business and into other "growth" projects if they cannot exit immediately. If the business cannot be milked, immediate exit may be preferable. The strategy alternative "Milk the Investment" connotes a draining of resources and cash without regard for long-term positioning. It means retrieving the value of earlier investments. Cash flows out, *not* in. This is the harvest strategy.

Endgame businesses which require frequent reinvestments due to technological needs cannot be milked effectively. (Even the best cost accountants and managers would have difficulty in squeezing cash out of a business that needed massive infusions of cash to continue operating.) Firms which find their endgame businesses have developed such traits may wish to exit soon.

Undepreciated Asset Values

If a firm possesses undepreciated and unsalable, business-specific assets, it would be expected that so long as the business's operating return (before corporate burden) exceeds the opportunity cost of capital for the company, the end-game assets would not be scrapped. An economic analysis of the abandonment decision should suggest that the firm would be indifferent in the short run between exit and continued competition provided its variable costs were covered. Fixed, or "sunk," costs would, theoretically, not affect its exit decision. Because firms must report losses on disposal of assets, however, sunk costs do influence these decisions. They can constitute a strategic exit barrier. However, if the endgame business's plant space, personnel, or other resources could be used more advantageously in another venture, it would be expected that the value of prolonged endgaming would be reevaluated to reflect this opportunity foregone.

Economic exit barriers are created when businesses are sold and resold because the value of a firm's goodwill is recapitalized each time a business is resold. Then depreciation schedules start anew to reflect the change in company ownership. Thus, a caution should be extended to firms which might contemplate scaling another strategic group's "mobility barriers"[6] to serve an enduring pocket of demand. Although it is possible for a firm entering endgame to assess which niches of demand appear to be most profitable, the firm must also assess which of these niches will be enduring and whether expenditures which would be required to enter them will be justified.

Summary of Economic Exit Barriers

The danger in feeding cash to endgame businesses whose technologies consume cash or in repositioning a firm in endgame is that there is a great risk that the value of such investments will not be retrieved. Even in a relatively stagnant technology that needs an infrequent reinvestment of the cash it generates, there is a risk that some catastrophic event will not permit a firm to extract all of the value it was planning to recover. Reinvestments will create economic exit barriers which will deter a firm from exiting even when it is earning subnormal returns. Therefore, it would be expected that when reinvestments occurred, they would occur early in the endgame and would be well considered. Similarly, it would be expected that firms would consider the costs of exiting when they enter a business and make provisions for these costs to facilitate timely exits later.

Factors Influencing the Volatility of Competition[7]

It would be expected that price warfare or other forms of volatile competitive behavior would be more likely to occur in industries where there are several strategic groups (whose strategic postures are significantly asymmetric) which are competing for the same customers' sales in a shrinking market. It would be expected that, in a concentrated industry structure where there are few strategic groups, improved coordination of competitive activities due to clearer signaling devices would enable these firms to avoid head-to-head competition and therefore to enjoy a more profitable endgame experience.

Within an industry's boundaries, there could be several different groups of customers, each satisfied by different types of competitors. To an outside observer, all of these firms would be considered to be in competition with each other. But, in fact, there actually may be several groups of competitors, each serving slightly different groups of loyal customers, who do not compete against other such groups of firms. These groups of competitors would have different strategic postures, different ways of evaluating the importance of the endgame to them, and different ways of competing. Their strategic postures would be asymmetric.

When demand for the endgame product declines, sales volumes may be lower in some markets than in others. Then firms whose plants are large may seek to invade the markets of other strategic groups in order to obtain enough sales volume to keep their plants operating at economic volumes. When more than one type of strategic group tries to serve the same group of customers, the potential for a volatile competitive environment is magnified. The extent of this volatility will depend upon (1) the extent of the asymmetries among competitors representing each strategic group; (2) the ways in which each competitor has operated in its market, historically; (3) the external strategic influences of parent firms upon diversified firms; and (4) the size and density of firms within adjacent strategic groups, as well as the firm's strategic group.

Strategic Groups

The relevant competitive unit for analysis within the endgame is the "strategic group" which will loosely correspond to the number of market niches which the endgame industry can sustain. If customers will pay for different product traits, the presence of differentiable products will enable more strategic groups to occupy an industry than will a product which has or is developing commoditylike traits.

It would be possible for one firm to comprise a strategic group. It would also be possible that all firms in the endgame industry will have very similar strategic postures with respect to their endgame business strategies and be in the same strategic group. It would be more likely that firms will all adopt similar strategic postures and endgame strategies only in industries which cannot sustain niches of demand because the endgame product has "commodity" traits. Where the firms are very similar, their mutual dependence upon each other to avoid creating price wars or other volatile conditions would be more quickly recognized.

The differences among strategic groups operating within the same industry are differences in their competitive postures for serving their particular customer market. Past investments which these firms have made in developing these strategic postures define the "mobility barriers" which potential entrants would have to scale in order to invade a particular firm's market niche. Strategic groups could be defined in terms of significant variations in their relative positions along several of the following competitive dimensions: (1) their relative cost positions, (2) relative prices, (3) width of product line, (4) extent of brand identifications, (5) product quality, (6) technological leadership or specificity of assets, (7) extent of service offerings, (8) degree of financial leverage, and (9) backward or forward integration within the business.[8] It is necessary to monitor the behaviors of competitors in adjacent strategic groups as well as within one's current group when demand is shrinking because similar competitors may be forced to compete in earnest against each other in the endgame even if they previously have had no experience in doing so. It would be expected that competition within endgame industries which have had few strategic groups (or highly dissimilar groups which are unlikely ever to meet) and a relatively long history of competitive interactions within these groups would be less volatile than endgame industries which have the potential for dissimilar strategic groups to clash.[9]

The major competitors within an industry may be thought of as existing on a map which depicts their strategic grouping, the similarities in the customer markets they serve, and other significant differences in firms' strategic postures. Porter suggested that this mapping could utilize shapes to depict differences in strategic group and distance between shapes to depict similarities in their customers or target markets. If an axis were used to designate differences between key factors in a firm's strategic posture, then positionings along these axes could also be used to depict similarities and differences between competitors.[10]

During tne endgame, competitors which may be scattered apart on the industry map are forced by shrinking demand to contract and refocus their selling efforts upon the remaining groups of customers. Frequently this brings into competition those firms which had previously enjoyed a quasi-monopoly and which are unfamiliar with the dynamics of some of the new rivals' modes of competing.

If there had not been competition between firms from different strategic groups prior to the endgame, it would not be expected that their market interdependencies had been recognized prior to endgame. In such a case, when firms must compete for the remaining customers in an industry, they could misread each others' tactical signals and exacerbate the tensions of uncertainty concerning how each will compete in the endgame. It would be expected that, until their interdependencies were recognized, firms could inadvertently trigger rounds of price cutting or advertising wars.

It would be expected that each firm would bring to the endgame its most successful competitive techniques and use them, if they are effective, against other competitors. The nature of firms' asymmetries in competition could be forecast from analysis of firms' historical bases for competition. From these analyses, firms could evaluate which endgames would be turbulent and which endgames would stay tranquil. Firms could use these differences to analyze the likely dynamics of endgame.

Interactions of Structural Factors as They Will Affect the Endgame Environment

The endgame environment will be influenced by interactions of the structural traits of the industry: (1) product traits, (2) customer characteristics,

(3) supplier characteristics, (4) economic exit barriers, and (5) factors influencing the volatility of competition. By analyzing the influence of these factors' interactions upon the endgame and each other, firms could estimate whether an industry will be potentially favorable (or unfavorable) for continued competition.

Unfavorable Industry Traits

It would be expected that there would be relatively low promise of a rewarding endgame in industries where demand for the product would be declining rapidly, the substitute products would be absolutely lower in cost and would be perfect substitutes, and the switching costs to the new products would be low. Firms would be unlikely to earn acceptable profits when the product has been developing commoditylike traits, customer industries have been concentrated and have exerted their power to extract rents in the past, the ultimate customers would be price-sensitive, and suppliers would be indifferent to the difficulties of the endgaming firms because they could sell their raw materials to other markets as well.

It would be expected that firms would encounter difficulty in exiting from an unfavorable environment where the assets in the industry are relatively undepreciated, the assets are highly specific to the endgame, and the firm recently acquired the endgaming business. Economic exit barriers would create an unprofitable endgame environment when other firms have lower-cost technologies at any scale, the firm's technology has high cash reinvestment requirements, and other firms' endgame facilities are part of integrated complexes which utilize shared resources with other prosperous, growing businesses, and therefore they will be unwilling to exit, too.

It would be expected that competition would be "volatile" in an unfavorable industry environment because there would be several firms from strategic groups which are quite different from each other who would be entering the remaining markets for the endgame product easily, signaling is and has been poor in the industry, fringe competitors would use price-cutting tactics to fill their oversized and underutilized plants (or the firm in question is not a dominant competitor, itself), and many rivals are pricing below their costs because external strategic considerations will not let them exit.

Favorable Industry Traits

By contrast, it would be expected that there would be relatively greater promise of a rewarding endgame experience in industries where the product could be effectively differentiated and protected from some substitution by patents; the substitute product could not unseat the endgame product in all markets; some pockets of demand for the product would likely be enduring; there would be some hope for revitalized demand (on a lesser scale); switching costs to the substitute product would be high; downstream industries would be weak or the firm has dealt directly with its customers; and the firm has very favorable long-term contracts for raw materials.

It would be expected that exit would be relatively easy for firms to attain and competition would be profitable in a favorable industry because the industry assets would be fully depreciated; there would be a ready market for used assets; the assets would be easily converted to other uses within the firm; the firm's technology would not require reinvestments for maintenance or technological changes beyond regular operation costs; and the firm would be the lowest-cost competitor operating a plant that breaks even at a low level of utilization.

It would be expected that competition would not be volatile in a favorable industry because there would be few strategic groups; all firms would recognize their interdependencies with respect to the other competitors; all firms' parents would have other businesses which are more important to them than the endgame business; there would never have been a price war; and competitive signals would be clear and easily understood.

Although these descriptions are extremes to some extent, they illustrate the types of factors which would cause an industry setting to be considered favorable or unfavorable when using this framework for analyzing industries for endgame strategy formulation. Analysis of these structural traits (and the interactions between them) will suggest the potential for profitability in a particular endgame environment. The commitment of competitors to the endgame industry would be estimated by analyzing whether any strategic exit barriers will keep a firm locked into the declining industry even when its industry traits appear to be unpromising.

Strategic Needs of the Firm Exogenous to the Endgame Industry

Corporate-wide strategies could influence a firm's formulation of endgame strategies. The corporate-wide priorities may dictate that endgame businesses serving profitable market segments should be terminated. Corporate-wide strategies may keep a firm invested in businesses which instead should have been abandoned due to low earnings.

External Strategic Influences

In comparing endgame competitors, the strategic postures of their parent companies (if the firm is not a single business company) should be analyzed.

It would be expected that if parent firms competed in other, viable markets, there might be a tendency for firms not to fight as viciously in a dying market where they are dominant if they fear cross-hauling, that is, retaliation in an attractive market where they are not dominant.

It would be expected that where resources are shared, exit barriers might be created. If the physical assets of the endgame business were integrated in a plant with the productive assets of healthy businesses, there could be unforeseen costs in shutting down the endgame operations, from tearing out plumbing, fixtures, and machinery or from disposing of other assets associated with the shutdown endgame business. Also, land-use plans (required following the dumping of effluents) must be disintegrated for future planning. The cost of satisfying these exit obligations could constitute a costly exit barrier, as well.

Competitors within the endgame may share a plant, or equipment, or personnel with other parent businesses. They may promote their endgame products along with other viable products using a common marketing program or common distribution channels. The same suppliers may provide raw materials to several businesses within competitors' parent firms. All of these external strategic factors might deter a timely exit.

Image Maintenance Goals

It would be expected that, other factors held constant, a firm which valued the endgame business highly for image maintenance reasons would face exit barriers. A firm might be willing to weather short-term losses if the firm sought to preserve the accumulated goodwill of its distribution channels for other existing or future products. The firm might willingly offer and honor customers' long-term supply contracts to keep customers' goodwill in other related markets. The firm might also manufacture replacement parts long after the product design is obsolete to show good faith to customers. In addition to the above, an endgame firm might offer employment assurances to disgruntled labor unions when shifting assets between businesses due to contractual obligations or a desire to avoid losing the benefits of an experienced workforce. All of these factors connote strategic reasons to continue investment in the endgame in order to maintain the firm's good image elsewhere.

By contrast, analysis of the firm's identity and what it had expected to attain by entering the business which is declining may suggest strategic reasons to divest the endgame business unit early. For example, it would be expected that firms which acquired a declining business as a part of a larger merger (the intention of which was to obtain the assets and market contacts of a viable part of the business unit) would be among the first companies to shut down or divest a sick endgame business after other exit barriers are overcome.

The "Single Business" Firm

It would be expected that, other factors held constant, firms which are single business entities would face high strategic exit barriers. Unless its shareholders seek liquidity, an endgaming single-business company will face major exit barriers because divestiture for it would constitute dissolution of the corporate entity. It would also be expected that single-business competitors would act like industry "mavericks." Although some single-business firms may milk their endgame assets to generate cash for their diversification ventures, other single-business firms are more likely to (1) sell themselves to a stronger competitor or (2) bloody the entire end-game industry in a bitter endgame price war to regain lost sales volumes if it cannot move resources to another business venture smoothly. It would be expected that the single-business firm would be dedicating its full resources to endgame, and, if it has attained significant staying power in the past, it will be a highly committed competitor which could exacerbate the severity of losses which might be suffered by firms which cannot exit due to their intrafirm linkages or other strategic exit barriers.

Short-term Reporting Goals

It would be expected that, other factors held constant, publicity-traded companies which "manage" their balance sheets for acquisitions purposes (or other reasons) would be deterred from exit by the recognition of write-off losses on disposal of their endgame assets. Economic exit barriers constitute factors which can deter firms from making timely departures from endgame businesses for strategic reasons as well as economic ones.

If the undepreciated, hence unrecovered value of an endgame business's assets is a large percentage of the profits reported in a particular fiscal year, the "height" (deterrent effect) of the strategic exit barriers may be substantial. (If the anticipated write-off loss would be insignificant as a percentage of a firm's reported profits, the height of the exit barriers would be less.) If the resale market for the firm's assets is thin, and their undepreciated value is high, a firm may accept a lower return than the corporate opportunity rate through continuing operations (and perhaps accelerated depreciation) rather than abandon the obsoleted assets immediately and recognize the write-off loss.

Because the availability of capital for future strategic projects is frequently tied to the pattern of corporate earnings performance, managers may strive to attain a smooth pattern in reported earnings, even where it might mean retaining a declining business unit which is earning less than the opportunity cost of capital. Because write-offs lessen confidence in the solidness of management's judgment and erode the firm's attractiveness as a merger partner, as a floater of corporate debt or equity, or as a partner in joint ventures, it would be expected that the firm would delay divestment of a declining business unit if it were pursuing a merger in another industry.

Managerial Exit Barriers

Corporate reporting conservatism reinforces *managerial* exit barriers in some cases. Some managers would balk at writing off obsolete assets where doing so would make their unit's performance look bad. Managers recognize that small losses on an obsolescing operation carried over several years look less disruptive to investors than a large loss on the corporate-reported earnings per share measure in the single quarter of diversiture. Consequently, managers may "carry" an endgame business or simply "mothball" the assets to avoid creating serious-looking reporting losses. Managers' behaviors are influenced by the communicated goals of the parent and by the reward system.

Vertical Integration Constraints

If the endgame business were highly interrelated with other business units in the company—if the firm purchased its supplies internally from another division, for example—it would be expected that there might be pressures from these internal suppliers to continue to produce the endgame products within the firm if they were earning a high return on transferring the units internally and if they had no outside markets. Similarly, if the endgame business produced components which were important inputs to another business within the firm, it would be expected that the internal customers of the firm would try to exert pressures to keep the endgame business operating, particularly if the units were transferred at cost and viable outside markets no longer existed to provide these components.

In such cases, the contributions the endgame business could make to corporate-wide profitability through the benefits of vertical integration might offset the perceived seriousness of the deteriorating demand encountered for the endgame business's products externally. The market for the ultimate product in a downstream transfer, for example, may be highly lucrative. If that were true, then intrafirm linkages could keep the firm invested in an endgame longer than would be economically advisable if the endgame investment were evaluated alone using only quantitative analysis.

Other Strategic Exit Barriers

In summary, strategic exit barriers are factors such as corporate image, a vertically integrated corporate structure, reciprocity or internal transfers of products, complementary product lines and/or distribution systems, other shared resources, or other types of barriers which could deter a company's disinvestment from declining businesses. It would be expected that a declining business would be retained because perhaps (1) it supplied components to other internal businesses' products, (2) it was inextricably identified with the corporate image, or (3) it was a significant purchaser of the products of another business within the firm's diversified structure even when it earned subnormal returns.

It would be expected that the presence of strategic barriers could lock in firms' assets, preventing weaker competitors from exiting and thereby exacerbating the likelihood that the performances of other rivals who were better suited to continue in endgame would also be adversely affected. It would also be expected that strategic exit barriers could impede the divestiture of an endgame business due to external needs of the firm such as its position in other markets, its relationship with critical external customers, or for economic reasons such as the shared burden on an integrated manufacturing plant.

The Endgaming Firm's Internal Strengths Relative to Rivals in the Declining Industry

Any firm which intends to reposition itself in endgame—perhaps by scaling the exit barriers of another strategic group—must have internal strengths which are relevant for its particular endgame. It would be expected that successful endgame firms would possess some such internal advantages relative to their rivals. Frequently, these strengths have been developed as a result of investments undertaken by a firm earlier in the business's evolution, and will differ depending upon the endgame industry. The appropriate strengths will be determined by the type of substitute products which challenge the endgame product, and by the type of market niches which remain. A firm which desires to remain in endgame could determine where its strengths lie by analyzing industry traits seeming to be most important in endgame, as well as by reviewing the value of the firm's history of previous investments and earlier successful competitive tactics. The firm must compare itself with other potential lasting competitors in the endgame.

Financial Advantages

It would be expected that an endgaming firm would have to possess financial advantages when it repositions itself into a new strategic group in order to overcome that group's mobility barriers. These strengths could emanate from favorable treatment in the capital markets if the firm's performance has been good. The support a firm receives through vertical integration could also be an important financial strength to the firm in executing endgame strategies if economies are available through shared facilities.

Firms would also receive a relative competitive strength from the collecting of financial information which would be necessary in order for them to make an intelligent evaluation of the abandonment decision. If the data needed to calculate the firm's "divestment value" were routinely collected, the firm might be aided in executing a timely divestiture. The financial information used to evaluate such endgame strategies is the salvage value estimates for shutting down the business and the alternative source (cost) information for the value the market would charge for the services the endgame business had provided if its products were used internally.

Marketing and Selling Skills

It would be expected that corporate direct foreign investments could constitute a marketing strength if multinational links enabled firms to continue to offer the endgame products in other, emerging markets. Demand grows and deteriorates at unequal speeds in different parts of a global arena. Extant demand overseas could provide (1) export targets that could be serviced by existing operations or (2) markets to be served by transferring technologies and portable manufacturing assets out of the dying market.

If demand were still growing in overseas markets, the manufacturing assets of nonmultinational competitors might become available at bargain prices when these firms abandon their domestic endgame investments and wish to sell these assets. However, multinational linkages could also constitute strategic exit barriers when a firm wishes to exit from an endgame if the overseas business unit were treated as a part of an integrated system that could *not* be shut down. It would be expected that an important marketing strength in endgame would be the absolute cost advantage of brand recognition. Brand loyalty would create mobility barriers that could protect a firm from the invasions of other competitors. The costliness of imitating a successful brand's marketing program would likely be prohibitive in endgame.

Although a wide produce line would be a strength in some endgame niches (it can enable the firm to "lock out" other competitors when shelf space becomes more scarce), it would be expected that profitability per unit may increase if some of the less marketable designs and colors in a wide-line product offering were pruned. If the offering of a wide line of endgame products is truly a desirable strength, it would be expected that the firm should be able to extract some bargaining advantages from its downstream customers which would enable the firm to enjoy better cash flows for the service of carrying a substantial inventory of these products.

Product Design and Engineering Skills

Although the firm may enjoy its reputation as the "technological leader" of the industry, this is not the type of strength which would be perpetuated in a declining market with great advantage. Engineering expertise is costly and must be well applied in endgame. The most desirable types of engineering strengths needed for endgame would be an able team of technicians who could repair or recondition physical assets inexpensively when they malfunctioned or rebuild them for other uses which would make them less specific.

Production Advantages

The most important strength to possess in endgame is that of the lowest-cost technology. That position could have been obtained through previous investments in patents, proprietary production processes or skilled personnel, and ownership of a favorable location near raw materials sources critical for lower production costs. It would be expected that a very favorable raw materials contract would give firms strengths as well.

It would be expected that an efficient firm could forestall conversion to newer technologies in the short term during endgame by cutting operating costs and exploiting the advantages of organizational learning and technical improvements by specializing its operations, sourcing parts or assemblies, and narrowing its product line.

An endgame firm's physical plant could offer strengths if it were very flexible for other operations or could be sold easily (these would be strengths needed in making a profitable exit from endgame). If it reached break-even volume at a low level of capacity, this would be a production strength as well.

It would be expected that a firm which has treated its customers and suppliers well might be able to borrow short-term cash from one of these sources—customers or suppliers—for revisions in the endgame manufacturing assets or for working capital loans. Such assistance would enable the firm to operate its fully depreciated but servicable assets for years longer if needed for the benefit of these upstream or downstream parties.

Managerial Exit Barriers

Firms may appear to act as if they believed that demand was not declining for the endgame products, or that demand was declining more slowly than economic facts would indicate. For strategic reasons (such as the firm is dominant in the industry, or the business's plants have been important research centers throughout the history of the firm), managers may not shut down plants as quickly as other indicators would recommend. For managerial reasons (the company is the only employer in the region, or managers fear they will be sacked when their business unit is retired), firms might give the declining business unit more opportunities to recover from operating problems before deciding that a shutdown is necessary. Thus, firms will not behave homogeneously when faced with declining sales volumes.

The resale market for firms' endgame assets (hence the height of firms' exit barriers) will be determined by firms' expectations regarding the likely viability of different pockets of market demand. If participants' expectations differ, sales of assets to other competitors may be possible. (Early exits and sales of assets are more likely to yield the recovery of a substantial part of the asset values that were invested in endgame than a late sale because later the market will likely be flooded with assets. Earlier, few firms will have recognized the need to exit.)

There could also be differences in firms' perceptions of a competitive event. If firms expect that demand will revitalize, they may be less disturbed by what they perceive as being a temporary slump in sales activity than firms which believe that demand will not revitalize. Competition in the endgame could be hazardous for firms which do not value their endgame business highly in a strategic sense because they will have to compete against the highly committed firms which will very likely be among the last firms in an endgame. The propensity of these latter competitors to use price warfare to retain a substantial share of the sales volume will be higher than for less committed firms.

A Simplified Strategic Matrix

An abbreviated framework for endgame strategies which abstracts the factors identified as being important above is presented in figure 2-1. This ma-

	Possess Relative Competitive Strengths	Have Relative Competitive Weaknesses
Favorable Industry Traits for Endgame	"Increase the investment" or "Hold investment level"	"Shrink selectively" or "Milk the investment"
Unfavorable Industry Traits for Endgame	"Shrink selectively" or "Milk the investment"	"Get out now!"

Figure 2-1. An Illustration of the Hypothesized Relationship between Endgame Strategy, Industry, and Competitive Factors

trix summarizes the relationships hypothesized to be significant in coping with the challenge of a declining business. Figure 2-1 suggests which strategies are likely to be appropriate given endgame industry conditions and the firm's relative position of strength.

The third dimension of the strategic matix, strategic importance of the endgame business to the whole corporate entity, has been omitted to simplify this presentation. The interpretation of that axis of the matrix would make predictions regarding the timing of (1) firms' exits from an endgame business or (2) the implementation of tactics designed to reduce firms' investments in endgame industries.

The strategic matrix suggests that certain generic strategies are more likely to be successful depending upon the relative hospitality of the industry's structural traits, the firm's relative competitive strengths, and given the relative importance of the business in strategic terms. Interpretive examples of the strategy matrix shown in figure 2-1 are given below.

Endgames differ across industries, in part, because some firms' industry environments are more conducive to successful execution of several strategies in decline than others (these are the favorable industries outlined previously). Within these industries, some firms' initial positions are more advantageous for sustained competition in declining markets than others. It is possible that different competitors within the same industry could cope with the endgame successfully, but in different ways.

The volatility of competition within an environment of declining demand has been hypothesized to derive from the number of strategic groups competing to serve the same market segments and from the asymmetries of these groups. The requisite internal strengths needed for performances in a particular endgame have been hypothesized to be influenced by the nature of the product, the industry environment, and the competitive postures of the other firms in the industry.

It would be expected that the presence of favorable industry structure attributes would create an hospitable structural environment for the execution of strategies calling for some form of continued presence. In such endgames, competitors could undertake reinvestments in assets in order to reposition to serve niches of enduring demand more advantageously.

It would be expected that the absence of these favorable traits or the presence of traits which are unfavorable would create a more hostile environment that would not encourage reinvestments in the industry. A prolonged presence within such an inhospitable environment could be risky for the ultimate success of firms which seek to retrieve the value of their asset investments from the declining business. It would be expected that firms' performances within an environment possessing unfavorable traits would be relatively poor.

The determination of these different characteristics—whether an endgame is a favorable environment or not—is based upon the framework using the industry structural analysis summarized previously. If a business is strategically important, it may be retained longer than the abandonment value analysis might suggest would be advisable. Then the more aggressive strategies for endgame would be considered feasible (assuming that they are executed in a timely manner).

"Increase Investment Level" (Gain Dominance)

If a firm is either (1) quite cost-efficient in producing the endgame product, (2) clearly identified as the industry "leader," or (3) sells a branded, well-accepted, or patented product, and has other corporate strengths, for example, in an industry which has (1) relatively low exit barriers, (2) few "maverick" competitors, or (3) a low rate of technological change by users, or other favorable characteristics, then the firm might consider the strategy of "increased investment" provided it is willing to make the necessary investments to support this strategy choice. Taking this risk could be quite rewarding if it is executed correctly. For example, a firm may be the lowest-cost producer of an obsolescing component which forms the foundation for very expensive, necessary testing equipment, and it may also be safely entrenched in its profitable market niche, pursuing a strategy which would be quite costly for its competitors to imitate. By purchasing the assets and proprietary product lines of rivals which are more eager than it to exit (by increasing its investment levels) and by adding such product lines to its own, a firm could conceivably erect mobility barriers and dominate the price-insensitive replacement market for those components, thereby extracting profits which would justify this aggressive strategy of "Increase the Investment Level."

From the firm's perspective, a favorable industry would be one where it would not be difficult to exit (if it were necessary to do so) because markets for its assets exist elsewhere, where it would not be difficult to respond quickly to competitors' maneuvers, where substantial reinvestments of earnings were not required, where competition was not on the basis of price, but rather where leadership could be attained instead through patents, brand loyalty, or other absolute cost advantages, and where demand was shrinking only in those market segments which the firm did not service, or at a slower rate in those segments where the firm *did* compete.

"Increase the Investment" could be an attractive strategy for a firm if a significant part of the firm's assets were committed to the endgame given that (1) the structure of the industry seemed favorable for it to recover the value of its investment later successfully and (2) the cash flows expected from continued participation were acceptable for the company. (However, given this context, the firm may wish to divest its endgame business immediately, instead of competing, and thus cash in on its dominance.) The most aggressive, hence the riskiest form of this strategy would be to "Increase Investment Level" by trying to invade other competitors' niches of loyal customers. In addition to good products and effective distribution systems, financial strengths would be needed if the firm wished to reposition its strategic posture in this manner. It would need to purchase whatever assets or intangibles constituted the mobility barriers of other successful strategic groups. Because of the risk involved in not recovering the value so invested, such an aggressive strategy would not be executed (even by firms possessing financial strengths who are very confident that such a venture would be successful) if industry traits or demand seemed to be unfavorable. A less risky way to achieve this posture might be through the acquisition of the assets of an exiting rival since the former act (building *new* capacity) would probably create higher economic exit barriers than would the latter tactic. (This assumes exiting competitors would sell their assets cheaply.) Helping competitors to exit can help the firm itself to achieve dominance.

"Hold Investment Level"

Holding the investment level in endgame would be an appropriate short-term strategy only when the industry's structural traits constituted an hospitable environment, for example, where its customers were price-insensitive, the firm operated at lower costs than its competitors, its brand was well differentiated or sold on long-term contracts to customers (which were either loyal to the product or bound to consume it by contract), and its suppliers were helpful in terms of financing terms, deliveries, and other services, or were a part of the firm's vertically integrated structure, and where the firm itself possessed the appropriate competitive strengths. Even if the firm occupied a particularly profitable niche within an otherwise unfavorable industry environment, there is always risk that the firm would be unable to recover the value of its investments in pursuing this strategy which calls for maintenance reinvestments in the endgame business. If the firm cannot convert its posture into one which appears to be largely favorable, immediate exit might be preferable.

"Hold the Investment Level" is a posture of waiting—for a stronger firm to exit, for a market niche to resolve its uncertainties, or for demand to revitalize (or clearly decline) in the markets the firm serves—and in the long run it is expected that the firm will either reposition itself to be dominant in the more promising markets or will retrieve its investment and exit. Firms which are locked into the endgame by exit barriers must be wary of this strategy. Unless these firms believed demand would revitalize in their markets or that they could gain some other advantage by remaining vital in this manner, a firm should not make the maintenance investments this strategy connotes. Like the strategy "Increase the Investment," this is an aggressive strategy which could be costly if the firm misestimated the potential profitability of the niche of the market it had sought to secure.

"Shrink Selectively"

It is expected that firms which are not in the strongest competitive positions within favorable industries might select a specialized, lucrative group of their customers to serve, and divest or shut down their other products and plants used in the endgame business. If the firms possessed competitive strengths and their businesses were important to them, "Shrink Selectively" might be an acceptable strategy even in a relatively unfavorable industry environment if there were niches of loyal customers which could be profitable to serve.

The successful execution of this strategy requires an assessment of the different market segments in an industry in order to assess whether there are profitable niches which could be served advantageously. It would be expected that firms would find it desirable to shrink down to niches where the buyers are not price-sensitive, do not have relative bargaining power, or do not choose to exercise their intrinsic bargaining power. It would be expected that a profitable niche might also have (1) rapid turnover demand (generating large cash flows), (2) good potential for creating "mobility barriers" (insulating it from crossover entries), and (3) a strong likelihood that demand in the niche could be prolonged because customers, who are using models of brands of endgame products sold by "adjacent" competitors (for example, Farina), would convert their taste preferences or applications to use products produced by the niche firm (in this case, by changing to Cream of Wheat) when the adjacent rival firms exited. Therefore, "Shrink Selectively" means redeploying assets to conserve a strong position in profitable niches, while releasing assets (disinvesting) in other, less desirable market segments.

It would be expected that where declining products are undifferentiated, the strategy "Shrink Selectively" would be foreclosed as an option to competitors (unless it were a multi-plant producer of the endgame product). If there are pockets of demand and the firm possesses some relative strengths but the industry has (1) relatively high fixed costs, capital-intensive technologies, or high exit barriers; (2) many maverick competitors who lapse into periods of cutthroat competition; or (3) if the endgame product is rapidly developing "commodity" traits, for example, then a strategy of shrinking to occupy a profitable niche may not be efficacious. A strategy of "milking" the investment to extract as much value as possible before demand deteriorates too much might be embraced instead because the outlook for profitable competition is relatively diminished.

"Milk the Investment"

It would be appropriate to "Milk the Investment" in industries where the firm assesses that its future in the industry will be limited. Firms may reach this conclusion because there do not seem to be enduring pockets of demand and the industry's structural traits seem unfavorable for continued competition, or firms may decide to milk a declining business that seems promising and hospitable because they do not possess the appropriate strengths for continued competition but cannot sell their assets. Where attractive alternative investments exist, and where the corporation needs cash to develop these new ventures, even a promising endgame may in fact be harvested early.

Some endgame businesses may be retained although their profit performance is lower than the corporate-wide criterion rate because they throw off good streams of cash. (In privately held firms, businesses may even show accounting losses while generating this cash flow.) Where an endgame business's assets are old and are fully depreciated, it would be expected that the endgame business would be retained until industry conditions deteriorated for the funds it could generate if the technology of the business did not need substantial reinvestments of cash.

"Milk the Investment" is a prevalent strategy in industries where firms find they face exit barriers. But if strategic exit barriers are also high, the relative staying power of rivals will *not* be determined merely by their inabilities to absorb short-term operating losses. Undepreciated, but obsolescing, unsalable and highly inflexible capital assets may lock rivals into prolonged endgame with potentially disastrous consequences. Therefore, it is particularly important to consider whether stronger competitors will also be locked into the endgame when analyzing strategies which might be effective.

Divest Now

Essentially, each firm competing within an endgame will strive to make the best of its performance, but, if industry conditions are *too* unfavorable for it, the firm will face increasing pressures to exit. If the firm lacks the relevant strengths and the industry is not particularly favorable for endgaming either, the strategic outlook for its endgame becomes rather bleak and the strategic framework suggests that the firm should sell its assets and get out of endgame as quickly as is feasible. Timing is crucial in executing this maneuver because other firms may be reaching a similar assessment. For that reason, the firm should prepare for the day when it must exit, perhaps by using its reserves to cushion the effect of an exit where the physical assets are undepreciated or time its exit to coincide with the recognition of gains from other assets which may be sold in order to cushion the effect of the large expected reporting losses. If downstream customers are powerful and seem to desire a continuing source of the endgame products, a firm may wish to try to sell its declining business unit to a strong customer or to a competitor in order to exit quickly.

Tactics for Managing the Endgame Strategy

The relative success of the firm in endgame will be determined by its experiences there. If the firm has exited in an orderly fashion without write-off losses or disruptions to other corporate businesses, it has exited successfully. If the exit occurred following a period of volatile prices and if a loss on disposal resulted, the firm's endgame experience was less likely to be successful. It would be expected that there will be some advantage (in favorable industries where the business unit has possessed competitive strengths, and where the firm is willing to reinvest some resources) in being able to commit oneself to an intelligent strategy, in the face of uncertainty, before one's rivals sort out the problem of endgame. Although it may seem desirable for the firm to wait to see what happens in the endgame before selecting an action plan, it would be expected that waiting could be suboptimal. It would appear that the firm cuts off the option of the strategic extremes (the increased investment and the early divestiture options) and their corresponding promises of profitable performance by waiting.

As demand shrinks, it would be expected that there would be adequate demand in endgame for only a few competitors to satisfy. If the industry signaling devices were effective, if a firm could communicate its binding commitment to the other rivals *early*, it might be able to preempt competitors from occupying the most desirable niches of customers. It may be able to signal in an unambiguous fashion that it intends to fight bitterly to retain this niche, once occupied. The firm may even be able to avert unwanted bloodshed if the industry consensus were (1) recognized among rivals and were (2) considered important to maintain for the mutual profitability of the participants.

This means that if a firm wishes to "dominate" in endgame, it appears to pay to *start early*. If one intends to "divest," it means that one would want to sell out before asset values drop too precipitously. Although some desirable cash flows could be enjoyed by firms in some endgames, there is empirical evidence also that other competitors have suffered losses in these same industries by not understanding the interrelationships of the forces in this environment as they affect the success of the firm's endgame strategy.

It is suggested that the endgame strategy selected should consider the industry structure and demand characteristics as well as the competitors and the internal characteristics of the firm under study. By recognizing the basic patterns which match strategy alternatives with these variables, the firm could better select and execute an optimal strategy in industry decline. Successful implementation of endgame strategies will require timely commitments and informed tactics. The risk of erring could be formidable. In practice, managerial exit barriers make implementation of endgame strategies difficult. Overcoming these exit barriers is a part of the challenge of managing a profitable endgame.

Notes

1. Richard E. Caves and Michael E. Porter, "From Entry Barriers to Mobility Barriers: Conjectural Decisions and Contrived Deterence to New Competition," *Quarterly Journal of Economics*, May 1977, pp. 241-261; Michael E. Porter, "Market Structure and Firm Profitability: The Theory of Strategic Groups and Mobility Barriers," Unpublished paper presented at the Marketing Science Institute Symposium, June 1977.

2. The author has benefited from exposure to the concepts contained in Catherine Hayden, "What Is a Harvest Strategy?" (Staff Paper, Strategic Planning Institute, July 1977).

3. The author has benefited from exposure to the concepts contained in Michael E. Porter, *Interbrand Choice, Strategy, and Bilaterial Market Power* (Cambridge, Mass.: Harvard Univ. Press, 1976), in developing this section.

4. M.E. Porter, "Buyer Selection," Course Note: Industry and Competitive Analysis, Harvard Business School, January 17, 1978.

5. The author has benefited from exposure to the concepts contained in Michael E. Porter, "Please Note Location of Nearest Exit: Exit Barriers and Strategic and Organizational Planning," *California Management Review* 19, no. 2 (Winter 1976): pp. 21-33; and R.E. Caves and M.E. Porter, "Barriers to Exit," in *Essay in Industrial Organization in Honor of Joe S. Bain* ed. Robert T. Masson and David P. Qualls (Cambridge, Mass.: Ballinger Publishing Company, 1976), in preparing this section.

6. The author has benefited form the concepts contained in Richard E. Caves and Michael E. Porter, "From Entry Barriers to Mobility Barriers," *Quarterly Journal of Economic*, May 1977, pp. 241-261; and M.E. Porter, "Market Structure and Firm Profitability: The Theory of Strategic Groups and Mobility Barriers" (Unpublished paper presented at the Marketing Science Institute Symposium, June 1977), in preparing this section.

7. The author has benefited from exposure to the concepts contained in Michael E. Porter, "Structural Analysis within Industries" (Unpublished manuscript, Harvard Business School, December 1977); and M.E. Porter, "The Structure within Industries and Companies' Performance," *Review of Economics and Statistics*, May 1979, pp. 214-267, in preparing this section.

8. For a more complete discussion of the differences between competitors, see M.E. Porter, "A Framework for Assessing Competitors" (Unpublished manuscript, Harvard Graduate School of Business Administration, October 1977).

9. There is support for some of these observations in the works of M.S. Hunt, "Competition in the Major Home Appliance Industry, 1960-1970" (Ph.D. diss., Business Economics Committee, Harvard University, May 1972) and H.H. Newman, "Strategic Groups and the Structure-Performance Relationship: A Study with Respect to the Chemical Process Industries" (Ph.D. diss., Business Economics Committee, Harvard University, December 1973). See also H.H. Newman, "Strategic Groups and the Structure-Performance Relationship," *Review of Economics and Statistics*, August 1978, pp. 417-427.

10. Porter, "Market Structure and Firm Profitability," 1977.

**Methodology of
the Endgame
Research Study**

The study's central hypotheses are that thé environments of declining industries differ, and that structural differences among industries are a central reason for these variations. Because the environments differ, there will be different endgame strategies. These hypotheses can best be tested by observing the experiences of a large number of different firms who managed declining businesses and by exploring the effects of industry structural traits upon endgame competition.

The rationale of the study's research design proceeds form three interrelated assumptions which are based upon empirical studies. These underlying assumptions are as follows:

1. There are and have been several business strategies which might be appropriate for coping with declining demand within a particular industry environment.
2. The declining business's industry structural traits define the endgame environment, and hence they influence the selection of strategies which might be appropriate for coping with declining demand.
3. The presence of differences among each industry competitor's perceptions, its strategic needs, and its internal corporate strengths suggests that, within the range of strategy options which might be appropriate for a particular industry endgame, different firms will choose different endgame strategies.

The major emphasis in the research design was placed upon evidence of persistent patterns of relationships among structural environmental traits, competitive performances, and endgame strategy decisions. It examined the experiences of fifty-two firms within seven industries.

Selection of the Sample

Although this study's framework argues that many traits are important to endgame strategy formulation, it would have been difficult to encompass all of these traits in a sample design. The characteristics which were selected for inclusion in the sample taxonomy are the central structural ones which correspond to the framework developed in the section describing the endgame paradigm. These traits are:

1. Concentration (number of competitors).
2. Potential for differentiation of the endgame business's products.
3. Height of exit barriers.

Figure 3-1 illustrates the cells which comprised the research sample.

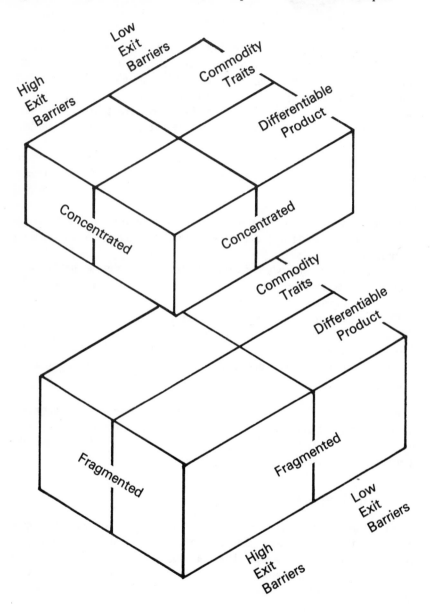

Figure 3-1. A Taxonomy for Classifying Endgame Industries

Industries were selected to conform to a taxonomy contrasting (1) high exit barriers (capital-intensive technologies and undepreciated, business-specific assets) with low barriers; (2) concentrated industry structures with fragmented ones; and (3) endgame products having differentiable traits (branded product strategies) with products having commodity traits. The sample design facilitated exploration of the influence of different corporate strategic postures upon competition while holding the environmental context constant. Moreover, the taxonomy focused upon *observable* traits of endgame businesses. The seven industries comprising the field research study are shown in figure 3-2. (An eighth industry, U.S. leather tanning, which was also studied is not contained herein.[1])

Summary and Comments Regarding the Field Research Study

The philosophy underlying the field research design was a desire to explore the variations in endgame strategy from the objective perspective of a diversified parent company in a manner which would incorporate the firms' strategic considerations outside of the endgame business as well as the manager's considerations inside the declining businesses. Yet, because the insights of some of these decision-makers might be subject to some biases due to their closeness to the problem, several replications of the interviews for each industry were considered to be necessary. The observations of parent corporations, customers, and suppliers, as well as industry trade

Concentrated Industries

Relatively High Economic Exit Barriers	Relatively Low Economic Exit Barriers	
Vacuum Receiving Tubes	Synthetic Soda Ash	Commodity Traits
Rayon and Cellulosic Acetate Extrusion	Baby Foods	Differentiable Product Traits

Fragmented Industries

Relatively High Economic Exit Barriers	Relatively Low Economic Exit Barriers	
Acetylene	Leather Tanning	Commodity Traits
Cigars	Electric Percolator Coffee-Makers	Differentiable Traits

Figure 3-2. A Taxonomy of the Industries Whose Members Were Interviewed in the Endgame Research Study

association representatives, were useful in cross-checking and abstracting the factors which may have led a firm to embrace a particular type of strategy in endgame.

The philosophy underlying the presentation of the data (in subsequent chapters) was a desire to segregate factual data from interpretations of them. The data are subject to certain limitations (which are explicated below). Therefore, the study has strived to maintain objectivity by not intermingling its findings with analytic treatments of them. The industries are traced from a touchstone or "Base Year" that facilitates cross-sectional comparisons. The integrating comparisons of the industries and competitors are presented separately from the data to facilitate an unprejudiced evaluation of the hypotheses.

A Description of the Data

The data are presented in the form of miniature industry studies, and include a qualitative analysis of the competitive activities within each of the seven endgames as the last part of each of these industry studies. A detailed background report regarding the structural characteristics of each sample industry and of firms competing during the base year (defined as a year prior to the endgame) was constructed for each of the seven sample endgame industries. A summary of the year-by-year competitive activities of each competitor within each industry during the endgame (the years from the base year to 1978) details how competitors responded to declining demand. An endgame competition chronology comprises the second section of each industry study. An analysis of the effects of the principal categories of variables believed to influence endgame strategy decisions—demand, industry structure, competitors' strategies and strengths and their resulting performances—follows in each data presentation chapter.

Limitations of the Data

The study of strategies for declining businesses examined a complex set of hypotheses using a cross-sectional research design and field studies as a means to gather the data. Its findings will have to be subject to numerous qualifications because of the disparity of the industries examined. The confidences with which conclusions could be stated in this study will necessarily be reduced by the strong element of judgment which will be needed in evaluating the findings as well as in describing a complex factual situation. Therefore, the data from this study will be handled with a lower degree of confidence regarding their generalizability than those of other empirically based research programs.

Note

1. The U.S. leather tanning industry endgame is described in K.R. Harrigan, "Strategies for Declining Businesses" (D.B.A. dissertation, Graduate School of Business Administration, Harvard University, 1979).

The Endgame in the Electronic Receiving-Tubes Industry

A receiving tube is an active electronic component capable of transmitting, detecting, and amplifying wireless electric signals. It is used as a key component in radios, television receivers, communications equipment, audio amplifiers, and many other electronic products. Receiving tubes had been the first electronic components and had been the basis upon which the modern electronics industry had been built. However, in the base year 1966 receiving tubes competed with transistors (invented in 1947) and integrated circuits (invented in 1958) for use in electronic devices.

Demand for receiving tubes had reached a second "peak" in 1966, with booming color-television set sales providing the major impetus. In this year, 282,677,000 receiving tubes were consumed for original-equipment (OEM) applications while 123,272,000 units were consumed for replacement purposes. By 1976 OEM consumption had declined by 98 percent (to 5,827,000 units); replacement demand had declined by 51 percent from the base year.

In general, the receiving-tube endgame was relatively "easy" in the sense of ease of extracting the value of firms' investments. Although competition had been fierce in earlier years of this endgame due to import competition in the OEM market, the later exits of competitors enabled the remaining receiving-tube manufacturers to exploit the relatively price-insensitive demand of the replacement-tube users. The endgame price ceiling on receiving tubes then became the "switching cost" of junking tube-technology electronic devices and adopting solid-state devices instead.

A Description of the Receiving-Tubes Industry

The Product

In a receiving tube, a metal filament or "cathode" was heated by electric current and emitted a stream of negative electrons which leaped across a vacuum to the positively charged anode or plate. The receiving tube was sometimes called a "vacuum tube" because of this vacuum. A grid or wire screen between the filament and plate controlled the flow of electrons by varying a small negative charge on the grid which tended to pass or repel the negatively charged electrons. Tubes had connecting pins for plugging them

I am indebted to Michael E. Porter for his technological assistance in revising this chapter.

59

into "sockets" in the electronic device to be powered, and each variety of tube had its own unique socket.

By 1966 the technology of receiving tubes was quite mature. While firms such as RCA held patents on some general-purpose receiving-tube designs, competitors could easily design around these patents and create a tube whose performance was equivalent. Receiving-tube manufacturers "cross-engineered" the tube designs of its competitors in order to have tubes which would be interchangeable. As a result, receiving tubes of competing manufacturers were essentially identical, though there were some specialized applications where proprietary technology was present. Receiving-tube technology which had been developed by RCA had been licensed to foreign electronics firms which had subsequently competed against the U.S. industry.

Markets

Receiving tubes were sold to a variety of markets, including OEM's, government, franchised independent dealers, other tube manufacturers, and private-label sellers. Each of these markets possessed somewhat differing characteristics, and receiving-tube manufacturers utilized strategies of careful market segmentation to preserve those differences.

The OEM Market. Receiving tubes were used by manufacturers of television sets, radios, audio components, instrumentation, and many other electronic products. Tubes were specially designed to meet the needs of OEM customers of significant size, and were manufactured to order in large volume. As a result, the inventory requirements for serving the OEM market were small. Television sets, and to a lesser extent radio receivers, represented the primary markets for tubes in 1966. Both industries were relatively concentrated. RCA held approximately 35 percent of the TV market in 1966, followed by Zenith at 20 percent, Motorola at 10 percent, GE at around 10 percent, and GTE Sylvania and Westinghouse with less than 10 percent each.

The receiving tube represented a small unit cost and relatively small proportion of the total value of the products in which it was a component, but its integrity was crucial to the operation of these products. So as a result, quality was critical and extensive inspection and testing characterized tube manufacturing. Price competition in receiving tubes had not been severe until the market entry of Japanese tube producers in the late 1950s.

Manufacturers sold to OEMs through their own sales forces, offering engineering assistance, special test data, and extensive service. The tube manufacturers with the best reputation commanded a slight price premium. Many large users of receiving tubes manufactured a significant proportion of their needs internally, particularly the major television-set producers. In addition, tube manufacturers sometimes purchased tubes from one another to fill out their lines in the case of low volume or especially costly proprietary tubes.

The Replacement Market. Replacement tubes for repairing electronic products were another important market for receiving tubes. There was a propensity to replace burned-out tubes with the tubes of the same manufacturer, if available, which created strong competition among receiving-tube producers to be designed into customers' sockets in the OEM market. Because of the proliferation of tube varieties for different OEMs, tube manufacturers often had in excess of 1,000 different varieties of tubes in inventory. Manufacturer investment in inventory to serve the replacement market was substantial in view of the need to provide good service and to stock these many varieties.

The demand for receiving tubes in the replacement market can be likened to the demand for spark plugs if, next year, diesel engines were mandated in all cars. Because all drivers would not purchase a new car with a diesel engine next year, there would still be a continuing demand for spark plugs due to the "switching cost" of replacing a useable automobile. Some switching costs associated with changing from receiving tubes to solid-state technology were similarly prohibitive.

For example, the cost of replacing a receiving tube in a television receiver would have been approximately $15; the cost of replacing the receiver itself would be $170 to $250. Some of the government communications equipment was twenty to thirty years old in 1966. Unless there were a technical or strategic reason to switch to solid-state equipment, even the military users of entertainment-grade tubes were reluctant to spend $50 million to do so when a few $7.50 receiving tubes could keep their equipment operating. Thus the demand for tubes was expected to be enduring.

Replacement tubes were sold through a number of channels. Most were sold through either independent or company-owned distributors to the thousands of dealer-affiliated and independent repair shops for electronic products. These same outlets often sold other products or components made by the receiving-tube manufacturers. Brand name and quality reputation as an electronics producer was critical in the independent service market, and there was substantial advertising of tubes both to service persons and to distributors.

Independent distributors were franchised and typically carried one major receiving-tube line and a secondary line to hedge against stockouts. Receiving-tube manufacturers employed sales forces to sell to their distributors and cultivated them with discounts off list prices, bonuses, trips, and favorable credit terms. Manufactuers often financed significant portions of the distributor inventory of their tubes in the form of accounts receivable.

There were two other markets for replacement tubes. One was to OEMs who had their own service organizations, such as Zenith. Tube-manufacturer brand name was less important in this market than in the independent servicing market, and OEMs often purchased U.S.-made or Japanese tubes with their own brand placed on them to lower costs. This was a part of the "private-brand" market. The other market for replacement tubes was to private-brand sellers of electronic products who had their own service organizations, such as Sears and Montgomery Ward. The market for these replacement tubes was known as the private-brand replacement market.

Governmental and Industrial. A limited quantity of receiving tubes was sold to government and industrial users for specialized applications such as communications equipment, process control equipment, weapons, and so on. These applications often required higher-grade technology and/or higher-fidelity tubes than so-called entertainment-grade tubes sold in the mass market.

The early 1960s was a period of rapid growth for receiving tubes because of the geometric growth in the use of tubes in color-television receivers. Radio receivers, the major user of receiving tubes in the 1950s and earlier, had contained five tubes or less. A black-and-white television set would use nine or ten receiving tubes, however, and a typical color-television receiver used twenty-three tubes in 1962. As color-television designs evolved, sixteen or seventeen receiving tubes were common in 1966. Later, hybrid solid-state-and-tube television receivers used five or six tubes. Hybrid solid-state and tube-television receivers were transitionary devices using both types of components. The first receiving tubes which were placed in hybrid televisions were the technologically simple tubes. It took a longer time to develop solid-state substitutes in some of the more complex, entertainment-grade receiving tubes.

Foreign Competition

Japanese companies had entered the U.S. receiving-tube market in the late 1950s, with a strategy of very low prices. Japanese manufacturers concentrated on the OEM market, which required low levels of inventory. Imports of Japanese tubes had grown rapidly since that time.

Japanese manufacturers had concentrated primarily on the high-volume OEM and private-brand replacement products and on the technologically simple varieties of tubes. There had initially been resistance to Japanese tubes due to lingering resentments from World War II, but as U.S. receiving-tube prices rose and Japanese tubes improved in quality, Japanese penetration began to occur. Japanese tubes were sold at discounts of up to 20 percent of the prices of domestically made tubes, but Japanese manufacturers provided little customer support or engineering assistance. They typically reverse-engineered domestic manufacturers' tubes. Japanese penetration of the independent service-replacement market had been due to the lack of distribution and dealer relationships.

Suppliers to the Receiving-Tubes Industry. Receiving-tube manufacturers used a great variety of materials, many of which were fabricated to meet their particular technical specifications. Some of the suppliers to the receiving-tube producers were small businesses which supplied a single crucial component to the receiving-tube manufacturers.

The receiving-tube producers themselves fabricated some of the other components used in their manufacturing operations. The major firms specialized in producing various low-volume components which they sold to each other. Most of the receiving-tube companies were partially backward-integrated. They drew their own wires and made some of their own parts. But backward integration could be costly and reduced flexibility. Major firms purchased their bases and bulbs from other sources such as Corning Glass Works or from other competitors which were backward-integrated into producing the particular components which were needed.

Manufacturing Technology of the
Receiving-Tubes Industry

The production process for making receiving tubes was relatively simple. The major steps from beginning to end included (1) fabrication of raw materials, (2) placing these components on structural jigs which held the materials in relative proximity to each other, (3) welding these pieces onto a base, and (4) sealing the assembly in an evacuated glass envelope.

Many receiving-tube manufacturers drew their own wires and produced their own cathodes, which were the rods which heated up in the receiving tube. Some receiving-tube plants wrapped their own grids and manually positioned them for welding operations. Other plants shipped their components to offshore plants for assembly and welding operations. In other offshore plants the raw-materials components were also fabricated.

The most critical assembly operation was the spraying of the cathode, a wire-wrapped nickel or other metallic rod. The cathode was sprayed with a special electron-generating coating. The cathode-spraying operation required crucial measurements and quality control. It determined the quality of the rest of the tube.

The "cage" of the receiving tube was assembled by placing the wire grids and wire-wrapped cathodes onto mica bases where they were welded into place. The glass envelope was shaped from glass tubes (usually purchased from Corning Glass Works) and was mounted and sealed. Gasses were then evacuated from the sealed chamber.

Most of the fabricating for receiving-tubes operations were labor intensive, though final assembly was done by machine. Quality control and meticulous testing were the keys to the consistent quality, and skilled labor was necessary for portions of the manufacturing process. The labor force for most receiving-tube manufacturers had been in place for several years. Receiving tubes were assembled inside factories which were clean and dustless to avoid any contaminating particles that could result in a malfunction. Plants frequently had work surfaces covered with tiles or parqueted hard wood. The tube-assembly operation was carefully supervised in these "clean" surroundings, but even then some technical difficulties occasionally occurred in the production process. Though manufacturing was relatively standardized, there was a certain element of "black magic" involved in producing tubes. There could be a run of defective tubes for unaccountable reasons, and this meant that extensive inspections were necessary.

By the mid-fifties, most producers of receiving tubes were making them on automated assembly lines. An efficient facility cost a minimum of $12 million in plant and equipment, and manufacturing receiving tubes also required significant investments in automation that had been, and continued to be, made by the major producers. Economies of scale increased significantly in the 1950s and 1960s.

Receiving-tube manufacturing shared few, if any, operations with the production of other electronic components or devices, and equipment for fabrication, assembly, and testing of receiving tubes was highly specialized. Each variety of receiving tube which was produced required a separate set-up on the assembly line. Economies could be enjoyed by producing long runs of various tube types, and the set-up costs necessitated runs of at least 10,000 units of a given type of receiving tube to break even. Since some tube designs broke even at such a high volume, tube-makers often sold to each other to round out their product lines. Direct and indirect labor were the major production costs in making tubes, comprising approximately 40 percent of the total. Materials costs were second in size. A substantial amount of testing and measurement equipment was also required as part of the manufacturing process for quality control. The savings involved in an offshore plant or a "feeder" facility could be substantial in receiving-tube production, given the high labor content.

Receiving-tube plants were free-standing buildings which could be converted to other uses. Although it would have been possible to convert these old, multi-story plants to transistor production, this practice was infrequent. Plants were more frequently converted to other mechanized operations or were torn down instead.

Economic Exit Barriers in the Receiving-Tubes Industry. The physical plants associated with receiving-tube manufacture did not constitute economic exit barriers because they were relatively well depreciated. Only those companies which had invested in automated processes recently were likely to face write-off losses on disposal of their receiving-tube business assets.

The relevant economic exit barriers in the receiving-tube business were created by working capital. Specifically, a receiving-tube corporation could destroy the distribution-channel goodwill it would need to distribute its solid-state devices later by acting imprudently with respect to tubes. The inappropriate timing of a firm's efforts to recover its inventory and accounts-receivable assets could erode or destroy the goodwill it had developed. For example, the receiving-tube inventory was relatively illiquid. It frequently contained over 1,000 different types of receiving-tube designs in order to provide good service to firms' distributors. Recovering these asset values by working off the inventory could require several years since some of the inventory turned very slowly. But selling the inventory in a lot size could cut off a firm's franchised distributors. A portion of a firm's accounts receivable were tied up in their distribution channels in the form of financial deposits. These working-capital assets were less collectible because any attempt to collect them could injure a distributor.

*A Historic Overview of the
Receiving-Tubes Industry*

Thomas A. Edison first noticed, in 1880, that a small metal plate or wire placed at the base of an evacuated glass-enveloped lamp became charged when the filament within the bulb was heated to incandescence. By the 1920s there were over 150 manufacturers of nearly 300 brands of receiving tubes who sold them to 150 to 200 manufacturers of radio sets. The major manufacturers of radio were RCA, General Electric, Philco-Lansdale, Atwater-Kent, Majestic, Emerson Electric, and Crosley. The receiving-tube producers of the 1930s included many "Ma and Pa" operations as well as some larger firms, including Sylvania, Ken-Rad (later General Electric), National Union, Raytheon, Westinghouse Electric, Arcturus, Hytron Electric (CBS), Philco-Lansdale, Johnsonberg Tube Company, Tung-Sol Electronics, and RCA Corporation.

Radio consumption of receiving tubes had plateaued by World War II; radio had become a mature product. However, postwar television production needed even more receiving tubes. Thus the industry thrived as television was commercialized.

After World War II, under the reconstruction policies of the U.S. government, receiving-tube manufacturers gave their technology to the defeated war powers. As a result of this technology transfer, the Japanese industry had developed to the point that exports became a significant factor by the late 1950s. Raytheon had sold its technology and some of its assets to Nippon Electric Company (NEC) in 1963. This enabled a Japanese producer to make a technological leap in matching the quality of U.S. tube producers. After NEC had done so, other Japanese tube producers learned to produce American tube varieties. By 1966, receiving-tube prices had dropped 40 percent since pre-Japanese times.

Substitute Technology. In 1948, two American Telephone and Telegraph employees at the Bell Laboratories discovered the transistor effect and subsequently described it in a research paper. Texas Instruments was among the first companies to try to commercialize the transistor, the first generation of semiconductors. Semiconductors or "solid-state" technology had inherent advantages over the receiving tube for most applications, including greater reliability, longer life, and ultimately lower cost.

In military markets, and other markets where extreme reliability and performance were crucial, solid-state technology was adopted while it was still quite costly. Receiving-tube use peaked in 1955 as transistors replaced receiving tubes in high-technology applications. In entertainment markets, cost was a primary consideration and penetration of solid-state devices was much slower.

In 1956, the year after the historical peak in receiving-tube consumption, some transistor manufacturers had predicted that half the TV sockets using tubes would be lost to transistors by 1961. Engineers at major TV producers like Zenith, Philco, Magnavox, Emerson, and the RCA Television Set Division recognized that solid state was inevitable once cost and reliability improved, but had predicted at this time that tubes would be in use for another ten to fifteen years. By 1966, solid-state technology had not been commercialized as quickly as had been expected by many observers, and a fully solid-state TV was not yet commercially feasible. However, in 1966, TV manufacturers were in the process of converting to a solid-state TV chassis.

The first firms to manufacture solid-state components were firms such as Texas Instruments, Transitron Electric Corp., and Hughes Aircraft. These were among the top five semiconductor devices producers in 1957, and none had produced receiving tubes. The production techniques involved in making transistors were completely different from those required in receiving tubes, although semiconductors were sold through the same basic distribution channels as receiving tubes.

In 1961, CBS and Philco had exited from receiving-tube production as well as television-receiver production. In that same year, General Electric closed its Scranton, Pennsylvania, receiving-tube plant and moved the plant's assets to the old Ken-Rad plant in Owensboro, Kentucky. The following year, General Electric closed its Anniston, Alabama, receiving-tube plant. It donated the building to the community and used the write-off for tax purposes. RCA closed its Indianapolis plant.

Despite the advent of solid-state technology, in 1966, color-television demand for receiving tubes had grown to a level which required the receiving-tube manufacturers' plant capacity to operate seven-day, multiple-shift operations in order to meet it. Although capacity was strained, no firms invested in new plant facilities. The tube shortfall was absorbed by imported receiving tubes.

Competition in the Receiving-Tubes
Industry in 1966

As a result of import competition, the pretelevision plateau in tube demand, and increasing automation, by 1966 there were only four major U.S. receiving-tube manufacturers: RCA Corporation, General Electric, GTE Sylvania, and Westinghouse Electric. Three domestic receiving-tube companies controlled 60 percent of the U.S. receiving-tube market's sales in 1966: RCA had 34 percent of the market in 1966; General Electric had 16 percent and GTE Sylvania had 30 percent. GTE Sylvania had 30 percent. Raytheon, Hytron (CBS), Philco, and Tung-Sol, which had previously produced both television sets and tubes, had discontinued both products. Of these, only Raytheon and Philco continued to merchandise replacement tubes under their own brand for their receivers; the tubes were purchased from other tube-makers. North American Phillips and Raytheon sold replacement tubes for use in repairing other manufacturers' sets as well as their own.

Firms such as Sears, Zenith, Motorola, Admiral, and Magnavox purchased and sold private branded tubes for their in-house repair operations. Imported receiving tubes competed with the domestic tubes for OEM applications. Major Japanese firms exporting tubes to the United States in 1966 included Matshusita, Hitachi, Toshiba, NEC, and Mitsubishi.

There were significant differences in the strategic postures of these firms. The most efficient manufacturers (firms like GTE Sylvania and General Electric) used feeder plants, offshore factories, or other cost-reducing techniques which were also intended to lower their relative fixed asset and human-resource investments. For example, GTE Sylvania's subassembly operations could be completed by contract firms which were not a part of the receiving-tube unit's corporate structure. Such precautions reduced the numbers of workers which would have to be absorbed into other operations when GTE Sylvania's receiving-tube operations were retired.

RCA Corporation. The RCA Corporation had pioneered the development of radio, black-and-white television, and color television and was considered the epitome of an electronics company. RCA was engaged in the manufacture of consumer products; commercial, military, and space apparatus; as well as computers and data-processing systems in 1966. RCA also operated television and radio broadcasting stations, a television and radio network, and supplied programming for broadcasting. RCA had other operations in book publishing, truck rental and leasing, and construction equipment, and operated extensive distribution and servicing network for its products. RCA was organized into twenty subsidiaries and one international division, and had sales of $2,548.8 million in 1966. As a corporate strategy, RCA tended to invest in technologically based new businesses, and had many investment opportunities in 1966.

RCA Receiving Tubes Division manufactured receiving tubes as well as consumer semiconductors, computer semiconductors, and memory products. RCA was heavily forward-integrated. RCA Corporation consumed receiving tubes internally in its television and radio receivers, public-address systems, transmitters, and aerospace products. Several military products produced by RCA Corporation also used specially designed receiving tubes. RCA held many patents on its earlier general-purpose receiving-tube designs and derived considerable income from licensed receiving-tube technology overseas. RCA helped to set up receiving-tube factories in other countries and collected royalties on their productive outputs, even if they exported them to the United States.

RCA receiving tubes had been historically manufactured at four plants: Harrison and Woodbridge, New Jersey; Cincinnati, Ohio; and Indianapolis, Indiana. The Harrison plant was the site of the original RCA facility. RCA had also produced receiving tubes at plants in Mexico and Brazil, although the output of these plants was usually consumed domestically in their respective locations. RCA had no offshore plants for production of domestically marketed receiving tubes.

RCA had closed its Indianapolis receiving-tube plant in about 1960, deploying the labor force to other RCA operations nearby. This decision was being severely criticized in 1966 as demand for tubes had increased rapidly in the color-television OEM market. In 1966, RCA produced tubes in facilities most observers believed to be less automated than those of its competitors. The three remaining receiving-tube plants in 1966 were also relatively old. RCA had made few apparent investments in receiving-tube manufacturing in the 1960s, and its production technology was more labor-intensive than that of other tube producers.

RCA's strong position in the receiving-tube market stemmed in part from the reliability of its product quality and its high level of service, as well as from its strong position in the television-receiver business. RCA's quality reputation was buttressed by research facilities which were unparalleled in the television-receiver industry. RCA engineers had helped Corning Glass to perfect the glass envelopes used in making receiving tubes and television picture tubes. RCA worked with receiving-tube customers such as Magnavox, Admiral, Philco, Muntz, and Emerson to produce high-quality television receivers.

RCA had created the "Nuvistor," a compact metal and ceramic tube, as a partial response to the transistor. Although the Nuvistor had been adopted in several RCA commercial applications and in some of RCA's military applications, it was not widely used because it had not proved to be a lower-cost product than the transistor.

RCA maintained strategically placed inventory reserves to help its customers to ensure they received quality components as needed for their plants to avoid production delays. This allowed OEM customers to hold minimal inventories of receiving tubes while RCA bore the cost of inventory. In addition to these warehouse services provided to OEM customers, RCA also helped to establish and finance independent electronics distributors who frequently carried only the RCA product line.

Approximately 80 percent of RCA's sales of receiving tubes in the replacement market were transacted through independent distributors, with much of the rest conducted through the RCA Distributing Corporation which was captive. RCA was very active in using promotional devices to stimulate the marketing of its receiving tubes in the replacement market. RCA introduced a trip program for its distributors in 1961.

General Electric Company. General Electric Company was the largest manufacturer of electrical equipment in the United States. It was engaged in the development, manufacture, and sale of apparatus, equipment, supplies, and appliances for the generation, transmission, and control of electrical power. General Electric's products ranged from lamps, household appliances, X-ray equipment, and industrial apparatus to complete utility power plants. General Electric was organized into six groups: the Aerospace and Defense Group; the Components and Construction Group; the Consumer Products Groups; the Electrical Utility Group; the Industrial and Information Group; and the International Group. Corporate sales were $7,177.3 million in 1966 and broken down as follows: industrial components and materials (33 percent); consumer goods (27 percent); heavy capital goods (22 percent) and defense products departments (18 percent). Receiving tubes were a part of the Components Group.

General Electric was the second-largest receiving-tube producer in earlier years, but it ranked third in 1966. General Electric had acquired Kentucky Radio Company (Ken-Rad) in 1944 in order to enter the receiving-tube business, and had been one of the last major electronics companies to enter the receiving-tubes business. It produced a relatively narrow line of tubes (over 900 tubes). At one time it had produced metallic tubes (like RCA's Nuvistors) but had discontinued that product line due to un-economic sales volumes.

General Electric was forward-integrated as well, producing television receivers, radios, and other kinds of products that used receiving tubes. General Electric consumer electronics products were sold through common independent and company-owned distribution channels and supported by an in-house service organization.

General Electric also produced substitute products such as semiconductors. It supported several research laboratories in electronic products.

Tubes were produced in domestic plants located in Owensboro, Kentucky, and Tell City, Indiana, in 1966. General Electric also operated an offshore plant in Singapore which enjoyed very low labor costs but required five-week lead times for shipping, processing, and repackaging even when using airlift transportation. In Singapore, receiving-tube components were mounted, soldered, and shipped to Owensboro, where they were sealed. Special tubes, low-volume tubes, and unique jobs were produced in their entirety in General Electric's domestic receiving-tube plants. While General Electric's plants were relatively old, GE had invested in developing cost-saving operations and equipment.

General Electric produced some proprietary tubes which it sold to the other manufacturers, and also bought tubes from other manufacturers to fill out its product line. In addition to purchasing tubes from RCA, GTE Sylvania, and other domestic tube producers, General Electric purchased the tubes of foreign producers as well.

General Electric was strong in the replacement market, and was the first receiving-tube manufacturer to introduce trips as premiums for distributors in 1960. It had built a strong system of independent distributors as its channel for merchandising tubes to the replacement market.

General Electric had strict financial performance goals, and the Tube Products Department maintained a policy of never undercutting competitors but rather of meeting price cuts if they occurred. Moreover, on several occasions General Electric initiated increases in receiving-tube prices.

General Telephone and Electronics Corporation (GTE Sylvania). General Telephone and Electronics Corporation (GTE) was a holding company which controlled more than thirty subsidiary domestic operating telephone companies and subsidiaries engaged in manufacturing radio, television, and electronics products; communications and industrial control equipment; data transmission and processing hardware; and specialized military and industrial communications equipment. Consolidated corporate sales in 1966 were $1,401.2 million.

GTE manufactured receiving tubes in its subsidiary, Sylvania Electric Products, Inc. (GTE Sylvania), which GTE had acquired in 1959. GTE Sylvania had produced sales of $454.1 million in 1959. GTE Sylvania was one of the largest manufacturers of electronic tubes, photoflash lamps, and fluorescent and incandescent lamps. GTE Sylvania also manufactured television and radio sets, semiconductor products, and cameras. It was a participant in national defense projects. Therefore, it was among the leading producers of traveling wave tubes, high power tubes, klystrons, and other industrial- and military-grade receiving tubes in addition to entertainment-grade tubes. In addition to its U.S. business, GTE Sylvania sold receiving tubes worldwide—to Canada, parts of Europe, and Latin America.

GTE Sylvania had been one of the first major tube manufacturers. As Nilco Lamp Company, it had produced receiving tubes for radio receivers. GTE Sylvania had also done extensive research with the U.S. military to develop "fuze" tubes for ordnance and subminiature tubes, such as lock-ins and guided-missile receiving tubes. Its very wide product line included government, industrial, military, and entertainment-grade receiving tubes.

GTE Sylvania pursued an aggressive differentiation strategy to serve the two principal types of receiving tube markets—OEM and replacement—maintaining two separate sales forces. As a special service to the OEM customers, GTE Sylvania offered customized engineering services. GTE Sylvania's engineering staff would design products to suit a customer's requirements or it would cross-design (reverse engineer) the receiving tubes manufactured by competitors to enable its customers to have a second source.

A replacement market sales force dealt with the over 700 electronics distributors who carried GTE Sylvania's receiving tubes. The replacement market sales force was given pricing discretion. It used promotion—trips, prizes, and incentive plans—to motivate its dealers to sell Sylvania components, though not to the degree that its competitors did. GTE Sylvania also helped its distributors financially. Both GTE sales forces also sold semiconductors.

GTE Sylvania was also forward-integrated into television and also produced a narrow line of consumer products—radio and television receivers and stereophonic phonographs. GTE Sylvania was one of two television producers which held out against using Japanese tubes. (The other was Zenith Radio, whose receiving tubes were supplied by GTE Sylvania.) GTE Sylvania's semiconductor division produced transistors and integrated circuits. GTE Sylvania maintained separate research laboratories for its entertainment products, electronics systems, parts, and semiconductor divisions.

GTE Sylvania produced receiving tubes in dedicated plants located in Altoona, Emporium, and Williamsport, Pennsylvania, and Burlington, Iowa. It also had a preassembly plant in Juarez, Mexico. GTE had invested heavily in automated tube assembly facilities from 1962 to 1966.

GTE Sylvania manufactured many of the components which went into its receiving tubes. It refined its own mica disks, drew its own wire, wound its own grids, sprayed its own cathodes, and at one time it had made the glass envelopes for the tubes. It also sold many of the tube components it produced to the other tube-makers.

Westinghouse Electric Corporation. Westinghouse Electric Corporation was engaged in the manufacture and sale of electrical apparatus and appliances for the generation, transmission, utilization, and control of electricity, and in the manufacture and sale of steam and gas turbines and associated equipment. Westinghouse Electric's products were highly diversified and included practically all electrical and related mechanical equipment required by electric power companies, electrified railroads, and the propulsion and electrical equipment needed by the navy and marine industry, as well as some equipment for the aviation industry. In addition to these heavy industrial products Westinghouse Electric produced household appliances, including radios and televisions. The electronics- (as opposed to the electrical-) related business of Westinghouse represented approximately 10 percent of corporate sales. Corporate sales in 1966 were $2,581.4 million.

Westinghouse Electric produced a small amount of receiving tubes in its electronic tube division which were sold internally to the unit which produced Westinghouse television receivers. Westinghouse Electric produced receiving tubes only for consumer products.

In addition to supplying its own internal needs for receiving tubes, Westinghouse Electric sold receiving tubes to small competitors which manufactured television or radio receivers and did not have the in-house capacity to manufacture receiving tubes. Westinghouse Electric's receiving-tube plant was located in Bath, New York, and had not been modernized. Lamp production operations were also active in that plant in 1966.

Raytheon Company. The Raytheon Comany engineered, manufactured, and sold electric equipment. An important part of its business was devoted to research, development, and production for the U.S. government of the navy's guided "Sparrow III" missile and the army's "Hawk" missile systems. Among its many products, the company also manufactured electronic tubes including klystrons and other power tubes; industrial- and military-grade receiving tubes; germanium semiconductor devices; silicon transistors; and many other electronic components. Corporate sales in 1966 were $709.0 million. Raytheon had acquired a television-receiver business in 1956 and sold its assets to Admiral Corporation. Raytheon had never been successful in the OEM entertainment business.

Raytheon receiving tube operations had been located in Newton, North Windham, and Quincy, Massachusetts. In December 1963 Raytheon announced that it would close the North Windham, Massachusetts, entertainment-grade tube plant, consolidating its tube operations and those of the Quincy, Massachusetts, tube plant operations in a plant at Newton, Massachusetts. The tubes Raytheon continued to produce were the industrial- and military-grade types. Earlier in 1963, Raytheon had closed a germanium semiconductor plant in Maine. (Germanium semiconductors were also technologically obsolete.) Soon afterward Raytheon divested its entertainment-grade receiving-tubes production facilities altogether. When it divested its entertainment-grade receiving tubes, Raytheon sold its equipment in Europe.

Raytheon contracted with Nippon Electric of Japan to supply it with receiving tubes which Raytheon merchandised to the replacement market under the Raytheon name. The Raytheon tubes were available only in the most popular, most rapidly selling models, and were sold at a modest discount to other tubes of the other U.S. manufacturers but at prices above those of Japanese firms. Raytheon's distributors carried Raytheon tubes as a second line, in addition to some other tube manufacturers' full lines.

Corporate Strategy Exit Barriers in the Receiving-Tubes Industry. It was important for a television-receiver producer to have an adequate supply of receiving tubes for its production needs and for its customers in the replacement market. After a TV producer had converted to solid-state components, there were no particular strategic exit barriers preventing that receiving-tube producer from exiting so long as (1) adequate world-wide production volume existed to satisfy the firm's strategic customer-service obligations through sourcing (PBR sales) and (2) a buyer could be located for the assets used to manufacture the "proprietary" tube designs which the particular receiving-tube producer had manufactured for the rest of the industry. It was acceptable in 1966 for a few competitors to merchandise receiving tubes (and divest their production facilities) as Raytheon had done provided adequate production capacity remained in operation to ensure that each television-receiver manufacturer's customer obligations could be met. This was important to avoid alienating customers' goodwill in markets served by other products also manufactured by the receiving-tube firms.

Strategically, there was a type of "reverse tying agreement" implicit in the sale of a television receiver containing receiving tubes. Corporations undertook an obligation to make replacement parts available to these customers in the future. The government, in particular, was dependent upon receiving-tube supplies long after the original equipment containing tubes ceased to be manufactured.

So long as an appropriate number of major receiving-tube companies stayed in the production end of the business to constitute "bankers of last resort," other receiving-tube companies could offer a truncated line of

PBR replacement tubes at lower inventorying costs. There was an implicit obligation upon the last receiving-tube manufacturer to retain efficient operating facilities and effective managers in order to serve the crucial industries which used receiving tubes and which could not afford to convert to solid state.

The receiving-tube competitors manufactured product lines of unequal widths. GTE Sylvania offered the widest product line. The imported PBR tube companies, like Raytheon, offered the narrowest tube product lines. All competitors' tubes were intended potentially to compete against each other.

Companies like GTE Sylvania and General Electric which had automated part or all of their remaining receiving-tube plants were economically more committed to the receiving-tubes industry. Also, firms which used fewer Japanese tubes, such as GTE Sylvania, were more committed strategically to participation in the replacement market. Because the strategic postures of the receiving-tube competitors were dissimilar but their products were fungible, the competitive environment of this industry potentially could be volatile in endgame.

Summary of Competitors in the
Receiving-Tubes Industry

In summary, the major brands of receiving tubes available in 1966 were produced or merchandised by companies who varied in their strategic postures along the following dimensions: (1) the extent of their automation of the tube-production process; (2) whether their tubes were preassembled or produced in offshore plants or in domestic factories; and (3) the relative importance competitors attributed to their receiving-tube business in 1966. For example, it may be inferred that receiving tubes were important to GTE Sylvania and RCA Corporation in 1966. GTE Sylvania had recently invested in the Altoona plant's automated equipment. RCA Corporation was closely identified with the receiving tube because its strategic image was that of an "electronics firm."

Strategic exit barriers kept several firms in the merchandising end of the receiving-tube business even after in-house production had been discontinued. The strategic exit barriers were relatively higher for Westinghouse Electric than for Raytheon because it had more recently placed television receivers into the consumer electronics market. Such barriers kept firms in the replacement market selling OEM domestic or Japanese-produced private branded receiving tubes for several years. The lower-cost, imported tubes kept price levels relatively depressed and forced some of the remaining producers to accept performances which were lower than their corporate criteria due to the influence of some of these strategic exit barriers on their behaviors.

A Mapping of Strategic Groups in the
Receiving-Tubes Industry

This section attempts to cluster the competitors along discriminating dimensions which will describe the differences in these firms' strategic postures. Using the dimensions described and discussed above one could analyze where competitors in the receiving-tube endgame differed in ways which might have constituted relative competitive advantages.

Within the receiving-tubes industry, there were two major strategic groups: (1) the producers and (2) the merchandisers. Within each of these two groups, classification of the firms according to the relative strategic importance of their receiving-tube products shows that the merchandisers (represented by Raytheon) regarded the receiving tube as being of low strategic importance:

	Receiving Tubes of High Strategic Importance	Receiving Tubes of Relatively Low Strategic Importance
Predominantly Produce Tubes Internally	GTE Sylvania RCA Corporation	Westinghouse Electric General Electric
Predominantly Sourced Tubes	Imports	Raytheon

Along these axes, the firms which were most committed to a particular chracteristic are positioned at the extremes of this "strategic space." For example, Westinghouse Electric's tube-making operations were small and it was phasing itself out of the OEM market. General Electric's sales of receiving tubes were a small part of its total corporate sales. Ample supplies of replacement tubes were available from other tube producers in the 1960s. Hence, receiving tubes were less important strategically for General Electric provided it could service the sockets it had created.

GTE Sylvania and Zenith Radio alone resisted the influx of imported receiving tubes in their OEM operations. (Zenith Radio never produced receiving tubes; it purchased them from other domestic tube producers, especially GTE Sylvania.) They were most committed to servicing their television-receiver customers with their own brand of replacement tubes.

RCA Corporation was most strongly identified with receiving tubes. It had access to good-quality receiving tubes from overseas, if necessary, because it had licensed its electronics technology to some foreign producers. Nevertheless, domestic receiving tubes were an important business to RCA Corporation.

Raytheon stayed in the replacement market merchandising business because the profit margins were better there. Raytheon was the lowest-cost producer because its tubes were sourced from NEC. It could easily "pull the string" which secured its position in receiving tubes and be divested cleanly in a few weeks.

The Endgame in the Receiving-Tubes Industry

Demand for receiving tubes declined sharply in 1967 as growth in color television slowed and OEMs continued converting to solid-state electronic components. However, receiving-tube demand recovered in 1969 and it was not until 1973 that the decline in demand began to accelerate. The conversion to solid state had taken longer than most observers had estimated, but by 1975 OEM demand for receiving tubes had shrunk to almost nothing. At the same time as industry sales declined, sales of imports were off sharply. Table 4-1 summarizes the demand for receiving tubes consumed in the United States during the endgame.

An Overview of the Endgame in Receiving Tubes

From table 4-1 it will be seen that the total volume of receiving tubes consumed declined by 86 percent from the base year 1966 to 1977. The average value of receiving tubes increased during this time due to changes in the market mixes of receiving-tube sales.

As the demand for receiving tubes softened in 1966, and the OEM market continued converting to transistorization, there was a significant change in the pricing structure and profitability of receiving tubes. The pricing structure had begun to soften in 1963. Manufacturers were pricing their tube products lower and accepting thinner margins on their sales. As demand for OEM receiving tubes shrank, the costs associated with servicing the replacement market—inventorying capital costs—became a disproportionate part of competitors' costs of being in the receiving-tube business. It was more expensive to operate in the replacement market than in the original equipment manufacturing market. When the OEM market became a lesser part of the total receiving tubes sales volume, the costs of participating in this industry were reexamined with greater scrutiny by corporate parents. Firms in weak replacement market positions reconsidered the attractiveness of their investments.

By 1970 the volume of receiving tubes sold in the replacement market exceeded the OEM market. As fewer and fewer receiving tubes were used in OEM applications, some of the Japanese producers exited from the U.S. market because their franchise in the replacement market was too thin. Imports of receiving tubes declined as follows:

Table 4-1
Manufacturers' Sales of Receiving Tubes by End Use
(add 000 units or dollars)

Year	Original Equipment Manufacturers	Replacement or Renewal	Export	Government	Total	Value	Average Unit Price
1939	65,284	25,375	7,841		98,500	27,985	$ .28
1940	72,249	28,994	7,233		108,476	27,610	.25
1941	92,031	33,782	10,025		135,838	47,500	.35
1942	64,640	36,495	6,612		107,747	43,000	.40
1943	54,507	19,637	3,106	32,828	110,078	51,000	.46
1944	60,207	20,899	4,552	43,405	129,063	62,140	.48
1945	57,235	40,462	4,995	36,786	139,478	68,500	.49
1946	129,637	65,228	9,991	361	205,217	101,000	.49
1947	131,987	43,530	23,184	833	199,534	107,000	.54
1948	146,162	47,056	10,687	815	204,720	112,000	.55
1949	147,298	39,696	10,073	1,686	198,753	119,000	.60
1950	301,483	69,325	10,768	1,385	382,961	250,000	.65
1951	247,855	94,597	24,438	8,754	375,644	261,000	.69
1952	241,406	83,843	13,935	29,335	368,519	259,116	.70
1953	293,601	112,785	20,614	10,091	437,091	303,675	.69
1954	246,729	115,358	15,922	7,080	385,089	275,999	.72
1955	288,810	150,718	24,442	15,832	479,802	358,110	.75
1956	262,898	166,558	25,397	9,333	464,186	374,186	.81
1957	240,708	184,493	23,378	7,845	456,424	384,402	.84
1958	191,832	167,805	24,597	13,132	397,366	341,929	.86
1959	227,669	170,729	19,969	14,569	432,936	368,872	.85
1960	200,362	161,092	21,375	10,226	393,055	331,742	.84
1961	188,176	150,249	22,245	14,336	375,006	311,098	.83
1962	190,140	134,390	19,804	16,905	361,239	301,525	.83
1963	233,668	133,016	16,958	11,902	395,544	297,000	.75

Table 4-1 *(continued)*

Year	Original Equipment Manufacturers	Replacement or Renewal	Export	Government	Total	Value	Average Unit Price
1964	212,010	125,006	20,430	10,642	368,088	272,000	.74
1965	232,921	130,325	17,198	16,108	396,552	282,000	.76
1966	282,677	123,272	19,335	17,595	442,879	301,000	.68
1967	179,763	111,183	15,353	17,050	323,349	210,000	.65
1968	163,717	113,094	13,716	11,099	301,626	196,000	.65
1969	143,227	112,547	14,864	10,245	280,883	283,691	1.00
1970	103,019	107,537	14,844	6,003	231,403	259,171	1.12
1971	101,530	101,813	13,671	6,393	223,407	261,386	1.17
1972	81,362	97,829	12,579	7,362	199,132	240,950	1.21
1973	51,871	96,190	13,267	6,670	167,998	204,244	1.22
1974	23,985	81,184	12,596	5,891	123,656	167,157	1.35
1975	8,557	67,944	8,056	6,784	91,341	152,215	1.67
1976	5,827	60,099	9,320	4,508	79,754	139,513	1.75
1977	n.a.	n.a.	7,319	n.a.	63,385	112,191	1.77

U.S. Imports of Receiving Tubes
(in $ millions)

1967	1968	1969	1970	1971	1972	1973	1974	1975	1976
21.3	18.9	18.4	17.6	18.0	18.4	18.5	11.9	10.1	9.6

Source: *Census of Manufacturers*, U.S. Bureau of the Census.

The price level in the replacement market had always been higher because (1) the Japanese producers could not penetrate it as effectively; (2) the customers in this market were less price-sensitive (they could pass on their increased costs); (3) these customers were less powerful in bargaining for price breaks or other advantages; and (4) the U.S. tube-makers avoided market-share raids through price-cutting after they had witnessed the poor profits of the OEM market which had resulted from price wars. As a larger proportion of the total unit volume of sales was comprised of replacement-market tubes, the average price levels reflected this change in their value increases.

A Chronological Description of the Endgame in the the Receiving-Tubes Industry

1967

By 1967, 73 percent of all phonographs and 90 percent of all radios had been converted to solid state. Color television had not yet become economical in solid state. But in the OEM market the Japanese receiving tubes were in full force, and OEM receiving-tube prices were declining.

The Electronic Industries Association (EIA) started litigation in the U.S. Treasury Department charging the Japanese with dumping receiving tubes in the United States. The Japanese producers had an annual capacity of over 200 million units. If this alleged dumping were not curtailed, the EIA charged, the imported tubes would exceed 80 percent of the OEM market. (This measure includes fully assembled OEM television receivers shipped into the United States from offshore plants.) The Treasury Department and Customs Office did nothing.

Westinghouse Electric. In 1967 Westinghouse Electric discontinued its manufacture of television receivers and, hence, of receiving tubes. Westinghouse Electric continued to merchandise receiving tubes which it sources from other manufacturers to be sold under the Westinghouse brand name. The inventory it held upon terminating the business moved very slowly.

Westinghouse sold its receiving-tube assets to a producer called Union Electric, which was located in Taiwan. The Westinghouse plant in Bath was converted to the production of high-discharge lamps. Westinghouse suffered some cash-flow disruptions in 1967 due to the unexpectedly slow turnover of the receiving-tubes inventory.

1968

Hitachi. Reflecting its overall "bullishness" regarding the future of Japanese tube sales in the United States, Hitachi allegedly expanded its receiving-tube capacity in 1968. It signed on International Importers, Inc., a manufacturers' representative company which had introduced Hitachi to the OEM market in 1957, to be its representative in the U.S. replacement market. Hitachi expected U.S. distributors to become more dependent upon Japanese receiving tubes in the future as more American tube-makers exited.

1969

In 1969 demand for receiving tubes in the OEM markets began to soften. More transistorized circuits were being designed into television receivers, and the remaining tubes in the hybrid televisions were the most costly, high-voltage, high-power entertainment tube types. The specialized tubes still used in high-fidelity stereo sets were similarly the costlier and technologically complex tube varieties. Over the next five years, prices on these complex tubes increased by 50 percent. A steady demand for industrial- and military-grade tubes continued.

RCA Corporation. In December 1969 RCA Corporation increased the price of its replacement receiving tubes by 8 percent. This was the first price increase of its kind since 1966. More and more of the technologically simple tube types were being produced for the OEM market by importers' Taiwanese plants.

Also in 1969 RCA completed its shutdown of its receiving-tube operations in Cincinnati. (Total disposals of RCA Corporation in 1969 were written down by $30,362,000. It is not known what portion of this was attributable to the retirement of receiving-tube capacity.)

GTE Sylvania. In 1969 GTE Sylvania closed its Burlington, Iowa, receiving-tube plant and sold it to a company which used it to make capacitors. The tube-making assets of Burlington were moved to Altoona, where they were consolidated with existing operations.

General Electric. Following the RCA Corporation's December announcement concerning a price increase for replacement receiving tubes, General Electric raised the price of the receiving tubes it sold to its replacement customers by 5 percent.

North American Philips. Amperex (North American Philips) indicated that it would study the RCA price increase. Amperex Electronics Corporation had entered the U.S. market in the 1960s when demand for tubes in color-television receivers had peaked. By 1969, its market share was 10 to 12 percent of the total receiving-tube market. (Philips owned a part of the equity in Mashusita.)

U.S. Treasury. In 1969 the U.S. Treasury ruled that EIA's charge of Japanese dumping was invalid.

1970

1970 proved to be the first year when industry sales of receiving tubes for the replacement market were greater than in the OEM market, as a major move to transistorization took place. 1970 also marked the introduction of large-scale integrated circuits.

General Electric. In 1970 General Electric raised its prices on replacement receiving tubes by another 5 percent. It discontinued tube production in its Tell City plant and converted the plant to other uses.

GTE Sylvania. Sylvania followed General Electric's price increase by raising the prices of its replacement receiving tubes 2 to 10 percent.

RCA Corporation. In 1970 RCA raised its prices on replacement receiving tubes by 2 to 5 percent. It closed the Woodbridge, New Jersey, and Cowansville, Quebec, receiving-tube plants, leaving only the Harrison, Pennsylvania, plant. Plants which were carried at book values of $30,806,000 (gross book values of $85,383,000) were written off. RCA noted in explaining its move that the original equipment market for receiving tubes had been all but eliminated by solid-state components. It expected that replacement-tube sales would also decline rapidly.

The Cincinnati and Woodbridge receiving-tube plants were sold to unrelated businesses. Usable receiving-tube equipment was moved to the old and inefficient Harrison research headquarters.

1971

RCA Corporation. In 1971 RCA Corporation repeatedly considered terminating sales of its replacement receiving tubes through independent distributors. RCA suggested that its in-house distribution organization should take over the regular sales of receiving tubes for the replacement market. However, RCA's independent distributors protested vigorously, and the company abandoned this tactic, which had been intended to improve its profit margins in the replacement market. The replacement market was becoming increasingly expensive to service as demand declined.

RCA raised the prices of 382 of the 1,000 varieties of entertainment receiving tubes it sold in the replacement market. RCA blamed higher labor and materials costs for the 6.6 percent increase it posted in July 1971. In December 1971 the Price Commissions, then in place, approved a 6 percent price increase for RCA entertainment-grade receiving tubes. RCA indicated that it would put the increase into effect immediately.

General Electric. In July 1971 General Electric followed RCA's price increase by raising its replacement-market receiving-tube prices by 6 percent.

1973

In 1973 a niche in the declining market for receiving tubes developed. Dynaco, Audio Research, and Jervis (Harmon Kardon) amplifier companies reported that demand for high-fidelity audio components in Japan was making it difficult for Japanese manufacturers of amplifiers to procure enough receiving tubes to meet Japanese demand. Tubes were still used on some high-fidelity audio components because of their special qualities.

1974

In 1974 the microprocessor was introduced; this was the fifth generation in active electronic components technology. 1974 proved to be a dismal year for the receiving-tubes industry. The overall effect of the recession slowed receiving-tube consumption. Television receivers were being converted entirely to solid-state components. Once one firm had a solid-state television set on the market, it became difficult to sell a set which contained receiving tubes. The last hybrid television receiver—the last TV set containing receiving tubes—was produced in 1974. Consumption of receiving tubes in OEM markets dropped dramatically. Some receiving-tube companies suffered losses as demand very abruptly and unexpectedly plummeted in 1974.

Matshusita. Motorola, Inc., sold its television-set business to Matshusita Electrical Company of Japan in June 1974. Matshusita was a significant exporter of receiving tubes in the United States. It renamed the television business "Quasar."

Philco. In June 1974 Philco (now a division of Ford Motor Company) announced it would discontinue manufacturing of radios and stereo component systems after its 1975 line was over. GTE Sylvania purchased the rights to these assets and the Philco brand name just as it had purchased Philco's receiving-tube business at an earlier time.

RCA. In June 1974 RCA announced that it would end its home audio line of radios, tape recorders and players, and phonograph equipment, including RCA's stereo line. In July 1974 RCA raised the prices on its entertainment tubes by 3.3 percent and on its industrial tubes by 13 percent.

General Electric. Industry observers noticed an apparent change in General Electric's receiving-tube strategy in 1974. General Electric had appeared to be "milking" its receiving-tube investment. It had closed its Tell City, Indianapolis, operation and moved the assets of that receiving-tube plant to its Hartford Road plant in Owensboro, Kentucky. Hence, there were no write-offs. The management staff at Owensboro had been curtailed and one of the two receiving-tube plants still operating in Owensboro was scheduled to be closed. However, in 1974 it appeared that General Electric had stopped the countdown to exit.

General Electric increased the number of marketing people employed by Owensboro despite depressed industry conditions. It began to emphasize selling receiving tubes to private-brand replacement markets and to larger-volume electronic-components distributors. The Hartford Road receiving-tube plant in Owensboro, which was scheduled to be shut down, was not written off but mothballed, to be held in reserve in the event that it might be needed again in the future.

GTE Sylvania. In October 1974 GTE Sylvania negotiated with Philco to obtain U.S. distribution rights to Philco-branded products. This arrangement gave Sylvania about 9 percent of the home television market and strongly improved its distribution system. Philco-Ford had 5,000 retailers and thirty independent and factory branch distributors. Under their agreement, Philco-Ford assembled color televisions and stereo consoles in Lansdale and Watsontown, Pennsylvania (the Watsontown plant was sold to Zenith), and black-and-white televisions in Taiwan (Sylvania later bought this plant from Philco) until April 30, 1975. At that time, Sylvania would manufacture and sell these products itself under the Philco name.

1975

North American Philips. Philips, which distributed tubes in the United States under the "Amperex" label, departed from the U.S. market in 1975. The abrupt decline in receiving-tube demand in 1974 had made North American Philips reconsider this business's attractiveness.

Westinghouse Electric. In 1975 Westinghouse Electric discontinued its receiving-tube merchandising activities. Westinghouse had discontinued receiving-tube production in 1967 but had continued to sell receiving tubes purchased from General Electric, GTE Sylvania, RCA Corp., and other (overseas) sources under its own brand name. Sales of receiving tubes no longer justified their inventorying costs. Westinghouse allegedly suffered losses from its merchandising services and reportedly sold the tube inventories it still held to a tube wholesaler at distress prices.

Toshiba. In 1975 Toshiba exited from the substantially less attractive U.S. receiving-tube market. Toshiba sold its receiving-tube assets to Samsung.

GTE Sylvania. GTE Sylvania bought the Taiwan plant and equipment from Union Electric (which had purchased them earlier from Westinghouse Electric). After GTE Sylvania found that the Union plant was uneconomic, it learned that it could enjoy certain tax benefits by transporting these assets out of the country. Yet because GTE Sylvania had no use for these uneconomic assets in the United States and wanted to retire them, it could not bring the assets to the United States. GTE Sylvania complied with the conditions of the tax laws by loading Union Electric's receiving-tube assets on a barge and burying them off the shore of Taiwan.

1976

RCA Corporation. In September 1976 RCA trimmed back its receiving-tube production by releasing 100 hourly and seventy-five salaried employees. Later that year, in the *President's Letter* of RCA's Annual Report, a closing date of July 30, 1976, was set for the shutdown of the Harrison tube plant, thus terminating RCA's production of receiving tubes. The company reported that it intended to continue to merchandise tubes and to sell replacement tubes from its inventories. The Harrison plant was a twenty-three-building complex covering 650,000 square feet. It was unlikely to be purchased by any tube-making competitors.

The Harrison receiving-tube plant had been the original RCA factory. It had been used by Thomas A. Edison. It was the oldest, most fully depreciated of RCA's plants. Over $100 million in working capital was tied up in financing the inventory, receivables, plant, machinery, and equipment of the receiving-tubes factory that was devoted primarily to the replacement market. This was 3 percent of the corporation's assets. Having decided to exit, RCA faced the problem of how to recover some of these assets and how to service its customers who relied upon RCA "single-source" tubes.

RCA actually closed its Harrison tube plant three months earlier than had been planned. It made "lifetime buy offer" to enable customers who used the 110 types of special receiving tubes RCA made to obtain their full anticipated inventory needs of these products. This was done because at the time RCA did not know whether it could sell the tube-making equipment used to manufacture these tubes. RCA loaded the market for an extended period of time through this lifetime buy offer in case it found no buyer. (This form of exit was similar to Raytheon's behavior in entertainment-grade receiving tubes when it made a lifetime buy offer before it divested itself of its tube-making assets.) RCA recognized a $10 million charge against earnings in closing the Harrison plant.

Ten percent of the RCA receiving tube equipment was sold to GTE Sylvania, in addition to the rights to produce Nuvistors and other exclusive products. GTE Sylvania purchased the tooling, equipment, raw materials, and work in process related to sixty receiving-tube types which had been produced only by RCA. The assets and designs of many of these tubes were moved to GTE Sylvania's automated plant in Altoona, Pennsylvania. The assets used to produce RCA's proprietary Nuvistor receiving tubes for military and some consumer electronics applications were moved to Emporium, Pennsylvania.

Even after RCA had divested its receiving-tube manufacturing assets, it maintained a service obligation to purchasers of the television and radio receivers which contained RCA tubes. RCA continued to merchandise receiving tubes until its inventory of tubes (which was sizable) was sold. It also sold maintenance contracts to companies and individuals in order to service their old television receiver sets, projectors, radios, or other RCA products for which replacement parts such as receiving tubes may be needed. It took two years for the RCA receiving-tubes inventory to be drawn down.

In calculating the cost of exit for the Harrison, New Jersey, plant, RCA management did not foresee the large number of workers' compensation cases which were subsequently filed against the corporation. According to these claims, workers allegedly sustained injuries while in the employ of the RCA Tubes Division which made them unable to assume other employment following the shutdown of the Harrison plant. The settlement proved to be very costly, on the order of $1 million.

Toshiba. The retirement of Toshiba from the U.S. receiving-tube market following upon the announcement of RCA's shutdown created a shortage of replacement-grade receiving tubes. Both General Electric's and GTE Sylvania's full tube output were needed to meet the 1976 receiving-tube demand.

1977

General Electric. Following the exit of RCA, the General Electric Tube Products Department again began production of metal receiving-tubes. After RCA's exit, the metal tubes were reintroduced by General Electric to serve the small, but price-insensitive, market for these tubes. The metal receiving-tube product had been manufactured by Ken-Rad Company, originally, prior to its acquisition by GE in 1945.

GTE Sylvania. Following the installment of the RCA equipment in its Altoona plant, GTE Sylvania began the weeding-out and reinvesting process in receiving tubes. It weeded out low-volume tube products and transferred their production to the Emporium tube plant. The automated Altoona tube plant was kept fully loaded with longer production runs. The tubes produced on these lines used general-purpose equipment and interchangeable tooling. They represented 90 percent of GTE Sylvania's sales volume.

Sole-source tubes requiring specialized equipment and special production techniques were produced once or twice a year at the Emporium receiving-tube plant. Also, low-volume, high-cost, and difficult-to-make receiving tubes were made there. The Emporium plant ran at only 10 percent of its engineered capacity most of the year. By producing these low-volume tubes for price-insensitive customers at this second plant, however, GTE Sylvania was able to retain the lowest industry costs for most of its tube output. This production strategy was supported by GTE Sylvania's aggressive sales efforts in the global replacement market for receiving tubes.

1978

RCA Corporation. In 1978 RCA finally completed selling off the inventory it had held at the time when it exited in 1976. After RCA's initial inventory holding had been worked off, the corporation remained in the receiving-tube market as a merchandiser. It purchased its receiving-tubes inventory from GTE Sylvania, General Electric, and other remaining global receiving-tube producers.

Others. As the value of the dollar fell, relative to the yen, U.S. receiving tubes grew more competitive with Japanese receiving tubes. The imported tubes challenge appeared to be fading as more and more receiving-tube producers like Philips, Toshiba, and Hitachi exited. The principal importers which remained in 1978 were Mashusita and the Nippon Electric Company (NEC).

Industry observers suggested that by the end of 1980, perhaps earlier, Mashusita might exit from the U.S. market. (Mashusita was 50 percent owned by Philips.) If Mashusita were to depart, this would increase the requirements of the U.S. market for receiving tubes which would have to be provided by the two remaining receiving-tube manufactuers in this country and by other global parties. If Mashusita (or NEC) were to exit, there could be greater hopes for profits to rise in the U.S. receiving-tube market, but there was also a risk of forcing faster transitions to transistorized technology.

In 1978 the supply of tubes manufactured by the two remaining U.S. producers was adequate to meet the demand. If one of them were to go out of business given existing demand levels, the other competitor would have been unable to satisfy all of the demand which was forecast into the 1980s. However, some of the assets of defunct U.S. receiving-tube produers were sold to companies overseas.

For example, industry sources discovered a small Indian company which produced American-designed receiving tubes. The origin of this small company's assets was unknown. (When a manufacturer of U.S.-designed receiving tubes divested, it would try to sell its equipment to retrieve as much value as possible; perhaps this Indian company had acquired its facilities from a secondhand junk dealer at the liquidation of a U.S. tubemaker.) The Russians, East Germans, Hungarians, and Yugoslavians were also manufacturing receiving tubes for popular European-type tube sockets in 1978. If one of the two dominant U.S. manufacturers of receiving tubes would find it necessary to exit, before the rate of demand for receiving tubes in the United States had diminished to the point where the capacity of the remaining competitors could satisfy that demand, it would be possible that the assets of the exiting competitor could end up in the hands of either the other competitor or one of the other remaining companies who manufactured receiving tubes in the global arena.

In 1978 GTE Sylvania and General Electric were both needed in order to supply the remaining demand for receiving tubes. The only remaining importers in the United States were Mashusita and NEC. Raytheon and RCA continued to merchandise their private brand tubes, respectively.

Since the last U.S. TV sockets requiring receiving tubes were manufactured in 1974, it would be a reasonable forecast that five years from that date—in 1979—the first replacement tubes for those television receivers would be needed. In order to satisfy this demand, a certain number of U.S. receiving tubes would have to be produced. If the tube merchandisers become greedy—if tube prices rise too high—it is predicted that consumers will throw away their old TV sets rather than pay the price of retubing them. But if pricing restraint can be exercised, the endgame could be more profitable and less volatile for the remaining competitors in the last years of the endgame.

Analysis of the Receiving-Tubes Endgame

There was little uncertainty among the competitors in the receiving-tubes endgame regarding the future of demand for this product. All firms involved in receiving-tube production recognized that eventually the solid-state technology would become commercially economic and would render obsolete the use of receiving tubes for most applications. All firms also recognized that a relatively predictable level of demand for receiving tubes in the replacement market would endure after tubes were designed out of major OEM markets, such as television receivers, and then acted in a way that would ensure that they could enjoy a profitable endgame in this replacement market by judiciously raising their prices and by tacitly following each others' leads when prices for replacement tubes were increased.

Demand during the receiving-tubes endgame was adequate to support one or more firms for a prolonged period of time, even at relatively higher price levels, because customers' switching costs (to replace their tube-television receiver units) were high. Investment was profitable for the remaining competitors because the customers in the replacement market were fragmented and not terribly price-sensitive. (They passed on the cost of replacement parts to their ultimate customers for receiving tubes.) Thus, this was one of the most "favorable" environments for continued investment during the endgame.

Exits from this endgame were orderly because rational decisions regarding which firms should remain in the endgame industry were easily made. It was clear who should remain in this endgame and who should exit. All of the firms producing receiving tubes in the endgame were diversified and hence there were few emotional exit barriers associated with this product. Their physical endgame assets were relatively depreciated. Hence, low to moderate economic exit barriers existed which could be easily overcome if a particular firm had to exit.

The competitors which remained in endgame were the lowest-cost competitors—those firms whose processes were most automated, most efficient, and utilized offshore preassembly plants. The competitors which exited were those firms which were less efficient or which possessed fewer strategic reasons to stay in this business. The firms in this endgame recognized their interdependencies and even produced and sold receiving tubes to each other to round out each other's tube lines while minimizing total production costs and increasing prices.

Because high switching costs for customers prolonged the demand for these products and because the exits of some competitors kept tube supply in line with demand, this was a profitable endgame for remaining competitors. There were few unforeseen write-off costs or other major expenses associated with firms' exits. There were few major disruptions to other corporate activities among the firms which did exit. The influx of imported receiving tubes in the OEM market in the early years of endgame had made profits rather thin in that market, but it was possible to earn returns of 25 to 30 percent on receiving-tube investments in the replacement market.

Characteristics

In the base year 1966 industry characteristics were as follows:

Demand. Within a reasonable price range, the demand for receiving tubes was price inelastic. The ceiling on prices for replacement tubes was the level at which users would abandon their tubed receivers and replace them with solid-state devices.

Product Differentiation. The receiving tube's design had to be interchangeable with the designs of other competitors' tubes. Thus the product possessed commoditylike traits. Companies differentiated their offerings on the basis of engineering services in the OEM market, and through promotional campaigns for their distributors in the replacement market.

Markets. In 1966 original entertainment equipment manufacturers consumed more receiving tubes than the replacement market, government prime market, PBR market, and export market combined. A substantial proportion of some tube-makers' sales were to internal (corporate) television-receiver manufacturing units in 1966.

Substitutes. Receiving tubes were rendered technologically obsolete by solid-state technology which was not yet economic for consumer electronics applications in 1966. The substitution of Japanese tubes for domestic receiving tubes used in OEM sockets was a more substantial threat to receiving-tube sales since exchange rates and operating efficiencies gave the Japanese producers lower costs.

Customer Industries. In 1966 the consumer electronics industry—notably television—consumed the greatest proportion of receiving tubes. An increasingly large proportion of receiving tubes was consumed in replacement sales to electronics-components distributors. Other major customers included other competitor television companies which were too small to produce their own receiving-tube components. Later, major tube producers which had shut down their operations became important customers.

Supplier Industries. Although a large portion of the raw materials used in receiving-tube production was fabricated internally, there were also small electronics companies which produced the low-volume but necessary components for the receiving-tube companies. The suppliers were small and did not seem to use their implicit bargaining power against the tube-makers.

Manufacturing Technology. The degree of automation used to manufacture receiving tubes varied by competitor. Some firms were highly automated. Some firms used offshore plants to perform the labor-intensive parts of the production process more economically.

Technological Innovation. Prior to 1966 some of the competitors in the receiving-tubes industry had made investments in process innovations to automate. Product revisions were made to suit customers' needs.

Capital Intensity. The cost of a receiving-tubes plant in the 1950s had been $12 million. Most of the receiving-tube plants were well depreciated in 1966. The value of newer-process innovations may not have been recovered at that time, however.

Competitive Structure. The competition in the OEM market was strong. Tube-makers tried to cross-design tubes into the television receivers of competitors' customers. The product they sold was standardized. Therefore strenuous competitive efforts were required to obtain and maintain OEM customers. In the replacement market, dealing, franchising, and flamboyant promotional campaigns were used to motivate distributors to push a particular brand of receiving tubes. Price competition by manufacturers was avoided.

As the number of television receivers, radios, and tape recorders which used tubes declined and the replacement market became more important, the prices of receiving tubes increased after years of stagnation. Companies which had not placed many sockets into the OEM market were unable to obtain adequate economies in the replacement market to continue to produce tubes. Because break-even levels of production were relatively high per tube variety, economic pressures forced several receiving-tube producers to exit. Notably, Toshiba, Hitachi, and North American Philips ceased producing receiving tubes in the United States. Westinghouse Electric ceased merchandising tubes when most of its television receivers were junked.

Analysis of Declining Demand for
Receiving Tubes

Demand for receiving tubes declined due to foreseeable technological obsolescence created by solid-state technology. Early in the endgame the
receiving-tube firms all recognized that there would be a lucrative replacement market for the product which could be served by one or two competitors' productive capacities. Demand for specialty products like the
metal receiving tubes could be forecast to be small but enduring. Receiving-
tube companies would know which products could replace the tube for
various applications because frequently they produced the electronic devices
which used receiving tubes and these firms produced the substitute semiconductor, integrated circuit, LSI, or microprocessor products, as well.

It had been expected that relative certainty among the competitors
regarding the rate and extent of obsolescence of an endgame product would
result in an orderly pattern of exits in which plant shutdowns could be
planned and executed in a manner which would result in no major write-off
losses or disruptions to other competitive activities. In most cases the certainty that the receiving tube would be designed out of most OEM devices
affected the endgame, as had been expected. Firms did not all correctly
estimate the speed of decline, however. Nor did they correctly identify
which firms would exit first. GTE Sylvania was best enabled to identify the
difficulties which would be encountered in commercializing the transistor
early in the 1950s. It exploited this knowledge by reinvesting in highly
automated receiving-tube plants which will likely enable it to be the last firm
in the lucrative endgame, as would be expected to occur when a firm
analyzes a declining market effectively and repositions itself advantageously.

It had been forecast that price increases could be easily accomplished in
replacement markets where the customers' switching costs to the substitute
technology were high. The high cost to consumers of replacing tubed television receivers enabled receiving-tube producers to raise tube prices several
times with success in the replacement market. This behavior was different
from the price-cutting which had been experienced to occur in the OEM
market, where import substitution was effective.

It had been expected that the presence of pockets of demand for endgame products which did not decline significantly would encourage firms to
remain invested in the endgame. Demand for industrial- and military-trade
receiving tubes, for example, did not decline; it remained steady. Although
each receiving-tube firm made these tubes, the success of GTE Sylvania and
Raytheon, two firms which continued to perform well in the receiving-tubes
endgame by pursuing aggressive postures (Raytheon brokered tubes for a
Japanese manufacturer), may have been further enhanced by their positions

as the major manufacturers of power tubes, traveling-wave tubes, klystrons, and other military and industrial tube designs.

Analysis of Endgame Industry Traits

It had been predicted that a "favorable" endgame environment would encourage some competitors to undertake reinvestments in assets in order to serve the niches of enduring demand most economically, and hence to become the last competitors remaining in such an endgame: favorable characteristics in this instance enabled two firms to reinvest in receiving-tube assets and to enjoy healthy profits successfully.

Product Differentiability Traits

The receiving tube was basically a fungible product, but firms which were able to sell customers specialized products, like RCA's Nuvistor metal receiving tubes, created for themselves (or for the firms which subsequently purchased their assets) niches of demand which were particularly price-insensitive.

Product Traits. In the OEM market, "copy-cat" price-cutters were producing many physically identical substitutes at lower prices because they manufactured receiving tubes in lower-cost surroundings or provided less service. The presence of some propriety tube designs in the replacement market as well as the inability of transistors to replace receiving tubes for particular applications quickly created niches of demand which endured and could be profitable for well-situated firms.

The domestic OEM receiving-tube manufacturers were able to preserve the profitability of their replacement market because (1) they possessed special manufacturing cost advantages in producing low-volume, high-power receiving tubes for television receivers, (2) importers had placed fewer tube-television receivers in the market, and (3) the nature of the buyer-supplier relationship in the replacement market made it difficult for the importers' tubes to gain a foothold because they would not undertake the necessary full-line investments to service distributors. Thus producers were able to increase prices selectively without opposition.

In the receiving-tube endgame, the tube designs which ultimately remained as a part of the active components in the television receiver the longest were the more complex and difficult-to-manufacture entertainment receiving tubes. These were the tubes which were also costliest to manufacture. Some importers were reluctant to tie up their working capital by holding these costlier, slowly moving receiving-tube varieties and were reluctant to provide the financing services to customers which were implicit in maintaining a ready inventory of these complex tubes.

Customer Traits. It had been expected that customer industries which were fragmented and which could pass on the costs of manufacturers' price increases in turn to their customers would not be particularly sensitive to higher prices during the endgame. The electronics-components distribution companies responded favorably to price increases since they too could extract higher prices for the receiving tubes when they resold them. Also, the customer industries were not powerful enough relative to the receiving-tube manufacturers to keep prices low. Therefore, receiving-tube producers were able to keep their tube prices high and to increase them during the endgame.

In summary, although the receiving tube was a commoditylike product, the high switching costs for customers in replacing devices which used tubes ensured an enduring demand for them. The relative lack of bargaining power of the distribution companies enabled the receiving-tube producers to extract the bulk of the benefits associated with servicing price-sensitive demand for a replacement product. These factors created a "favorable" environment for continued investment by those firms which could serve these markets in an orderly fashion.

There were strategic reasons for a few firms to remain invested in receiving-tube production even when profit margins in the OEM market became very thin. Although all tube manufacturers produced tubes which were interchangeable for a particular socket, at least one firm had to remain in the industry to produce these tubes. Those firms which had recently sold tubed electronics products were obliged to merchandise replacement tubes appropriate for these products because chemical process plants, government communications, and high-fidelity applications could not be cut off from at least one source of receiving tubes.

Technological Characteristics

The most important product trait in this endgame was the cost of the component. The automated receiving-tube competitors who used offshore preassembly plants and subcontracted work to noncorporate feeder electronics plants possessed the lowest operating costs and were best suited to remain invested in this industry.

Technological Innovations. Improvement in raw materials, work methods, and materials handling continued to be made through the early years of the endgame. These technological improvements enabled some receiving-tube competitors to become more efficient than other competitors and constituted one of the more important elements of "staying power" which permitted some of them to endure longer than others.

Economic Exit Barriers. The physical assets which were least fully depreciated in endgame were those investments which had been made to automate or to improve a receiving-tube plant's work methods and production process. The RCA labor-intensive technology was more expensive to divest than had been anticipated due to the relatively permissive treatments of workers' compensation claims in that particular situation. This finding suggests that if labor becomes more like a "fixed cost" due to continued difficulties in retiring employees, it should be included as being a potential form of economic exit barrier in the analysis of endgame industries.

The most significant economic exit barriers in the receiving-tubes endgame were not the physical plants and equipment. Many of these had already been depreciated in full before the decisions of most firms to exit occurred. The expenditures made on plant and equipment to conform to environmental pollution requirements or to convert from one form of energy to another represented another relatively insignificant type of economic exit barrier and they were expensed as well. The most significant economic exit barriers were the working-capital requirements (inventory) of the receiving-tube business. These affected the timing of firms' exits from merchandising after production had been discontinued.

Firms such as RCA, which undertook a service obligation to service their products for many years after the basic piece of television equipment had been sold, carried large receiving-tube inventories as a crucial part of their corporate strategies. The inventory in the receiving-tubes business appeared to represent about two years of replacement receiving-tubes stock. Unless this inventory could be sold to another tube-maker, a former receiving tube producer's continued participation in the endgame as a "merchandiser" was almost guaranteed due to these economic exit barriers.

It had been forecast that the timing of firms' exits from the endgame would be influenced by their relative abilities to recapture the value of the assets they had invested in the endgame. GTE Sylvania bought such firms' receiving-tube assets in order to help them to exit more rapidly.

It had been expected that high fixed costs due to capital-intensive technologies would raise economic exit barriers in the short run, and would increase the likelihood that price-cutting would be used to fill competitors' plants to an efficient capacity. Since those firms which apparently faced lower economic barriers exited when industry demand could not absorb all of the output of all of the major receiving-tube producers, price-cutting has not yet been necessary in this industry. Moreover, when the capital-intensive receiving-tube assets were moderately depreciated, producers faced relatively lower fixed costs, and hence less temptation to cut their prices in order to fill those receiving-tube plants. The "Major Plant-Minor Plant" loading scheme of GTE Sylvania was an example of the efficient use of the most capital-intensive plant—with its automated operations—in order to maximize the length of production runs for popular, relatively standard designs of receiving tubes. The less-standardized, low-volume, or technologically complex receiving varieties were no less capital intensive than the other tubes. However, in endgame they were manufactured infrequently on specialized assets kept in the "Minor Plant," as if they were produced in a job shop in order to maximize the economies available in operating a fully loaded, capital-intensive receiving-tube plant as well as to avoid writing off the "Minor Plant" before it was well depreciated. (GTE Sylvania would be facing economic exit barriers of a significant magnitude if it were to contemplate exit at the present time due to its capital-intensive technology and reinvestments. It is not clear whether it would cut prices if demand fell.)

Competitive Characteristics

It had been expected that price-cutting could erode profit margins in industries where competitors were significantly asymmetric in their strategic postures, for example, where their cost structures differed, but it was also expected that a concentrated industry structure could facilitate some coordination of competitive activities, and perhaps lower prices. Orderly exits were expected because uncertainty regarding competitors' relative strengths and regarding demand for the product would be low and because after the receiving-tube firms had experienced the thin profit margins of the OEM market (where imported-tube producers competed) they tacitly understood the need to refrain from price-cutting tactics when serving the replacement-tube market.

The cost structures of receiving-tube competitors differed because their respective levels of automation differed and consequently each required different production volumes to break even. Also firms' expectations regarding the rate at which demand would diminish differed and, accordingly, their reinvestment patterns differed. Given these asymmetries in cost structures, it is surprising that price levels in the replacement market could remain as steady as they did. Yet, the concentrated structure of the industry did enable competitors to avoid price-cutting as a means of competing.

Thus, the nature of the endgame product—its linkages to larger value products of the tube-makers and its importance to their corporate strategies—influenced the way in which receiving-tube manufacturers competed and the types of strategic business reinvestments which were made in the endgame. Because their product was standardized and their industry was capital-intensive (in terms of working capital as well as physical assets), it could have been predicted that competition would be on the basis of price in the OEM market where Japanese imported tubes competed, but that the endgame would not be volatile in the replacement market where importers were not strong competitors. Although their capital asset investments made their cost structures dissimilar, the competitors' concentrated industry structure enabled them to ease out excess capacity in an orderly manner. They were motivated to do so because they recognized the potentially lucrative opportunities of this market.

Analysis of Corporate-wide Strategic
Needs of Competitors

It had been predicted that an "important" endgame business might be retained longer than economic analysis might suggest was advisable and that the presence of "strategic exit barriers" might influence the timing of firms' exits or the implementation of tactics designed to reduce firms' investment levels. Strategic exit barriers did retard the exit of one firm from the receiving-tubes endgame. The influence of these barriers upon that competitor was perceived and understood by the other firms in the industry and they adapted their behaviors to keep the replacement market lucrative despite the behavior of the affected firm.

Corporate Goals. It had been expected that retention of the receiving-tube business would be important for firms such as RCA which had been identified closely with electronics. It is suspected that this corporate identification acted as a strategic exit barrier in earlier years, detering the early retirement of inefficient receiving-tube plants. But the examples of Raytheon and Westinghouse Electric, which were able to eliminate their production operations while still servicing their television receivers customers with replacement parts, dispels some of the belief that an electronics company had to manufacture its own receiving tubes in order to "maintain a presence" in the industry. The existence of alternative suppliers of a wide line of replacement receiving tubes reduced the perceived "disgrace" of exiting while one's sockets were still in the market.

Vertical Integration. Strategic exit barriers were important in tempering the timing of divestiture plans by the receiving-tube producers. The linkages among television-receiver companies, components suppliers, and their consumer entertainment electronics products were important to firms' corporate strategies. As long as a substantial number of a firms' sockets remained in use in the market, a television-receiver company had to offer replacement tubes for its electronics products. The ease with which the electronics firms' service department could replace burned-out receiving tubes with other private brand renewal (PBR) tubes quickly affected their willingness to formulate an exit strategy for this business, particularly when the asset values involved in selling plant and equipment were low or would require some writing off of undepreciated assets upon exit. When firms' strategic obligations could be satisfied by purchasing other tube manufacturers' outputs, the ease of exit was increased for firms in weak cost positions.

Even where perceived disgrace ("corporate image") was not an effective deterrent to exit, it had been expected that the economic considerations of supplying downstream customers was an important strategic barrier in this industry. As long as receiving-tube producers also manufactured television receivers, they manufactured replacement tubes internally, but when a subtantial volume of tubes was no longer required, other sourcing arrangements were sometimes utilized. The receiving-tube producers themselves manufactured the semiconductor devices which replaced tubes and were thereby able to forecast the expected demand for replacement (and OEM) tubes.

The upstream integration into raw materials was not a significant detriment to divestiture and downstream integration was not an important barrier if other PBR tubes were available. It really did not matter if the tubes were obtained from sources inside the firm rather than outside the firm, as long as a reliable supply of tubes were available.

Other Strategic Exit Barriers. Other strategic exit barriers receiving-tube firms faced included factors which eroded corporate goodwill and relationships with distributors or other, smaller and nonintegrated competitors which had purchased their tubes. The goodwill of independent distribution channels which also dealt with a firm's competitors was an important strategic asset for the promotion and support of the firm's other electronic components, such as semiconductors. Although receiving-tube volume was a small part of these companies' total business, it was irritating for them not to have the necessary replacement parts. Therefore, it was expected that firms such as RCA would not discontinue merchandising activities abruptly even after they had sold their original inventory of receiving tubes.

A substantial number of households which still viewed television receivers containing some receiving tubes would be alienated by an electronics company which did not make replacement tubes available bearing their brand names or using their specifications. This strategic exit barrier tended to temper firms' decisions to exit completely by obliging them to maintain at least a merchandising participation in the industry.

Analysis of Endgaming Firms'
Competitive Strengths

It had been predicted that firms possessing the relevant relative competitive strengths which were appropriate for profitable longer-term participation in a particular endgame environment would be better suited to pursue some of the more aggressive strategy options in coping with declining demand. A comparison of the strategic postures of firms in this endgame (when considered in light of the industry's traits) indicated that some firms did possess competitive advantages which made them better suited to remain in this endgame than other firms.

All of the competitors reviewed here were forward-integrated and placed their tubes in their own or other companies' television receivers, high-fidelity amplifiers, or other electronic products. All of the competitors reviewed above were diversified into the production of the solid-state electronic devices which were substitutes for receiving tubes, so these aspects did not constitute competitive advantages which enabled one firm to distinguish itself over another. Those firms which possessed important competitive strengths were the firms whose technologies enabled them to enjoy lower production costs or whose market position enabled them to place many receiving-tube sockets into the lucrative replacement market.

Vertical Integration Advantages. It had been expected that a large market share in television receivers would be necessary in order to place many tube sockets into the replacement market and that such a competitive advantage would provide a competitor with the cash flows needed during the 1960s and early 1970s to remain competitive in the OEM market, provided a firm's cost structure were advantageous. Vertical integration proved to be a strength to the extent that it created an internal, captive market for receiving tubes because break-even volumes for tube production were high.

Where the corporation's consumer products department was not obliged to buy its receiving tubes internally, however, they sometimes used the less expensive imported receiving tubes in their television-receiver sockets even in the cases of some of the major receiving-tube manufacturers. In other cases, common types of receiving tubes sold to outside customers were actually sourced from an importer in order to take advantage of these lower costs. Therefore, in order to capture a large market share a firm had to have been among the lowest-cost competitors in the market and kept its plants fully loaded in order to enjoy the economies created through its R&D investments. Fully loaded plants depended upon an aggressive sales force to merchandise the firms' tubes or tubed product. Therefore, the firms which enjoyed the most rewarding endgames had all of these strengths—internal markets, external markets, R&D skills, and the lowest-cost technology—in order to succeed.

Product Design and Engineering Skills. It had been expected that those firms which had invested in R&D frequently to improve their products' quality or their production process's efficiency would possess a competitive strength which was important in the OEM market. When selling television receivers in competition against sets containing imported receiving tubes, it was necessary to have the lowest possible costs in order to remain price-competitive. Firms which had invested in cost-cutting automation in the early 1960s were best suited to compete against the imported tubes and thus to place more sockets into the more lucrative replacement market. Also, the use of offshore preassembly operations gained a competitive cost advantage.

Production Advantages. It had been expected that the greatest production advantages would be those relating to automated production processes, lower-cost raw materials, and proprietary technologies. (The value of proprietary products such as the Nuvistor or GE's Compactron were not truly cost advantages—rather these were examples of products which had been designed into military and consumer applications by aggressive and effective sales representatives.) Competition in the OEM market had squeezed receiving-tube prices close to their costs. (Note the relatively low increases which occurred in receiving-tube price levels relative to many other types of products' price changes over a twenty-year span.) The firm or firms which remained to serve the dwindling demand for receiving tubes in the replacement market were those which possessed relative production strengths.

Analysis of Firms' Performances in the
Receiving-Tubes Endgame

Given the "favorable" industry structural traits, some reinvestments would be expected in this endgame. Given the differences in firms' strategic postures in this well-understood endgame, some orderly exits were expected and some continued investments were anticipated.

Westinghouse Electric was the only firm examined which exited completely during this study of the receving-tubes endgame. Raytheon had already exited from production of tubes and RCA discontinued production relatively late in the study. While Westinghouse Electric and Raytheon recovered the value of their receiving-tube investments, RCA encountered unforeseen difficulties involving employees in executing the retirement of its manufacturing activities.

Firms Which Exited Early. It was expected that the most significant internal strengths in the receiving-tubes endgame would be (1) production advantages coupled with (2) the scope and quality of producers' distribution channels, especially in reaching the replacement market.

Firms such as Raytheon and Westinghouse had not been sufficiently successful in the television-receiver business to justify continued production of tubes because they had not placed enough sockets into the television market in order for demand for their replacement receiving tubes to be sufficient to help their poor performances in the OEM market (where they had been pitted against the lower-cost imported tubes).

Firms Which Exited Late. RCA, the least efficient producer of receiving tubes, was actually helped by the discontinuation of receiving-tube production internally and sourcing of replacement tubes from other manufacturers. Raytheon, an early exit, enjoyed a "rewarding" endgame experience as a merchandiser because it presented an advantageous access to a wide distribution system. Thus a firm could enjoy a lucrative participation in the receiving-tubes market by being among the first to sell its receiving-tube assets and its technology while maintaining its favorable relationships with the components distributors.

Early Exit: "Milk the Investment"

Westinghouse Electric. It had been expected that since Westinghouse Electric's television receivers did not have product quality which was as high as the other manufacturers' receivers and because Westinghouse Electric had not been able to market its television receivers as extensively as the other producers, it would not manufacture receiving tubes in the endgame very long after it had divested its television investment. The receiving-tube business at Westinghouse Electric was treated as a part of its television-receiver business, which was divested in 1967 when a buyer for those assets was available.

Because Westinghouse was not well entrenched in the television-receiver market, the relatively small demand for Westinghouse replacement tubes made continued operation of its receiving-tube plant somewhat uneconomic. Because Westinghouse Electric was relatively inefficient in tube production and was not in a relatively strong position in receiving-tube production, it would be expected to exit with difficulty.

After Westinghouse had sold its receiving-tube plant in Taiwan in 1967, it sourced replacement tubes from other producers to maintain its service obligation to television customers, but industry sources suggested that the tube inventory Westinghouse held moved very slowly. Although Westinghouse had recovered part of its investment by selling the plant and equipment, it could not make a clean exit. The tube-merchandising business which was undertaken as a customer service was costly. When Westinghouse ceased these activities in 1974, it sold the remaining inventories to a tube wholesaler at a distress sale price.

Raytheon. In contrast to Westinghouse Electric, Raytheon had sold its television-receiver business ten years earlier. It had worked off its tube inventory and had aggressively merchandised high-volume receiving tubes which could be used in any producer's television receivers. It would be expected that the first firms which exited would find buyers for their assets, as did Raytheon and Westinghouse Electric. Because Raytheon sold its tube-marketing assets before demand for receiving tubes used in television receivers had peaked, it could have been forecast that these assets and the knowledge of tube production which Raytheon sold should enable the firm to profit from this sale.

After Raytheon had sold its technology to Nippon Electric Company, Raytheon served as a "broker" to NEC (which produced its tubes in a joint venture with a Korean company) and became the domestic price leader in the replacement-tubes market because its prices were among the lowest due to their offshore production costs. As a broker, Raytheon sold only the most popular, easy-to-produce tubes both under its own name and under other brands. Raytheon was in a relatively liquid position with respect to its receiving-tubes participation and would have encountered the least difficulty in discontinuing its small investment in the receiving-tubes business because it held little inventory. Raytheon kept its prices low, but in proportion to the higher-quality brands. Because it sold the tubes of the lowest-cost foreign producer, Raytheon enjoyed a highly lucrative endgame.

Late Exit: "Milk the Investment"

RCA Corporation. Although RCA possessed the largest market share in television receivers and receiving-tube sales, its exit from tube production made sense because it possessed manufacturing cost disadvantages. In retrospect, its delay in exiting did *not* make economic sense.

RCA operated its oldest, least-efficient receiving-tubes plant while it closed down other plants. RCA did not follow the other tube-makers when they invested in devices for mechanically shaping, firming, aligning, sealing, and packaging their receiving tubes. Instead, RCA retained its labor-intensive technology. Additional high labor costs were incurred because RCA did not use offshore feeder plants. At the time of RCA's exit, the wages it paid in New Jersey were approximately ten times higher than those paid in the Orient. Because RCA used more costly labor to perform preassembly tasks and because it was not as automated as were the other major receiving-tube competitors, the steep differential between their labor costs could have influenced RCA's decision to exit. Also, RCA was plagued with excessive overhead. For example, it retained receiving-tube design engineers (who were no longer needed) years after it had switched its television receivers to solid-state technology.

RCA lost money because it did not respond well to the economic dynamics of the depressed 1974 receiving-tubes market. When RCA designed receiving tubes out of its TV receivers, it could have discontinued its tube production as well. It is unclear whether RCA's tardiness was due to inadequate market intelligence concerning its high-cost position or whether the strategic exit barriers associated with its corporate image kept RCA invested longer than seems to have been economically rational.

RCA was, however, a vibrant marketer. Its distribution services division was competent and relationships with its independent distributors were strong. As long as there were competitors who could supply RCA with receiving tubes bearing its brand name, RCA did not perceive itself to be suffering any particular competitive disadvantage when it finally discontinued tube production. Profit margins on reselling activities were still good in the receiving-tubes replacement market. Therefore, RCA managed to milk its investment rather well in light of the highly illiquid, oversized inventory it was carrying. (Because it was "RCA's" inventory, it was worked off in only two years.) RCA sold the receiving tube assets needed to supply its proprietary tubes to GTE Sylvania, who produced these tubes for RCA to resell. From RCA's perspective, it has retained its necessary strategic relationships yet it has exited from receiving tube production relatively successfully. RCA received much of the book value of the $100 million it had tied up in inventory, although it earned no return on it when opportunity costs are considered.

Continued Competition: "Hold Investment Level"

GTE Sylvania. It would be expected that GTE Sylvania would enjoy success in this endgame because GTE Sylvania possessed the greatest technological advantages in receiving-tube production. It had invested in an automated plant and had developed designs to fit every customer's sockets (wherever the designs were used in economic volumes) and had developed overseas markets in addition to domestic distribution. GTE Sylvania had purchased the Philco and Westinghouse Electric tube assets, respectively, and had used them as constructively as was feasible. When RCA exited, GTE Sylvania purchased its Nuvistor tube-producing assets and the tooling for several other RCA "proprietary" designs. The RCA tubes were proprietary to the extent that only RCA had manufactured them. RCA had sold these specialty tubes to governmental users by using its highly successful marketing powers. There was no technological superiority to these tubes except that they had been designed into devices which locked their users into purchasing replacement tubes only from RCA because no other tube-makers bothered to "cross-engineer" these designs.

As a PBR supplier to RCA, GTE Sylvania's market performance shared in RCA's marketing successes. GTE Sylvania also used an aggressive sales force of its own to keep its own market share in the replacement market equivalent to General Electric's market share.

During endgame, GTE Sylvania repositioned itself in order to be in the best competitive position for sustained competition. GTE Sylvania had been "shrinking selectively" by closing plants, consolidating physical assets, developing improved product designs, and acquiring the assets of other tube-makers. After RCA's exit, when GTE Sylvania had acquired and digested the valuable portions of RCA's tube business, GTE held its investment positions while it monitored the likely demand for future receiving tube demand.

General Electric. It was expected that General Electric would maintain the most conservative policies regarding its strategic posture in the receiving-tube investment because the company was considered by some observers to have "written the book" on how to manage a declining business most profitably. The company was very conservatively managed and it carried a very lean overhead. When RCA appeared to be unwilling to exit, General Electric started to milk its investment rather than invest in any more competitive expenditures to reestablish its receiving-tubes position and upset the market. Consequently, General Electric could execute a clean exit if it wished to do so because it had kept its investment level low but efficient.

Like GTE Sylvania, General Electric changed its endgame strategy from a conservative milking activity to a more aggressive posture after RCA exited. The receiving-tubes business had been a cash generator and a success story within General Electric. Yet it was in a declining market, and the timing of exit was a very important consideration for General Electric because it wished to recover its receiving-tube asset values but not injure adjacent relationships with its excellent distribution channels. Therefore, the General Electric problem of managing decline was one of *not* releasing its resources too soon while also trying to avoid making excessive commitments in terms of cash, or in terms of people, resources, and bricks and mortar when the long-term demand for receiving tubes is uncertain.

The discontinuities in the observed behavior of General Electric in recent years could be traced to several significant factors: (1) a discontinuity in the leadership of this particular department with respect to the marketing managers, (2) changes in corporate leadership, and (3) the softening demand due to the 1974 recession frightened some of the companies still producing or merchandising receiving tubes. In scrambling to respond to what looked like a doomsday situation, companies like General Electric sold off assets, terminated personnel, or relocated some of their resources because they expected the future to be blacker than it turned out to be with respect to demand for receiving tubes. The market for receiving tubes improved substantially following RCA's exit for the two remaining domestic competitors, GE and GTE. Indeed, in 1977 domestic industry sales volume in receiving tubes was better than that of 1975. General Electric understood that the replacement market would need its productive capacity once RCA shut down.

General Electric was not as automated as GTE Sylvania at the time when RCA's exit enabled GE to remain profitable in the endgame. General Electric's offshore plant was in Singapore. Although GE carried five weeks' inventory to turn around the operations in its feeder plant and thus was somewhat less flexible than GTE Sylvania's feeder plant in Mexico, General Electric's offshore plant was also less costly to operate.

The philosophy of General Electric's management regarding the timing of its exit has been to maintain its financial flexibility by remaining lean and by seeking profitable markets. The following factors might make this a feasible strategy for General Electric: (1) the domestic receiving-tubes building is old and has been completely written off; (2) the automated equipment improvements made there have been fully written off; (3) the Singapore feeder plant has been rented, and therefore it constitutes a very low barrier when General Electric evaluates whether to exit; and (4) the working capital investment is being managed in such a way that it will be worked down by the time the company is in a position to exit unless demand falls too drastically. The inventory position will be General Electric's major concern. In 1978 inventory position—representing approximately two years of receiving-tube stock—is not exceedingly salable except through attrition.

It could have been forecast that GTE Sylvania and General Electric were most likely to remain in the receiving-tubes endgame after RCA overcame its strategic exit barriers because their operating cost positions were most advantageous. The product possessed commoditylike traits which enabled any receiving-tube producer to manufacture the same tubes as the other producers. A lucrative market could be anticipated due to the high switching cost barriers faced by users of tubed electronic devices and the strategic need of firms which discontinued receiving-tube production to merchandise their branded tubes to customers for a reasonable time after the sale of the original equipment. GTE Sylvania or some firm operating its assets will likely be the last producer of tubes in this endgame because it faces the highest exit barriers at the present time and the lowest operating costs.

The Endgame in the Synthetic Soda-Ash Industry

Synthetic soda ash (sodium carbonate) is a granular, basic chemical which has been processed commercially in the United States for sixty years or more for use in several manufacturing processes. Only six firms have manufactured this commodity in large quantities in the United States since 1882.

Consumption of synthetic soda ash peaked in 1966. In 1968 the first synthetic soda-ash plant was shut down. In 1967 only 73 percent of the soda-ash needs were satisfied by synthetic soda ash. Demand for soda ash itself is not declining; rather demand has been satisfied by the use of a new product, natural soda ash. Excess natural soda-ash production capacity, built in anticipation of future soda-ash demand, has kept the price of all soda-ash products relatively low. The synthetic soda-ash producers have been forced out of business by their inability to achieve satisfactory profit margins as a result of these low prices.

Natural soda ash could be produced less expensively but it requires higher transportation costs to reach the eastern soda-ash-consuming customers. Demand for synthetic soda ash was expected to endure several years longer than it did, but tightened pollution control laws forced many synthetic soda-ash plants to be shut down prematurely.

A Description of the Synthetic Soda-Ash Industry

The Product

"Soda ash" is the common name for a crystalline substance (sodium carbonate) which is manufactured in two principal grades, light and dense, which differ minutely only in physical characteristics, such as bulk density, size, and shape of the soda-ash particles. Other physical properties, such as noncombustibility, nontoxicity, and solubility in water, are common to both grades of synthetic soda ash. Light soda ash can be used in the same applications as dense ash, but it gives a finer texture and a more thorough premixing when combined for chemical processing. The physical differences are indistinguishable to the naked eye. Both soda ashes are white, anhydrous granular materials containing well above 99 percent sodium carbonate when shipped. Ninety percent of the soda ash produced in 1967 was

105

manufactured using the Solvay process, whose by-product, calcium chloride, had been simply discharged into a nearby body of water until legal chloride concentration limits were lowered in the 1970s and chlorides became a major problem for synthetic soda-ash producers.

Table 5-1 summarizes the historical total dollar sales volume for all types of soda ash.

The growth in dollar sales volume shown in table 5-1 disguises the gradual encroachments natural soda ash made upon synthetic soda-ash producers' markets. Table 5-3 shows the growth of this substitute product more clearly. As the economy expanded its need for soda ash, investments were made in *natural* soda ash instead of synthetic soda ash because the return on the Solvay process (explained below) did not justify new investments. More than one alkali produced the oxide which synthetic soda ash had provided historically; many were less costly in 1967.

Markets for Synthetic Soda Ash

Soda ash is a basic chemical finding some use in virtually *every* industry. Major uses for soda ash have included (1) glass manufacture; (2) chemicals processing; (3) pulp and paper manufacture; (4) sodium compounds; (5) soaps and detergents; (6) water treatment; (7) aluminum preparations; (8) petroleum refining; and (9) sealing ponds from leakage. It is an essential raw material in the chemicals industries, but the major demand for soda ash has been in glass manufacturing (50 percent). In 1967 glassmakers consumed about 2.8 million tons of soda ash. Glass container manufacture grew rapidly in line with nonreturnable bottle growth and the banning of plastic soft-drink bottles made from acrylonitrile. Substantial quantities of soda ash (10 percent) are also consumed by flat glass producers for automotive windshields. Table 5-2 summarizes the major uses for soda ash. Soda ash is used to produce sodium phosphates for detergent formulations. Sodium phosphate improves a detergent's grease-cutting, wetting, and rinsing properties. But, since the cutback in the manufacture of phosphate detergents, soda ash has been used for producing nonphosphate detergents instead (these latter detergents require even *more* soda ash in their manufacture than did the phosphate detergents).

Table 5-1
Total Value of Industry Shipments of All Soda Ash
($ millions)

1959	1960	1961	1962	1963	1964	1965	1966	1967
125.5	119.2	120.6	122.3	123.6	135.4	124.0	136.9	132.2

Source: *Census of Manufacturers*, U.S. Bureau of the Census.

Table 5-2
Major Markets Consuming Soda Ash in 1967

Use	Volume: Million Tons Short/Yr.	Percentage of Total Market	Estimated Rate of Growth (percent)
Glass Manufacture	2.8	38	4
Flat glass	.5	7	n.a.
Chemicals processing	2.5	34	3
Sodium phosphate manufacture	1.0	21	5
Pulp and paper production	.5	7	2
Exports	.3	4	3
Other uses	1.2	16	n.a.
Total	7.3		

Source: Compiled from researcher's estimates and field interviews.

Substitutes for Synthetic Soda Ash

Natural Soda Ash. Natural soda ash possesses identical traits to those of synthetic soda ash and is produced less expensively. Most "natural" soda ash is made by mining and milling a mineral ore called "trona" found in the Green River formation in southwestern Wyoming. The mineral trona, which consists mainly of sodium sesquicarbonate, was laid down some 50 million years ago during the middle Eocene epoch, when an alkaline lake which occupied the area evaporated.

Green River trona is an ideal source for mining natural soda ash because the seams are pristine and of a constant thickness throughout the area, making conventional mining techniques feasible. The processing of natural soda ash from trona is both simple and inexpensive, but synthetic soda-ash producers historically have had a cost advantage nevertheless, due to their proximity to customers east of the Mississippi. The freight differential from western, natural soda-ash-producing locations has generally been over $20 per ton. The introduction of large hopper cars reduced some of the freight cost disadvantage, but in 1967 the synthetic soda-ash producers could still make a profit from operations when undercutting natural soda-ash prices.

Table 5-3 shows that the proportion of natural soda ash to synthetic soda ash produced over time had been rising slowly, from 12 percent in 1958 to 27 percent in 1967. The rate of increase in total soda-ash usage was less than the national rate of economic growth, however, because other substitute alkali chemicals were available and would be used if it were more economic to do so.

Caustic Soda. While soda ash has many end uses where it is the preferred alkali because it is a solid (for example, in glassmaking) it must compete on an economic basis with other alkalis, particularly caustic soda, or sodium

Table 5-3
Volume of Shipments for Soda Ash
(short tons)

Year	Natural Soda Ash	Synthetic Soda Ash
1967	1,748,271	4,848,905
1966	1,738,000	5,071,005
1965	1,494,000	4,928,421
1964	1,275,000	4,947,901
1963	1,119,000	4,681,765
1962	978,000	4,606,663
1961	784,626	4,516,368
1960	789,707	4,557,770
1959	715,330	4,903,979
1958	626,000	4,661,000

Source: Series M28A, Department of Commerce.

hydroxide, which is generally a coproduct of chlorine manufacture. The many chlorine-caustic plants built in the 1960s to meet industry's demand for chlorine (Cl_2) spewed out an average of 1.1 tons of caustic soda (NaOH) for every ton of chlorine product (Cl_2)—customers or no customers. Because caustic soda could be very low in price, demand for soda ash became a derived function that fluctuated over time in response to the availability and price of the competing product, caustic soda.

A reliable alternative source of soda ash could only be attained over time by maintaining a continuing buyer-seller relationship with a soda-ash producer, because when demand outstripped the supply of hydroxides, supplies of soda ash became "tight." In periods of tight supply, soda-ash producers tended to give preference in deliveries to their older, established customer accounts. A major market for synthetic soda ash was the producing firm itself. Firms engaged in chemical processing activities consumed 25 percent or more of their soda-ash output internally, processing it into higher-margin chemical products. In order to ensure a reliable source of supply, some synthetic soda-ash firms also bought a part of their soda-ash needs from outsiders (in some cases paying a premium for the privilege of doing so).

Soda ash was shipped directly from the producers' factories to consuming firms. The chemicals producers maintained a marketing staff and one common sales force sold the many different chemicals of the firm. Although there was a posted price list in the industry, buyers and sellers negotiated for actual sales prices. Soda ash was merely one of several chemicals which the soda-ash producers sold to their customers. Because price increases in one market might be offset by bargain prices negotiated in another market, price increases for synthetic soda ash became somewhat difficult to sustain. The bargaining power of the soda-ash producer relative to the soda-ash buyer was that of a member of a concentrated industry sell-ing to a member of one of several concentrated customer industries such as glassmaking, chemical-processing, or paper-producing firms.

Soda-ash producers tried to differentiate their synthetic soda-ash offer-ings on the basis of services (mainly timely deliveries), corporate reputation, or personal working relationships. The physical product itself did not offer much opportunity for differentiation. Each synthetic soda-ash producer tended to serve those customers nearest to its plants, but customers for soda ash could afford to be price-sensitive when abundant supplies of caustic soda were available and ignored years of trading relationships with syn-thetic soda-ash manufacturers when reliable, low-priced natural soda-ash supplies become available.

The western, natural soda-ash producers tried to make a market for their soda ash during the 1960s by holding their prices very close to their costs. In some cases during these years of "penetration pricing," some natural soda-ash producers may have absorbed freight costs which made it difficult for eastern, synthetic soda-ash producers to earn acceptable profit margins.

When, in October 1965, Diamond Shamrock tried to raise the price of soda ash $2.00 per ton to $33.00 per ton, the western soda-ash firms were not supportive. Allied Chemical and FMC Corporation declined to go along with the increase. Allied Chemical had announced its natural soda-ash plant in 1965.

Industry-wide soda-ash prices stayed uniform, as a consequence of this competitive behavior, for several years and this eroded the historic loca-tional advantage of the eastern synthetic soda-ash producers.

Suppliers to the Synthetic Soda-Ash Industry

Synthetic soda ash was manufactured from sodium chloride and calcium carbonate. Synthetic soda-ash plants therefore tended to be located in eastern regions where the basic raw materials—salt and limestone—as well as the soda-ash customers were abundant. Most of the synthetic soda-ash manufacturers had captive sources of these materials at their locations in the natural salt-bed regions of the Great Lakes—Detroit, Ohio, and Syracuse; Virginia; and the Gulf Coast—Louisiana and Texas. Some pro-ducers of synthetic soda ash were backward-integrated into limestone-quarrying activities and mined these raw materials in locations near an inex-pensive source of hydroelectric power and a river for waste disposal.

The Manufacturing Technology of Synthetic
Soda Ash

The Solvay Process. The first step in the Solvay process consisted of crushing limestone (calcium carbonates) and mixing it with coke. The mixture was then burned in enormous lime kilns. Carbon dioxide was recovered from the top of the kiln; lime was taken from the bottom.

Purified salt brine was pumped to the top of an absorption tower, filled with small ceramic tiles. Ammonia gas was delivered to the bottom of the tower and, as the brine flowed down from one tile to another, the ammonia was absorbed in it, forming ammoniated brine which was pumped to the top of seven-story soda-ash columns. Carbon-dioxide gas from the lime kiln was pumped into the bottom of these columns and bubbled up through the ammoniated brine, producing crystalized sodium bicarbonate and ammonium chloride in solution. The sodium-bicarbonate and ammonium-chloride slurry was pumped to filter wheels which separated the two. The sodium bicarbonate was fed into dryers which removed moisture and carbon dioxide, leaving sodium carbonate (soda ash). The ammonia was recovered for reuse by treating the ammonium chloride with burnt lime, yielding the by-product calcium chloride, which was usually discharged into a nearby body of water.

The Solvay process was extremely capital-intensive. As a continuous process it needed few laborers, except to transport materials. Although some of the physical assets involved might be used for other applications, many of the assets which comprised a soda-ash plant were highly specific to that use and costly. The approximate cost of constructing Olin Corporation's 350,000-pound-per-year soda-ash plant in 1933 (the minimum efficient size for a synthetic soda-ash plant) had been $6.5 million. In 1951, when PPG Industries bought out American Cyanamid's share in their soda-ash complex in Corpus Christi, the purchase price of a soda-ash plant had more than doubled. (In 1978 the cost of constructing a Solvay soda-ash plant would have been $250 million.)

The older Solvay synthetic soda-ash plants had a tendency to become voracious consumers of cash needed to repair minor operating problems because they were worn out. The pollution-control devices required for the chlorides problem were frequently more expensive than the net book values of the synthetic soda-ash plants themselves. Pollution-control investments exacerbated the tendency of plants to become "cash consumers" where previously they had been good "cash generators" for the corporation.

The high capital costs of maintenance and pollution-control devices also made the break-even level of capacity utilization relatively high (near 90 percent) and significant diseconomies were incurred by operating a Solvay process plant 25 percent below its engineered capacity. The Solvay process was extremely energy-intensive and inefficient (50 percent of direct costs), making operating costs high as well.

The Trona-Mining Process. By contrast, when the trona ore was brought to the surface, it was crushed and screened and passed to tanks where water heated to 90° C. dissolved the sodium sesquicarbonate and insoluble matter such as shale and rock was removed from the solution in settling tanks and by filtration. The dissolved sodium sesquicarbonate was recovered by cooling the solution under vacuum and then passing it to calciners where it was held for twenty minutes at 240° C. There the sodium sesquicarbonate decomposed into sodium carbonate (soda ash), carbon dioxide, and water and the soda ash that emerged from the calciners was ready for shipment.

The pollution problems were minimal in this process. The capital investment was less than half of that required for the synthetic process, and although the mining and processing of trona required large amounts of energy and labor, the energy required was only half that of the synthetic Solvay soda-ash process.

Economic Exit Barriers. The undepreciated values of subsequent reinvestments in maintenance or pollution control equipment would be the only write-off losses directly related to the shuttering of the old synthetic soda plants, however, if the synthetic soda-ash plants were physically integrated into a chemical complex which (1) had been built upon soda ash as its central "hub" and for which (2) the soda-ash plant had been bearing much of the overhead costs, and if closing down the synthetic soda-ash plant were to make these other operations bear their full overhead burdens after the elimination of synthetic soda-ash operations, then it would be expected that economic exit barriers might deter the exit of a firm. The plants of BASF Wyandotte and Diamond Shamrock, for example, loaded soda ash most heavily in this manner.

Economic exit barriers could also originate from the clean-up costs associated with the discontinuation of a synthetic soda-ash plant. The plant had to be literally disentangled, pipe by pipe where possible, to close a part of an integrated chemical plant. Also, there were environmental maintenance costs of a contingent liability nature in the event that a subsequent tenant of the land was found to be damaged due to substances dumped into the land or water by a chemicals company. The fines on failure to remedy such emissions ranged from $1,000 per day upwards.

A Historical Overview of the Synthetic
Soda-Ash Industry

Soda ash has been known and used as an alkali since early historic times. A primitive method of removing impurities from dried lake-bottom deposits of soda ash was used until a chemist, Nicholas LeBlanc, developed a way to convert common salt into soda ash by a chemical route involving the intermediate production of sodium sulfate. Although great progress had been made in using the LeBlanc process, the high consumption of fuel and labor, as well as the disagreeable waste materials associated with the process, encouraged researchers to find a simpler method of producing soda ash from common salt. In 1863 the Solvay process was developed. Synthetic, Solvay-process soda ash was first produced commercially in 1874. The Solvay process was introduced to the United States in 1881 at Syracuse, New York, where large underground deposits of natural salt were known to exist near sources of suitable limestone. The Allied Chemical Corporation's synthetic soda-ash plant in Syracuse operated commercially in 1882.

Some of the older Solvay plants had been allowed to deteriorate during the war emergency of the 1940s but several firms did undertake renovation or rebuilding of their soda-ash plants after the war rather than build new soda-ash plants. No new synthetic soda-ash plants have been built since 1934, but Allied Chemical rebuilt the Syracuse plant in 1948.

In 1953 FMC Corporation built the first trona-based mining operation for producing soda ash in Green River, Wyoming. When it became evident that FMC's venture was a commercial success, the synthetic soda-ash industry watched with fear and dread in 1963 as Stauffer Chemical Corporation also commercialized a trona mine. FMC Corporation was an outsider to the soda-ash industry, but, more importantly, FMC Corporation and Stauffer Chemical Corporation were large consumers of soda ash. In 1965 Allied Chemical Corporation also announced its intention to build a natural soda-ash plant in Green River, Wyoming. Allied Chemical Corporation already operated three synthetic soda ash plants.

Also at this time pollution-control investment costs were increasing. As the parts-per-million criteria tightened, firms which used old technologies like the Solvay process were faced with unsettling alternatives: (1) invest several million dollars in pollution-control equipment or (2) leave the industry. In 1955, natural soda ash had represented 12 percent of total soda-ash production. By 1965 it represented 30 percent.

Competition in the Synthetic Soda-Ash
Industry in 1967

Six producers operated the ten synthetic soda-ash plants in 1967. Three other firms made soda ash using natural processes. The largest four producers of soda ash in any form represented 68 percent of total industry capacity in 1967. In 1952, before the entry of FMC into natural soda-ash production, the four largest producers of soda ash had represented 80 percent of total industry capacity, all in synthetic soda-ash capacity. By 1967 natural soda ash had accounted for all of the industry's expansion.

Allied Chemical Corporation was the largest synthetic soda-ash producer (29 percent of the market) and the oldest. Diamond Shamrock (10.5

percent), Olin (10 percent), PPG Industries (12 percent), and BASF Wyandotte (10.8 percent) were approximately the same size in terms of synthetic soda-ash capacity. Dow Chemical's output, which operated a caustic carbonation soda-ash plant, represented only 1 percent of total industry capacity.

Allied Chemical Corporation. Allied Chemical was one of the largest diversified U.S. chemical enterprises with a strong position (over 65 percent of sales) in basic industrial chemicals. Its principal products were inorganic and organic chemicals, including petrochemical products. Total 1967 corporate sales were $1,243 million, of which 11 percent was in alkalies, chlorines, and chromium compounds, approximately $135 million per year. Allied Chemical produced a wide range of alkalies and sold them in several different user markets, and also consumed a portion of its soda ash and other alkalies internally. They were important products for Allied Chemical, which also produced caustic soda and chlorine, bicarbonate of soda and ammonium compounds, and calcium chloride in its Solvay process division.

Allied Chemical was the largest U.S. synthetic soda-ash producer in 1967. The Solvay Process Company, the oldest U.S. synthetic soda ash company and one of the five firms creating the Allied Chemical Corporation, was also the oldest of Allied Chemical's businesses.

Allied Chemical Corporation maintained research and development laboratories at the Syracuse location, which had a capacity of approximately 1 million tons per year. Other Allied Chemical synthetic soda-ash plants were located at Detroit, Michigan (450,000 tons per year), and Baton Rouge, Louisiana (800,000 tons per year).

Allied Chemical maintained that its product policy for soda ash would be to provide its customers with the best service while providing the corporation with good profit performance. It was the only synthetic soda-ash producer who had made investments to mine trona for manufacturing natural soda ash in Wyoming. Given that 1967 industry-wide synthetic soda-ash capacity utilization was only 83 percent, the commercialization of a new natural soda-ash plant by Allied Chemical implied that somebody's synthetic soda-ash plant would be eliminated unless consumption of soda ash increased dramatically.

Olin Corporation. The Olin Corporation was a major diversified producer of chemicals, metals, packaging materials, drugs and pharmaceuticals, and sporting arms in 1967. The Olin Chemicals Division made basic inorganic chemicals such as chlorine, caustic soda, and soda ash, as well as organic chemicals, plastics, and agricultural products. Olin's total chemical sales were approximately $198 million of total corporate sales of $792 million in 1967. Its Chemicals Division produced industrial chemicals, petrochemicals, urethane chemicals, and other specialty products which were sold to industrial markets. Olin Corporation was a significant consumer of its own soda-ash production. It upgraded the soda ash into higher-margin chemicals such as sodium phosphates.

Olin Corporation's oldest business was the alkali operations, which began in Virginia in 1892 as the Mathieson Alkali Works. The Saltville, Virginia, synthetic soda-ash plant was Olin-Mathieson's oldest plant. It was located along the relatively shallow Holston River, above a bed of natural salt deposits. The mother plant in Saltville had a 1967 capacity of 365,000 tons per year. The other Olin Corporation synthetic soda-ash plant discharged calcium chlorides into the brackish waters of Lake Charles, Louisiana. Its capacity was 400,000 tons per year. Olin owned no trona reserves.

PPG Industries, Inc. Pittsburgh Plate Glass Company was one of the two leading U.S. producers of plate glass used by the automobile industry in the form of safety glass in 1967. PPG ranked as one of the leading producers of sheet or window glass, as well. It also produced paints, varnishes, brushes, mirrors, and cement. Sales of PPG Industries' basic inorganic chemicals represented approximately $142.3 million in 1967, and PPG Industries ranked fifteenth in sales of resins, coatings, and industrial chemicals.

PPG Industries had entered the chemicals business to obtain a ready supply of soda ash for glass production through the Columbia Chemical Company. Incorporated in 1899, Columbia Chemical had a Solvay-process soda-ash plant at Barberton, Ohio, whose capacity in 1967 was 600,000 tons per year. In 1931 PPG Industries, Inc., had joined American Cyanamid to form Southern Alkali Company, a synthetic soda-ash and other alkalies venture in Corpus Christi, Texas (250,000 tons per year). PPG Industries bought American Cyanamid's 49 percent share of this joint venture in 1951 and became one of the first chemicals firms to venture into the Gulf.

Diamond Shamrock Corporation. Diamond Shamrock was a diversified company with interests in chemicals and oil and gas. Its corporate sales were $498 million in 1967. Its chemicals unit manufactured a wide variety of chemicals and plastics. Its oil and gas unit produced natural gas and crude oil, refined crude oil, and sold petrochemical products.

It produced soda ash in the Industrial Chemicals Division, which manufactured and sold a large number of basic inorganic chemicals, including synthetic soda ash, chlorine and caustic soda, laundry soda, soda crystals, detergents, and special alkalis. Approximately 25 percent of Diamond Shamrock's sales were in these types of chemicals, approximately $125 million in 1967. Although the company had successfully diversified its source of earnings, synthetic soda ash was still an important business to Diamond Shamrock in 1967.

Diamond Shamrock produced soda products for the glass, pulp and paper, chemical, soap, nonferrous metals, iron, steel, paints and pigments, textiles, and food-processing industries. Diamond Shamrock tried to serve its traditional customers well with fast deliveries. Many of Diamond Shamrock's customers relied upon the firm for their major supply of soda ash. Diamond Shamrock consumed as much as 25 percent of its soda-ash production internally. Like the Olin Corporation, Diamond Shamrock upgraded its soda ash to produce higher-margin chemicals and it owned no trona reserves in Wyoming. Much of Diamond Shamrock's captive consumption of soda ash was used to produce sodium silicates, bicarbonate of soda, chromates, and chrome chemicals for specialty tanning compounds.

Diamond Shamrock's Industrial Chemicals Division operated a synthetic soda-ash plant in Painesville, Ohio, which had been built in 1912. Corporate research and development laboratories were also at Painesville, the mother plant of the corporation.

BASF Wyandotte Chemicals Corporation. The Wyandotte Chemicals Corporation produced soda ash, caustic soda, chlorine, glycols, oxide products, cleansing and sanitizing products, and paint and coatings. It was closely held in 1967. Total corporate sales were $134.8 million. The Wyandotte, Michigan, soda-ash plant, which was commercialized in 1927, provided alkalies for internal use and many nearby customers in the automotive industry. It was the site of corporate headquarters and of a research facility and was Wyandotte Chemicals' mother business. The soda-ash plant faced the Detroit River in Michigan.

Dow Chemical Company. The Dow Chemical Company manufactured a diversified line of organic and inorganic chemicals, plastics, bioproducts, and metals in 1967. The Dow Chemicals group produced a wide variety of basic inorganics such as caustic soda, chlorine, and magnesium oxide. Its 1967 sales were $1,382 million. Dow produced small amounts of soda ash for internal consumption at its chlor-caustic plant in Freeport, Texas, which also produced chlorinated hydrocarbons and magnesium, acetylene and polyvinyl chloride, and other organic chemicals.

Dow Chemical's synthetic soda-ash plant used the caustic carbonation production process. Under this process, excess caustic soda was used by Dow Chemical to make soda ash. This use of caustic soda had to be abandoned when economic demand for caustic soda increased in the late 1960s. The soda-ash facility was nonoptimal in design since it was intended to support the other chemical operations at Freeport, *not* to produce and sell soda ash in a merchant posture.

Corporate Strategy Exit Barriers in the Synthetic Soda-Ash Industry

All of the firms producing synthetic soda ash consumed a part of it internally. Thus, strategic exit barriers could exist where a chemical complex was dependent upon a supply of synthetic soda ash for internal consumption and none was available from outside vendors. Another strategy consideration which might keep a firm invested in this industry longer than the time which might have appeared to be economically most desirable was an unwillingness to permit more profitable, strategically important businesses from being closed down due to a reallocation of overhead which made the promising businesses look less so.

Soda ash had been important to the image of some firms because a position in soda ash defined the basic, industrial nature of a chemical company. For them, the divestment of a firm's synthetic soda-ash business could be a traumatic decision because it altered the definition of the firm's basic business ("Diamond Alkali," for example). Most of the synthetic soda-ash plants were the "mother plants" of the corporation and soda ash was their founding business.

Summary of Competitors in the Synthetic Soda-Ash Industry

In summary, the synthetic soda-ash industry was concentrated. The plant capacities of many of the competitors were approximately the same size. Their mission for the soda-ash business was approximately the same; soda ash was a reliable, cash-generating business. The competitors' histories in soda ash were similar. The competitors were quite symmetrical in their competitive postures.

There were not meaningful bifurcations between strategic groups within the synthetic soda-ash competitors' ranks. Only Allied Chemical produced both synthetic and natural soda ash. All of the synthetic soda-ash firms consumed some portion of their soda-ash output internally and sold the remainder to traditional customers with whom they had done business for several years and in several chemicals. Soda ash alone was no longer a large portion of the sales of any of the competitors. All of the soda-ash producers also manufactured chlorine and caustic soda, a substitute for soda ash.

A Mapping of Strategic Groups in the Synthetic Soda-Ash Industry

The synthetic soda-ash producers could be grouped according to (1) their dependence upon soda ash or internal consumption, (2) their share of production which was sold externally, or (3) whether or not they held a position in the production of natural soda ash. These differences can be graphed on axes which help to identify the strategic groups in this industry. The firms who were most dependent upon soda ash for internal consumption were PPG Industries and Dow Chemical. Although Diamond Shamrock, Olin Corporation, and BASF Wyandotte consumed some of their output internally, they sold more than 50 percent of it. Allied Chemical was the only firm which produced both natural and synthetic soda ash. These groupings are summarized below:

	Produced Soda Ash Primarily for Internal Consumption	Sold More than 50 Percent of Soda Ash Output
Produced Only Synthetic Soda Ash	PPG Industries Dow Chemical	BASF Wyandotte Diamond Shamrock Olin Corporation
Produced Both Natural and Synthetic Soda Ash		Allied Chemical

The Endgame in the Synthetic Soda-Ash Industry

Excess capacity held down the price of soda ash in 1967. Stauffer Chemical and Allied Chemical had exacerbated this condition by building natural soda-ash plants in Wyoming. Until supply could be brought in line with demand, price increases appeared to be unlikely. Yet increasing pressures from environmental-protection laws made a price increase imperative for the synthetic soda-ash producers. Energy costs were increasing rapidly as well. As the operating costs of the synthetic soda ash producers climbed, the delivered price of natural soda ash became more competitive and the future of the Solvay process seemed increasingly depressed. Table 5-4 summarizes the volume of shipments of synthetic soda ash during the endgame.

In 1967, the most recent synthetic soda-ash-plant modernizations (those of Diamond Shamrock and BASF Wyandotte) were at least ten years old. Most soda-ash plants were even more highly depreciated. Allied Chemical's last significant investment in synthetic soda ash was the 1947 rebuilding and modernization of its Syracuse synthetic soda-ash plant. Only Olin Corporation had made significant investments in its synthetic soda-ash plants in recent years. It was expanding the capacity of its 1892 Saltville, Virginia, soda-ash plant in 1967.

A Chronological Description of the Synthetic Soda-Ash Endgame

1967

Olin Corporation. In November 1966 Olin Corporation commenced a multi-million-dollar modernization program at its oldest (1892) soda-ash

Table 5-4
Production of Soda Ash during the Endgame of Synthetic Soda Ash

Year	Natural Soda Ash (Short Tons)			Synthetic Soda Ash (Short Tons)			All Soda Ash
	Production	Estimated Capacity	Estimated Percentage Excess Capacity	Production	Estimated Capacity	Estimated Percentage Excess Capacity	Total Value ($1000s)
1977	6,227,918	8,760,000	41	1,811,669	2,080,000	15	—
1976	5,216,291	7,500,000	44	2,343,772	2,680,000	14	155,315
1975	4,352,743	6,460,000	48	2,802,231	2,870,000	2	165,941
1974	4,048,140	5,100,000	26	3,506,895	3,880,000	11	157,534
1973	3,706,680	4,400,000	17	3,813,395	3,880,000	2	131,028
1972	3,128,773	4,400,000	40	4,304,869	4,580,000	6	145,218
1971	2,864,742	3,850,000	34	4,297,846	4,945,000	15	129,856
1970	2,678,103	3,050,000	14	4,393,096	4,945,000	13	131,487
1969	2,494,690	3,050,000	22	4,540,193	5,045,000	11	127,034
1968	2,043,000	3,050,000	49	4,595,719	5,445,000	18	129,498
1967	1,748,271	2,450,000	40	4,848,905	5,445,000	12	132,181
1966	1,738,000	2,450,000	41	5,071,005	5,445,000	7	136,997

Source: Bureau of the Census; *Chemical Marketing Reporter* ; and author's estimates.

plant in Saltville, Virginia, to place Saltville in compliance with existing effluent standards and to improve the cash-generating performance of the Saltville plant. Lime and caustic-soda production were discontinued to increase dense soda-ash production. New rotary kilns were added to replace the vertical lime kiln, and coal-fired conversion furnaces were also replaced.

The Olin Corporation's modernization investment increased soda-ash production at Saltville by more than 45,000 tons per year. The only problem was one relating to its location in Saltville on the Holston River, where Olin Corporation had been dumping calcium-chloride wastes into the river since 1895. The river was very shallow; this magnified the effect of the effluent's damage.

The Western Natural Soda-Ash Miners. In 1967 the Wyoming governor signed into law a bill to facilitate trona mining in alternate sections of land by giving an operator the right to dig relatively inexpensive tunnels connecting mining operations in two or more sections that touch only at the corners (checkerboard fashion) rather than exploit each parcel individually.

Allied Chemical, Diamond Shamrock, FMC Corporation, Olin Corporation, Philadelphia Quartz, Philips Petroleum, Texas Gulf Sulphur, and BASF Wyandotte Chemicals Company, companies which either produced trona already or were seriously prospecting, leasing, and evaluating the Green River trona lands, supported this revision in land-use laws.

1968

Demand for soda ash softened as a result of a seven-week strike in the glass-container industry during 1968, and the price of caustic soda was falling. Despite this temporary dip in demand for soda ash, producers indicated in their annual reports that they believed the long term outlook for soda ash was encouraging.

Olin Corporation. The Saltville modernization proved to be a failure in 1968 because the expected production rates were not achieved and capital spending was approximately two times what Olin Corporation had budgeted.

Allied Chemical. Allied Chemical accelerated its program "(a) to identify and eliminate marginal business, and (b) to sell off idle or otherwise unneeded properties and assets" in 1968. As a part of this program, Allied Chemical brought on stream the efficient Green River, Wyoming, natural soda-ash facility and closed the inefficient seventy-one-year-old synthetic plant in Detroit, Michigan, its oldest plant. Retirements of undepreciated physical plants including the Detroit soda-ash plant comprised a write-down against income of $138,100,000 for Allied Chemical in 1968, of which Detroit comprised less than 1 percent.

The timing involved in coordinating the Detroit shutdown and the opening of Green River's soda-ash plant was off by a few months, creating a temporary shortage of soda ash which facilitated a price increase to $35.00 per ton. This was the first price increase that had been seen in the industry since FMC's natural soda-ash plant had started to operate in 1956. The price of soda ash had previously remained constant at $31.00 per ton.

1969

Allied Chemical. Allied Chemical computerized soda-ash production scheduling at Green River, Wyoming, Baton Rouge, Louisiana, and Syracuse, New York, in 1969 to streamline delivery logistics. The investment was consistent with Allied Chemical's policy of serving its customers well while providing good profit performance for the corporation.

1970

In 1970 tightened state-level parts-per-million (ppm) standards for emissions of chlorides into rivers and lakes had a disastrous effect on several synthetic-soda plants since approximately 1.3 tons of calcium chloride are created for every ton of synthetic soda ash.

Olin Corporation. Olin Corporation announced in July 1970 that it was being forced to close its 1,000-ton-per-day, seventy-five-year-old Saltville, Virginia, soda-ash plant and lay off 700 Saltville residents (25 percent of the town's population) because the company was unable to meet Virginia's tightened water-pollution standards which placed stricter limits on the discharge of chemicals into the river than any previously imposed. Olin Corporation had no technological, economic, or practical solution to the problem of meeting the Saltville waste problem without a price increase, so Olin tried raising its soda-ash price to $39.50 per ton. But few customers would support this price increase. In 1970 Olin's Saltville plant had been operated at full capacity until Olin raised its price. Then demand fell, so that the plant was only operating at half the previous rate and operating costs per unit of synthetic soda ash rose disastrously because the announcement of the Saltville plant closing, coupled with Olin's recent price increase, encouraged Olin's customers to seek other suppliers of soda ash.

Because closing down Olin Corporation's synthetic soda-ash production facilities at Saltville would also mean the shutdown of existing by-product facilities for carbon dioxide and bicarbonate of soda, which had been fed from the soda-ash unit, the shutdown resulted in an extraordinary net charge of $10 million after taxes which was recognized in Olin's 1970 Annual Report. (The before-tax extraordinary charges in that year exceeded $20 million.)

Olin Corporation requested and received an extension of the mandatory shutdown deadline until December 31, 1972, to lessen the impact upon its employees, the community, and customers. The firm continued to run out the plant (operate it with minimal expenditures for maintenance) after recognizing this loss. The shortage in soda ash from the shutdown in Detroit, the rumored shutdown of Saltville, and the general furor over stringent 1972 water standards for chloride emissions enabled soda-ash prices to stay at $39.50 even as more applications using soda ash switched to caustic soda because the price of caustic soda was also increased.

Dow Chemical. On August 1, 1970, Dow Chemical discontinued production of soda ash at Freeport, Texas, because of "uneconomic production factors in the existing plant." Dow Chemical had been producing soda ash from excess caustic soda and had been consuming most of its soda-ash production internally. When the price of caustic soda rose, this practice was no longer economic and was discontinued. The captive output in question was a relatively small amount (1 percent of industry capacity). The Dow Freeport chemical complex housed several other nonrelated chemical processes including its carbon-based chemicals works (acetylene and PVC). Hence, discontinuing the production of soda ash did not close down the entire Dow Chemical complex.

Wyandotte Chemical. In 1970 Wyandotte Chemical Corporation was acquired by Badische Anilin & Soda Fabrick GmbH U.S. (BASF), a subsidiary of BASF, West Germany, one of the world's largest chemical companies. BASF GmbH placed an infusion of capital into Wyandotte Chemicals during the transition period and sales for the consolidated firm (BASF U.S. and Wyandotte) exceeded $200 million in 1970.

PPG Industries. PPG Industries announced that a shutdown of its Barberton, Ohio, soda-ash plant seemed imminent. Ohio state chloride emissions standards would also be tightening effective January 1972. At Barberton, PPG Industries had been discharging chlorides into the rivers at the rate of about 1,200 ppm from its 6-million-tons-per-year plant. Like Olin Corporation, PPG Industries had no means of lowering the chloride concentration sufficiently while also remaining competitive with the prices of the natural soda-ash producers.

1971

PPG Industries. In May 1971 PPG Industries announced that the shutdown of the Ohio soda-ash plant would also close the calcium-chloride and bicarbonate-of-soda satellite units. In total, these three Barberton-produced products accounted for about $19 million, or about 6 percent of PPG Industries' chemical sales and less than 2 percent of the company's total sales in 1970.

Allied Chemical. In July 1979 Allied Chemical earmarked $14 million for expenditures to improve pollution controls at the firm's synthetic soda-ash plants in Syracuse, New York, and Baton Rouge, Louisiana. An Allied Chemical spokesperson indicated that these installations were "in pretty good shape" in contrast to other synthetic soda-ash plants in the industry. Allied Chemical also announced an expansion of its Green River, Wyoming, natural soda-ash plant in July 1971.

1972

Allied Chemical. In 1972 Allied Chemical expanded its calcium-chloride processing facilities at Syracuse. Allied Chemical's facilities would enable it to produce for sale the anhydrous form of calcium chloride, a salt which, as a pollutant in Virginia and Ohio, was forcing other synthetic soda-ash manufacturers to shut down.

1973

As a consequence of alleged price-cutting by Wyoming natural soda-ash producers, the returns on synthetic soda-ash firms' investments were just barely adequate in 1973.

PPG Industries. In 1973 PPG Industries, Inc., finally closed the Barberton, Ohio, synthetic soda-ash plant, which had originally been slated to be shut down in 1972, showing an extraordinary charge of $11.3 million in that year. Although PPG Industries reported that the physical condition of the plant would make it operationally impractical to continue beyond 1972, the company had continued to run the plant while new capacity was being brought on stream by western soda-ash producers because PPG needed a reliable supplier for its own soda-ash requirements before it could afford to shut down its plant.

New Entrants into Natural Soda Ash. Because there were shortages of caustic soda *and* soda ash, the remaining synthetic soda-ash plants were pushed to maximum output levels during 1973 despite increased energy costs and increasingly costly environmental problems, and a scarcity of soda ash was foreseen. Texas Gulf announced an investment in a million-tons-per-year natural soda-ash plant and FMC Corporation invested to increase its Green River capacity by 750,000 tons per year. Kerr-McGee Chemical invested to build a 1,300,000-tons-per-year soda-ash plant in California.

1974

BASF Wyandotte. In December 1973 BASF Wyandotte Chemical announced a price increase of $2.50 per ton in bulk quantities and $5.00 per ton in bagged shipments. This would make the new prices $42.00 per ton in bulk and $44.50 per ton in bags if the prices held.

FMC Corporation. FMC Corporation responded in January 1974 to BASF Wyandotte's price increase by raising both bag and bulk prices $2.50. The other soda-ash producers followed FMC Corporation's lead. Stauffer Chemical posted a $2.50-per-ton boost across the board.

PPG Industries. In May 1974 PPG Industries raised its soda-ash prices $6.00 per ton or 12 to 16 percent, depending upon the type of shipment. PPG Industries listed its new price for 100-pound bags of soda ash at $48.00 per ton. Soda ash in bulk form would sell for $44.00 per ton if PPG Industries' price held. FMC Corporation did not challenge this price increase either.

Allied Chemical. Allied Chemical Corporation reported adverse performance in its inorganic chemicals in 1974 due to the start-up and construction-related costs of a completed expansion and a further expansion of its Green River, Wyoming, soda-ash facilities. These start-up costs resulted in a pretax loss of $24.8 million for the soda-ash business reported in Allied Chemical's financial statements in 1974, a loss of 1 percent on sales. (Allied Chemical's corporate sales in 1974 were $2,216 million.)

1975

By the end of 1974, operating costs for energy at synthetic soda-ash plants had increased approximately three to four times per Btu from previous energy costs. Steam coal, the principal fuel at the synthetic soda-ash plants (which had been selling at a delivered price of $8.00 per ton, $5.00 per ton FOB), quadrupled to an average price of $20.00 per ton (before delivery).

Several natural soda-ash expansions were completed in 1975 and several more were announced. In 1975 FMC Corporation announced an additional 800,000-tons-per-year expansion at Green River and Allied Chemical announced an expansion as well. Stauffer Chemical announced a 200,000-tons-per-year expansion in 1975.

Allied Chemical. In April 1975 Allied Chemical announced that it would close its Baton Rouge synthetic soda-ash plant in a move "designed to place greater marketing emphasis on capacity development in its Green River, Wyoming, natural soda ash installation." This would result in a substantial cost savings for Allied Chemical. Baton Rouge was closed in May 1975, yet Allied Chemical reported continuing losses in the start-up of its natural soda-ash business due to escalating construction, labor, and energy costs, together with a shortage of skilled labor and a strike in Green River, Wyoming. No loss on disposal of the Baton Rouge synthetic soda-ash plant was reported, however.

Olin Corporation. Olin Corporation announced that it would close its Lake Charles, Louisiana, synthetic soda-ash plant in September 1975 for "economic reasons" and because of "higher energy and raw materials costs" as well as an increase in the substantially less expensive production of natural soda ash. Olin's last soda-ash plant was producing at a capacity of only 280,000 tons per year before it closed down. Arrangements had to be made to supply Olin's internal needs for soda ash—about 85 percent of the plant's output—before the plant could be shuttered.

Olin Corporation provided for extraordinary losses on disposition of certain operations ($2.6 million) and on the permanent loss of utility of an unprofitable manufacturing facility ($4.7 million) in its 1975 annual report. The portion of these charges which were related to the shut down of the Lake Charles synthetic soda-ash plant was not detailed, but it is likely that $4.7 million was incurred in closing down the synthetic soda-ash plant.

1976

Diamond Shamrock. Diamond Shamrock announced that it would close its 800,000-tons-per-year Painesville synthetic soda-ash plant by December 31, 1976, because the energy costs at Painesville had risen by 300 percent since 1968. (Energy represented over one-half of the cost of manufacturing a ton of synthetic soda ash.)

The decision to close down the Painesville soda-ash plant reflected the combination of (1) an aging plant, (2) increasingly stringent pollution-control standards, (3) escalating costs of the energy-intensive synthetic soda-ash process, and (4) increasing competition from energy-efficient natural soda ash. Diamond Shamrock recognized a $5 million writedown from the shutdown of the Painesville chemical works in 1976.

1977

The price of soda ash had been increased to $55.00 per ton FOB Green River in 1977 from $42.00 per ton in 1974. In the East, the price was $85.00 per ton FOB Syracuse in 1977. But despite the expected salutary effect of these price increases, firms such as BASF Wyandotte forecast in 1977 that they would be unable to operate beyond the time when stringent water-pollution regulations came into effect.

In 1977 Texas Gulf, Tenneco, and Phillips Petroleum announced plant expansions or new natural soda-ash plants and promised favorable prices in order to penetrate the existing soda-ash market. These announcements made the soda-ash industry look even less favorable for continuing competition by synthetic soda-ash firms whose operating costs were quite high compared with the delivered costs of the natural soda-ash firms.

PPG Industries. PPG Industries announced in 1977 that it would close its last synthetic soda-ash plant, located in Corpus Christi, Texas, by March 1978. The decision was attributed to increased costs of energy, maintenance, repairs, raw materials, and government regulations. No write-down loss was reported in PPG Industries' 1977 Annual Report.

1978

BASF Wyandotte. Late in 1978 BASF Wyandotte announced that it would close its 800,000-tons-per-year plant located at Wyandotte, Michigan. The vice-president of BASF Wyandotte's industrial chemicals group called the Environmental Protection Agency's pollution-control requirements "unrealistic, unreasonable, and uncompromising." He also conceded that the Solvay process for manufacturing synthetic soda ash was obsolete because it was labor- and energy-intensive. BASF Wyandotte had spent $10 million on improvements to the soda-ash plant between 1964 and 1974 which had enabled BASF Wyandotte to set new production records at this old plant, but after 1974 the investment went sour. The older, more experienced personnel had retired and the plant was not highly automated. Hence, operating problems developed. The plant's steam utility became inefficient. Profitable production volumes could not be achieved by running at only 60 percent of engineered capacity, but because BASF Wyandotte could not fill its plant, it retired the plant earlier than its forecasted horizon of 1983.

The state of Michigan had sued BASF Wyandotte in September for non-compliance with pollution-control requirements. The remedies sought would have cost BASF Wyandotte $2 million or more which it could not afford. The estimated cost of building a new Solvay process synthetic soda-ash plant in 1978—$250 million—was also not cost-justified for BASF Wyandotte.

At the end of 1978, only Allied Chemical in Syracuse, New York, continued to operate its synthetic soda-ash plant. Although Allied Chemical did not seem to be threatened by competitive or environmental problems at that location, it expected some problems if it could not replace a major customer, Church & Dwight, in 1980. Church & Dwight, a nearby manufacturer of Arm and Hammer bicarbonate of soda, was building a new bicarbonate-of-soda plant in the West which would use natural soda ash as raw material.

Although some of the exits from the synthetic soda-ash industry were orderly and could have been planned, others were less so. Overall, this endgame environment did not seem to be favorable for continued participation by the synthetic soda-ash producers. There was some stickiness in exits, due to the force of some of the strategic exit barriers explained in the analysis above. In general, however, there seemed to be generally recognized industry agreement that exit from the endgame was necessary.

Analysis of the Synthetic Soda-Ash Endgame

There was relatively little uncertainly among the competitors in the synthetic soda-ash endgame regarding the future demand for this product as the endgame progressed. All of the synthetic soda-ash producers recognized that eventually the operating efficiencies of natural soda ash would enable the natural soda-ash producers to underprice soda ash produced from the energy-intensive, highly polluting Solvay technology. The synthetic soda-ash firms also recognized that the firms which were located nearest to their customers (relative to the western natural soda-ash producers) would be in the best relative cost positions (due to lower delivery costs) until rising energy costs also made their products too uneconomic compared with natural soda ash.

Despite this recognition of the prevailing economics of soda ash, there was uncertainty regarding the rate at which natural soda ash would become competitive with synthetic soda ash. The synthetic soda-ash producers expected that they would remain cost competitive with the natural soda-ash producers for a longer time than they, in fact, could be. The firms participating in this endgame did not foresee the impact which the following factors would have upon the price of soda ash, and hence upon their own soda-ash economics: (1) water pollution control legislation, (2) capacity expansions by the existing natural soda-ash producers, and (3) entries into natural soda-ash production by additional new firms.

The endgame became less profitable because the endgame product was being replaced by a chemically identical substitute which was less costly to manufacture. The customers which each synthetic soda-ash producer served were price-sensitive; the natural soda-ash producers kept their prices depressed. As synthetic soda-ash producers' operating costs rose, and they sought some support from their customers, they learned that customer loyalties to a particular soda-ash vendor were low. In summary, this was one of the more "unfavorable" environments for continued investment.

Exits from this endgame were chaotic and disruptive to the respective firms. There was no industry consensus regarding which firms should remain in the industry, largely because much of the uncertainty regarding which competitors could remain in the industry was created by uncontrollable external factors (pollution standards). There were managerial exit barriers associated with leaving the synthetic soda-ash businesses, and economic barriers because some synthetic soda-ash assets had recently been renovated or supplemented by pollution-control devices. This meant that several synthetic soda-ash producers carried relatively undepreciated assets in 1967.

By 1979 the only synthetic soda-ash producer which remained was one of the lowest-cost plants. It had been renovated in 1948, was the "newest" of the synthetic soda-ash plants, possessed the most eastern location (giving it lower delivered costs), and it had no pollution problem. For most firms, this was a difficult endgame. The firms which exited from this industry possessed high operating (energy) costs and faced steep reinvestment requirements for pollution-control equipment. These firms recognized large write-off losses because these legal requirements forced them to exit prematurely in some cases. The industry's characteristics in 1967 are summarized below.

Characteristics

Demand. Demand for alkali chemicals was inelastic but the availability of substitute products made demand for soda ash price-elastic. Caustic soda was becoming more available and this condition imposed a price ceiling on synthetic soda-ash prices.

Product Differentiation. There were no significant differences between natural and synthetic soda ash, only differences among vendors who could offer more frequent delivery or better service based on personal working relationships.

Markets Where Sold. Synthetic soda ash was sold by the boxcar or the bag through direct negotiation with the producing firm. There were no middlemen. The glassmaking industry was most firmly dependent upon a supply of soda ash because its technology would have to be changed significantly to use some other alkali such as caustic soda. Chemical processing users could switch alkalies more easily.

Substitutes. Caustic soda and lime could provide the same oxide as soda ash, but natural soda ash (trona) was a more frequent substitute for synthetic soda ash.

Structure of Customer Industries. Customers for synthetic soda ash were concentrated industries which were not particularly dependent upon soda ash for their oxide needs. All of the synthetic soda-ash producers consumed a part of their soda-ash needs internally. A producer's own internal needs for soda ash could be a strong strategic exit barrier.

Structure of Supplier Industries. The raw materials required—salt and limestone—were usually captively held or were located near an inexpensive source of electricity.

Manufacturing Technology. Soda ash was a continuous process using old, technology-specific assets. There were few R&D improvements to the old Solvay process, which was very capital-intensive, extremely energy-intensive, and needed frequent repairs and maintenance. Pollution-control investments were required.

Capital Intensity. The physical assets used to produce soda ash were, on the average, forty years old in 1967 and a high level of capacity utilization was necessary to obtain efficient operating costs in production.

Competitive Structure. There were six competitors producing synthetic soda ash in 1967, each of which was similar in capacity and use of soda ash internally. In 1967, synthetic soda-ash capacity was 70 percent of total soda-ash capacity.

By the end of 1978 all of the synthetic soda-ash capacity was held by one firm, Allied Chemical. Industry-wide, approximately 4.4 million tons per year of synthetic soda-ash capacity had been retired while approximately 6.4 million tons per year of natural soda-ash capacity came onstream in the ten years following the base year, 1967.

Analysis of Declining Demand for Synthetic Soda Ash

Synthetic soda ash was replaced in all applications by an alternative, chemically identical material, natural soda ash, which was substantially less expensive to produce while environmental pollution standards were tightening, requiring synthetic soda-ash producers either to make the mandatory reinvestments in pollution-control equipment or exit.

It had been expected that where a substitute product, such as natural soda ash, exists which is increasingly more cost-competitive with the endgame product due to the learning curve's effect, lower conversion costs, and higher energy costs for synthetic soda-ash production, the outlook for continued participation in the endgame will not be promising. In this example consumption of synthetic soda ash became residual demand when its price could not be kept low.

It had been expected that where manufacturers of the less expensive substitute product expanded their capacity in anticipation of growth in demand while keeping their prices low to create a market for this newly added capacity, the likelihood of profitable prices for the endgame product would be low. It was found that natural soda-ash producers would not raise their prices until sufficient synthetic soda-ash capacity had been retired to keep supply in line with the quantities of soda ash demanded.

It had been expected that the uncertainty concerning the need to exit would exacerbate the difficulty of serving contractual customers where firms also served other product needs of these customers and could damage their goodwill. It was found that the need to maintain this goodwill acted as an exit barrier for some soda-ash producers.

It had been expected that uncertainty among competitors regarding the rate and extent of replacement of the endgame product by its substitute would result in a pattern of ill-timed and chaotic exits. An abrupt pattern of exits occurred in the synthetic soda-ash endgame and the write-off losses which some soda-ash producers faced upon exit was large. Their exits seemed to be unplanned and were disruptive to firms' other activities where firms in this endgame did not correctly estimate the speed with which natural soda ash would come onstream to replace synthetic soda ash.

In summary, the transition from synthetic soda ash to natural soda ash was more rapid than some firms which were involved in this industry had anticipated. The factors which precipitated the rapid demise of the synthetic soda-ash demand were uncontrollable. There were significant differences in the sizes of the write-offs firms recognized when closing their soda-ash plants which may have been due to internal, strategic factors rather than to characteristics in this particular industry.

Analysis of Endgame Industry Traits

In this industry environment, there were no enduring niches of demand, there were few benefits for remaining in this endgame that justified doing so, given the costliness of the reinvestment requirements, and many firms reduced their commitments to the industry. It did *not* appear to be a favorable endgame environment.

Product Differentiability Traits

Natural and synthetic soda ash were fungible. In industries where the end-game product possesses commoditylike traits, the competitors which possess the lowest costs frequently also possess the greatest staying power. In the synthetic soda-ash industry, energy costs (fuel types) and pollution-related expenses were important in determining how long firms would be able to remain invested.

Product Characteristics. The commoditylike characteristics of synthetic soda ash lessened the range of options which a firm could pursue so that the "Shrink Selectively" strategy would be an option only in geographical terms. Natural soda ash was replacing synthetic soda ash in *all* applications. There were no niches of demand that synthetic soda ash alone could exploit. It had been expected that where the market's needs were similar in each segment (in this case, a need for oxides) and the product was commoditylike, the range of endgame strategies would be narrowed and the ways of executing a strategy would also be reduced. Moreover, where no differentiating attributes could be used to justify a higher price for synthetic soda ash than for natural soda ash, synthetic soda-ash firms' profit margins would be endangered in the endgame. Since the substitutes for synthetic soda ash were perfect substitutes, no justification for higher synthetic soda-ash prices existed and synthetic soda-ash producers suffered from depressed prices which were inadequate to cover rising energy costs.

Customer Traits. It had been expected that price-sensitive customers would not accept price increases in purchasing synthetic soda ash when a lower-priced alternative was readily available and that quasi-contractual customer relationships would be abrogated when lower prices were available by using natural soda ash instead. It had been expected that price increases would be accepted where customers faced "switching costs" in changing to an alternative raw material. In the short run, glassmaking customers would possess the least flexibility because soda ash is a solid, and caustic soda is supplied as a liquid. It was found that price increases could not be posted if switching costs were relatively low.

Competitive Characteristics. It would be expected that competition would not be volatile in this industry because the industry structure was concentrated and the competitors' strategic postures were symmetric. The competitors possessed similar diversification patterns and competed against each other in several other markets. The synthetic soda-ash producers, as a group, were struggling to remain efficient against the common enemy, which was natural soda ash, caustic soda, and lime substitute products. Hence, they tried to avoid price-cutting against each other.

In summary, the opportunities for a long and prosperous endgame were precluded by the presence of a perfect substitute available at a lower price. Although this situation was quickly recognized, there were some substantial exit barriers which deterred firms from leaving this endgame. Although economic pressures to exit from this endgame were strong, the combination of economic and strategic exit barriers were frequently strong enough to keep a firm locked into this industry.

Analysis of the Corporate-wide Strategic Needs of Competitors

It had been expected that an "important" endgame business might be retained longer than economic analysis might suggest were advisable because "strategic exit barriers" could influence the timing of firms' exits or the execution of tactics designed to reduce firms' investments in the endgame industry. Strategic exit barriers influenced the timing of exits where firms were obliged to provide customers with a reliable supply of soda ash due to other marketing relationships. Internal dependence upon a reliable supply of soda ash for corporate consumption was also a strategic exit barrier.

In summary, the synthetic soda ash had formed a visceral part of the industrial chemicals companies' corporate strategies. Physically and strategically, the synthetic soda-ash firms would encounter difficulties and recognize losses by shuttering their synthetic soda-ash plants. Consequently firms delayed doing so for as long as their particular strategy postures would allow.

Linkages inside the synthetic soda ash plants and linkages to customers of substantial importance to the corporation influenced the timing of firms' exits. The threat of recognizing large write-off losses upon retirement of the synthetic soda-ash plant (which may have included undepreciated renovations, expansions, or pollution-control devices) also influenced the timing of firms' actual exists. In summary, the timing of firms' decisions in this endgame was influenced more significantly by the strategic considerations than was the basic decision whether or not to exit.

Analysis of Endgaming-Firms' Competitive Strengths

It had been predicted that firms possessing the relevant relative competitive strengths would be better suited to pursue some of the more aggressive strategy options for coping with declining demand. A comparison of the strategic postures of the firms in the synthetic soda-ash endgame indicated that some firms did possess slight competitive advantages which made them suited to remain in this endgame longer than other firms. Competitors' strategic postures in the synthetic soda-ash industry were similar along several dimensions because they were all diversified into other industrial chemicals, produced chlorine (and caustic soda), and consumed their soda ash internally—in differing relative amounts. Firms served the same markets, and their industrial (inorganic) chemicals divisions' sales volumes were similar in 1967. The most significant internal competitive strengths possessed by firms in the endgame were (1) locational advantages near raw materials and near soda-ash customers, (2) technological advantages in improvements to their plants which gave them better efficiencies, and (3) local pollution standards (this is actually a part of locational advantages which could be used to forecast when firm's synthetic soda-ash plants would be shut down).

Locational Advantages. It would be expected that firms which were located near salt deposits, limestone quarries, a cheap supply of energy, and a *deep* river or other body of water would possess the greatest raw-materials cost advantages. Of these, the factors which proved to be most decisive in determining which firms could remain in endgame longest were the deep body of water for effluents and an inexpensive source of energy.

Also, the plants nearest to their synthetic soda-ash customers (relative to the western, natural soda-ash producers) possessed longer staying power because they could offer lower delivered prices when prices were quoted in FOB terms.

Technological Advantages. It would be expected that the newer synthetic soda-ash plants might have incorporated technological improvements used in older plants. The newest synthetic soda-ash plants were Allied Chemical: Baton Rouge (1934) and Syracuse (rebuilt in 1948); BASF Wyandotte (1927); Olin Corporation (1934 at Lake Charles); and PPG Industries (1931), and they were among the last plants to be retired because there were economies of scale in operating larger, up-to-date synthetic soda-ash plants. In both cases, the Allied Chemical plant at Syracuse possessed the greatest relative technological advantages—it was the newest and the largest plant, it was located near a salt mine and a limestone quarry, and it possessed a safe outlet in which to dump its effluents.

Natural Soda-Ash Plants. It would be expected that if a synthetic soda-ash producer were also invested in natural soda ash, it would be able to shut down its synthetic soda-ash plants at times which could minimize the impact of any undepreciated asset values upon its corporate financial performance. Allied Chemical, which did invest in a massive natural soda-ash plant, was able to shut down two synthetic soda-ash plants while recognizing scarcely any write-offs on disposal.

Cash-Flow Requirements. During the 1960s most producers of synthetic soda ash made the necessary reinvestments in pollution-control equipment ($1 to $5 million) to accommodate existing pollution-control standards and treated these investments as tax deductions or credits. Mandatory investments were rare until 1970, and there was a limit to how much benefit could be obtained from reinvesting in small increments to upgrade seventy-five-year-old, continuous-process chemical plants, unless they were rebuilt as Allied Chemical had done with its Syracuse plant. Eventually, the cash outflows became too large to be accepted.

Managerial Exit Barriers. The synthetic soda-ash business was the "mother" business for many of these competitors, and their plants were in rural locations where the firms had the social responsibility of being the sole employer in the region. Industry sources have suggested that some soda-ash producers which investigated the option of investing in natural soda ash did not do so because they would have to shutter their Solvay process plants to do so. Demand, at the time of their analysis, for soda ash did not appear adequate to sustain the presence of many soda-ash plants.

Analysis of Firms' Performances in the Synthetic Soda-Ash Endgame

Given the "unfavorable" industry structural traits in this endgame, and the large size of the required pollution-control investments, compared to the small expected benefits (*not* economically justified) of making these reinvestments, firms would not be expected to remain in this industry. Instead, they would be expected to exit when they could no longer justify operating their soda-ash plants and would not make additional investments in their synthetic soda-ash plants once they had recognized that their plant would be unable to meet future parts-per-million effluent requirements. Given the well-understood dynamics of this industry, it would be expected that firms whose strategic postures were similar would act similarly but that the timing of their exits might vary.

Olin Corporation encountered the most significant exit barriers. Its poor performance was due in part to Olin's slowness in trying to extract the value of its soda-ash investments. Other firms hurdled barriers which were less severe—economically and strategically—than were Olin Corporation's exit barriers. An analysis of the participants' strengths and the success of the strategies they pursued in the endgame follows.

Although the timing of their exits differed, the six synthetic soda-ash firms all eventually milked their investment in preparation for exit. Differences in the outcome of their individual endgame performances may be explained by differences in the initial conditions of each firm and in the maneuvers they executed in the earlier portions of the endgame.

Early Exit

Dow Chemical. It would be expected that Dow Chemical could dispose of its synthetic soda-ash investment without difficulty because the synthetic soda-ash plant's output was consumed internally and Dow was in the best geographic location to purchase soda ash in the market inexpensively from tne western soda-ash producers.

Dow's original synthetic soda-ash investment had been a way to dispose of excess caustic soda which, in 1956, had little economic value to any producer. When caustic soda began to command a higher price than the cost of the soda ash Dow Chemical could process from it, Dow closed down its soda-ash operations, sold its caustic soda in the open market, and subsequently purchased the soda ash it needed from other firms.

Late Exits

Olin Corporation. Olin Corporation would not be expected to retrieve a substantial portion of the investments it made in the mid-sixties successfully when information about the regulatory environment of this endgame became clearer. Saltville could have been forecast to be one of the first synthetic soda-ash plants to be unable to comply with the more stringent parts-per-million guidelines because the plant was located on a very shallow river. The relative amount of effluent mud Olin Corporation dumped into the Holston River made this plant especially costly to put into compliance.

Olin made substantial ($4 to $8 million) reinvestments in its Saltville synthetic soda-ash plant around 1967 to put it into compliance with then-existing statutes regarding industrial effluents. Olin was willing to reinvest in this business because (1) it had underestimated the willingness of the western natural soda-ash producers to keep prices low for so many years; (2) it had misjudged the willingness of its customers to absorb price increases which would help Olin Corporation weather bad times in the soda-ash industry; (3) it had underestimated the difficulty which would be encountered in renovating its 1892 Saltville soda-ash plant; and (4) it had underestimated the attractiveness of the trona mine investments to its customers. Olin Corporation had correctly forecast that demand for chemical oxides would increase. But it had misjudged the importance and cost-effectiveness of substitute oxides, especially the economic viability of natural soda ash (compared with synthetic soda ash) in satisfying this growing demand.

While Olin was focusing its attentions upon saving the Saltville soda-ash plant, the Lake Charles synthetic soda-ash plant was permitted to deteriorate. (In effect, by pouring resources into the Saltville plant, Olin neglected to make maintenance investments at Lake Charles.) When Olin tried to bring Lake Charles into compliance, the effort was in vain. The cost of shutting down each plant was high—$10 million after tax ($26 million before tax) for Saltville and $2.6 million after tax ($7.3 million before tax) for Lake Charles.

Diamond Shamrock. Because Diamond Shamrock's synthetic soda-ash plant was in a relatively stronger position to endure during this endgame, it would be expected that Diamond Shamrock would be successful in milking its synthetic soda-ash investment if it tried to do so. Diamond Shamrock operated a relatively young plant (1912) which had had major renovations in 1951, and environmental pollution controls did not seem to encumber the Painesville soda-ash operations.

Rising energy costs seem to have been most devastating for Diamond Shamrock, which, unlike the Baton Rouge, Lake Charles, and Corpus Christi soda-ash plant locations, where relatively inexpensive energy sources were available, was operating a soda-ash plant in Ohio, where energy costs were substantially higher. Despite its plant's operating efficiency and its managers' efforts to operate the synthetic soda-ash plant efficiently, it had to be shut down by 1976 when Diamond Shamrock's energy prices quadrupled.

The factors which influenced the speed with which Diamond Shamrock could exit were the availability of an alternate source of soda ash for its internal needs and for its contractual customers. Diamond Shamrock had begun sourcing a portion of its own soda-ash needs from three other producers of soda ash when in 1975 it recognized that its own exit would be inevitable. Diamond Shamrock also felt an obligation to carry its regular soda-ash customers until their needs could be satisfied as well since this was consistent with its corporate strategy and because it sold other products to these same customers. Thus, strategic exit barriers were important for Diamond Shamrock in managing its endgame strategy in the synthetic soda-ash business.

Diamond Shamrock is more fortunate than many of the other firms in the soda-ash industry because it had some time to milk its investment successfully before its exit. Nevertheless, Diamond Shamrock reported an extraordinary charge of $5 million for costs associated with shutting down this plant.

PPG Industries. PPG Industries would not be expected to remain in the synthetic soda-ash endgame long because it possessed no unusual strengths which would enable it to remain invested longer than other firms. Because PPG Industries consumed much of its synthetic soda-ash production internally to manufacture glass, it delayed both the Barberton, Ohio, shutdown and the Corpus Christi shutdown beyond the court-ordered dates to run its soda-ash plants for as long as was possible. Industry sources alleged that PPG could not negotiate a contract for a reliable supply of soda ash (for its internal needs) with the remaining soda-ash producers in 1973.

PPG Industries incurred costly fines for noncompliance with local water standards when it did not shut down plants on schedule, but was able to recover more of the undepreciated value of the plants than if it retired them (with no recovery values expected) on schedule. The write-off on the Barberton soda ash was approximately $11 million. No writedown was disclosed for the Corpus Christi plant.

BASF Wyandotte. BASF Wyandotte would be expected to be one of the last firms to exit because it possessed a location near the glassmaking industries which supplied the automotive industry and its parent, BASF GmbH of Germany, evaluated this business (or the satellite businesses it supported) as being worthy of reinvestments in the synthetic soda-ash plant to keep it efficient. Until the western natural soda-ash producers could overcome the freight differentials involved in their distant locations, BASF Wyandotte's position as supplier to the automotive industry had seemed secure, although it was also clear that pollution-control requirements would force the plant to shut down eventually. This temporary reprieve enabled BASF GmbH to milk the value of its previous investments in an orderly manner. Because BASF Wyandotte's synthetic soda-ash plant's operations also supported other chemical operations which the German parent wanted to maintain, shuttering the synthetic soda-ash plant was undesirable (because it would likely close down physically integrated operations elsewhere in the Wyandotte complex, or shift a large share of corporate overhead to other products, making them appear to be uneconomic). BASF Wyandotte would not have been able to recover the $10 million it had invested in plant renovations if it could not operate the plant long enough to depreciate it through operations. The abrupt BASF Wyandotte decision to shut down its synthetic soda-ash plant illustrates the perilous nature of this endgame with respect to asset retrieval. It is not known whether BASF recovered these costs, and the size of the write-off associated with this shutdown has not been disclosed.

Continued Competition

Allied Chemical. Allied Chemical was in the best position in the synthetic soda-ash industry because it had invested in a natural soda-ash plant in 1965, and the synthetic soda-ash plant at Syracuse was inherently more advantageous to operate than were other synthetic soda-ash plants because it had the most eastern location. This was important because it enabled Allied to sell soda ash from its Syracuse plant to its customers more cheaply than natural soda-ash producers. Also, Allied Chemical's Syracuse plant was located on a benign saline lake whose environmental balance would not be disturbed by chloride effluents and it had been rebuilt in 1948 after technological improvements from the Diamond Shamrock, BASF Wyandotte, or PPG synthetic soda-ash plants could be incorporated. Allied Chemical recovered the chloride effluents from the synthetic soda-ash operations and sold them as snow-removal salts in northern markets.

Allied Chemical had timed the closing of its Detroit and Baton Rouge synthetic soda-ash plants to correspond with expansions of its natural soda-ash plant, in Wyoming (in order to keep prices firm). Nevertheless, there were allegedly some managerial efforts to boost the productivity and to cut the costs of operating the Baton Rouge plant to preserve it before it was closed down. Here, Allied Chemical management worked at cross-purposes with the firm's corporate strategy because managers in charge of the soda-ash plant did not want to give it up.

The Allied Chemical strategy was not costless. Although it recognized write-offs of approximately $1 million on Detroit and less on the Baton Rouge plants, it exited without much disruption to other businesses. Allied Chemical did recognize a pretax loss of $24.8 million in 1974 on the new, natural soda-ash capacity it was bringing on line by contrast.

In 1967 Allied Chemical had produced at a combined capacity that represented 29 percent of all soda-ash capacity. A forecast of plant expansions and shutdowns suggests that in early 1978 Allied Chemical's soda-ash capacity was 33 percent of total industry capacity, but by 1979 Allied Chemical alone produced synthetic soda ash.

The Endgame in the Baby-Foods Industry

Baby foods are commercially processed formulas or special foods strained to a very fine consistency to be fed to infants. Baby foods are consumed primarily by children from birth to the age of approximately two years. The number of new births had reached a peak in 1957, and baby-food manufacturers had publicly estimated a 16 percent increase in births beyond that level by the mid-sixties and had built capacity in anticipation of this forecast. Instead, births had declined 12 percent from the 1957 level by the mid-sixties, resulting in significant excess capacity in the industry.

A Description of the Baby-Foods Industry

The Product

Baby foods are chopped, strained, or pureed dairy products, fruits and vegetables, or meats processed for consumption primarily by infants. The principal types of baby foods include (1) juices and soups; (2) precooked cereals; (3) strained and chopped vegetables and meats; (4) fruits; (5) desserts; (6) junior cookies and teething biscuits; (7) egg yolks; and (8) meat base and milk formulas. These types of baby foods could be grouped into three categories: (1) formulas, manufactured mostly by subsidiaries of drug companies; (2) infant foods; and (3) "junior" formulations of infant foods. "Junior foods" were more coarsely ground in texture than infant foods. The food in each category was consumed by babies progressively as they matured and their diets became more varied.

Formulas, juices, and cereals were the first products eaten by a child. Canned baby foods are consumed by babies between the ages of two months and eighteen months. Commonly, physicians recommended that the child add fruits and vegetables to its diet in the second month, and meats during the third and fourth months. Chopped junior foods are introduced to the child's diet in the ninth or tenth months. As soon as the baby can consume solid foods with ease, baby foods are no longer included in its diet. Therefore baby-food demand was a function of births and of the proportion of babies being fed commercially prepared baby foods. Consumption of baby foods had been growing slightly faster than the rate of population

I am indebted to Michael E. Porter for his assistance in editing this chapter.

growth because a growing proportion of babies were being fed commercially prepared baby foods.

Baby foods could be physically differentiated by the quality of raw materials used, flavors, and packaging. Strict sanitation requirements in production facilities ensured that all baby-food brands were equally free from contamination. Most brands of baby food offered the same flavors in a wide assortment of products. However, perceived product differentiation in baby foods seemed to transcend physical differences; mothers seemed to believe there were differences among brands of baby food and they were loyal to their brands. Extensive promotional outlays were used to differentiate baby foods and ensure that they received wide grocery store shelf space.

Commercially prepared baby foods were close to being necessities for infants' feeding in 1965. Some mothers prepared homemade baby foods, and the development of food-processing home appliances (blenders, food grinders, and so on) had made the preparation of home-cooked baby foods somewhat easier. However, less than 5 percent of babies were fed with homemade baby foods in 1965.

Births had reached their absolute peak rate in 1957, when 4.308 million babies had been born. By 1965 births had fallen to 3.76 million babies. Consumption of baby foods in 1960 had amounted to 872.8 million pounds, or approximately 233.1 million at manufacturers' prices ($266 million at retail). Approximately 42.1 percent of this volume was made up of fruits processed for baby foods ($98.1 million); 29 percent meat products ($67.6 million, which includes both meat packing *and* full-line baby-foods processors who produced baby foods); 17 percent vegetables ($39.6 million); 12 percent custards and puddings ($27.9 million). Sales of baby-food cereals accounted for another $23.3 million.

In 1958 the marketing department of Gerber Products had forecast that births would increase from the 1957 peak of 4.308 million to 4.4 million births by 1965 and predicted a 16 percent compound growth rate in births from 1965 to 1970. This optimism regarding future growth in births was widespread in the baby-food industry and new plants and warehouses were being built on the basis of such forecasts in the 1960s.

Markets

While the ultimate consumer of baby foods was the infant, the purchaser was usually its mother. The principal outlet where baby foods were sold in 1965 was the grocery store, which accounted for 90 percent of baby-food sales. Convenience stores also sold some baby foods. Originally, baby foods had been sold through drug stores as a high-margin medicinal product. By

1965, however, baby foods were a lower-margin, higher-turnover grocery-store item. Grocery stores carried only a limited number of baby-food lines, making shelf space competition crucial.

In addition to branded sales through grocery stores, there was a private-label market for baby food. Private-label brands represented approximately 5 percent of the total U.S. market. There was also an institutional market (for example, hospitals and nurseries) which purchased some of its requirements either from the major baby-food producers or from companies who specialize in private brands. Because institutions were very much interested in low prices, private-label brands were quite successful in some institutions. Other institutions preferred branded baby foods because of the quality of care they connoted.

Different brands of baby food had tended to be favored in various parts of the country, and not all baby-food manufacturers merchandised their products in the same geographic markets. Beech-Nut baby food was most intensely distributed in New England and was also sold on the West Coast, with little or no representation in the Midwestern markets. Swift had its strongest position in the Midwest. By contrast Gerber and Heinz sold to the entire United States.

Marketing

The two most important factors which seemed to motivate purchases of a particular brand of baby food were brand awareness and the shelf space devoted to the brand. Baby-food companies were selling mothers reliability and nutritional expertise. Some brand names had become synonomous with high-quality care for babies and baby-food processors spent considerable sums to develop and retain their image of reliability. Although the baby-food companies had spent considerable sums to differentiate their products, demand was still somewhat price sensitive. Gerber-brand baby foods could sell for a penny or so more at retail (an 11 percent premium), but price differentials beyond that could shift customer purchases to other brands.

The number of sidings (shelf space) devoted to a particular baby-food brand was related to but did not necessarily reflect fully that brand's share of the market. For example, although Gerber Products had held a 62 percent market share in baby-food sales in 1962, a shelf-space study conducted that year found the following shelf-space allocations within a typical baby-foods display: Swift & Company received 3 percent of the shelf space; Clapp, 16 percent; Heinz, 18 percent; Beech-Nut, 21 percent; and Gerber Products, 36 percent. By 1965, however, the declining numer of births, and hence baby-food sales volumes, had been clearly noticed by grocers. As the demand decreased, grocers began to carry only one or two branded baby-food lines.

Since the Gerber brand was best known in the United States, it was usually one of those brands, and pressure on the smaller producers had intensified.

In the early 1960s, when births had been near their peak, grocery stores had used the baby foods as traffic-building sale items. However, as volumes decreased, grocers were demanding wholesale price reductions, rebates, discounts, and off-invoice inducements to carry a particular brand, and these were widespread in 1965. Grocers also received promotional displays, coupon deals, and other merchandising aids to turn over the inventory they did carry. The retail price of baby foods had gone up as grocers stopped passing on their discounts to customers in 1965.

There was a high degree of product turnover in baby foods. Gerber Products estimated, for example, that 40 percent of its 1965 sales volume had been in products introduced in the previous ten years. Consequently, much of the R&D investment required in order to compete in the baby-food markets was used in the production of new varieties of baby foods. The baby-food producers were appealing to the babies' mothers when they insisted that it was believed to be necessary to introduce improved versions of baby foods as well as completely new flavors on a regular basis to maintain consumer confidence. Firms engaged in significant R&D to create new varieties of baby foods.

Advertising and Promotion. Baby-food companies used direct customer communications to move their baby foods off the grocers' shelves. The principal promotional tools used were direct home mailings, hospital samples, and advertising. Advertising emphasized the nutritional quality of the brand as well as the brand name. In 1960 Gerber Products had spent $3,771,000 on media advertising, or about 3 percent of its sales. Gerber Products' total advertising *and* sales-promotion expenditures amounted to 6.8 percent of its sales. In the same year, Swift & Company spent $620,000 on media advertising, or 5.5 percent of Swift's baby-food sales, and its total advertising *and* sales promotion expenditures amounted to 15 percent of its baby-food sales.

Sales and Distribution Tactics. Baby foods were sold to grocery stores either through wholesalers or directly to grocery chains by using a salesforce and "detail men." Baby-food detail men went into grocery stores to check inventory levels, to take orders, and to place the baby foods on the shelves for sale to the ultimate customers. The practice of sending a sales representative to shelve baby foods in the grocery stores was very expensive for companies who produced a very narrow line.

Leading firms also had medical detail sales representatives who called upon obstetricians and maternity and pediatric wards of hospitals, as well as pediatricians, to establish the nutritional value of their respective firm's baby foods. Doctors' recommendations were also sought by baby-food companies in order to sell their particular brand. Free samples were usually distributed to convince mothers of the reliability of a particular brand.

Physical distribution of baby foods occurred through regional warehouses and also direct from plants in regions near the producers. As a special service, some baby-food companies offered inventory reserves to their customers.

Suppliers to the Baby-Foods Industry

Although several of the baby-food companies had considered backward integration, only H.J. Heinz Company owned and operated farms which supplied some of its food-processing needs in 1965. The other baby-food packers contracted for crops on a yearly basis with farmers in choice regions where good soil or fertile orchards were located and with nearby meat packers. Some companies developed their own seed, distributed it to their growers, and hired field men to supervise the care given to crops on contract farms.

Because crops were seasonal and most foods were perishable, there were limits to the length of time produce could be stored. Therefore, baby-food producers had to arrange their production schedules to accommodate the harvest dates of the various crops they used.

Manufacturing

The assets used to produce baby foods were (1) the physical plant and warehouses; (2) general-purpose stainless-steel food-processing machinery, such as grinders and pressure-cooking equipment; (3) specialized machines associated with a particular raw material, such as pear-coring machines; and (4) some specialized equipment (strainers, for example) used only in the preparation of foods of the consistency of baby foods, or to automate a particular operation such as stacking or sterilizing the small containers characteristic of baby foods.

In order to make baby foods, the raw materials—fruits, vegetables, and proteins—are cleaned, inspected, cut or eviscerated, and cooked. Dry ingredients are weighed, inspected, and blended before cooking. Vacuum steam-cooking processes are used to preserve vitamins and minerals. Cooked ingredients are strained and flavorings and vitamins are added. High temperature cooking may follow, then jars and cans are filled and capped by special machines. Some cooking in jars to sterilize after filling follows. The containers are washed, labeled, or lithographed, and packing machines put them into cartons which are date-coded and shipped. Many inspections are interspersed between these steps and production is highly automated. Several hundred thousand cartons of baby food can be processed in a week with speeds varying depending upon which flavor or type of baby food is being produced. Special-purpose, high-speed machines were created for the unique needs of the baby-food processors.

Quality control is crucial in baby-food production. The third shift of every baby-food plant was devoted to steam-cleaning the stainless-steel machinery. The cans and jars had to be date-coded to ensure that they did not exceed their shelf lives. The average inventory replacement cycle for baby foods was over a year—largely because some crops were available only once a year.

Capital requirements in the industry could be estimated from historical outlays on facilities by industry participants. In 1947 the Beech-Nut baby-foods plant in California had cost approximately $6 million, including warehouses and equipment.

Gerber Products constructed a North Carolina baby-food plant in 1958 for $4 million, and a plant plus warehouses in 1964 for $10 million. Although the cost of a complete baby-foods complex was relatively high, the cost of adding an incremental production line within a general-purpose, food-processing complex was considerably less expensive.

There did not seem to be significant economies of scale in production. The more than 100 different varieties were produced several times per year by the major firms.

Economic Exit Barriers in the Baby-Foods Industry. Because assets used to produce baby foods in 1965 were not unlike those used to process foods for adult consumers, much of the value of assets used in a baby-food plant could be retrievable if these assets could be sold to another food-processing firm. If a baby-food producer were diversified into the processing of other foods, such as ketchups or tomato puree, the straining, cooking, and packaging machines could be readily converted to the processing of ketchup and tomato puree. The grinders and cooking equipment used in preparing some of the ingredients used for baby foods could be converted to the production of pet foods.

A baby-food processor which was backward integrated into the production of cans or the lithographing of cans could use its unutilized baby-foods packing capacity for packaging other products. If a baby-foods company were already engaged in packing foods for adult markets, economic exit barriers from the baby-foods business should be relatively low.

A Historic Overview of the Baby-Foods Industry

In 1900 babies had been fed farina and other cereal preparations eaten by adults. The first cereal expressly for babies was Pablum®, introduced in 1915.

The first canned foods produced especially for babies were sold through drug stores as medical prescriptions. Several origins have been suggested for the baby-foods industry. According to one source, the canned baby-foods industry had its beginning in 1921 when Harold A. Clapp, a Rochester, New York, restaurant owner, prepared a formula composed of beef broth combined with vegetables and cereals and reduced it to a puree to feed his ailing baby daughter. Clapp's product was soon merchandised through drug stores for 30 to 40 cents per can.

In 1928 Dan Gerber, whose father owned a Fremont, Michigan, vegetable- and fruit-packing plant, conceived of the idea of volume processing of vegetables for babies which could be merchandised inexpensively in grocery stores like adult food products. Increased competition from Gerber's products forced Clapp to begin selling his baby foods through grocery stores, and their price was reduced to 14 to 15 cents per can.

In 1947 Swift & Company pioneered processed meat products especially for babies. Gerber Products quickly followed Swift's lead by signing a copacking agreement with Armour & Company, another meat-packing firm. Heinz introduced baby meat products in 1952, and Beech-Nut began copacking baby meat products with Hormel & Company in 1955. The introduction of baby meat products was a significant product innovation, and most recent such innovation in the industry.

While these firms were competing in the baby-foods industry in 1965, there had been some unsuccessful entrants into the baby-foods business. The Hygeia Company of Buffalo entered the baby-foods business in 1930, selling its products through the drug trade. After two or three years Hygeia had left the industry, having been unable to mount the necessary marketing effort. Stokley-Van Camp had entered the market in the late 1930s and distributed its baby foods in a few areas, but had withdrawn from the market by early 1947.

Libby, McNeil also had entered the baby-food business in the mid-1930s and offered a complete line of baby-food fruits, vegetables, vegetable-meat combinations, and juices on a national basis for several years. While Libby, McNeil had done quite well through World War II, it began to slip badly in 1947. By the mid-1950s Libby had only two or three markets where it had a significant share and its share was only 2 to 3 percent in those markets. Libby discontinued its baby-food line in 1960. Campbell Soup had attempted to market four or five varieties of baby soup in the late 1940s but had failed to establish itself in the business. In 1959 General Foods had test-marketed a limited line of baby foods under the Birds-Eye label. It then launched a substantial advertising and promotional campaign and moved out of its test market. However, Birds-Eye baby foods were withdrawn two years after introduction when the operation did not prove to be profitable. Since 1955, infant cereals have accounted for about 10 percent of the baby-food industry, excluding juices and formulas. Mead, Johnson was first to enter the cereals market in 1915 with its Pablum cereal. In 1956 Mead, Johnson's Pablum cereal had about 50 percent of the market and Gerber's infant cereals had about 25 percent. By 1962 these market shares had been reversed; Mead, Johnson had 21 percent of the cereals market; Gerber had 50 percent.

Competition in the Baby-Foods Business in 1965

Six companies produced baby foods or formulas in 1965. The sales of the leading three producers of baby food comprised approximately 91 percent of industry sales in 1965. The three leading baby-food companies all merchandised a full line of baby fruits, vegetables, meats, desserts, juices, and cereals. The competitors were not equally represented in all parts of the United States. Gerber had approximately 70 percent of the West and Southwest. Heinz and Clapp shared the remaining 30 percent in the West, with Swift and Beech-Nut only minor factors.

Gerber Products Company. Gerber Products was a specialist in baby foods. From 1943 until 1960, baby food had been its *only* business. By 1965, Gerber Products also owned Knoll & Company (which produced vinyl baby pants and bibs) and Kapart (which produced stretchwear outer garments for infants). These were a minor portion of Gerber Products' 1965 sales volume of $194.0 million, but represented a Gerber strategy of garnering "more bucks per baby." Gerber's sales were primarily domestic, with only 10 percent coming from foreign operations.

Gerber Products had been the industry leader in baby foods since its 1928 decision to sell baby foods in grocery stores. Its cherub-faced corporate trademark was synonymous with babies, and Gerber had a reputation for high quality. Every year some 3 million mothers received samples of Gerber cereals through the mails soon after the birth of their child. Later they received strained-food samples when the infants were old enough to consume them. Gerber also supported its products by sponsoring television shows, advertising in magazines, and through cooperative promotional programs with hospitals and obstetricians.

Gerber Products offered the widest line of baby foods in the industry. It produced many flavors and consistencies of fruits, vegetables, meats, juices and soups, precooked cereals, desserts, cookies and teething biscuits, egg yolks, and infant formulas. Gerber devoted considerable attention to developing new products for babies to appeal to mothers' desires for improved baby foods. During 1964 Gerber had dedicated a new research facility which it had constructed in Fremont, Michigan, at corporate headquarters. The research lab developed new baby foods and methods of packing them. In

1964 almost 40 percent of Gerber Products' sales volume had come from products which it had introduced from its labs the previous decade.

In the infant formula market, Gerber had tried to capture a significant market share with its "Modilac® " product. Gerber's efforts to become the leading full-line baby-food company—from formula to toddler meals—were not fully successful, however, because Gerber's sales of formula never achieved a critical volume. Consumers seemed to feel that a formula producer should be affiliated with a pharmaceutical laboratory.

Because Gerber Products was so dedicated to the production of baby foods, its plants were the most specialized in the industry. Gerber Products produced baby foods in plants located in Fremont, Michigan (built in 1928); Oakland, California (1943); Rochester, New York (1950); Asheville, North Carolina (1959) and Fort Smith, Arkansas (1965), in the United States. Gerber also had several international licensees (Australia, France, Germany, Italy, Japan, Phillipines, South Africa, and the United Kingdom), and subsidiaries in Canada (1950), Costa Rica (1968), and Mexico (1959).

These plant locations also served as warehouses and Gerber had 100 percent distribution to ensure rapid shipments through supermarkets and other large food stores using a sales force of 1,200. Gerber Products was particularly well positioned to service the southern, southwestern, and western market regions. Gerber purchased fruits and vegetables from farmers in the several regions where its plants were located. Some Gerber foods—particularly its meats and fruit juices—were produced under contract for Gerber by nearby food processors and by meat-packing plants.

In 1958, the year after the peak number of births (4.3 million), Gerber had forecast 4.2 million births in 1960; 4.4 million births in 1965; 5.1 million births in 1970; and 5.8 million births in 1975. The new Asheville, North Carolina, and Fort Smith, Arkansas, plants reflected this long-range forecast.

Beech-Nut Foods. In 1965, the Beech-Nut Packing Company was a part of Beech-Nut Life Savers, Inc., which manufactured chewing gum, candy, coated gum, cough drops, chocolate products, fresh baked pies, coffee and tea, mints and fruit drops, paper cartons, cosmetics and toiletries, and baby foods. Corporate sales were $206.2 million in 1965.

The company was divided into operating groups by its ten plant locations and also by the assets of each company. Beech-Nut Packing Company had merged with Life Savers Corporation in 1956, and, prior to the merger, sales had been $83.5 million, with a return on sales of 3 percent. In 1965 Beech-Nut Foods contributed 30 percent of corporate sales and 35 to 40 percent of corporate income.

Beech-Nut Foods offered a line of baby-food products that was nearly as wide as that of Gerber Products. In addition to offering a wide line of products, Beech-Nut had also tried to lead the industry through research and development in baby nutrition, through the introduction of new products, and through the continued upgrading of existing products. In 1965 Beech-Nut Foods was attempting to increase its share of the U.S. market. Beech-Nut had scarcely touched the growing opportunities for export sales, foreign licensees, and foreign subsidiaries, in 1965.

Beech-Nut Foods distributed its baby foods in the same manner as did Gerber Products. However, Beech-Nut foods were not distributed in all parts of the nation. Beech-Nut operated baby-food plants in the following locations: Canajoharie, New York (1899); Rochester, New York (1955); and San Jose, California (1947). Beech-Nut Foods had also purchased a plant site at Three Rivers, Michigan (1953), for possible expansion of baby-food facilities. In 1965 *Barron's* reported that Beech-Nut Life Savers was planning to build a baby-foods plant in Michigan in anticipation of the next baby boom.

Beech-Nut Foods was not vertically integrated. Like Gerber Products, it processed produce which it had purchased from farmers. Its baby meat products were packed for it under contract by Hormel & Company.

H.J. Heinz Company. The H.J. Heinz Company was a widely diversified, vertically integrated food processor in 1965 whose principal products included soups, ketchups and other tomato products, pickles, vinegar, baked beans, spaghetti condiments, individual plate lunches, baby foods, and many other food products. The many different types of foods produced by Heinz and its subsidiaries were sold by H.J. Heinz in the United States under the Heinz label and the trademark "57 Varieties." H.J. Heinz also sold tuna and fish products under the name "Starkist" and pet foods under the trade name "9 Lives." Heinz operated eleven plants and numerous raw-materials receiving stations and warehouses. Most of these properties were leased.

Corporate sales of H.J. Heinz Company were $519.6 million in 1965, of which 46 percent were international. U.S. baby-food sales represented about 10 percent of the Heinz USA food division.

Heinz was the largest baby-food company on a worldwide basis, but it had achieved its greatest successes in the baby-foods business abroad. Heinz had 80 percent of world sales of baby food. Its subsidiaries—Plasmon (Europe), Alimentos Heinz C.A. (Venezuela), and H.J. Heinz Company of Australia, Ltd.—had achieved a rapid growth and a market dominance which Heinz USA could not duplicate in its home market. Heinz was an innovator in baby-foods worldwide but *not* in the United States for this reason. When Alimentos Heinz C.A. (or Plasmon) had developed a new baby-food product, it was tested in markets where Heinz was the leading baby-food brand. Then, if it were successful there, the innovation might be introduced in the United States.

Heinz offered 185 varieties of infant fruits, vegetables, meats, cereals, and other preparations overseas but only 115 varieties in the United States market.

Heinz USA competed on price, when it was necessary to do so, to hold its desired market share. Brand loyalty to Gerber Products was not so strong that a one-cent or more differential could not entice some mothers to purchase Heinz baby foods instead. Generally, this price strategy gave Heinz baby foods an image of lesser quality than Gerber's.

Three U.S. plants were dedicated to processing H.J. Heinz baby foods. They were located in Pittsburgh and Chambersburg, Pennsylvania, and Tracy, California. Heinz baby foods were distributed through the same logistical systems used for other Heinz products. Some of its products were produced for it by copackers and were sold under the Heniz label.

Swift & Company. Swift & Company was the largest meat-packer in the world in 1965. It was engaged in meat-packing and produced related food lines throughout the United States and to some extent abroad, through forty-six packing houses.

Principal products were meats and meat products; poultry; butter, cheese, margarine, and ice cream; eggs; hides, skins, wool, and leather; cotton-seed products; soybeans, peanut oils, peanut butter, cooking oils, and other vegetable compounds; phosphate rock; plant food, livestock and poulty feed, and pet foods; and industrial chemicals, among other prodducts. Consolidated Swift & Company sales in 1965 were $2.75 billion.

Swift & Company was a very specialized producer of baby foods. It manufactured *only* baby meats, egg-yolk dinners, and other high-protein baby foods. Swift had been forced to follow a narrow-line product strategy by the provisions of a consent decree in the 1920 meat-packing antitrust suit against the five major meat-packing firms. The suit precluded packers from expanding into other food products.

The Swift & Company baby meats were produced at three meat-packing plant locations, located in East St. Louis, Illinois; St. Paul, Minnesota; and Fort Worth, Texas. These plants were also engaged in other types of packing operations including pet foods.

Swift research chemists had developed the baby meats in 1946 as a product to take up slack in underutilized meat-packing plants. Swift & Company's sales force had promoted the new product successfully as being a specialized high-protein supplement designed to satisfy the special nutritional needs of infants relatively late in the feeding cycle. Sales of Swift & Company baby meats had peaked in 1954, eight years after their introduction. The subsequent decline was due in part to the fact that Swift's initial success was imitated by others in the baby-foods business who added meats to their already wide lines of fruits, vegetables, juices, and cereals for babies.

Later, in an effort to better use its assets, Swift copacked high-protein meats for other baby-food companies who did not themselves produce a line of baby meats. Swift packed meat for babies under the Beech-Nut and Topco labels, as well as for other private label accounts. The volume of meats packed for Beech-Nut and Topco represented 30 percent of the baby meat volume produced in the Swift & Company plants in 1965.

The East St. Louis plant producing baby meats and other products was being closed down in 1965 and there was also excess capacity in both the Fort Worth, Texas, and St. Paul, Minnesota, plants. This slack enabled these plants to produce the baby meat products formerly packed at East St. Louis.

Mead, Johnson & Company. Mead, Johnson & Company manufactured over 185 consumer products including nutritional products for infants and all ages, and pharmaceuticals and contraceptives whose usage depended mainly upon prescription. Mead, Johnson also introduced "Metrecal®" for weight reduction in the nonprescription market. Its corporate sales in 1965 were $22.9 million.

Mead, Johnson offered a very narrow line of baby foods, consisting of three items. Mead, Johnson produced "Pablum® ," a precooked cereal for infants; "BiB" juices, and "Enfamil® ," an infant formula. Mead, Johnson had gotten its start as a company with Pablum® cereal around 1915. Pablum® cereals, BiB juices, Enfamil® infant formula, and other special-purpose nutritional products of Mead, Johnson & Company were marketed through grocery channels by the Edward Dalton Division.

Although sales of Enfamil® had risen 16 percent in 1965 and had made inroads into competitors' market shares of the $100 million infant-formula market, sales of Pablum® and BiB juices had recorded declining sales volumes in 1965. Pablum cereals and BiB juices were priced competitively with the brands of Beech-Nut, Heinz, and Gerber, although Heinz may have been one cent cheaper at retail. BiB and Pablum® were nevertheless losing share. Mead, Johnson's share had eroded over twenty percentage points since 1955, thanks largely to Gerber. But Enfamil® had become second in infant formula sales to Abbott Laboratories (who produced Similac®). Profits for Mead, Johnson's Pablum® and BiB juices were holding stable in 1965 as sales volume waned, largely because promotional expenditures supporting these products had been reduced.

Abbott Laboratories. Abbott Laboratories was leading domestic producer of pharmaceuticals, hospital products, medicinal chemicals, antibiotics, bulk intravenous solutions, and vitamin products. Abbott Laboratories also manufactured and distributed chemicals for agriculture and industry. Its corporate sales in 1965 were $236.8.

Abbott Laboratories' subsidiary, Ross Laboratories, which was acquired in 1964, produced Similac® , a nondairy (hence hypoallergenic) infant nutritional formula for the baby-food market. Ross Laboratories was located in Columbus, Ohio, with plants in Sturgis, Michigan, and Mitchell, South Dakota. The company also produced "Pream," a nondairy coffee creamer, and other products. Pediatric products contributed approximately 17 percent of Abbott Laboratories' total corporate sales in 1965.

Abbott Laboratories specialized in infant formulas within the baby-food market. Although Abbott Laboratories rarely advertised its infant feeding formula, Similac was the leading product of that type sold in the United States. Abbott Laboratories used the same "medical detail" salesforce to convince doctors to recommend Similac to new mothers and to sell doctors on the use of Abbott Laboratories' intravenous solutions and other products. The medical salesforce added credibility to the formula's claims of nutritional value, and doctors' recommendations to mothers to use the formula had greatly increased the product's credibility with mothers.

Corporate Strategy Exit Barriers in the Baby-Foods Business. Baby-food firms would face exit barriers which may have deterred them from (1) using their baby-foods plants and equipment for the production of some other canned foods or from (2) dropping some of the duplicative or unprofitable product varieties in a wide product-line strategy. For example, Gerber Products and Beech-Nut Foods had a strategic resistance to canning other types of foods using their baby-food assets. The idea that their assets could be used to process products other than baby foods was repugnant to their management. Similarly, some baby-food companies would not reduce their wide prolifieration of product offerings because a full product line (over 100 items) was believed to be necessary in order to keep competitors' products off the grocers' shelves. Therefore, competitors would subsidize their losing products rather than delete them.

Thus, if it was a part of a firm's strategy to offer a wide variety of canned products, baby foods might be important to it. For Heinz and Swift, U.S. baby foods were only a small part of their corporate sales. For Swift, baby foods were, in fact, a minor business, originally designed to fill excess meat-packing capacity. But Swift believed in its posture as a "pioneer" in baby protein needs. Thus Swift & Company remained in the baby foods business to preserve this image. Similarly, H.J. Heinz remained in the U.S. baby-foods industry because it was the dominant global baby-foods company. Corporate pride would not let the U.S.-based global baby-food firm abandon a position in its native markets, just as Swift apparently could not concede that Gerber had outperformed it in baby meats for many years.

Single Business Firm Strategic Exit Barriers. For Gerber Products and the management of Beech-Nut Foods, the baby-foods industry was important because they were among the earliest businesses of the companies and because they comprised a larger part of the firms' total corporate sales. By contrast for Heinz, the overseas sales were quite important (46 percent of sales), but for Gerber Products foreign baby foods represented less than 10 percent of sales. Since these firms met in the overseas arena, some of the seemingly futile price-cutting of H.J. Heinz in U.S. baby-food markets might have been intended to weaken the potential threat of Gerber baby foods overseas.

The baby-foods production assets could have been used for other manufacturing uses, but the value of goodwill and brand identification which had been developed through years of advertising and communicating with the babies' mothers acted as a deterrent to exit for successful firms. Such strategic (as well as emotional managerial) exit barriers could upset the timing of an exit or the valuation of baby-food firms' reinvestment decisions (such as new advertisement expenditures, decisions to renovate rather than to close down plants, or tactics involving new product introductions in endgame). Such strategic (identity) barriers could delay a baby-food firm's exit decision until competition had become quite uneconomic.

Summary of Competitiors in the Baby-Foods Industry

Baby-foods producers pursued one of two product strategies for baby foods: (1) they offered a wide line of baby fruits, vegetables, cereals, juices, meats, and proteins; or (2) they specialized in a narrower group of baby foods, for example, infant formulas or baby meats. Most of the baby-food companies were diversified into other businesses in addition to baby foods. Gerber Products, alone, had not diversified out of the baby business because Gerber was a specialist in baby foods possessing the largest market share. Beech-Nut Foods, which had been heavily invested in its baby-food packing activities in the 1950s, possessed the second-largest market share.

Baby foods were important to Gerber Products in 1965, but less important to Beech-Nut Foods and to Mead, Johnson. Swift & Company was highly diversified and produced baby meats, in 1965, as a means of absorbing excess capacity in meat-packing plants which otherwise might have been shut down prematurely. Baby foods were also less important to H.J. Heinz and to Abbott Laboratories because their distribution systems were already used to sell other products.

A Mapping of Strategic Groups in the Baby-Foods Business

Within the baby-foods industry, there were two major strategic groups: (1) wide-line producers and (2) specialized or narrow-line producers. Within each of these groups, a classification by importance of the baby-food products relative to total sales is also possible. Thus, members of the majority strategic groupings could be delineated as shown below.

	Baby Foods of High Strategic Importance	Baby Foods of Low Strategic Importance
Wide-Line Product Strategy	Gerber Products Beech-Nut Foods	Beech-Nut Foods H.J. Heinz
Specialized or Narrow Product Strategy	Mead, Johnson	Abbott Laboratories Swift & Company

Along these axes, the firms which were most committed to a particular characteristic are positioned at the extremes of this "strategic space." For example, Mead, Johnson considered baby foods to be important in its product mix, but it offered a relatively narrow line of products. Gerber Products offered the widest product line; baby foods were very important to it. Swift & Company and Abbott Laboratories offered the narrowest product lines and were the most diversified into nonfood products. Baby foods were of relatively low strategic importance to these firms when evaluated as a percentage of sales or in only the U.S. arena.

Summary of Competition in the Baby-Foods Industry. In summary, the baby-foods industry was concentrated, and the market shares of the firms in it were unequal. There were differences in firms' geographic distribution patterns as well as differences in their strategic postures. Consequently, the competitive environment of this industry could be potentially volatile in endgame within markets where asymmetric competitors met and demand for their products was shrinking.

The Endgame in the Baby-Foods Industry

There proved to be a considerable gap between the baby-food producers' expectations concerning the birth rate and the actual number of births over the 1960 to 1978 period. None of the baby food companies believed that the birth rate would decline as much as it did (42 percent) for as long as it did (twenty years). Figure 6-1 compares Gerber Products' 1958 forecast with the actual number of births which occurred from 1960 to 1975. Gerber Products was expecting almost 6 million babies in 1970. Instead, only 3.7

million arrived in 1970, a 38 percent discrepancy that reflected the fact that the postwar baby boom of the 1950s was an aberration.

A shrinking number of births led to strongly increased competition in the baby-foods industry. Grocers demanded a higher margin for devoting shelf space to baby-food producers' lines as unit demand fell. The number of shelf facings (space) allocated to baby foods in grocery stores was reduced.

Millions of Births

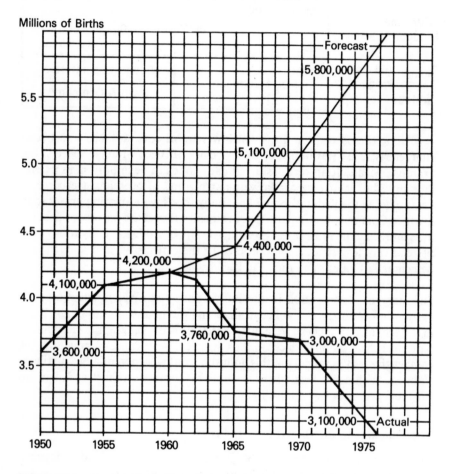

Sources: Gerber Products' Long-Range Forecast, Annual Report, 1958; U.S. Bureau of the Census.

Figure 6-1. Comparison of Forecast Birth Rates with Actual Birth Rate (1950-1975)

Retailers raised their baby-food prices by a few cents while baby-food producers lowered their prices to retailers in an industry-wide price war for shelf space. Pricing in the industry was disrupted by the imposition of price controls in 1971. The relative percentage of baby foods sold in grocery stores had increased by 1971 when a larger percentage of infant formulas began to be sold in grocery instead of drug-store outlets, which, in conjunction with a shift away from breast-feeding, caused sales of infant formula to grow rapidly. In 1974 more mothers began to supplement their babies' diets with homemade baby foods in response to the heavily publicized criticisms of the baby-food producers leveled by *Consumer Reports* and other consumerists.

A Chronological Description of the Endgame in the Baby-Foods Industry

1966

Gerber Products. In 1966 Gerber Products discontinued its copacking agreement with Armour & Company and began to produce its baby meat products internally. Similarly, production of juices, which had been packed by other processors under Gerber's supervision, was brought inside to plants in Asheville, North Carolina; in Rochester, New York; and in Fremont, Michigan. Additional freezer capacity was planned for Fremont to support the new, internal production of Gerber baby meat products. The cold-storage facility at Asheville was also scheduled to be doubled.

In 1966 Gerber also introduced new juices, cereals, and desserts to widen its product line. In addition to Gerber's "Modilac® " infant formula, "Meat Base" and "Lambase" infant formulas were also marketed heavily in 1966 to capitalize upon the growing acceptance of commercially prepared infant formulas.

Gerber Products also continued its strategy of related diversification. In 1966 Gerber entered the life-insurance business, using an existing, successful marketing channel—direct mailings. Parents of newborn babies received mail solicitations from Gerber Insurance Company to purchase low-cost life insurance for *young* adults. Gerber also introduced a line of babywear in early 1966 manufactured by its Kapart subsidiary.

Swift & Company. In an effort to lower their unit cost of distribution, Swift & Company experimented with a cooperative distribution system whereby Beech-Nut Foods' sales representatives would shelve Swift-brand—as well as Beech-Nut—baby foods during their regular sales calls. This program was unsuccessful because of the significant geographical differences in the markets the two firms served. Beech-Nut brands were well developed in the East and thinly distributed in the West, except for California. Swift & Company had enjoyed its greatest popularity in markets such as New York or Chicago as well as in the western states where Beech-Nut was *not* distributed. Swift & Company also had better-developed distribution channels in western states.

By the end of 1966 Swift & Company found it necessary to cancel this cooperative program and to reinstitute its own shelving program, resulting in higher costs.

1967

The birth rate continued to fall in 1967, as did the absolute *number* of babies born.

Swift & Company. In 1967 Swift & Company offered a rebate to grocers which it called an "in-lieu-of-service" discount, in conjunction with a boost in its advertising expenditures. This campaign was undertaken to encourage dealers to stock their own shelves with Swift baby meat products. Although this advertising campaign and grocer's discount gave Swift & Company a higher cost per unit than its competitors this action was in fact *less* expensive per unit than the cost of Swift's providing its own detail persons as the other firms had been doing.

The in-lieu-of-service discount did *not* improve Swift's competitive position. Sometimes the Swift & Company baby meats were shelved with Swift meat products instead of with the other baby-food products.

Gerber Products. In 1967 Gerber tested some products which could utilize its excess packing capacity. Gerber had chosen to try to introduce high-margin, gourmet foods since it recognized that it could not compete effectively in selling the low-margin, high-volume food products against the established food packers. Its first "single-service" (in glass jars) adult foods were Beef Burgundy and Turkey Mornay. They looked like baby foods. Gerber Products also tried to expand the usage of baby food by developing and promoting baby foods as an ingredient in preparing other foods. It issued cookbooks which used its baby foods as ingredients or as sauces in an effort to sell more jars of baby food.

1968

In 1968 the cost of glass jars rose due to a prolonged strike in the glass industry. Freight cost increases also added to the pressures upon the baby-food firms for a price increase. However, prices remained at 14 or 15 cents per jar, the same as the 1930's levels. Producers' profitability was generally depressed even more when some members of the baby-foods industry started cutting prices to grocers on some products.

H.J. Heinz, USA. Heinz USA tried to counter the sagging demand for its baby-food products by increasing its advertising expenditures and by lowering some of its prices to grocers. Heinz reported that these activities had been successful, and claimed a significant increase in sales volumes and an improved U.S. market share. Beech-Nut and Gerber followed the Heinz wholesale price cut to maintain their grocery-store shelf facings.

Beech-Nut Foods. In 1968 Beech-Nut Life Savers was acquired by E.R. Squibb Company, a pharmaceuticals firm, which had been affiliated with Olin-Mathieson. Squibb produced prescription drugs, cosmetics, medical chemicals, household products, and medical diagnostics. The absorption of Beech-Nut Foods into a pharmaceutically based corporation should have given Beech-Nut an entree into the manufacture of infant feeding formulas. None was introduced, however. Instead, new funding was used to make Beech-Nut Foods more aggressive in its existing retail markets for baby foods.

Several new baby foods were introduced by Beech-Nut during 1968. Efforts were made to introduce the Beech-Nut line of baby foods into new major geographic markets where it had not previously been available. This was supported by a 9 percent boost in an already expanded advertising campaign and by lowered prices to grocers. Beech-Nut *did* become better established in the northeastern markets and it was able to move rapidly into new markets as a result of this campaign. The market share it captured was frequently at the expense of Gerber.

Gerber Products. Gerber's "Toddler Meals" in a jar were introduced in the Northeast and East Central states. "Playbox Cookies" and "Gerber Pretzels" snack foods were introduced nationally. A new junior cereal was introduced by Gerber in its eastern markets. These product introductions were frequently made in Beech-Nut's home market in order to bolster Gerber's slightly deteriorating market position there.

Gerber increased its efforts to market pureed fruits, vegetables, and meats to the institutional market. Larger containers and increased advertising in the appropriate trade and professional journals supported this particular marketing effort.

Gerber's sales in 1968 were the highest in the company's history. Much of this performance was due to Gerber's diversification into other nonfood products used for babies.

Swift & Company. In 1968 the second Swift & Company meat-packing plant which had produced baby foods—in St. Paul, Minnesota— was closed. At this same time, the Fort Worth, Texas, meat-packing plant was no longer operating at full capacity. Therefore, the Fort Worth plant began to produce the high-protein baby meat products which had been manufactured in Minnesota.

Mead, Johnson and Company. In 1968 the Bristol-Myers Company acquired Mead, Johnson. It invested several million dollars in the company and launched a multi-million-dollar advertising campaign for Enfamil® infant formula. Bristol-Myers management discontinued the Pablum® cereals and BiB juices, however. The increasing aggressiveness of Gerber Products in these markets made continued competition for a share of a shrinking business seem unwise.

1969

By July 1969 the actual number of births had risen by 2 percent over that of the previous twelve months. Though this respite from decline proved not to last through the year, the pricing skirmishes and battles of 1968 were temporarily resolved when baby-food prices were increased across the board in July 1969, with all the major producers joining in. This harmony was shortlived, however. Battling tactics again erupted, with H.J. Heinz leading the price reductions. As price-cutting became widespread, advertising budgets were cut by most of the competitors. These "price promotions" in the industry dragged on, with periods of temporary truce, until July 1974.

H.J. Heinz USA. Heinz USA boasted in 1969 that its baby-food market share had climbed significantly for three successive years and that new items such as junior fruit pies, pureed foods, and sauces had been introduced successfully in 1969.

In the face of excess capacity H.J. Heinz relocated and consolidated its Heinz baby-food operations in its Pittsburgh food-processing facilities. Pressure cookers were substituted for kettles. Heinz also continued to build a network of distribution centers, strategically located to serve markets across the United States. Since Heinz sold other products besides baby foods to its grocery channels, some economies in shipping costs could be anticipated when this network was completed.

Since H.J. Heinz did not have adequate volume to fill its plants, it continued to cut its prices to grocers on baby foods, starting in Detroit, where Gerber Products had been most strongly entrenched. This was the beginning of a long, continuing price war. Beech-Nut Foods and Gerber Products were forced to respond when their unit volume declined too much in a particular regional market by also lowering their prices to grocers.

Beech-Nut Foods. In its 1969 Annual Report the Squibb/Beech-Nut Company hinted that although its market share increases were satisfactory in its baby-foods and other specialty products, these products did *not* make an acceptable contribution to profits in 1969. The profitability of baby-food sales, Squibb/Beech-Nut reported, continued to be hampered by severe price competition and by increased manufacturing and marketing costs. In order to bolster its sagging sales volume and to fill the unused capacity in its baby-food plants, Beech-Nut Foods had cut its baby-foods prices.

Gerber Products. Gerber's market share had historically hovered around 60 percent. When the price war commenced in Detroit, Gerber's market share there fell to 30 percent; overall Gerber's market share fell to 53 percent.

Gerber entered the price war though it maintained a one-cent-per-jar retail price premium between it and the other brands. Whenever the pricing spread between Gerber and the other brands opened up to 1.5 or 2.5 cents per jar, Gerber's market share would start to erode severely.

Gerber Products continued its strategies of vertical integration and related diversification. If acquired Cornucopia Farms, Inc., a small fruit supplier and a chain of children's day-care centers. Gerber Products also completed construction of its new Asheville, North Carolina, juice-processing facility in 1969 and began to process fruit juices internally.

Gerber Products also expanded its international involvement. In 1969 Gerber Products licensed CPC International to sell baby food in the European Economic Community and the United Kingdom. Gerber derived approximately 10 percent of its revenues from foreign sales in 1969, and had exported baby foods to more than seventy countries. As living standards improved in less-developed countries, foreign operations were expected to play an increasingly important role in the baby-food industry for all of the United States firms.

1970

In 1970 the rate of decline slowed; the baby-food firms seemed to read the slowing of the rate of decline to mean that the demand for their products would soon revitalize.

Abbott Laboratories. In May 1970 Abbott Laboratories increased its investment in infants' nutritional products. It announced that a $10 million infant formula faculty would be built at Altavista, Virginia. The plant was scheduled for completion in 1972. Sales of Similac® had been up by 20 percent in 1969 as more mothers became convinced that a hypoallergenic infant formula was valuable. The baby-formula unit had thus outperformed all other Abbott Laboratories product groups.

Beech-Nut Foods. In 1970 Beech-Nut Foods opened a new baby-cereal plant in Fort Plain, New York, but it phased out the old baby-food plant at Rochester, New York, leaving only the Canajoharie, New York, baby-food plant operating. Both the Rochester and the Canajoharie plants had been operating with much excess production capacity.

H.J. Heinz. Heinz cut its baby-foods salesforce in half, retrained the survivors, and set up a new distribution system to cope with its shrinking baby-food sales volume. Heinz also lowered its prices, again. Overseas, Heinz baby-food sales were still doing well. Heinz had launched a new marketing campaign in Copenhagen, and had just build Europe's largest and most modern baby-food factory in Italy. Heinz waited for births to increase in the Unites States.

Gerber Products. In 1970 Gerber Products devoted intense efforts to developing the "toddler," or older baby market. Gerber introduced separate advertising campaigns to promote the cereals, pretzels, cookies, soups, and desserts it had recently introduced for the older baby market.

Gerber Products also continued its strategy of "related diversification" by acquiring the Hankscraft line of vaporizers, humidifiers, and nursery products in 1970. Hankscraft produced a high-quality line of humidifiers, which fit well with the high-quality image Gerber had sought to maintain.

Swift & Company. Swift's in-lieu-of-service rebate had enabled Swift & Company to maintain distribution of its baby foods, but its competitive position did not improve and sales were declining in absolute terms. In 1970 Swift & Company announced that it would close the meat-packing plant in Fort Worth, where its baby meats were currently being processed.

Although the major baby-food firms expected that the absolute number of births would soon increase, Swift & Company chose not to continue production of its baby meats. Instead, Swift negotiated a copacking agreement with Armour and Company (who had been copacking baby meats for Gerber Products until 1966). All advertising support was withdrawn by Swift & Company from the product.

1971

The price of baby food was controlled in 1971 under the federal price controls program. But the prices of many of the raw materials used in processing baby foods were not controlled. Meanwhile the prices of baby food had been lowered by another round of price warfare. These were the prices which were locked in by government controls.

Approximately 3.6 million babies were born in 1971, a decrease from the number of births in 1970. The birth rate had not increased as baby-food companies had hoped it would. Because some firms had built plants on the basis of their expectations, considerable overcapacity plagued the baby-foods industry in 1971.

H.J. Heinz. Heinz's prices stayed down. Under its price-cutting program, Heinz's U.S. baby-food sales had increased by 10 percent and its market share hit a modern high point. Heinz undertook a comprehensive "profit improvement" program in 1971 in order to reduce its operating costs without deteriorating the quality of its baby-food products.

Beech-Nut Foods. Beech-Nut Foods' profits were squeezed, and there were corporate grumblings that the recently acquired baby-food unit was not making an acceptable return.

Gerber Foods. Gerber Products had tried repeatedly in its annual reports and in other published materials to coax up the price of baby foods. The purchasers of baby foods were becoming more price sensitive and less brand loyal.

1972

There were 72,000 fewer births during the first quarter of 1972 than during that same period in 1971. Profit margins continued to be squeezed.

Around June 1972 H.J. Heinz again cut the price of its baby food in an effort to wrest market share away from Gerber Products. The cut hurt Beech-Nut Foods more than it did Gerber. Many grocers were cutting back on their shelf space dedicated to baby foods. Usually, either Beech-Nut or Heinz brands tended to be displaced when shelf space was reduced. In order to stay on the shelves, Beech-Nut retaliated to Heinz's price cut with a price cut of its own.

Beech-Nut had been losing money for Squibb/Beech-Nut. When Beech-Nut matched Heinz, Gerber's share of the market was squeezed. As its market share deteriorated, Gerber, too, had to enter the price war.

Gerber Products. Sales volume decreased for Gerber Products in 1972, the first such decline in Gerber's history. Gerber stopped TV advertising and lobbied successfully to receive a 2 percent price increase for baby foods from the price-controls board. Gerber shortened its motto to read, "Babies are our business . . . ." Formerly Gerber's well-known motto had read, "Babies are our business . . . our *only* business."

H.J. Heinz. Heinz USA made several major capital investments to improve efficiency in baby-food production through the upgrading of its plants and equipment in 1972. Among the improvements announced were equipment to increase its strained baby-food capacity at Pittsburgh; the completion of the eighth canned-foods distribution center in Iowa City, Iowa; and the construction of expanded warehouse capacity in Arlington, Texas. All of these improvements would also be helpful in Heinz's other food businesses.

In its overseas subsidiaries, H.J. Heinz used many of Gerber's diversification tactics as the birth rate also declined in the European Economic Community. Heinz promoted a line of babywear, infants' clothes, and premiums. It also began advertising the nutritional value of its products compared to the home-prepared equivalent in order to increase the usage of its products in Europe.

Beech-Nut Foods. In following industry price cuts, Beech-Nut baby foods were no longer making a satisfactory contribution to E.R. Squibb. Discounts off grocers' list prices were frozen at high levels. Rather than precipitate another round of price cuts, Beech-Nut Foods chose to withdraw from markets where it had achieved only spotty distribution, thus conceding the shelf space vacated to Heinz or Gerber, or both.

Squibb had lost over $5 million in its baby-foods business in 1972 and expected to lose that amount again in 1973. It decided to sell its Beech-Nut baby-foods unit, and sold out at a giveaway price.

1973

Beech-Nut Foods. In March 1973 Squibb Corporation at last succeeded in selling the Beech-Nut baby-foods unit. The purchaser, Baker Laboratories of East Troy, Wisconsin, borrowed the cash to pay Squibb. The 1973 Annual Report of Squibb showed a loss on the sale of its baby-food business of $15,429,000. A question which occupied Squibb management's attention was whether the spun-off Beech-Nut baby-food company could survive long enough to pay off its debts to the parent. Would the loss to Squibb be even larger in fact?

Swift & Company. During 1973 Swift & Company terminated the copacking contract with Armour & Company and left the baby-foods business entirely. By the time the courts ruled that Swift & Company might be permitted to offer nonmeat baby foods (an exception to the earlier antitrust decree), it was too late.

Gerber Products. Gerber's profit growth was inhibited by the events of 1973 (spiraling inflation, significant raw-materials cost increases, the price war, and a further decline in the number of babies born). Yet Gerber completely remodeled its Fremont, Michigan, baby-food plant in 1973. A new baby-cereal facility was also being built in Fremont, Michigan. All of Gerber Products' other plants were reputedly in excellent condition, although having excess capacity in the industry.

In 1973 Gerber's diversification strategy seemed to be running into some trouble. Gerber had diversified into markets dominated by firms such as Cheseborough-Ponds and the baby-powder king, Johnson & Johnson. A Gerber toiletries line, which included shampoo, oil, lotion, powder, and cotton swabs, had gone national in January 1973. Also the rubber-panties market, which Gerber had dominated, was being rendered obsolete by disposable diapers. A Gerber day-care center venture and the mail-order life-insurance business were also losing money in 1973.

Gerber Products tried to utilize its excess food processing capacity by introducing Gerber peanut spread and ketchup. But selling ketchup brought Gerber into conflict with H.J. Heinz.

H.J. Heinz. Heinz USA was renovating its plants despite the reportedly miserable profit performance of its baby-food products in 1973. It was also backward-integrating into can-making facilities. Heinz consolidated eastern can-making operations at Pittsburgh, including baby-fruit-juice cans. A new western canning facility at Stockton, California, ensured that the Heinz plant at Tracy, California, would have cans for its full range of production needs (which included tuna fish, tomato products, pet foods, and other canned foods). New production facilities at Tracy made it possible for Heinz to produce a fall line of junior and strained baby foods there. The Pittsburgh baby-food factory began full-time use of a hydrostatic, continuous sterilizer for baby foods (or other canned products).

In September 1973 a truce was reached in the baby-foods price war. Discounts off list to grocers were halved or, in some markets, disappeared completely. Retail baby-food prices went up in some cases by over 40 percent.

1974

In 1974 only 3.1 million babies were born. The 1974 recession dampened forecasts for an increase in the 1975 birth rate. Price controls were lifted on April 30, 1974, enabling baby-food competitors to adjust their selling prices upward to absorb rising costs. Discounts vanished and prices went up, with Gerber leading the increase.

Gerber Products. In 1974 the famous Gerber Products motto about babies disappeared completely from Gerber advertising. Previous year's profits plunged 27.9 percent. In 1974 Gerber still had a 62.2 percent share of the strained baby-foods market; 65.1 percent of the junior line; and 82.7 percent of baby cereals. Seventy-two percent of Gerber's sales volume was still in domestic baby foods ($205.5 million). The Gerber diversification had taken Gerber into the following businesses by 1974: *Gerber Babywear*: vinyl pants, bibs, knit shirts, socks, and training pants; *Geralco Containers*: metal cans for Gerber juices (a backward integration); *Gerber Life Insurance*: direct-mail life and health insurance (not profitable); *Spartan Graphics*: printing and graphics service center for other businesses (a backward integration); *Gerber Children's Centers*: twelve child-care centers in five metropolitan areas (not profitable); *Hankscraft*: vaporizers, humidifiers, nursing bottles, infant-care items, and infant-care accessories (a highly successful subsidiary); *Babygro*: stretchwear outer garments for infants and toddlers; *Atlanta Toy and Novelty*: plush stuffed toys and novelties; *Cornucopia Farms*: fruit for nearby Gerber plants (a backward integration move).

During the year 1974 Gerber acquired the Walter W. Moyer Company, a manufacturer of quality underwear and other knitwear. Moyer had been a supplier of infant shirts, socks, and training pants to Gerber for many years. Gerber's nonfood products were now marketed in drug, mass merchandising, and other new channels of distribution.

H.J. Heinz. H.J. Heinz controlled about 22 percent or $100 million in annual domestic retail sales of the baby-food market in 1974. Although Heinz had increased its share of the baby-food market, Heinz had experienced an 8 to 10 percent drop in its sales volume of baby foods since 1970. Heinz attributed this fall-off to the declining number of births. In 1974 Heinz repackaged the entire baby-food line. Its new promotional campaign stressed the nutritional value and the confidence inspired by the Heinz label on baby foods.

Beech-Nut Foods. In 1974 Beech-Nut Foods had a 20 percent share of the baby-foods market. New management reported that the company was profitable, although Squibb had lost $5 million in its last year of ownership. No advertising expenditures were made for the years 1974 and 1975 by Beech-Nut.

1975

The number of births increased in 1975 by approximately 200,000 babies. Per capita baby-food consumption actually declined slightly. The key development, however, was the charge by consumer groups that baby foods were not as wholesome, nutritious, and safe as baby-food manufacturers represented them as being. All manufacturers came under fire.

Gerber Products. A major communication effort was launched by Gerber Products in 1975 to answer the consumerist charges. The Gerber formulations, processes, and quality control checks were reexamined to ensure that the baby foods were of high quality. Phone-in questions from mothers were fielded by a panel of experts in a special "Ask Gerber" telethon effort.

Gerber repeatedly stated in its annual reports, that the number of babies being born would eventually increase. To raise incremental revenue, however, Gerber sold market-research services for noncompetitive products and used surplus production capacity at Fremont, Michigan, for processing food products (peas) for other, noncompetitive processors.

Gerber Products had long considered its corporate name, "Gerber," to be one of its most valuable assets and had historically been very selective about the use of the name. When its plants were severely underutilized, Gerber had tried to use its well-known brand name to sell other products. The "Gerber" image was so firmly entrenched in the minds of consumers, it discovered, that the nonbaby products had done very poorly.

Despite these problems, Gerber's share of the shrinking baby-foods market grew even larger than before. In March 1975 *Barron's* estimated that Gerber possessed well over 80 percent of the cereal market and 65 percent of the strained and the junior foods markets (compared with 70, 55, and 55 percent, respectively, in 1970). Moving to consolidate this position, Gerber returned to advertising its products on television in 1975.

Beech-Nut Foods. Beech-Nut Foods was losing market share to Gerber as it struggled to survive. In retrenching and turning the company around, Beech-Nut had released its salesforce and placed its baby food with food brokers in an effort to reduce overhead.

1976

The number of births stayed level at 3.1 million in 1976—too little for the industry's current plant capacity. *Consumer Reports* had advised readers, "We suggest making your own, until the baby food industry makes its own better."

Gerber's share of the declining market was 70 percent. Heinz had captured 16 percent, but its plants were running with as much as 50 percent excess capacity. Both Heinz and Gerber had tried to comply with consumerists' requests for quality products. By the end of 1976, however, an unexpected turn of events made both firms scramble for position as Beech-Nut interpreted the consumerists' demands differently.

Beech-Nut Foods. On December 27, 1976, Beech-Nut Foods launched a campaign publicizing its reformulated baby-food products which contained no added salt and little, or no, added sugar. The new products also contained no chemical preservatives and no color enhancers. Retail pricing was expected to be one cent higher than Gerber Products' baby foods.

One of Beech-Nut's new products, an unsweetened juice packaged in a glass jar—with a "new" twist-off cap to accommodate easy application of a standard-sized nipple—was introduced in late 1976. Chairman Frank Nicholas himself promoted the juices, suggesting that glass was *safer* than cans (which could leach metallic substances into the juices). A $1 million campaign was launched by Beech-Nut Foods to urge mothers to "read the product's label" and educate themselves regarding the clearcut choice the newly formulated Beech-Nut baby foods offered them.

H.J. Heinz. Apprised of the Beech-Nut Foods product change in late 1976, an H.J. Heinz spokesperson announced that Heinz would remove salt from 108 of its baby-food products, sugar from seventy-two products.

Gerber Products. A Gerber spokesperson noted that Gerber had begun removing the sugar from various items in 1974. Of 150 Gerber items, eighty-nine contained no sugar. Fifty-four baby-food items contained no salt, while other Gerber baby foods contained the 0.5 percent salt which the National Academy of Sciences had recommended as being an essential nutrient. However, Gerber promised that added salt would be removed from 104 of Gerber's 152 baby foods.

1977

In 1977 Beech-Nut Foods had enjoyed some success from its gamble as consumers responded positively to its reformulated products, forcing Gerber and Heinz to follow. 1977 ended on a hopeful note for the baby-food firms as the number of births started to increase.

Beech-Nut Foods. What Beech-Nut foods had lacked in a war chest of cash, it made up in a warlike spirit and a nose for newsworthy events. Much "free" air time was obtained through interviews on local talk shows. Beech-Nut chairman Frank Nicholas himself made over 300 such appearances in 1977. The free publicity created an impression of innovative management at Beech-Nut. By the end of 1977, Beech-Nut Foods' sales volume had increased by 29 percent over the previous year.

Gerber Products. In June 1977 Gerber Products announced that it would join with Beech-Nut and Heinz in removing salt from those baby-food products which still contained some salt. Although Gerber contended that some salt was important as a nutrient, it indicated that consumers were confused by the many arguments concerning salt. Gerber admitted that the change would require time. "No-salt-added" products would become available in the autumn.

A 1977 market survey of homemakers indicated that of the respondents who purchased baby foods, 24 percent *said* they purchased the Beech-Nut brand of baby foods—a number considerably in excess of historic purchasing patterns. By October 1977 Gerber's reformulated foods became available. Consumer loyalties drifted back to Gerber, but there was no doubt that the industry's self-proclaimed "maverick" had made an impression on the market.

Even though Gerber was backward integrated into can-making operations and had recently acquired a metal lithographing company to further integrate, Gerber followed the Beech-Nut lead by introducing its juices in glass jars in 1977. Within six months, industry sales of baby fruit juices were up 300 percent.

H.J. Heinz. H.J. Heinz terminated a contract for copacking of baby fruit juices marketed under its label in 1977. The baby-food juices were packed at the Pittsburgh plant starting in 1977. Heinz reported that it was enjoying significant savings as a result of this change.

In May 1977 H.J. Heinz announced its intention to close its Chambersburg, Pennsylvania, baby-food plant. The company attributed the closing to a long-term decline in consumption of processed baby food. Heinz noted that its share of the baby-food market had remained approximately constant over the previous four years but that the volume of baby food consumed dropped 23.7 percent during that time.

Heinz disclosed that the Chambersburg baby-food plant had been operating at about 50 percent of capacity for the past several years and production at its Pittsburgh plant had also been well below capacity.

By the end of 1977, Heinz reported that its baby foods were reformulated to eliminate all salt and reduce the amount of added sugar in them.

1978

In 1978 demographers forecasted 4 million births annually by 1982. The birth rate in 1978 indicated 3.2 million babies would be born.

Beech-Nut Foods. The first significant product innovation since baby meats was introduced by Beech-Nut Foods in January 1978. The new product, Cera-Meal, was actually licensed to Beech-Nut Foods by a West German firm.

H.J. Heinz. Heinz executives showed less confidence concerning demographers' forecasts than Gerber. Heinz's market share was 15.5 percent in 1978, compared to 69 percent for Gerber. Its plants were reported to be utilized at 75 percent of capacity. When asked whether Heinz might exit, a Heinz spokesperson commented that it would be difficult to sell off *any* baby-food company except Gerber given the current economic conditions.

A Heinz spokesperson suggested that H.J. Heinz was not optimistic about the future of the U.S. baby-foods industry. "Even using some fairly generous projections for the 1980s," he suggested, "the market will be smaller than it was [in 1958] twenty years before. That's not what I call a growth industry."[1]

All of the firms who fought in the price war suffered significant losses, especially Swift & Company's baby meat business. Yet it was likely that demand would level off at a substantially reduced rate and would continue to need servicing by at least one baby-food processor. Overseas markets would likely also require expanded baby-food plant capacities in the future. Therefore, competitors did not see many motivations to exit.

In general, the baby-foods industry had a long-term perspective which sometimes caused it to overlook the more immediate competitive or strategic needs of the firms. For example, Swift & Company may have mistimed its exit because it was caught up in the image of being a "meat specialist." Beech-Nut Foods may have overextended itself because it was caught up in the image of being the "industry maverick." Gerber Products, itself, may have misestimated the importance of industry innovations, such as the hypoallergenic formula, the "no-salt, no-sugar" baby food, the screw-top juice jar, or the instantized baby granola product. Gerber Products had become paternalistic due to its previous successes. This factor may have impaired its timing as well in responding to challenges in the endgame. Although Gerber Products never reported an accounting loss due to its baby-foods business, some investment sources have accused Gerber's top management of being slow to recognize the implications of environment characteristics as they may affect Gerber Products.

Analysis of the Baby-Foods Endgame

There was great uncertainty among the competitors in the baby-foods end-game regarding the level of future demand. All firms recognized that some babies would continue to be born. But competitors differed in their forecasts regarding the rate with which the number of babies born would increase. Despite evidence to the contrary, the baby-food firms did not change their expectations regarding the likelihood of revitalization of this industry. The baby-food firms comforted themselves by believing that the young mothers created by the postwar baby boom would soon be giving birth, even when in 1978 the oldest of these potential mothers were thirty-one years of age. Thus, there was difficulty in predicting future demand for the product and the differing expectations of the competitors was reflected in their expansions (or contraction) of capacity.

Demand during the twenty-year decline in the number of births was not adequate to support all of the productive capacity which was dedicated to baby-food production. The industry had offered very attractive profits in the past and all of the major participants believed demand would soon revitalize. Therefore, none of the competitors would take its plants out of the industry, and, because excess capacity pervaded the industry, price increases were difficult to execute and price-cutting plagued the manufacturers. During the endgame, participation was less profitable than it had been when capacity was closer to demand, but during most years of the endgame the baby-food companies suffered from reduced profits rather than from losses. (Beech-Nut Foods in 1972 and 1973 is an exception here.)

There were few exits from this industry because there were high expectations regarding the future profitability of the industry. None of the entrenched competitors would concede that it should exit to relieve the industry's excess capacity. Swift & Company was squeezed out of the industry after years of incurring higher marketing costs than the other competitors, yet it too must have enjoyed an acceptable level of profits in order for it to have persisted so doggedly in producing its baby-protein products. Emotional exit barriers were high because firms which had been identified with the specialized baby-food market were reluctant to exit and strategic exit barriers deterred some firms from deploying their relatively flexible assets for other food-processing businesses. In general, exit barriers were difficult to overcome in this industry, but the exit barriers were not economic in nature. The industry conditions in the baby-foods business in 1965 are reviewed below.

Characteristics

Demand. Baby food was a necessity to babies, but it could be produced at home. Demand for branded baby food was price-sensitive. A differential of about 1.5 to 2.5 cents would be adequate to encourage brand-switching behavior. (This suggests that "Gerber" could command a 10 percent price premium.)

Product Differentiation . Baby foods could be differentiated by the quality of the raw materials used, the taste, the physical appearance, the flavors produced, and the packaging. There was active brand differentiation of baby foods which was supported by advertising campaigns, "medical detail" sales representatives, and direct-mail communications.

Markets. In 1965, 89 percent of the baby foods produced were sold through grocery-store outlets. The major purchasers of baby foods were mothers.

Substitutes. Baby foods could have been produced at home, but not necessarily more cheaply (if a mother's time has value) or as antiseptically as a commercially processed baby food. The benefit which canned baby foods provided was their convenience.

Customer Industries. Although there were many grocery stores which purchased baby food in the United States, within a particular region there were few customers. Many of the customers were chains of grocery stores representing large sales volumes for the baby-food producers but a relatively insignificant purchase for the customer grocer stores (0.5 percent).

Supplier Industries. Although there were many farmers and meat-packers who produced the raw materials used to produce baby foods, the baby-food companies usually negotiated for the harvest of a particular group of farmers. Some baby-food companies owned their own farms or orchards in 1965.

Manufacturing Technology. The processes used to prepare baby foods were highly automated in 1965. The assets were similar to those used in packing other, "adult" foods, and were not specific to baby-food production.

Technological Innovation. Frequent flavor, processing, or packaging changes were made in 1965. Product turnovers were high. There had not been a significant new baby-food product since the creation of baby meats twenty years previously.

Capital Intensity. The baby foods production processes required a plant and equipment costing approximately $4 million. If the warehouses, handling equipment, and other machinery used in a baby-food plant were included in this cost in 1965, a $10 million investment would have been required.

Some of the plants were relatively new in 1965. They had been built after 1957 in anticipation of the next wave of rising population.

Competitive Structure. The baby-foods industry had a very competitive, concentrated structure in which one firm dominated the market (with a 60 percent share of the market). The other firms could use price competition to obtain shelf space, sometimes to the detriment of the larger company. In 1965 almost all of the productive capacity of the baby-foods industry was held by the four largest firms: Gerber Products, H.J. Heinz, Beech-Nut Foods, and Swift & Company. Some private-label brands produced by one of these firms were sold by grocery chains. A sizable infant formula market had been developed by 1965. Other pharmaceutical competitors produced these infant formulas successfully.

Although dollar sales volumes of baby food were increasing as the price eased upward at retail, fewer babies were being born in the United States during the endgame. In 1970, 3.7 million babies were born. Three years later, only 3.1 million babies were born. When the birth rate finally "rebounded" in 1978, 3.2 million births were forecast, but this did *not* represent a large absolute increase in demand for baby foods. The plants and productive assets used to process baby foods were yet only 75 percent utilized.

Demand for baby food declined due to an unexpected decline in the number of births. Early in the endgame, none of the demographers could recognize that the birth dearth would be as enduring as it was. Consequently, capital investments were made on the basis of expectations which were grounded in a high degree of certainty that the number of births would occur. The forecasts were wrong. Only a different forecast (one which was less pleasant to accept) could have alerted baby-food firms to the expectations of young couples.

It had been expected that relative uncertainty among competitors regarding the rate and extent of declining demand would result in chaotic industry conditions in which (1) excess capacity would not be retired; (2) orderly exits would not occur; (3) major losses would be suffered by some competitors; (4) price-cutting could erupt into open price warfare; and (5) companies would encounter difficulty in deciding whether to stop reinvesting in the declining business. In the baby-foods endgame, competitors had apparently concluded that baby foods was still an attractive business for reinvestment. Plant retirements were accompanied by reinvestments elsewhere. Only Swift & Company exited. Squibb/Beech-Nut suffered major losses (5 percent of gross profits) and price warfare erupted. The "natural" foods product transformations required sizable reinvestments in the baby business. In 1978 all three of the major baby-food processors were apparently even more committed to this industry because they were certain that the market would revitalize.

It had been expected that price increases would be difficult to execute where the customers' switching costs (at the retailer level, to another brand of baby food; at the consumer level, to homemade baby foods) were not high and where the industry suffered from severe excess capacity. Price-cutting in the wholesale markets broke out during endgame as firms each tried to fill their baby-food plants by loading grocers' shelves with their respective brands of baby food. Price increases occurred, but the success of these increases was due to the competitive structure of the industry—not to a recognition that the depressed level of births would be long-term. It had been expected that where the competitors expected the decline in sales to be temporary, not permanent, there could be industry-wide price-cutting which could damage the industry's membership permanently. Had the baby-food firms recognized in 1968 that the decline in births was more en-during than they had anticipated, they might not have competed so bitterly for so long to retain their former respective volumes of the shrinking shelf space allocated to baby-foods distribution. In the baby-foods endgame, the true nature of demand was not recognized by all competitors. Hence, they could not act in a nondisruptive fashion.

Analysis of Endgame Industry Traits

It had been predicted that a "favorable" endgame environment might en-courage some competitors to undertake reinvestments in assets in order to serve niches of enduring demand most economically. Only the infant form-ula market experienced growth during this endgame and Abbott Lab-oratories which served this "niche" of demand, expanded its capacity to cope with its success in the grocery channels. There were other attributes of this industry's structure which baby-food producers believed were favorable, including: baby foods were not replaced by a "substitute" pro-duct, and there was a relatively steady replacement rate of babies at the new, lower birth rate; thus, some firms could continue to service the de-mand which would remain.

Product Differentiability Traits

Although baby foods appeared to be similar, Gerber Products baby foods commanded a 10 percent premium, suggesting that the baby-food product could be differentiated. Because buyer loyalties could be strong, grocers controlled the shelf space, but the ultimate consumers could exert some pressure over grocers in order to obtain the brand of baby foods they desired, and much of the value-added of the baby food product was controlled by the food processors themselves, who advertised and promoted their foods using many marketing tools to retain their customers' loyalties.

Product Traits. It had been expected that the creation of and maintenance of a brand name or a well-recognized corporate name which connoted product quality could be used as a competitive tool and as a justification for higher prices because the trust associated with the brand name made the product seem to be more acceptable to a market of customers which valued high quality in baby foods. In this endgame, Gerber Products was able to charge slightly higher prices for its brand of baby foods while the brand name Heinz apparently was associated with lower-margin products (ketchup). Hence Heinz could not sell substantial volumes of its baby foods at prices which were the same as Gerber's. Heinz could appeal to a market that valued lower prices, but it could not convince most consumers that its value equaled Gerber's.

Baby foods were very high-margin products largely due to the risk customers perceived in feeding infants low-quality foods, and therefore an image of high-quality specialization in the care of feeding infants could justify industry-wide high prices (relative to their costs), provided price-cutting or other activities did not erode the potential profitabilty of these products. Apparently, there was some "mystique" associated with being identified as a baby-food company which the food processors were most unwilling to diminish. (This attitude may have been the basis for the strategic exit barriers which deterred baby-food producers from using their assets for other food-processing activities during difficult periods.)

Customer Traits. Grocers were price-sensitive because they could not pass on substantial price increases to their customers (the mothers and fathers) easily. As the demand for baby foods declined and inventory turnover slowed, grocers used their power over shelf space to extract some of the baby-food producers' high profit margins by demanding lower prices from baby-food manufacturers. It had been expected that price-sensitive customers would encourage grocers to seek to extract relatively high fees from the producers for stocking a particular baby-food processors' products because grocers were limited in the price increases they could make on baby foods, and slower retail turnovers for stock keeping units (SKUs) reduced the grocers' profit margins. In this endgame, grocers reduced the amount of shelf space devoted to baby foods and encouraged the baby-food manufacturers to buy their shelf space (that is, give grocers price breaks).

It was found that beyond a price premium of 15 percent, the ultimate customer did not tend to value one brand of baby food over another, which meant that if competitors lowered prices enough they could buy market share away from the dominant firm. Because the premium required to invade Gerber's markets was a few cents (at retail), the endgame became volatile (and unprofitable for manufacturers) when Heinz initiated the price war. When this occurred, the industry's customer industry, the grocers, did not enhance the attractiveness of this endgame for reinvestments or for increasing commitments through their behavior; rather, they exacerbated the price war.

Supplier Traits. It had been expected that a supplier industry whose members were fragmented and which sold its entire output to one of the baby-foods processors would not possess much bargaining power, and therefore the farmers and orchardists were not expected to charge unusually high prices for their produce. Because there was a relatively ready supply of farmers, vertical integration did not seem to be necessary in order to ensure produce quality and reasonable prices.

In summary, the relative bargaining power of the grocers did not enable the baby-food producers to extract the full value of their brand names and accumulated customer goodwill. The baby foods were differentiable, however, and this enabled the food processors to enjoy healthy profit margins for their products. Thus, in balance, the potential differentiability of the endgame product enhanced the attractiveness of this industry environment even under conditions of declining demand.

Technological Characteristics

It would be expected that firms whose physical assets were flexible in their usage (that is, they could be used to process other foods in addition to baby foods) would have been able to shut down operations or to process other foods in their plants if they expected that demand would continue to decline. In this endgame, such expectations proved to be the key consideration in the deployment of baby-food processing assets. During the early 1970s Gerber temporarily tried to sell "gourmet adult foods," using its food-processing assets to fill its plants to an efficient level of utilization, and it tried to reach the toddler market. At last, when the recession depressed expectations severely, Gerber temporarily packed peas for a private-brand company on its underutilized baby-food assets.

Heinz built its baby-food plant in physical proximity to its tomato-sauce plant to take advantage of locational economies. Apparently Heinz was less concerned whether its food-processing assets were used to produce baby foods or other foods than were Gerber and Beech-Nut. (Swift & Company produced baby meats to fill underutilized capacity in its meat-packing plants.)

In summary, if a baby-food firm wished to exit from this business, a market very likely existed for its food-processing assets. Only the highly specialized processing machines were not readily convertible for use in another foods' production line. Of the baby-food firms, only Gerber, which possessed the newest and most efficient baby-food-processing plants, was likely to face the problem of inflexible (hence irrecoverable) asset investments because only Gerber operated highly specialized baby-food machinery.

Competitive Characteristics

It would be expected that price-cutting could erode profit margins within industries where competitors such as these were asymmetric in their strategic postures, for example, where their cost structures differed, but that some coordination of competitive activities should be possible within such a concentrated industry. The price war could be ended and prices could be increased successfully in this industry during 1973 (after price controls were eased up) because signaling in this market was effective and competitors' strategic postures were similar enough to recognize a common need for "breathing space" or a time of "truce" in the price war. Thus the competitors apparently could agree on behaviors to benefit the industry, ultimately.

Gerber possessed the best operating economies, but it appeared to possess no desire to exploit this advantage by increasing its share of the market beyond 70 percent (perhaps due to the undersirable effects of antitrust prosecution it would incur). By 1973 competitors were aware that a decreasing trend in birth rates had prevailed rather than the increasing trend they had forecast. This meant that competitors recognized a need to act in a more restrained fashion in the event that the depressed number of births was more than a temporary phenomenon. By 1973 Squibb had divested Beech-Nut Foods and the new management of Beech-Nut needed time to assess where the baby-food market was going (and what its role within it should be), and H.J. Heinz was encountering declining demand in its overseas markets and also needed breathing space. Therefore, after the baby-food firms had experienced the thin profit margins of their price war, they tacitly recognized the need to refrain from price-cutting tactics for a time in 1973. (One could infer from published statements during the summer of 1973 that the two major competitors—Gerber and Heinz—were expecting that Beech-Nut's productive capacity would be retired during 1973 even if the price war were ended.)

It would be expected that a floundering "single-business" company such as the new Beech-Nut Foods firm would resort to desperate tactics in order to remain viable in the endgame competition, and thus Beech-Nut Foods raised the stakes of this competition by creating a demand among purchasers of baby food for its "natural" baby foods. This was a highly risky tactic which was costly for the entire baby-food industry because it raised customers' expectations and made it necessary to reinvest unknown amounts of R&D to produce the products Beech-Nut Foods had promised to babies' parents.

In summary, the baby-food industry was volatile because (1) all of the competitors serviced the same segments of the market; (2) competitors did not all perceive that the birth declines were enduring, hence demand may have been without hope for much revitalization; and (3) customer industries were encouraging competition in the form of price-cutting and other dealing activities.

But because the baby-food product was highly differentiable, competition could have been along nonprice dimensions. The physical assets were flexible enough that an exit would have been easy to execute, and a baby-food plant could have been closed down without difficulties because signaling devices were relatively well established when the competitors wished to coordinate their industry activities. Therefore, the structural traits of this industry were relatively favorable. The competitors' expectations, the lack of well-established pockets of demand, and the strategic postures of these firms were more contributory to the unrewarding competitive conditions in this endgame than were other structural traits which were identified above.

Analysis of the Corporate-wide Strategic Needs of the Competitors

It would be expected that firms might keep an "important" endgame business longer than economic analysis might have suggested was advisable because "strategic exit barriers" might influence the timing of firms' exits or the timing of the implementation of tactics designed to reduce firms' investments in the endgame industry. In this endgame, two firms were virtually single-business companies by 1973, and their incentives to remain in this industry were strong. Even H.J. Heinz may have considered that its multinational position as the major baby-food firm required it to remain a participant (albeit a small participant) in its home market's baby-food business.

Corporate Goals. Although expectations influenced their asset deployment decisions heavily, it would be expected that for firms such as Gerber (and later for Beech-Nut Foods), which had been closely identified with the United States baby-food business, the retention of the plants which produced baby foods would be important and that this corporate identification with babies may have acted as a strategic exit barrier in deterring firms from early retirement, "mothballing," or another use of the baby-food processing plants.

It was found that baby-food firms had copacked their products to achieve industry-wide economies in the past (for example, Swift & Company copacked with Armour, and Gerber sourced several foods), and that copacking had become an acceptable way of expanding a baby-food firm's productive capacity during periods of high demand without investing in new bricks and mortar. But this cost-saving technique was unworkable among competitors which remained during the baby-food endgame because (1) each firm expected that the number of births would soon increase and wanted to have adequate plant capacity; (2) each baby-food processor was reluctant to source foods from a competitor and to deploy its plants for other uses because these plants also served as strategically placed warehouses for servicing unforseen (emergency) demand for baby foods and for monitoring conditions in important markets; and (3) some competitors could not retire or mothball a plant because of the duty they believed they owed to their employees. Therefore productive capacity exceeded the demand for baby-food products, yet none of the baby food companies would retire any plants warehouses, meat lockers, and so on in order to rationalize supply in this industry. They apparently believed that the baby-food business would revive and thrive, and hence they stayed invested and endured the competitive turbulence they created in this endgame.

In summary, there were strategic reasons for firms to remain invested in the baby-foods business which may have justified enduring a decade of declining sales volumes and thin profit margins. The product was inherently profitable if it could be sold to the grocers without excessive discounts and incentives, and if there were once again more than 4.3 million babies, so that the productive capacities of the baby-food producers were filled, the industry could be a profitable one. But even during the years when 3.1 million babies were born, firms stayed invested in the baby-food business because (1) they faced significant strategic exit barriers such as the need for a U.S. presence in baby food due to multinational involvement in baby foods, a shared distribution system, or a need to offer several different canned grocery products to customers; or (2) they were single-business firms heavily invested in the baby-foods business. In 1978 baby foods still represented 82 percent of Gerber Products sales; baby foods were 100 percent of the "new" Beech-Nut Foods' sales. With few investment alternatives, these firms must continue to compete in the baby-food business and hope that the number of babies born increases.

Analysis of Endgaming Firms' Competitive Strengths

It would be expected that firms possessing relative competitive strengths which were appropriate for competing in this endgame would be better suited to pursue some of the more aggressive strategy options (described in chapter 2) for coping with declining demand. In the baby-foods endgame, the firms which possessed important competitive strengths were (1) the firms whose past R&D expenditures and promotional campaigns had created for them goodwill and a substantial share of the market; (2) the firms whose baby-food plants possessed the lowest operating costs; (3) the firms whose distribution systems were most effective; and (4) the firms whose assets were relatively flexible.

Advertising and Marketing Expenditures. It would be expected that the goodwill accumulated in the baby-foods industry from direct mailings, public recognition of brand names and trademarks, and a reputation for quality such as those enjoyed by Gerber could be a competitive strength when, during the endgame, prices fell so close to costs that advertising expenditures could not be afforded. Another advertising strength in the baby-foods industry was enjoyed when firms such as Beech-Nut Foods created "newsworthy" media events which gave the firm free television or radio publicity and created cumulative goodwill which might build brand loyalty.

It would be expected that the distribution systems employed in the baby-foods industry could also constitute a strength because the use of shelf servicing and "medical detail" men could help to reinforce the quality image of a particular brand of baby food. The use of detail men was a costly way to distribute baby food, and it was best suited to competitors which sold large volumes of baby food, hence it served as an entry barrier.

The innovative use of food brokers to sell baby food proved to be a competitive strength for a smaller firm, such as Beech-Nut Foods, because this method of distribution had never been used in the baby-foods business before Beech-Nut tried it, and the use of food brokers may have shaken up Beech-Nut's grocery-store competition temporarily. (This would be a system whereby the brokers had their own territories and were highly motivated to push their products into grocery stores and onto the shelves.)

It would be expected that firms whose market shares were large because of selling strengths would enjoy advertising economies, distribution economies, and purchasing economies in addition to manufacturing economies which are associated with large market share. The competitive requirements of the baby-foods industry penalized small market-share firms like Swift & Company, which was obliged to engage in the same competitive tactics as did the larger firms but which incurred expenses which were a larger proportion of its sales volume than were Gerber's expenses.

Product Design and Research-Development Skills. It would seem that there could be competitive advantages in the baby-foods endgame from the cumulative goodwill earned from years of infant nutritional research or from maintaining high standards of quality, and that there would be great success associated with the introduction of jars of juice which used a screw-on nipple to facilitate easier feeding of infants away from home. Apparently, if a true innovation of quality were introduced (like this juice jar which Heinz first introduced in South America in 1969), a competitor could gain a sales advantage from doing so.

Production Advantages. It would be expected that firms which possessed lower operating costs would be in relatively better positions to endure the damages of a price war. Gerber possessed the most automated and lowest-cost baby-foods processing plants in this endgame, and, at the end of the price war which squeezed Swift & Company out of the market, Gerber Products emerged profitably and with an even larger share of the baby foods market (which may suggest that other strengths were operative but also that Gerber's plants possessed low operating costs).

Well-established Channels of Distribution. It would be expected that there would be an absolute cost-competitive advantage in the baby-foods industry to firms which possessed well-located, well-established distribution channels and warehouse locations. A well-controlled logistics system of shipping schedules and transshipment points could be an advantage in this endgame if it lowered unit handling costs, as could an effective system of detail men.

Flexibility of Asset Use. It would be expected that there could be competitive advantages in the baby-foods industry from having alternative uses for the baby-food processing assets. For example, if a firm copacked baby foods under private labels for grocery chains or retailing cooperatives, these sales could provide some of the volume necessary in order for the firm to run the baby-food-packing equipment efficiently. Or, if a firm produced other products which used the same or similar food packing assets, the other product lines could be used to absorb excess capacity when demand for baby foods declined. Strategic (or managerial) exit barriers might have prevented some firms in the baby-foods industry from offering copacking services, however, in this endgame.

Diversification. It would be expected that there could be an organizational strength from being diversified, from not being a single-product company in the baby-foods endgame, and, during the years of declining demand, successful diversification could be a financial and moral strength to firms because they would not be dependent solely upon the welfare of an industry like baby foods which was locked into a price war for so many years.

   In summary, the most significant strengths enjoyed by the firms in the baby-foods endgame were those that (1) enhanced their flexibility or (2) represented goodwill from past investments. The financial and organizational advantage of having other businesses to generate cash flow or alternative uses for the food-processing assets was a strength. The established reputation of a baby-food firm's product was not lost if a year of advertising were skipped, and this was also a strength since it gave the firm bargaining power in negotiating for shelf space from grocers and in encouraging the consumers to purchase its baby-food products.

Analysis of Firms' Performances in the Baby-Foods Endgame

Given the relatively "favorable" industry structural traits of the baby-foods industry and the certainty that some demand for baby foods would remain, some reinvestments would be expected in this endgame. Given the relatively high percentage of asset values which the baby-foods processing plant assets and brand-name goodwill comprised of firms' total assets, major competitors would not be expected to overcome their exit barriers and close down baby-food production facilities. The nature of demand in this endgame was unclear and the uncertainty regarding its duration tended to keep firms relatively heavily invested because they expected a revitalization of demand.

There were no early exits from the endgame, and only one firm exited from this industry, Swift & Company. Although Swift was effectively out of this endgame when it closed the Fort Worth plant in 1970 and copacked its meats and proteins under an agreement with Armour & Company, Swift still maintained a presence in this industry until 1973 because it was uncertain whether adequate demand would be generated from future increased births to sustain its participation in this industry.

Firms Which Exited: "Milk the Investment"

Swift & Company. Swift was not expected to perform well in this endgame because Swift was stymied strategically by the prohibition of the consent decree and was the highest-cost competitor. Swift & Company possessed the weakest position among competitors in the baby-food industry, and although Swift created a significantly improved food for babies, it was clear that Swift needed the introductory benefits of its own brand of cereals, juices, and canned vegetables in order to be trusted by mothers when it came time to add meats to babies' diets. Because Swift was prohibited from producing and selling those products, it was placed at a multiple disadvantage with respect to Gerber Products. Swift could be expected to encounter competitive cost disadvantages because Swift was production-oriented in this business, not marketing-oriented. The original Swift "baby meats" product innovation had been production-oriented in spirit and the production of its baby meats was used to absorb excess productive capacity in Swift & Company's meat-packing plants and to bear part of the corporate overhead burden. It was only after Gerber, Heinz, and Beech-Nut (Hormel) had imitated the new meat product that Swift worried about how to market it, and then Swift & Company was at a disadvantage in marketing because its costs per unit were higher than those of the other competitors as it tried to match their product differentiation expenditures in order to develop its own customer loyalties.

Swift & Company would not be expected to encounter exit barriers when it left the baby-foods business because no meat-packing plant was devoted exclusively to baby meats. Although Swift & Company's economic exit barriers were low, however, it faced strategic exit barriers because it still believed that it was a "nutritional pioneer" long after Gerber had surpassed its sale volume in baby meats and many industry observers had forgotten which firm created baby meats. Consequently, when Swift copacked its baby meats in an effort to milk its investment of any residual goodwill associated with the Swift & Company baby meats image, it may have been incurring instead an opportunity cost for its corporate parent.

Continued Competition: "Milk the Investment"

H.J. Heinz. Heinz would be expected to be able to recover much of the value its U.S. baby-food investment without needing to reinvest in this business because (1) its corporate name was well recognized; (2) its production facilities were flexible for use to process other foods; and (3) Heinz was well diversified in a manner which minimized its dependence upon baby foods.

Heinz USA did not compete from a base of strong product recognition in baby foods, but its corporate names and logo ("Heinz—57 Varieties") were well known. Although Heinz held between 16 and 22 percent of the baby-food industry's sales during endgame and offered a complete line of baby food products, as did the other major firms, Heinz was not an aggressive baby-food company in the United States. Heinz's overseas baby-food operations were more profitable and its global market share was larger (in dollar sales volume) than its U.S. baby-food company's share. Heinz traditionally had used its overseas markets to introduce new ideas and to develop new, nutritional baby-food products while remaining quite conservative in its competitive tactics in the United States. Heinz USA did not innovate in baby foods, but it imitated because Heinz found that there was no competitive advantages to taking risks in a market dominated by Gerber Products.

Heinz would not be expected to face strategic (or managerial) exit barriers if it needed to use the baby-food plant assets to process other foods. The Heinz plants were flexible because a typical complex produced tomato products, sauces, meats (or tuna), and baby foods (Heinz packed baby foods in cans), and when Heinz reinvested in baby-food assets, it was to add machinery which had other production applications, in addition to baby foods. The attitudinal difference between H.J. Heinz and Gerber Products was one of devotion to their respective baby-food investments. H.J. Heinz was diversified into other products which used its assets and into other businesses which provided better cash flows, and its plants were leased. Heinz had developed an integrated food-distribution system that spanned the country which it used to distribute its canned products. Because Heinz had maintained a relatively flexible position in this industry, it would not seem difficult for Heinz to exit or to recover value from the baby-foods investment when it was necessary to milk it.

"Hold Investment Level"

Mead, Johnson and Abbott Laboratories. The firms serving the infant formula market would be expected to perform well in endgame. Infant formulas had been among the top fifty, fastest-growing grocery-store items for several years since the product had been moved from the drug store to the supermarket and the infant formula producers served a specialized niche which was protected (to some extent) by mobility barriers. A credible producer of formula was usually affiliated with a pharmaceutical laboratory, thus Silimac® (Abbott Laboratories) and Enfamil® (Mead, Johnson) enjoyed greater success than did Gerber's Modilac®.

Abbott Laboratories built a new formula plant to accommodate its increasing demand. Mead, Johnson's corporate parent, Bristol-Myers, divested Mead, Johnson's other baby-food products (BiB juices and Pablum® infant cereal). The strength of both of these firms was that they had identified a favorable niche to serve and they stayed in that niche (thereby avoiding competition with Gerber) where they possessed greater strengths.

"Increase Investment Level"

Beech-Nut Foods. Beech-Nut Foods would not be expected to perform well after it had been divested by Squibb because it seemed to be in a weaker position relative to the other major baby-food firms. Its distribution coverage was spotty, it was not well distributed in some of the growing regions of the United States, and, after Squibb divested Beech-Nut, it was very heavily dependent upon the success of its baby-foods business. The company was highly leveraged and quite vulnerable to a bad year of depressed sales and thin profit margins.

The success of the Beech-Nut strategy depended upon maintaining its ability to keep its plants filled to an efficient volume. Because Beech-Nut Foods had contracted for a large debt servicing requirement, the firm would be in a precarious position if it could not generate the necessary cash flows. Due to these expenditures and its strategic commitment to the baby-food business, Beech-Nut Foods faced the highest exit barriers. Beech-Nut Foods was trying to expand its market share and claim the crown of "industry innovator" from Gerber Products. Given these desperate odds, it should not have been surprising that Beech-Nut management took a gamble to try to save the company.

The centerpiece of the Beech-Nut strategy was a gamble that the company could develop the product consumers thought they wanted. When they had developed this product, Beech-Nut Foods used food brokers instead of shelf-servicing sales representatives. Instead of relying upon doctors' recommendations and hospitals adoptions to create customer demand, Beech-Nut Foods management "went public" and created "media events" to publicize its newly formulated, healthful baby-food products. These tactics lowered Beech-Nut Foods' distribution costs. The company used its potential savings from this tactic for large outlays for R&D. (The Beech-Nut R&D and advertising commitments were especially large.)

The company did create a demand for its product and it forced the other firms to imitate its strategy. But the company is privately held and does not divulge performance information. Therefore, like the demand for baby foods, there is substantial uncertainty concerning the long-term financial viability of this firm.

Gerber Products. Gerber Products would have been expected to possess the greatest competitive strengths and success in endgame since (1) it held the largest share of the market (in all baby foods except infant formula), (2) its specialized plants enjoyed the lowest unit costs, and (3) Gerber had become well diversified. Gerber Products had been a very profitable company for many years. It was cash-rich and had always paid a dividend to its shareholders. Moreover, it was conservatively managed and carried little debt. Gerber pursued a wide-product line, vertically integrated strategy in baby foods, and all of its diversifications were closely related to existing baby-product businesses. Gerber Products maintained an R&D laboratory which specialized in nutritional research. Professors of nutrition sat on the Gerber board of directors and advised the firm.

Gerber's five baby-food plants were located in regions which were either thriving, or which occupied special strategic significance. During the baby-food endgame, Gerber Products kept all five of the baby-food plants operating, even at low levels of capacity utilization, because it faced economic and strategic exit barriers which kept Gerber from closing down one of its baby-food plants. The baby-food plants were relatively new, specialized, and undepreciated. Gerber Products was firmly committed to its belief that the capacity of these five plants would be needed soon, and thus Gerber would not close down a baby-food plant because it anticipated that the plant would be needed again in two or three years.

Gerber Products had a very effective salesforce in terms of medical-detail and shelf-servicing operations. The brand name and cherub-faced trademark of Gerber baby foods had accumulated so much consumer goodwill that almost every U.S. grocery outlet carried Gerber baby-food products. Furthermore, Gerber was expanding its operations overseas and continued to invest in its baby foods and baby-related products during the endgame. Since the company's strategy was dependent upon babies, it strived to earn "more bucks per baby" as the number of births leveled off considerably below the number of births in 1957, when Gerber Products announced construction of its last two baby-food plants. The firm's strategy was based upon competitive advantages and it was expected to be successful.

Note

1. Reprinted from the 16 October 1978 issue of *Business Week* by special permission, ©1978 by McGraw-Hill, Inc. New York, NY 10020. All rights reserved.

7

The Endgame in the Electric Percolator Coffee-Maker Industry

An electric percolator coffee-maker (perc) is a pot which brews coffee using a percolating flow of heated water. Prior to the introduction of the automatic drip coffee-maker (ADC), the electric percolator coffee-maker had been the principal type of coffee-maker and had represented the largest annual sales volume of coffee-maker devices. Demand for the electric percolator coffee-maker declined because the technologically superior, automatic drip coffee-maker replaced it.

A Description of the Electric Percolator Coffee-Maker Industry

The Product

In an electric percolator coffee-maker, heated water is driven, in a percolating action, from the pot's base to the top of the pot through a hollow stem, to where coffee grounds are suspended in a basket perforated with tiny holes. The grounds basket is contained within the coffee pot, which boils the water. The brewing coffee passes through the grounds again and again until the desired strength of coffee is attained. Some electric percolator coffee-makers keep the coffee warm until consumed, but many do not.

The principal components of the electric percolator coffee-maker are the pot, the heating element, the electric cord, and the coffee-grounds basket. The best-known model of electric percolator coffee-maker is the "cold water" pump model, first introduced by Universal (GE) in 1908. In this model, a small well, or recess, in the base of the pot, around which the heating element was brazed, concentrated heat on a small quantity of water. This started the perking action in only two or three minutes. Formerly, the entire pot of water had to be heated before the brewing of coffee could commence.

Electric percolator coffee-makers may be made of glass, aluminum, stainless steel, porcelain-clad steel, or polypropylene plastic (poly percs). High-priced stainless steel and aluminum percolators were used as attractive serving pieces at social functions, but they developed an interior stain with time that was difficult to clean. Glass percolators were easier to clean but they were banished from the dining room because they did not make attrac-

185

tive serving vessels. Percolators were sold in a variety of kitchen fashion colors such as white, turquoise, avacado, gold, or poppy red, in addition to the shiny, metallic-surfaced models. Percolators were also available in several sizes.

Electric percolator coffee-makers which brewed one to sixteen cups were called "percolators." Electric percolator coffee-makers which brewed more than sixteen cups were called "urns" or party percs. The average life of a perc was five years. In 1972 more than 90 percent of U.S. households owned an automatic coffee-maker (up from 49 percent in 1962) and most of these automatic coffee-makers were percolator-sized coffee pots, ranging in size from two-to-four-cup models to twelve-cup models, with the most popular size being eight-to-ten-cup models.

Manufacturers shipped 8.5 million coffee-makers in 1969, of which more than 76 percent were electric percolators, representing approximately 16 percent of the total U.S. households. In 1972, 10.1 million coffee-makers were sold by manufacturers, as more households were forming, of which approximately 75 percent were electric percolators. Seventy percent of the percolator sales volume was in replacement sales because the market for electric percolator coffee-makers was mature. In 1972, 95 percent of the total United State households owned at least one electric percolator.

Markets

Electric percolator coffee-makers were merchandised through department stores, drug chains, discount chains, catalog showrooms, mail-order chains, stamp plans, mom-and-pop stores, gasoline stations, supermarkets, housewares departments of hardware stores, and variety stores in 1972. Within the percolator market, there were two major submarkets: a higher-priced market where higher-quality appliances were sold, and a lower-priced market where private-label, regional firms' products, or other less expensive models, were sold in competition with nationally advertised, low-priced, branded models. Approximately 35 percent of the sales of electric percolator coffee-makers were made in department stores, specializing in higher-margin and heavily advertised branded coffee-makers. Many discount stores also preferred to carry branded electric percolator coffee-makers, which they would discount heavily as traffic-builders for their other appliance products.

A major change in discount houses' methods of merchandising consumer electric housewares was their reliance upon a computerized ordering and inventory-control system which had the effect of increasing the frequency of orders, lessening the overall amount of housewares inventory held, and reducing the number of vendors with whom business was transacted. As a result of these changes in merchandising, specialized manufacturers of electric percolator coffee-makers became increasingly dependent upon wholesalers to place their percolator products on distributors' shelves. Department stores found that in order to carry a wide variety of brands, prices, and colors representative of the potential differences among percolators, an inventory of at least twenty percolator models was required. An inventory of only ten to twelve models would have been carried by a discounter at this time.

In 1972 electric housewares retail distributors such as department stores were striving to decrease the variety of electric percolator coffee-makers they carried and to concentrate upon middle price points in an effort to maximize their inventory turnover. Drug chains were limiting the brands they would stock to those for which cooperative advertising support was available. Catalog houses were reducing the number of catalog pages devoted to electric housewares. Mom-and-pop stores carried only one or two models (one low end, the other high) of percolators manufactured by one or two companies. The percolator and other small electric housewares had become primarily "traffic" items for many of these retail channels.

Electric percolator coffee-makers were sold to households both as original equipment and as a replacement product. In 1972, 70 percent of the percolator coffee-makers were sold to a replacement market. Demand in the OEM market was partially a function of demography. Electric percolator coffee-makers tended to be purchased by consumers when new households were formed. Newly married couples and first-time apartment dwellers were likely to purchase their first coffee-makers when they commenced housekeeping duties. Demand for electric percolator coffee-makers in the replacement market was influenced by the technological life and performance of the consumer's previous coffee-making unit, which was usually a percolator coffee-maker as well.

Marketing

The technical life of an electric percolator coffee-maker was usually three to five years. A new coffee-maker would be needed when an electric percolator coffee-maker became discolored to an extent which could affect the taste of coffee brewed in it even if cleaned. The typical customers for such small appliances could be "traded up" to a new coffee-maker that offered the "latest gadgets and fashion colors" when they replaced their old coffee pot. "Trading up" means selling customers a more expensive replacement model. Frequently these replacement appliances offered new features or minor styling changes. The percolator coffee-maker customer who was in the replacement market had usually been away from the market for several years and frequently could be amenable to buying improvements in the product when he or she replaced the older coffee-maker. The life-span of a particular model of electric percolator coffee-maker was short, but yearly changes in colors, decorations, sizes, materials, and styling features abounded.

Household customer purchases were motivated by attractive colors, materials, sizes, quality, and prices. Electrical percolator manufacturers tried to reach these customers through both advertising expenditures and a proliferation of products, prices, and styles.

Manufacturers of perculator coffee-makers differed in the amount of price dealing they would offer to their retail channels to help them sell percolators. The major electrical housewares manufacturers offered two types of percolators—a "price-football" or lower-priced percolator for those promotional purposes, and the medium- and higher-priced percolator lines where price-cutting was rarely used in 1972.

Discounters believed that it was particularly important for their images to carry a lower-priced and nationally advertised branded price-football type of percolator. Both discount houses and department stores used these percolator coffee-makers as traffic builders once a month or every six weeks. Both types of outlets advertised percolators, although discount stores did so more frequently than did department stores. Discount stores carried the lower-priced polypropylene (plastic) percolators which retailed for less than $10.00 on a regular basis.

The medium- and high-quality percolator coffee-maker products provided manufacturers with medium profit margins during most of the year. Manufacturers would support their retail channels in using price promotion on these relatively stable-priced percolators during biannual "special" sales. Price footballs would be brought in for other promotions which were run more frequently.

The low-quality percolator coffee-maker products were used for aggressive price-cutting activities throughout the year. Unlike the medium- and high-priced lines, which were usually sold near list prices, the price-football products were sold to retailers at cut-rate prices. Discounters took only narrow profit margins on these low-priced traffic-building percolators when reselling them; they literally "gave their profits away." This type of promotion was backed by heavy advertising expenditures made by both the manufacturers and the retailers in order to push these low-priced percolators to the ultimate consumers.

Major small electrical appliance manufacturers competed for retailers' shelf space using cooperative advertising, the power of "national brand names," and aggressive salesforces who were empowered to use pricing and additional promotional materials to pull a full line of appliance products through these channels. Manufacturers spent increasing sums on special merchandising campaigns and other dealer incentives and also sponsored television programs using media advertising and other promotional gimmicks to support their full line of percolator products. Keeping at least one percolator coffee-maker unit in an appliance company's product line was important for the major electrical housewares manufacturers even if the percolator itself did not break even after corporate burden had been charged against it. Percolators were a vital part of a full-line product offering, used not only to keep out competition and to put their new products on retailers' shelves easily, but also to attract more shelf space away from narrow-line or more specialized competitors. Product proliferation was a special form of competitive tactic in this business. There were many different types of percolators being sold in different types of retail outlets for different prices in 1972.

Substitutes. The automatic drip coffee-maker (ADC) was an innovation. It was a substantial improvement over some of the problems which had plagued percolator coffee-maker use. Percolator-brewed coffee was not always good, a fact which could be embarrassing when users were entertaining. Automatic drip coffee-maker brewed coffee, by contrast, was easier to make, faster, and it was alleged to taste better because water passed through the grounds chamber once. (Percolators forced boiling water through grounds compartments over and over again. This destroyed the delicate flavor of coffee beans.) With time, percolator interiors would become more bitter, and this built-up emulsion also effected the taste of the coffee brewed. Percolators had to be cleaned and polished frequently, as well.

Suppliers

Electric percolator coffee-makers were manufactured from electrothermostats or other heat-control devices, rolled metallic bodies, or blow-molded plastic bodies, heating elements, electrical cords, and metallic grounds baskets. Some percolator coffee-maker producers, such as aluminum firms, were backward-integrated to provide some of these raw materials to their electrical housewares operations. The electro-thermostat controls were manufactured by two large firms, Texas Instruments and Emerson Electric, and several small companies. Major firms such as Sunbeam Appliance and Proctor-Silex, who assembled their own percolators, sourced some of their cords and electrical devices from suppliers such as these.

Rolled-aluminum or stainless-steel bodies were supplied by metals-fabrication companies. No percolator firm was backward-integrated to produce its own plastics, but plastics were supplied by many small companies.

Mirro Aluminum and Wear-Ever (ALCOA) supplied their own metal sheets for percolator bodies. Major firms such as General Electric sourced rolled bodies from other suppliers or subsidiaries.

Manufacturing Technology

The essential tools used for percolator manufacture were dies, a hydraulic press, injection molding equipment, and certain fabricating equipment unique to percolators. The investment in tools and dies needed to fabricate aluminum percolators was approximately $60,000 in 1972. Annual sales volume of $500,000 was needed to justify investing in a simple facility to produce percolators. Break-even volume for such a plant which fabricated its own aluminum was approximately 400,000 units.

If the appliance firm fabricated its own aluminum, entry costs would have been lower since the firm's production of percolator coffee-makers would have represented a small incremental investment added to a firm's total activities in rolling aluminum. Polypropylene percolator coffee-makers could also be produced with a relatively low incremental entry investment in dies and blow-molding equipment if the manufacturer already possessed the basic plant, equipment, and experience of producing and selling similar plastic products. If a firm bought most of its components from outside suppliers, manufacture of percolator coffee-makers would be primarily an assembly operation and the capital costs of a percolator plant could be kept low by leasing the plant and equipment needed to assemble purchased components. Sourcing agreements were also used by some of the smaller appliance firms in order to have a percolator to offer as part of their full product line without investing in plant or equipment for producing the percolator.

Because the assets used to fabricate glass, aluminum, or polypropylene into percolator coffee-makers were not specific to percolator manufacture, an appliance firm which produced other small appliance products could convert some percolator assets for other uses inexpensively. The percolator manufacturers which would be most badly hurt by declining demand for percolator coffee-makers would be those firms which (1) produced percolator models which were quickly cannibalized by the automatic drip coffee-makers and which (2) possessed few internal alternate uses for undepreciated percolator-specific assets. (The assets used to produce ADCs were different from those used to produce percolator coffee-makers. Only the heating rods and other small components were similar.) But where the value of the assets used to manufacture percolator coffee-makers had been completely depreciated, they could simply be mothballed until demand for percolators or some similar product was resuscitated. Because assets which had not been fully depreciated would have to show some write-off losses within a reasonable time after shutdown and because there was a thin resale market for them, the assets used to manufacture percolator coffee-makers were frequently mothballed (rather than "junked") if no other product line could use them.

Economic Exit Barriers. Technologically, the barriers to exit were not high because the plants where percolator coffee-makers were assembled were not inflexible for use in manufacturing other small electric appliances. Sometimes, two products were produced in the same plant—each giving and taking floor space relative to their sales volumes. Nonintegrated firms could exit by running out aluminum or stainless-steel inventories and converting their leased plant space to other products. Integrated (rolling mills) manufacturers could use production facilities to fabricate another metallic product. If other polypropylene blow-molding operations were also executed in a percolator plant, the capacity vacated by exit could be converted to the other products easily; but the sunk cost of the dies for the percolator designs, if undepreciated, would not be recoverable. For glass percolators, exit might be more difficult unless other glass housewares utensils or appliances were also produced at a percolator plant site.

Because entry de novo into most small appliance businesses required a high capital investment per unit of value added, manufacturers of electric percolator coffee-makers were usually diversified into either metals-fabricating or other appliance-manufacturing activities if they fabricated their own components. Economic exit barriers became significant for electric percolator coffee-makers where the producer did *not* offer a wide line of other products which could readily absorb the abandoned production assets but where several other products were being produced within the plant, using the same basic technology, the write-off cost for polypropylene or aluminum electric percolator coffee-makers could be low because much of the vacated capacity and assets could be diverted to other products. In some cases, entire plants were dedicated to the manufacturing of electric percolator coffee-makers. Some of these plants were leased, and in many cases the assets used to fabricate electric percolator coffee-makers were well depreciated. Because private-brand percolators were readily available, a company enjoying these conditions could exit economically from this business but maintain a presence strategically by sourcing its percolators from other companies. The lowest exit barriers were faced by firms which assembled sourced components in leased plants.

A Historical Overview of the Electric Percolator Coffee-Maker Business

Pots for brewing coffee had been sold in the United States since before the turn of the century. In 1908, Universal (now GE) introduced the cold-water pump coffee-maker, which brewed coffee far more rapidly than earlier models. Metal Ware Corp. improved upon this design by developing a valveless pump immersion heating device, which facilitated easier cleaning of the device as well as greater brewing speeds. Two problems which had plagued the early coffee-maker units were (1) their tendency to overheat, causing fires, and (2) their costliness. S.W. Farber Incorporated, introduced an electric percolator coffee-maker which offered one way of coping with the electrical burnouts problem. Farber patented a rotating disc fuse which guarded against earlier coffee-makers' electrical fires caused by coffee-maker burnouts. Features such as these fuses and other safety devices were offered more frequently on the higher-priced percolator coffee-makers in the 1920s. Mirro Aluminum Company of Manitowac, Wisconsin, provided a solution to the problem of costliness. Since Mirro, a manufacturer of aluminum cookware, operated its own rolling mills to produce its own sheets from raw aluminum ingots, it sometimes had excess capacity which it used to produce a low-priced aluminum percolator coffee-maker, and it captured 50 percent of the market for domestic coffee-makers with this low-priced entry in the 1920s.

Although Mirro Aluminum dominated the market for low-priced coffee-makers in the 1920s, its market share was eroded in the 1930s by the introduction of a glass percolating coffee-maker, the Silex, which used the percolator principle to drive water, contained in a glass orb, heated from below by a flame, into a chamber containing coffee grounds. During World War II the Silex coffee-maker had been the dominant type of coffee pot because of shortages of aluminum and stainless steel, used in the war effort. By 1947 only 33 percent of U.S. households preferred aluminum coffee-makers, and approximately 60 percent preferred the glass, Silex-type coffee-maker.

After World War II the unfilled, excess capacity of the Silex Company doomed it to bankruptcy and the Silex Company was acquired by the Proctor Electric Company. By 1950 Universal, Sunbeam, and General Electric held a total of 52 percent of the nonglass percolator coffee-maker market, and continued to represent over 50 percent of the total market throughout the 1950s. In 1965 the General Electric Company acquired Landers, Frary and Clark, maker of the Universal-brand coffee-makers, thus consolidating GE's position as the leading manufacturer of electric percolator coffee-makers. In 1965 Walter Kidde & Company acquired the S.W. Farber Company, a manufacturer of high-quality, stainless-steel percolators. In 1966 SCM Corporation acquired Proctor-Silex, and West Bend, a manufacturer of porcelained appliances and cookware (then the fourth-largest producer of electric percolator coffee-makers), was acquired by Dart Industries, a highly diversified holding company. Scovill, which owned the Hamilton Beach and Dominion brands, acquired the Westinghouse Electric small appliance line in 1972.

Competition in the Electric Percolator Coffee-Maker Business in 1972

Firms in the small electrical household appliance business produced two types of products: (1) basic or fundamental appliance units which had high consumer saturation levels (many households used these appliances); and (2) high-margin, highly advertised "fad" items whose investment could be recovered quickly. In 1972 percolators were still thought to be "staple" products, but if they were to become fad products reinvestments in the percolator coffee-maker business were not likely to be made because most percolator coffee-maker producers' original percolator investments were well depreciated in 1972.

Table 7-1 lists the major producers of percolator coffee-makers in 1972.

Table 7-1
Thomas Register List of Firms
Manufacturing Percolator Coffee-Makers in 1972

Aluminum Specialty Co.
American Production Co.
Amrum Metal Industries
Buckeye Ware, Inc.
Club Aluminum Products Co.
Corning Glass Works
Cornwall Corporation
Cory Corporation
Dominion Electric Corp. (Scovill)
Enterprise Aluminum Co.
Ershler & Krukin
S.W. Farber (Walter Kidde Co.)
Forman Family, Inc.
General Electric Company
The Hoover Co.
John Oster Mfg. Co.
Harold Leonard & Co.
Leyse Aluminum Co.
Metal Ware Corp.
Mirro Aluminum
National Presto Industries, Inc.
Nicro Steel Products Co.
G. Parkwood Co.
Proctor-Silex (SCM)
Regal Ware, Inc.
Revere Copper & Brass, Inc.
Sun-Chief Electrics, Inc.
Sunbeam Corp.
United Metal Goods Mfg.
Wear-Ever Aluminum, Inc. (ALCOA)
West Bend (DART)
Westinghouse Electric

Source: *The Thomas Register of American Manufacturers*, (New York: Thomas Publishing Company, 1972). Reprinted with permission.

Many of these firms served only regional markets and the Bureau of the Census reported that only nineteen of them sold more than $100,000 of percolators annually.

The coffee-maker industry's geographic location was confined primarily to the Great Lakes region, with eight firms in Wisconsin, five in Ohio, four in Illinois, and five in New York state. Many firms listed as being manufacturers of coffee-makers in 1972 were also aluminum fabricators, requiring access to waterways in order to minimize transportation costs for their raw materials.

General Electric. General Electric was the largest and best-known manufacturer of electric percolator coffee-makers. The principal businesses of General Electric included consumer products, industrial power equipment; industrial components and systems, aerospace products, a vast research and development center, an international division, and a finance-company subsidiary. In 1972 General Electric operated 210 U.S. plants and eighty international plants (in twenty-three other countries). Total corporate sales were $10,239.0 million in that year. Consumer products represented 27 percent of General Electric's worldwide sales.

In 1972 General Electric produced electric percolator coffee-makers within the Housewares Division of the Consumer Products Group, which also produced air conditioners, clothes washers and dryers, dishwashers, lamps, personal and portable appliances, radio and television receivers, ranges, refrigerators, stereo equipment, and tape recorders. Its group sales for 1972 were $2,782.0 million.

General Electric represented 23 percent of national percolator sales volume, roughly $15.6 million in manufacturers' shipments, but only 0.5 percent of its Consumer Group Sales.

General Electric had entered the electric percolator coffee-maker business through an acquisition of a percolator company in the early 1930s which made General Electric one of the largest factors in the percolator business, and the second-largest-selling brand. (The leading model was the Universal-brand coffee-maker, acquired by GE, in 1965.)

In 1972, General Electric was the leading department-store brand of coffee-makers, with a market share of 17 percent. Thirty-five percent of all coffee-makers were sold through this channel. Thirty-three percent of all GE-brand coffee-makers were sold through department stores.

Despite the large sales volume of General Electric's electric percolator coffee-makers, the product was not relatively important to the Housewares Division because over 100 different types of small electrical appliances were produced within it. In 1972 General Electric offered six basic designs of percolators. There were two different sizes in its aluminum line, three different styles in its stainless-steel line, and a specialty model which was made of nickel.

The General Electric stainless-steel percolator coffee-maker retailed for more than $30 (twelve-cup). The immersible aluminum percolators retailed for approximately $25 (nine- or ten-cup). The other two General Electric aluminum percolator coffee-maker models retailed for $15 and $20, respectively, in 1972. General Electric also offered a four-cup aluminum percolator for less than $10 which was popular in discount outlets. (This was GE's price football.) General Electric's percolator coffee-makers were heavily promoted by corporate advertising, and cooperative advertising allowances and were distributed nationally. Although department stores were an important distribution channel for General Electric percolator sales, the prominence of the General Electric brand name also made it an attractive product for discount channels and catalog showrooms to sell.

General Electric percolator coffee-maker components were manufactured, in part, by foreign subsidiaries whose local sales were poor and who had no good alternatives to fill their plants. This linkage could have represented a strategic exit barrier to General Electric for models such as the P-15 because discontinuing that product would have meant closing down the factory which produced its aluminum, specular body.

Components for General Electric's percolator coffee-makers were produced in several locations. The Universal coffee-maker plants were located in Fort Smith, Arkansas, and New Britain, Connecticut. Stainless-steel bodies were sourced from Denmark and the United Kingdom as well as Allentown, Pennsylvania.

Dart Industries, Inc. (West Bend). Dart Industries was a conglomerate whose subsidiaries manufactured and sold housewares, glass containers, architectural, pharmaceutical (Rexall Drug) and health-care products, chemicals, and plastics through multinational divisions. Its total corporate sales were $888.0 million in 1972, of which the Consumer Products Group represented 16 percent. The group produced a broad line of cookware, electric housewares, humidifiers, electronic air cleaners, copper giftware, and vacuum products. Sales for 1972 were $146.0 million, of which percolators were 6.5 percent.

Percolator coffee-makers which were produced by the West Bend Company in West Bend, Wisconsin, represented a relatively important product with a national market share of 14 percent in 1972, making West Bend a major factor in the electric percolator coffee-maker business. In 1971 West Bend had introduced its multi-colored nine-cup aluminum electric percolator coffee-makers, which were priced below $20 at retail, and a ten-cup unit which retailed for approximately $25. West Bend was popular with discount houses, ranking fourth (below Regal Ware, GE, and Sunbeam in the lower-priced markets), but it ranked second in national sales volume because West Bend sold coffee-makers to retailers such as Montgomery Ward, J.C. Penney, and W.T. Grant as a private-brand manufacturer.

Sunbeam Corporation. The Sunbeam Corporation was a holding company whose businesses included household electrical appliances, electrical instruments, industrial heat treating furnaces, bedcoverings, copiers, water treatment, scales, and industrial air pollution control devices, among others, with multinational subsidiaries on three continents. Total corporate sales were $453.2 million. Household appliances were important to the Sunbeam Corporation since before 1960 its primary business had been appliances. In 1972, percolators represented 1.9 percent of corporate sales. In 1972 Sunbeam Corporation produced electric percolator coffee-makers in the Sunbeam Appliances Company, which manufactured food mixers, blenders, can openers, fry pans, irons, toasters, waffle-bakers, and coffee-makers, among other products. Sunbeam Appliance products were sold under the Sunbeam Appliance trademarks, Sunbeam and Coffeemaster (and the Oster Corporation trademark, Osterizer) and were manufactured in a South Carolina plant which was completely dedicated to production of five basic percolator bodies (facilitating a large number of product variations in styling).

Sunbeam was the "Cadillac" of the small electrical household appliance industry. It offered fewer price-football units than did the other major appliance companies and was able to avoid much of the lower-priced market's shelf-space jostling and price-cutting by virtue of its large market position and the quality of its wide percolator line which, represented 13 percent of the national percolator coffee-makers sales volume. This multitude of percolator coffee-maker and other appliance product offerings available in a wide range of prices gave Sunbeam substantial bargaining power with respect to its distributors. In 1972 Sunbeam Appliance percolator coffee-maker designs were available in stainless steel, colored aluminum, and glass. Moreover, for Christmas 1972, Sunbeam's Oster Corporation introduced a ten-cup percolator coffee-maker made of transparent polysulfone, an unbreakable plastic. Sunbeam Appliance purchased the necessary electrical cords, thermostats, and heating elements from outside suppliers. It fabricated the grounds baskets and vessels internally in its South Carolina plant. Sunbeam's glass percolators captured approximately 20 percent of the glass coffee-maker market; the aluminum and stainless-steel units represented 11 percent of the nonglass market. Sunbeam also carried a "price-protected" line (under the now-defunct "fair trade" laws) called Vista, which represented the highest-quality Sunbeam percolators.

Sunbeam did not advertise its percolators as heavily as did General Electric. As late as 1971 Sunbeam still promoted its percolator coffee-maker on the basis of the value of the corporate name. This meant that a large corporate identification campaign was launched in which a percolator coffee-maker would be one of many appliance products featured in the advertisement.

Corning Glass Works. Corning Glass Works was a leading manufacturer of products made from specialty glasses and related crystalline materials. The company also produced integrated circuits, medical instruments, and electronic devices, as well as a limited line of appliances. Corporate sales in 1972 were $714.6 million. The Consumer Products Division which produced housewares for cooking, preparing, serving, and storing foods and beverages represented 28 percent of Corning Glass Works' total sales. Other consumer products manufactured in this division included glass ceramic counter-tops for cooking ranges and Steuben Glass. Division sales for 1972 were $200.6 million. Percolators represented 4 percent of division sales.

The Corning Ware electric percolator coffee-makers were part of a growing line of Pyrex® and Corning Ware® housewares which Corning Glass Works had introduced with great success. In addition to its regular ceramic percolators, Corning Glass Works had created a separate, high-quality line of pyro-ceramic coffee-makers called Electromatic percolators, and, between these two lines of percolators, Corning made about fifteen different models.

Corning Glass Works' percolator products represented 12 percent of national percolator sales volume and represented the highest percolator prices and quality. Corning offered only a specialized, narrow line of electrical housewares, like its cookware line of Pyrex® and Corning Ware®. Corning Glass Works had just launched an expensive advertising campaign for its new Electromatic percolator, which included new designs and packaging as well as increased advertising expenditures, when the automatic drip coffee-maker was introduced at the end of 1972.

SCM (Proctor-Silex). SCM Corporation (Smith-Corona-Marchant) was a highly diversified operating company whose principal products included typewriters; electrostatic office copy machines and other office equipment; coatings, resins, and chemicals; food products; pulp, paper, and paper products; teleprinter communications equipment; and portable electric appliances. SCM operated seventy-four plants twelve of which were overseas). Total corporate sales were $917.8 million in 1972, of which the consumer-appliances and typewriters group represented 19 percent. In 1972 SCM Corporation produced electric percolator coffee-makers within its Proctor-Silex Company, which included SCM typewriters, as well as irons and ironing tables, vacuum cleaners, and percolator coffee-makers. Group sales for 1972 were $174.4 million, of which percolators represented 4 percent.

The Proctor-Silex salesforce was highly deal-oriented, and aggressive price-cutting (below list) occurred routinely in the Proctor-Silex lines because high sales volume was an important part of the Proctor-Silex percolator sales strategy. Proctor-Silex sold 80 percent of the glass percolator sales volume—approximately 10 percent of total percolator coffee-maker sales. Unfortunately this particular product looked most like the glass carafes used in the automatic drip coffee-makers. Thus, glass percolators were likely to be among the first percolators eliminated from store shelves by distributors. (It would have seemed like a duplication of scarce retail shelf space to continue to stock glass percolator coffee-maker inventories.)

Proctor-Silex percolators competed in the low end of the market where inexpensive coffee-makers abounded. Although the suggested retail prices of Proctor-Silex percolators were nearly $20, the ten- and twelve-cup models were frequently discounted so that Proctor-Silex's glass percolators competed with Regal Ware's polypropylene percolators.

Percolator coffee-makers were manufactured in the Baltimore, Maryland, Proctor-Silex plant. Ironing tables were also produced at this factory. Proctor-Silex's asset investment was somewhat flexible with respect to percolators. Proctor-Silex made its own electrical controls and heating elements. It bought its glass from Corning Glass Works. The Proctor-Silex percolator coffee-maker was a high-margin product for the firm because it used the least expensive raw material, glass.

Mirro Aluminum. Mirro Aluminum manufactured and sold aluminum cooking utensils, boats, aluminum siding, and aluminum foil. The company's principal diversification was into the manufacture of intermediate-sized fiberglass pleasure boats. Total percolators represented approximately 3 percent of corporate sales and were Mirro Aluminum's largest category of kitchen products in 1972. The company also manufactured aluminum cookware, electric cookware, and pressure cookers and manufactured electric cookware and percolators under the Sears, Roebuck label, as well as its own Mirro-matic label.

Mirro-matic percolator coffee-makers had been promoted using ample advertising allowances (about twenty times more than General Electric per sales dollar). Because Mirro Aluminum was small, it did not enjoy economies of scale in advertising but it needed the heavy advertising investment in order to compete strongly against the many cat-and-dog companies who also produced and sold low-priced percolators. Percolator coffee-makers were produced at Mirro's Manitowoc, Wisconsin, plant, where Mirro also operated its own aluminum-rolling mill. These operations gave Mirro the lowest costs in the aluminum-percolator business. The percolator product it offered was mature and few revisions of its design (and hence its dies) had been made for several years. The percolator coffeemaker business shared the rolling-mill and aluminum-smelting facilities with the other kitchenware businesses.

Regal Ware, Incorporated. Regal Ware was the largest privately owned U.S. housewares manufacturer and the dominant firm in the lower-priced percolator coffee-maker business. Its major product was the polypropylene percolator (the poly perc), a very low-cost unit. In order to support this low-cost product policy, Regal Ware cut manufacturing costs wherever possible in its assembly operations, using polypropylene instead of metal in the percolator's body or components, for example, in the grounds basket. Regal Ware was not encumbered with undepreciated fixed assets in this business because it purchased materials and was predominantly a blow-molding and assembly operation. This competitive posture enabled Regal Ware to enjoy relatively greater economic flexibility than did its higher-cost competitors, smaller regional plastics firms who produced a few poly percs.

Regal Ware promoted its polypropylene percolator coffee-maker using catalog advertising and a program of premium sales. Regal Ware's product strategy was to provide good quality at a low price. The Regal Poly Perk®, which retailed at $7.99, was discounted to $4.99 by distributors to build traffic for their other housewares products.

Walter Kidde & Co., Inc. (Farber, Inc.). Walter Kidde was a conglomerate whose products and services were in the fields of safety, security, and protection; industrial and technological products; and commercial and consumer products. Corporate sales were $832.2 million in 1972, of which consumer products represented $33. In 1972 Walter Kidde produced high-quality electric percolator coffee-makers in its consumer and commercial products group, which also manufactured incandescent and fluorescent lighting fixtures; temperature-controlled showcases and display fixtures; commercial aircraft fixtures (galley equipment, passenger and crew seats); and electric appliances and cookware. Group sales in 1972 were $274.8 million.

When Walter Kidde acquired S.W. Farber, a manufacturer of high-quality, aluminum-clad stainless-steel and electrical appliances, it broadened the Farberware brand's exposure in retail channels. Where formerly Farberware had been pursuing a very selective distribution strategy commensurate with its high-quality image, Kidde sold Farberware through medium-level department stores, but not to discounters. Farberware sales were high in department stores because S.W. Farber supplied demonstrator-sales clerks in stores where Farberware appliances were sold.

Farber percolator coffee-makers retailed for $30 and sometimes for $35 in 1972. They were available in limited models but were of high-quality craftsmanship, and were promoted using an advertising campaign which spent less per sales dollar than General Electric's campaign. Farberware was most popular on the East Coast, particularly in New York, near the S.W. Farber Bronx factory, in stores like Bloomingdale's.

Corporate Strategy Exit Barriers. In the consumer housewares business, carrying a full line of appliances was important in order to "lock out" competitors from scarce distributor shelf space. Thus, appliances like percolator coffee-makers were continued after their volume fell below their break-even levels. The strategic deterrence of the full-line policy explains why few firms would discontinue their offerings of electric percolator coffee-makers completely. The percolator would likely stay in an appliance manufacturer's catalog even it if were incurring a loss, to maintain a presence in percolator coffee-makers.

The appliance companies which might have suspected that automatic drip coffee-makers would be more than a fad in the United States had too much at stake strategically in their percolator business to undermine it by selling ADCs, and were thus slow to produce the substitute product. The first companies who did offer automatic drip coffee-makers were not encumbered by their percolator exit investments or previous marketing investments in percolators, as were the major household-appliance companies.

Summary of Competitors' Profiles

In summary, several different strategic groups served the electric percolator coffee-maker markets. The competitors differed with respect to (1) the width of their housewares line and of the percolators' relative importance to that housewares line; (2) whether firms fabricated percolators internally, using assets which were shared with other products; and (3) which niches of the coffee-maker market a firm's percolator coffee-makers were positioned to serve.

Wide-line Appliance Companies Affiliated with Large Corporations. Wide-line appliance firms heavily advertised their percolator coffee-makers or their corporate trademarks and brandnames. They engaged in the occasional "dealing"—special price concessions, cooperative advertising, promotioned budgets, and other retailer incentives—that was necessary to gain shelf space and to sell large volumes of percolators. Because these firms offered wide product lines, they could offer percolator coffee-makers in several price niches.

Individually, the percolator coffee-maker line was not relatively important to wide-line appliance companies. There were too many other products which comprised the appliance firms' lines. Yet, at least one percolator had to be retained in their lines in order to offer a full line of appliances. Wide-line appliance firms varied in the amount of internal fabricating they undertook. Some firms sourced many of their components and assembled them in a plant near their markets. Other firms performed the fabrication task internally to ensure quality control in their percolator production.

Specialized Product Lines—Housewares Companies. Housewares companies who offered only one or two electrical appliances frequently diversified into percolators as a logical extension of proficiency with a particular raw material—glass, pyroceramics, or aluminum, for example. Frequently they offered dishes, cookware, or other utensils in addition to the percolator coffee-makers.

Specialized housewares firms advertised their percolator coffee-makers, as did the wide-line appliance companies, but, because they did not offer a wide product line, sometimes they relied upon wholesalers to place their products on store shelves. Wide-line appliance companies employed an in-house salesforce to push their products through channels in addition to using outside wholesaling channels.

The specialized percolator coffee-makers were frequently aluminum fabricating companies such as Mirro Aluminum, Metal Ware Corporation, Wear-Ever Aluminum, Inc., or Aluminum Specialty Co. The Corning Glass Works percolators were fabricated from the glass-works technology it had previously developed. Revere Copper & Brass fabricated percolators from the metals it used for other products. Some of the percolator coffee-maker firms did not use their raw materials and assets for other housewares, however. Some small companies were so specialized that they provided *only* percolators to private-brand customers.

A Mapping of Strategic Groups in the Electric Percolator Coffee-Maker Business

Within the electric percolator coffee-maker business, the competitors could be arrayed along the dimensions of (1) wide product line versus specialized, or narrow, product line; (2) firms which were predominantly appliance companies versus firms which were predominantly aluminum, or other raw-materials, fabricators; and (3) higher-quality and priced versus lower-priced products. Within these classifications, the electric percolator coffee-maker firms could be grouped into strategic clusters which depict their similarity to each other as follows:

	Predominantly Appliance Companies	Predominantly Materials-Oriented Companies
Wide Product	General Electric Sunbeam Appliance Hamilton Beach West Bend	
Narrow or Specialized	Proctor-Silex Toastmaster Regal Ware, Inc. S.W. Faber	National Presto Industries Mirro Aluminum Corning Glass Works

Along the axes of this cluster diagram, the firms with the relatively widest and most narrow product lines are positioned at the extremes of this "strategic space." For example, General Electric and Sunbeam Appliance offered the widest product lines. They are depicted as major appliance companies. By contrast, Mirro Aluminum and Corning Glass Works had specific raw-materials orientations. Each of them offered a few housewares such as pots, pans, or utensils. Each offered a very limited number of electrical appliances. They are depicted as being similar to the many other small, regional fabricators whose primary electrical-appliance offerings were percolator coffee-makers.

The complex differences among competitors in the electric percolator coffee-maker endgame might also be considered in terms of the differences between the producers of high-priced percolators and of lower-priced percolators, as well as between those whose percolators were relatively important in the firms' product mixes and those which were less important.

General Electric and Sunbeam Appliance offered percolator coffee-makers which served almost every market segment (except, perhaps, the private-label market). Thus they competed with all of the other percolator firms. Toastmaster, Hamilton Beach, and Westinghouse Electric served a higher-priced market than did some of the other wide-line product strategies. The product lines of Proctor-Silex, S.W. Farber, and West Bend still offered a wide variety of electrical appliances, but they were narrower than the other wide-line appliance firms.

Mirro Aluminum, Regal Ware, and Corning Glass Works offered specialized product lines. In each case, the percolator coffee-maker was their only electrical housewares appliance. Presto Industries produced slightly more housewares than did these firms. It was backward-integrated like most of them, as well.

Montgomery, Ward and Sears, Roebuck, as retailers who featured private brands, competed with most of the other percolator coffee-maker firms. However, these retailers differed in their product emphasis and pricing postures with regard to percolators. Sears, Roebuck offered top-of-the-line, stainless-steel percolators as well as aluminum percolators. Montgomery, Ward emphasized the lower-priced, colored aluminum percolators.

The Endgame in the Electric Percolator Coffee-Maker Industry

Although Europeans had used the drip coffee-maker method of brewing coffee for a long period of time before ADCs were commercialized successfully in the United States, automatic drip coffee-maker designs imported from Europe had never captured U.S. consumer interest. When Mr. Coffee, the first automatic drip coffee-maker designed especially for U.S.

markets, was first introduced, it appeared in department stores where a huge cooperative advertising allowance (of $5 per unit) and a generous mark-up ($22 wholesale, marked up to $40 retail) made it worthwhile for distributors to push the product.

Mr. Coffee was launched at Christmastime 1972 in Abraham & Strauss in New York City. Most producers of percolator coffee-makers did not consider that Mr. Coffee might be anything more than a passing fad, but, with heavy promotional support during this introductory period, Mr. Coffee sold 12,000 units per week in one store. The "new" automatic drip coffee-maker was more convenient to maintain and easier to operate. Consumers were assured by "Joltin' Joe" DiMaggio that the coffee it brewed did indeed taste better. The introduction of the automatic drip coffee-maker *helped* percolator sales for approximately eighteen months (1973 and part of 1974). Then percolator coffee-maker sales volume plummeted. Table 7-2 summarizes the sales volumes of these products at the manufacturer's level and at retail. The responses of many major percolator coffee-maker producers were to advertise more heavily at first but to cut back on advertising as the automatic drip coffee-makers became more popular, and then to enter the automatic drip coffee-maker business themselves.

A Chronological Description of the Percolator Coffee-Maker Endgame

1973

West Bend. West Bend reduced the number of percolator coffee-maker styles it offered and invested heavily in assets to produce automatic drip coffee-makers at its large, multi-building appliance complex in West Bend, instead. By being one of the first coffee-maker manufacturers to offer drip coffee-makers, West Bend cashed in on the benefits of a relatively unsaturated market for these coffee-makers. Soon West Bend was producing automatic drip coffee-makers for other housewares appliance companies who wished to hurry into the drip coffee-maker market, and with time West Bend's percolator assets were squeezed off of the production floor and into storage.

Corning Glass Works. In 1973 Corning Glass Works created a separate product division for its electrical housewares products because these products had grown rapidly and become increasingly important. To support this venture, Corning introduced new percolator designs in glass and ceramic materials and launched a heavy promotional campaign.

Table 7-2
Quantity and Value of Manufacturers' Shipments

	1969	1970	1971	1972	1973	1974	1975
Manufacturers' Quantity (thousands of units)							
Electric coffee-makers, vacuum and percolator types	6,496	6,124	7,002	8,188	8,720	8,662	6,675
Electric coffee-makers, urn (party perc) types	2,526	2,370	1,785	1,984	1,936	1,625	1,234
Total, electric percolator coffee-makers	9,022	8,494	8,787	10,172	10,656	10,287	7,909
Manufacturers' Value (thousands of dollars)							
Electric coffee-makers, vacuum and percolator types	53,267	52,402	62,311	67,800	78,404	92,386	90,291
Electric coffee-makers, urn (party perc) types	21,432	20,643	15,291	16,500	15,682	13,240	10,797
Total, electric percolator coffee-makers	74,699	73,045	77,607	84,380	94,153	105,626	101,088
Average Manufacturers' Price per Unit (dollars)							
Electric coffee-makers, vacuum and percolator types	8.20	8.56	8.90	8.28	8.99	10.67	13.53
Electric coffee-makers, urn (party perc) types	8.48	8.71	8.57	8.31	8.10	8.15	8.75
Total electric percolator coffee-makers average price	8.28	8.60	8.83	8.84	8.84	10.26	12.78

Source: Bureau of the Census, *Census of Manufacturers.*

Mirro Aluminum. In 1973 Mirro Aluminum added a new roll grinder to its aluminum-rolling mill. Of the $2.2 million Mirro Aluminum spent for capital improvements, the largest portion of the monies was devoted to expanding its rolled-body aluminum percolator production capacity.

Proctor-Silex. Proctor-Silex introduced new percolator products for 1973, targeted to the upper end of the percolator coffee-maker market, which were higher-quality extensions of their successful polypropylene-rim-and-base, glass percolators which had been introduced in 1972. This product strategy was a significant departure from the market Proctor-Silex usually serviced.

General Electric. In 1973 the nickel-plated percolator coffee-maker design and two stainless-steel bodies were phased out by General Electric to be replaced by another stainless-steel percolator design with more added features. This product turnover was a part of General Electric's regular upgrading of products and not a response to the automatic drip percolator invasion. Its effect, however, was to reduce the number of percolator designs carried in General Electric's inventory. In most cases, when General Electric removed a percolator coffee-maker from its catalog, it did not hold inventory to supply its distributors with the deleted unit, but the very high-quality nickel and stainless steel percolators were an exception. Production of them was discontinued in 1970, but slow inventory turnover made them available until 1973.

In 1973 General Electric also introduced two plastic percolator coffee-makers, a blue model selling for $20.98 which was immersible (meaning all of the electrical connections were sealed, permitting the coffee-maker to be dunked in water), and a yellow model retailing for $15.98 which was not. The General Electric plastic percolators were a disaster because Regal Ware and Cornwall Perkette® plastic percolators were lower priced, undercutting General Electric in the lower-priced market. Meanwhile, the new automatic drip coffee-maker was creating a sensation in the higher-priced coffee-maker market where the plastic percolators had originally been positioned.

Sunbeam. The Oster polysulfone plastic percolator was also a failure when automatic drip coffee-makers were introduced. The Oster model was of tinted clear plastic and retailed for $35.

1974

Proctor-Silex. When automatic drip coffee-makers began to erode the sales volume of Proctor-Silex's glass percolators in 1973, Proctor-Silex responded by offering new percolator coffee-maker models in 1974 which it hoped would revive its flagging sales volumes. One new higher-priced percolator coffee-maker unit was targeted to compete directly against the automatic drip coffee-makers when their prices declined. The other percolator was a low-priced, eight-cup polypropylene model priced at $13, which was intended to challenge Regal Ware's highly successful poly perc and General Electric's two new polypropylene percolators.

Proctor-Silex tried to sell its poly-perc product through K-Mart and similar discount stores. The plastic percolator was discontinued in 1975. Proctor-Silex also introduced an automatic drip coffee-maker unit called Coffee Magic® in 1974.

Corning Glass Works. In 1974 Corning's new glass and ceramic percolators maintained a successful presence in the coffee-maker market, even as other competitors' percolators performed poorly, and continued to hold their high prices against the automatic drip coffee-makers.

1975

By 1975 a major market bifurcation in percolators had occurred; the price-football models and the high-quality models endured. Prices for low-end average stainless-steel percolators declined 45 percent in two years while high-end average stainless-steel percolator prices increased 47 percent in two years. As the prices of many automatic drip coffee-maker units declined, similarly priced aluminum percolator coffee-maker units were eliminated. The retail prices of stainless-steel coffee-makers increased in the high-quality market but were discounted severely as traffic-building items in other retail channels. Although the price of glass percolators decreased at retail by almost 10 percent, the prices of aluminum percolators increased by approximately 15 percent because aluminum had become quite expensive inasmuch as more of it was used in automobiles. Sales volumes for both percolator types decreased drastically.

During Christmas 1973, electric percolator coffee-makers still had been given as gifts. The most popular units were the high-quality models—Farberware stainless-steel percolators from $19.99 to $29.99 and Corning Glass Works; Electromatic percolators at $29.95. Similarly, in 1975, the most popular percolator gift items were the high-quality models—Farberware stainless steel (a two-to-four-cup percolator at $24.99), General Electric's Universal coffee-maker at $30, and Corning's glass percolator at $25.

In the low-priced coffee-maker market, discounters discovered that shoppers would still choose percolators priced below $15 over automatic drip coffee-makers priced at $20 if the percolator coffee-makers offered appeared to be a good value. (In 1975 drip coffee-makers became competitive with percolator coffee-makers around the price of $15.) Therefore, low-priced percolators remained important to discounters even though their sales volume was off by 30 to 50 percent from 1972 volumes.

General Electric. In 1975, after General Electric had announced that it would study its percolator coffee-maker products in order to eliminate redundancies, it retained the popular stainless-steel models (SSP-10 at $38.98 retail and the SSP-12 at $43.98) but restudied the viability of the aluminum P-15 line. There were four models in it which might be uneconomic, General Electric suggested.

Proctor-Silex. In 1974 Proctor-Silex eliminated the Dura-Perk polypropylene percolator which had been introduced in 1974 because the stain-resistant and easy-to-clean percolator had not been well received. In 1975 Proctor-Silex also issued a general recall of its new automatic drip coffee-maker units because a defective fuse in them had resulted in fires in two kitchens. The automatic drip coffee-maker was repaired and reintroduced later in 1975, but the Proctor-Silex Coffee Magic coffee-maker did not achieve the desired market penetration and Proctor-Silex redesigned it in 1976.

1976

Sunbeam Appliance. When Sunbeam Appliance reduced its percolator coffee-maker line to four stock-keeping units in 1976, many styles and sizes (such as the turquoise-colored percolators) were eliminated. In the conventional-style Sunbeam coffee-makers, two units remained: the polished-aluminum and the harvest-gold styles. In the glass-style coffee-maker, avocado was eliminated; only the harvest-gold-colored glass percolator was retained. In the stainless-steel model the seven-cup no. 15-20 model was discontinued while the twelve-cup model was retained. In Sunbeam's aluminum percolator line, the avocado-colored model no. 15-62 was discontinued.

West Bend. West Bend also reduced its percolator coffee-maker line by eliminating marginal colors, such as poppy red. West Bend retained the harvest-gold, avocado, and polished-aluminum percolator models in its one-to-fifteen-cup model units.

General Electric. In 1976 General Electric phased out the white-colored plastic bases on its nine-cup P-15 aluminum percolator coffee-maker (it was still available in gold, avocado, and black). The SSP-12 (twelve-cup) stainless-steel percolator, which had replaced the nickel-plated percolator (and other two stainless-steel bodies), was made immersible and the SSP-10 ten-cup version of this percolator) was discontinued due to lack of demand.

S.W. Farber. Farber's stainless-steel-clad aluminum percolator coffee-maker was still an important product for its retailers, who feared that Farberware percolators would either be discontinued or not be supported in 1976. Although it had made no design revisions in its basic percolator product line 1976, Farber assured its retail customers that it would stay in the percolator business and raised its prices. (Trade rumors reported that some Farberware percolators were being sold in discount channels in late 1976. If this were true, it would be a major change in Farber's distribution policies.)

Mirro Aluminum. Because Mirro Aluminum made no revisions to its percolator coffee-maker products in 1976, its retail distributors feared that they would be eliminated. A Mirro spokesperson assured retailers that no Mirro-matic percolators had yet been discontinued and that they were destined to be around, selling at $15 retail or lower, for a long time.

Proctor-Silex. In 1976 Proctor-Silex reduced its glass percolator line to two ten-cup and two twelve-cup models after revising several models and styles of successful percolator units to capture their best features, but sales did not improve. The necessary breakeven volume to bear its traditional burden of corporate overhead could not be attained because Proctor-Silex's glass percolators were being cannibalized by their glass automatic drip coffee-makers. When its total percolator coffee-maker volume had fallen to less than 10 percent of capacity, SCM halted production of Proctor-Silex percolators at their leased Baltimore plant. At this same time, the Proctor-Silex ironing-tables line, which shared plant space with the glass percolators business, was offered to a smaller competitor. (Ironing tables were also a declining business.)

Corning Glass Works. In 1976 Corning Glass Works discovered that 1974 models of their Electromatic coffee percolators contained faulty epoxy joints which caused the handles of some of these percolators to become unstuck and to burn users with hot coffee. In its recall of these percolators, Corning spent over $100 million on display kits for its 90,000 retailers to recover some 360,000 units. At that time, Corning still manufactured its fifteen percolator models.

Given the unfavorable publicity toward Corning concerning the product recall plus the deteriorating demand for percolators, Corning abruptly cut the promotional support for its percolator coffee-makers and discontinued both lines. Corning did not warn retailers of the discontinuation of its premium-priced Electromatics, leaving them with inventories of the product.

1977

Proctor-Silex. In March 1977 SCM Corporation announced its intentions to close permanently the leased Baltimore, Maryland, Proctor-Silex plant where glass percolator coffee-makers, automatic drip coffee-makers, and ironing tables had been produced. The automatic drip coffee-maker assets were relocated at the Altoona, Pennsylvania, Proctor-Silex plant and the ironing-table production assets were sold to another company. When no buyer could be found for the glass percolator business, which included three glass models at that time, SCM Corporation mothballed the physical assets at the Altoona plant but retained the automatic drip coffee-maker units, which did not share assets with the percolator coffee-makers.

Corning Glass Works. In 1977 Corning Ware and Electromatic percolator production was officially discontinued and Corning percolators that were already in the channels were allowed to sit on retailers' shelves.

Sunbeam Appliance. When it became evident that Sunbeam could not sell percolators because the public wanted drip coffee-makers, Sunbeam ran a large lot of its most popular stainless-steel model and dismantled its percolator equipment. Sprinklers, lawn mowers, and other types of outdoor appliances were subsequently produced in the South Carolina plant. The one popular percolator continued to be carried in Sunbeam's inventory to maintain a "presence" in the industry.

1978

Table 7-3 summarizes which percolator coffee-maker units were still on retailers' shelves in summer 1978. There were no glass percolators and the Corning pyroceramic percolators listed appeared to be units which had not yet worked their way through the distribution channels. Five stainless-steel percolator coffee-maker models were available and nine aluminum percolator models were offered. Three plastic percolator models were offered nationally, but only a few of these percolator coffee-makers were carried in any single discount store. A distributor chose two or three of the best-selling percolator units to carry, instead of a wide line of percolators.

In 1978 S.W. Farber led the stainless-steel percolator coffee-maker market, which was predominantly sold through department stores (and catalog showrooms); General Electric led the aluminum percolator coffee-maker market, which had predominantly sold through discount stores and catalog showrooms. Some aluminum percolators were also sold in drug stores and hardware stores. Regal Ware led the plastic percolator coffee-

Table 7-3

Electric Percolator Coffee-Makers Available in National Markets in 1978
(suggested retail prices)

Type	Capacity	Price
Stainless Steel		
General Electric	12-cup	38.98
Sunbeam	12-cup	42.95
Farber	4-cup	27.99
	8-cup	37.99
	12-cup	41.99
Aluminum		
G.E. Universal	8-cup	19.95
General Electric	8-cup	21.98
	9-cup	27.98
West Bend (Colored)	9-cup	17.95[a]
Mirro (Colored)	10-cup	26.95
	10-cup	29.95[b]
Plastic		
Regal Ware	4-cup	12.95
—[c]	8-cup	13.50
Ceramic		
Corning Glass Works	8-cup	—[d]
	10-cup	
	12-cup	

[a]West Bend also offered a five-cup colored aluminum percolator coffee-maker. No price could be found for it.

[b]Mirro Aluminum also offered two nine-cup colored aluminum percolator coffee-makers. No prices could be found for them.

[c]Mirro Aluminum also offered an eight-cup plastic percolator. No price could be found for it. Industry sources indicate it was priced too high and that its styling was inappropriate.

[d]These were left-over inventory units. Corning does not appear to be in the percolator business in 1978.

maker market, which was predominantly sold through discount houses. Mirro Aluminum sold its plastic percolators in hardware stores, as well. One of the most important outlets for percolator sales in 1978 was the relatively innovative catalog showrooms such as H.B. Davis, True Value, and Sentry.

Many aluminum fabricators, such as Aluminum Specialties and Westinghouse Electric, sold their assets to other appliance companies. Cornwall Corporation went bankrupt. Other nationally known appliance companies such as Dominion, Hoover, Oster, Presto, and Wear-Ever simply discontinued percolator production and sold off their inventories.

By 1978 Farber, General Electric, and West Bend percolators had joined Mirro Aluminum and Regal Ware percolators in the discount channels, where they were promoted as price footballs, which meant that manufacturers' representatives cut prices more frequently to retain shelf space in the lower-priced outlets. Although percolators were still sold in the department-store channels, the greatest sales volume was attained in catalog sales outlets and discount stores in 1978.

The chronological description of the endgame, above, has described the difficulties of some firms, most notably Proctor-Silex, whose sales volume in percolators fell while it could not launch a successful replacement product (automatic drip coffee-maker) quickly enough to avert the impact of this product's decline. The future of demand for percolator coffee-makers is quite uncertain, given the faddish nature of the small electrical housewares business. Firms which mothballed their assets could return to percolator production if it were appropriate to do so. By contrast, if demand for percolator coffee-makers does not resuscitate, corporate pressures to continue to inventory percolators may be overcome eventually when most of the remaining percolator users have switched to other coffee-brewing devices or have died.

Analysis of the Electric Percolator Coffee-Maker Endgame

The manufacturers of electric percolator coffee-makers were able to adapt to the challenge of automatic drip coffee-makers easily due to previous related experiences with declining products and to favorable industry characteristics. A brief summary of these environmental conditions in 1972 follows.

Characteristics

Demand. In 1972 demand for percolator coffee-makers had plateaued and was slowly increasing as more households were formed. Demand for lower-priced percolators was price-sensitive. Demand for the high-quality percolators was not as price-sensitive, but fewer units of these types of coffee-makers were sold annually.

Product Differentiation. Percolators could be physically differentiated by size, materials, color, and price. They were branded and promoted as being part of many major small electrical appliance companies' lines.

Markets. In 1972, 70 percent of the percolators purchased were replacement units. Percolator coffee-makers were merchandised through department stores, drug stores, discount houses, catalog showrooms, hardware stores, variety stores, and as premiums in promotional campaigns.

Substitutes. The automatic drip coffee-maker captured the imagination of customers and replaced their old coffee-maker units. The ADCs invaded first the higher-priced markets and then the middle-priced markets. Only the lowest-priced percolators and a few distinctive high-quality percolators were not driven off the retailers' shelves by the ADC.

Customer Characteristics. The retailers who distributed percolators and ADCs were most strongly influenced by cooperative advertising allowances and brand names. Price deals were also important in competing for shelf space. The retailers eventually refused to carry some percolator models because their turnover was too slow.

Supplier Characteristics. If a percolator were made of aluminum, there was competition for a coffee-makers' raw materials from the automotive industry. Firms who fabricated their own metals held an advantage in obtaining these raw materials. The percolator business was more important to the small plastics firms who supplied the industry and no materials shortages occurred in this segment of the business.

Manufacturing Technology. Aluminum percolators required rolled bodies. Plastic percolators could be blow-molded. In each case, dies were required for each percolator design. Some of the large percolator manufacturers sourced the components used to manufacture percolators and assembled them internally. Exit barriers were low.

Technological Innovation. Percolator coffee-makers were very mature. No new production techniques had been developed for several years, but new designs were introduced frequently. Some companies tried to introduce percolator coffee-makers in new materials in 1973, even after the ADC had been introduced.

Capital Intensity. If a percolator plant were constructed and operated, sales volume of $500,000 would be required to break even. Like many small electrical housewares investments, the dies and other tooling associated with new percolator designs had to be expensed quickly. Many firms sourced components and assembled percolators rather than invest in the machinery needed to fabricate them.

Competitive Structure. Although there were thirty to forty companies selling percolator coffee-makers in 1972, only a few of them were national brands. Competition for retailers' shelf space was intense between companies, but competition was by appliance manufacturers' lines, not by items within them. The percolator was part of the total appliance product offering, whether it was placed on the retailers' shelves by a manufacturer or by a wholesaler.

By 1975 there was little uncertainty among the manufacturers in the electric percolator coffee-maker endgame regarding the future of demand for this product. The small, electrical household appliance industry enjoyed relatively short product life-cycles, and companies were able to cope with the decline of the percolator (once they acknowledged that it was a declining product) as adeptly as they had coped with the decline of other fadlike products. The percolator coffee-maker was being replaced by the automatic drip coffee-maker, but hopes that the percolator could someday revitalize did not act as a deterrent to timely, rational exits during this endgame.

The petrified demand for percolators was relatively price insensitive and retailers who were engaged in discounting activities believed that they needed to carry the percolators as traffic builders, even in endgame. Hence, although prices could be raised somewhat, firms trimmed back the variety of percolators they offered, retired capacity, and continued to supply percolators (when customers requested them) at their regular prices instead of flooding the market. Exits from production in this endgame were orderly and firms executed them in most cases without incurring significant losses. The firms which were bound by strategic considerations to offer a percolator product frequently served this demand from a large inventory and exited from production as well.

Most of the percolator manufacturers also offered the substitute product, automatic drip coffee-makers, during the endgame. Firms which were slow to introduce ADCs and whose percolator coffee-maker sales volumes fell significantly during the endgame were most severely damaged by this loss of sales revenues. There was a lag time between a firms' recognition of the inroads made by automatic drip coffee-makers and its successful introduction of a competitive product which proved to be particularly crucial in evaluating some firms' performances in endgame. Percolator sales continued to be as profitable to manufacturers in endgame as many other small household appliances. But the nature of the percolator business, particularly in light of its reduced sales volumes, was no longer as attractive as it had once been.

Analysis of Declining Demand for Percolators

If firms could not ascertain whether the automatic drip coffee-maker was merely a fad, it would be expected that such firms would encounter difficulty in timing their retirements of productive capacity. In the percolator endgame, this uncertainty deterred firms from cutting down percolator production lines in a timely manner and from introducing automatic drip coffee-maker units earlier. For example, firms such as Proctor-Silex continued to invest only in its percolator business eighteen months after the successful introduction of the automatic drip coffee-maker unit. If it had been able to determine with greater certainty that the ADC was a substantial substitute product, and not a fad, it may have avoided making some of the reinvestments it made in the percolator business after the base year.

Percolator coffee-makers had been one of the five "staple" appliances sold each year by small electrical household appliance manufacturers. When manufacturers found that percolators had to be managed like other fad products, and executed the needed changes, they cut their losses successfully. But firms which had not responded in this manner to their falling percolator sales volumes were somewhat of a disadvantage.

Some customers still purchased percolators in 1978. Some "old-fashioned" customers—particularly older people—who still believed that percolators made the best coffee wanted to purchase percolator coffee-makers, and customers looking for a low-priced coffee-maker also purchased them. Since low-priced percolators were important to a discounter's image, percolator coffee-makers had to be sold in those channels long after the successful introduction of ADCs.

It would be expected that where the substitute consumer product represented a newer technology that was heavily advertised and well promoted within its retail channels such that it attained a high level of consumer acceptance quickly, the endgame product would be most successful if it competed in either specialized or lower-priced markets rather than competing head-to-head with the new product. In the percolator coffee-maker endgame, the automatic drip coffee-maker was an attractive new consumer product which was heavily supported with promotional allowances and corporate advertising to penetrate the percolator market. Percolators continued to be competitive in lower-priced markets and in the higher-priced stainless-steel-clad servingware markets even when automatic drip coffee-maker sales volumes grew to represent a larger proportion of the total coffee-maker market and an increasingly large number of consumers switched to the newer-technology coffee pot rather than replace their older units with percolator coffee-makers.

The automatic drip coffee-makers were well promoted by using television advertising, offering cooperative advertising allowances, and emphasizing substantial retailer mark-ups in a business where, traditionally, retailers had given away the profits on most of the small electrical housewares they merchandised. The retailers helped the drips to render obsolete the percolator coffee-maker by giving larger shares of ADCs shelf space, preferential location, and price (discounting) promotions. Seeing that the success of the ADC was based on its attractiveness to retailers, the percolator appliances manufacturers quickly introduced their own versions of the automatic drip coffee-maker. As might have been expected, the attentions given to the new, higher-margin product by percolator producers forced the endgame product to decline faster because its distribution coverage was lessened when percolator coffee-maker companies (such as West Bend) who introduced models of the popular automatic drip coffee-maker promoted it heavily while funds used to promote the percolator coffee-maker were withheld or reduced.

It would be expected that if the manufacturers of percolator coffee-makers were able to raise their prices during the endgame, their direct customers, the retail distribution channels, would not balk at price increases which they could pass on to their customers. (Margins were very low on percolators due to their traffic-building role in the endgame.) Price increases were facilitated by the relative price insensitivity of consumers who still desired to purchase percolator coffee-makers and by the high price of the substitute product.

In summary, uncertainty regarding the duration of demand for automatic drip coffee-makers deterred some coffee-maker firms from discontinuing percolators and introducing drip coffee-makers. The substitute product seemed to appeal to consumers at first on a fashion or fad basis; hence, producers believed there was a remote possibility that demand for percolator coffee-makers could be revitalized in the future if the fad for percolators returned. This uncertainty, added to the high cost of introducing a new product like the ADC, may have deterred some firms for whom percolators were important from reacting faster to flagging percolator demand.

Analysis of Endgame Industry Traits

It had been predicted that an "unfavorable" endgame environment would discourage competitors from reinvesting in physical assets or in advertising in order to serve customers for a product which is recognized as being a declining business. The combination of flagging demand characteristics, industry structural traits, and the aggressive way in which the substitute product was being promoted did not seem to constitute an industry environment where many reinvestments were justified, and, after competitors understood the impact of the automatic drip coffee-maker, few reinvestments in capital assets were made.

Product Differentiability Traits

The electric percolator coffee-maker was physically differentiable and this differentiability allowed several niches of customer demand to coexist in the endgame. The demand for the percolators in different niches declined at unequal speeds. The regional cat-and-dog percolator producers which competed by selling at low prices were frequently squeezed by national brands. The nationally advertised brands which had developed brand-name recognition among customers continued to compete successfully on a lesser scale in endgame because a pocket of demand which they satisfied remained viable in the endgame. Although discounters sold even the highest-priced percolator brands during the endgame, percolators made by "General Electric" or "Faberware" retained their images of quality and their attractiveness to customer groups who preferred percolator coffee-makers.

Product Traits

It would be expected that niches of demand would emerge in this endgame and that the firms whose products were best entrenched within the remaining pockets of demand would enjoy the best staying power in serving this demand. In this endgame, S.W. Farber held its relative position in the high-quality, high-priced market for percolators. Regal Ware, Inc., and Mirro Aluminum continued to serve the lower-priced, discount markets where customers wanted percolators because they were a less expensive way to brew coffee. Percolator coffee-makers had been available in several different designs, and it was easier for percolator manufacturers to phase out a few designs and to narrow their product lines before they discontinued production altogether, and to do so without alienating their retail channels. Yet, given the markets' traits, percolator coffee-makers were not expected to become commodities when fewer models became available because a large part of a percolator's intrinsic value in endgame would be created by its brand image or corporate name. These quality images enabled producers to justify price increases in markets where quality was an effective differentiating characteristic, giving them access to a pocket of relatively lucrative demand to satisfy in endgame.

Customer Traits

It would be expected that retailers would cut back the size of their inventories of percolator products as demand diminished. Over fifteen varieties of percolator were required to show the different product variations in a typical manufacturer's line. As fewer ultimate customers for percolators remained, retailers cut back on their offerings to a few percolator models or they discontinued them because they refused to devote SKUs to a slow-moving product. The retailers who continued to stock percolators were those who discounted them heavily. For them, percolator "specials" continued to be an important part of their discounters' image.

Customer "switching costs" (to switch to the newer technology) were low, and as the endgame progressed, the cost of the automatic drip coffee-makers rivaled the prices of the more expensive percolator coffee-makers. The core of customers which continued to purchase percolators did so because of their personal preferences.

Technological Characteristics

The actual cost of producing a percolator coffee-maker included initially high fixed costs and necessitated large production volumes. There was a significant cost disadvantage incurred by running small appliance plants below capacity, which is why some appliance firms sourced individual products from other housewares producers.

Exit barriers were low in this industry because assets were well depreciated at the time of their retirement and could be mothballed, to be resuscitated later for a long production run of percolators for inventory if an electrical appliance company needed to maintain a presence in the percolator coffee-maker business only for strategic reasons. (The most significant exit barriers in the electric percolator coffee-maker business were "strategic," and not economic.)

It would be expected that exit from the percolator coffee-makers endgame would be easily implemented because the technology of coffee-makers did not create high economic exit barriers and many percolator manufacturers had invested in percolator production in such a way that exit was not difficult to execute, particularly if percolator manufacturers (1) had leased much of the plant space and equipment they needed; (2) had sourced many of the components required; (3) were backward-integrated into metals or plastic fabrication; or (4) had kept their asset exposure low in other ways. When percolator assets were mothballed, their residual value was simply written off in the year production was discontinued, and other activities were started at their plants.

The assets used to manufacture percolator coffee-makers were specific (dies and some finishing equipment), but the plants could be used flexibly. (No productive assets were moored to the floors in a manner that would have been difficult to remove.) The specific assets used to manufacture percolators or many other shortlived small electrical household appliance products were usually expensed quickly in order to recover their value. Given the thin resale market for percolator-producing assets, firms would have to do so because otherwise they would not be able to recover the value of the goodwill and other investments which were a part of their percolator business.

In summary, exit from percolator coffee-maker manufacturing was not difficult. The capital-intensity of the physical plant associated with production did necessitate large-volume runs, but this trait precipitated an exit decision for firms whose sales volumes flagged relatively early in the endgame. Exit barriers were low because few firms had made technological reinvestments which raised these barriers.

Competitive Characteristics

It would be expected that because different percolator market niches could be filled by different manufacturers, some percolator coffee-maker producers could be present in endgame yet not compete directly with one another, and these firms were more likely to endure.

Firms such as S.W. Farber, which served the high-priced, luxury percolator coffee-maker market, which yielded very slowly to substitution by ADCs, sustained their important percolator businesses, suffering less damage to profitability than other firms which suffered significantly declining sales volumes.

It would be expected that firms which continued to manufacture percolator coffee-makers which were in demand would enjoy satisfactory profits because the manufacturers could sell their percolators to the retailers at their usual mark-ups. The volatile price war between percolators and automatic drip coffee-makers existed primarily at the retail level, where it was used as a traffic-building device. Price competition did not erupt because major firms such as Sunbeam did not push their percolators in endgame to the detriment of their profits. It would be expected that the portion of the percolator market where the ADCs competed most directly would be most quickly eroded by the substitute product. In this endgame, the medium-priced aluminum percolator coffee-makers began to compete more intensely against the lower-priced polypropylene percolator coffee-makers, in the lower-priced niche where automatic drip coffee-makers were not competitive. It is not clear whether these manufacturers used price warfare to place their percolators on retailers' shelves because many of these companies did not depend so heavily upon percolator sales volumes that they would bother to erode the small profitability they earned on the coffee-makers to gain more shelf space. Before long, aluminum prices increased and made aluminum percolator coffee-makers even less profitable in the lower-priced market and this competition subsided.

In summary, because the economic exit barriers associated with this business were low, orderly retreats from this market were possible. The timing associated with executing the various strategies firms pursued in endgame were not encumbered by these barriers. Niches existed which sustained the profitability of various competitors' markets and marketing advantages helped the high-priced and large-volume competitors while low operating costs kept the lower-priced market niches profitable.

Analysis of the Corporate-wide Strategic Needs of Competitors

It had been expected that firms might keep an "important" endgame business longer than economic analysis might suggest was advisable because "strategic exit barriers" would retard the timing of firms' exits or their decisions to mothball their assets. In this endgame, firms which had postured themselves as major wide-line small electrical household appliance manufacturers were more likely to retain some form of participation in this industry than were specialty-fabricator firms which produced percolators in addition to other products from a raw material such as aluminum or plastic.

The wide-line appliance manufacturers tried to satisfy retailers' requests for percolator coffee-makers but they possessed no loyalty per se to this particular product. Many firms quickly invested in automatic drip coffee-makers. Even firms where percolators had been relatively important, such as West Bend, gave much of their promotional attention to ADCs. Firm's long-range corporate goals were not defined in terms of being percolator manufacturers. Hence, these firms were not deterred from reducing their investment levels or exiting.

Cash-Flow Traits. The typical small electrical household appliances products possessed a short life-cycle; they were essentially fad products, but the percolator coffee-maker had been an exception to this behavior. For many years, it had served as a stable generator of cash flows. Firms in the small electrical housewares appliance business were accustomed to feeding a particular product with cash in the hope that a few of these products would become popular and would generate good cash inflows which would fund the next generation of fadlike products. When percolator coffee-makers became obsolete, appliance manufacturers changed their policies regarding the management of percolator products and treated them like a short horizon fad product.

Strategic Exit Barriers. The wide-line appliance manufacturers, such as General Electric, Sunbeam Appliance, and West Bend, were not expected to exit entirely from the electric percolator coffee-maker business because, in order to maintain a full-line electrical appliance offering, these companies had to show a percolator in their catalogs even if they no longer manufactured it. That is why some appliance firms sourced percolators or held large inventories of them which they had run before closing their plants rather than exit totally from the percolator business.

Single-business percolator manufacturers and other firms for whom the percolator represented a significant portion of sales were expected to try to capture sales volume by undercutting competitors' prices and were expected to be less willing to exit than firms which were well diversified would be. Firms such as Regal Ware and Mirro Aluminum which did rely upon percolator sales reduced their costs and corresponding prices whenever possible in order to keep their percolator coffee-makers viable in the market, and small regional percolator manufacturers did use price-cutting to obtain shelf space. But because these smaller firms' brand names were not well known by consumers, they did not have the drawing power of a "General Electric" or "West Bend" percolator and consequently they were not effective against the better known percolator brands.

Analysis of Endgaming-Firms' Competitive Strengths

The percolator manufacturers which would be best suited to remain as producers in the endgame were (1) firms whose products were nationally advertised, hence best known by consumers; (2) firms which served some special niche of demand which other competitors tended not to service; and (3) firms whose production costs were among the lowest so that they could provide low-cost percolators to their effective retail channels of distribution. (These categories correspond roughly to the market niches where demand for percolators remained viable during the endgame.) A comparison of the other aspects of firms' strategic postures indicates that some firms were more or less advantageously endowed with competitive strengths. Some firms operated their percolator factories every week during the endgame while other firms held inventories or sourced percolators instead. Differences in how firms coped with declining percolator demand were due, in part, to differences in firms' competitive advantages.

Marketing and Selling Strengths. Significant internal strengths had been created by past marketing and product development expenditures, and these absolute cost advantages continued to be important in endgame, where prices had to remain relatively low. The creation of an image of high quality as a result of advertising and marketing channel development expenditures constituted a strength for firms which occupied the higher priced niches of the market, firms like S.W. Farber which did not cut price and tried to persuade its distribution channels to avoid price-cutting deals. (Farber tried to avoid selling its percolators to discount outlets because it would have eroded the "mystique" of high quality that had been created and supported Farberware's higher prices in department-store outlets.) Neither Farber nor General Electric would support price-cutting since it would be tantamount to destroying their products' niches, and, by maintaining their high-quality images, they became even more attractive to discount channels.

Possession of an overseas percolator subsidiary would not necessarily be expected to constitute a competitive strength for percolator firms because European percolator designs did not appeal to U.S. tastes. Multinational linkages where an affiliate or subsidiary marketed products overseas could not always provide a marketing arm or a source for manufactured components. (In the case of General Electric, a subsidiary did produce components for percolators, but it also constituted an exit barrier for GE.)

The strategic posture of being a wide-line appliance company was expected to become more of an operational deterrence to exit than a competitive benefit in an endgame where demand was deteriorating rapidly and the substitute product was a highly effective substitute. As was explained above, retailers did not carry all items which comprised a full line if some of those items moved slowly. Hence, a wide-line company had to retain the capacity to supply percolators even when demand for them was so low that maintaining a production line to manufacture percolators or an inventory of percolators was uneconomic.

Absolute Cost Advantages. It would be expected that manufacturing efficiencies would be a competitive strength, particularly if a percolator firm competed in the lower-priced market. Other advantages which would seem to be important in lowering costs included a location near a supply of critical raw materials (for example, for Mirro Aluminum, its location near an aluminum foundry), and well-established, cooperative distribution channels—wholesalers and retailers. However, distribution advantages were more frequently associated with additional strengths such as brand-name advantages.

Managerial Exit Barriers. It would be expected that if resistance to the decision to eliminate percolator coffee-makers were to develop within an organization, it would be more likely to emanate from the ranks of top management (from managers who believed that the corporation's image was inextricably tied to percolator production) than from the line management (which was evaluated on the basis of the declining product's performance). In the percolator coffee-maker business, management's efforts to eliminate percolator products were thwarted in some cases by the chairman of the board, Chief Executive Officer (CEO), or other high-ranking executive who believed the firm should continue to carry at least one percolator product as a part of its strategic mission.

In summary, by the fifth year following the introduction of the automatic drip coffee-maker, the percolator coffee-makers which continued to be competitive were those which were either low priced or were of high quality and higher priced. Hence the most important competitive strengths associated with performing well in endgame were those related to maintaining firms' respective mobility barriers—the higher-priced, high-quality market or the lower-priced (lower operating costs) markets.

Firms which were serving the high-priced markets had to maintain an image of quality while minimizing their reinvestments in percolators. Firms which were serving the lower-priced markets had to keep their costs per unit very low in order to offer the necessary cooperative advertising allowances to retailers yet still earn enough in gross margins to justify the investment strategically if not economically. Firms which were broadly based in appliances had to inventory source, or manufacture percolators in order to be able to offer them as a part of their wide appliance lines.

Analysis of Firms' Performances in the
Percolator Coffee-Maker Endgame

Because firms did not all perceive immediately that the automatic drip coffee-maker was an effective substitute for the percolator coffee-maker, their behaviors were dissimilar. In particular, the timing of firms' exits or plant shutdowns in response to the changes in the coffee-makers demand was not uniform. There were some similarities in the behaviors of firms once their problem of reduced demand was recognized, however. The speed with which firms responded to the challenge created by ADCs influenced the success of their tactics in the coffee-maker business. Although firms such as General Electric performed well, others like Proctor-Silex did not.

Given the uncertainty concerning demand for percolators and the relatively unfavorable industry environment which evolved as the automatic drip coffee-maker made sizable inroads into the coffee-maker market, few reinvestments were expected in this endgame. If reinvestments did occur, they were expected early in the endgame before the uncertainty surrounding the substitute product was resolved. Given the relatively low percentage of total asset values the percolator coffee-maker business comprised for many firms, it would be expected that some coffee-maker companies would close down percolator production or eliminate their percolator offerings completely. Because the duration of demand for percolators was uncertain, and thus the endgame was not well understood by the industry participants, some confused behavior would be expected in the earlier years of endgame.

Corning Glass Works and Proctor-Silex, the only firms which exited completely from their percolator businesses, were the firms that would be most likely to do so because both firms manufactured glass percolators, the products most similar to automatic drip coffee-makers. Sunbeam Appliance and West Bend also exited from the production of percolators (but they retained a presence in the industry through their merchandising positions) while other firms reinvested in this industry. General Electric, Mirro Aluminum, Sunbeam (Oster), and Proctor-Silex each introduced polypropylene percolators which were not successful. Proctor-Silex, General Electric, and Corning Glass Works each promoted their percolators heavily through 1974. But by 1975 Proctor-Silex and General Electric each also sold an automatic drip coffee-maker under their brand names.

By 1978 the following major percolator companies had discontinued their percolator coffee-maker operations: Proctor-Silex, Hamilton Beach, Toastmaster, Cornwall, Corey, Empire, Hoover, Merit Enterprises, Oster, Presto, Aluminum Specialty (Chilton), Corning Glass Works, Van Wyck, Revere Cooper and Brass, and Ekco. Regal Ware had enjoyed considerable success with its plastic percolator coffee-makers throughout endgame. Mirro Aluminum and Metal Ware (Empire) had also introduced less successful plastic percolators. Cornwall, the other major plastic percolator firm, had gone bankrupt, and only the Regal Ware percolator was well received.

The Farber and General Electric models represented the only companies whose higher-priced percolator lines endured. Corning Glass Works' units were still on retailers' shelves in 1978, but Corning was no longer producing or competing in the percolator business. Percolator coffee-makers had been an important staple business and cash generator for S.W. Farber, more important to Farber than they were to many remaining appliance companies. General Electric, Sunbeam, and West Bend, the full-line appliance companies, maintained a presence in the percolator endgame by merchandising their products, but only General Electric had adequate volume to operate its percolator line on a daily or weekly basis.

Firms Which Exited Early. It would be expected that the firms whose markets had been eroded away by the glass-carafed automatic drip coffee-makers would exit relatively early if they had no other percolator products to offer. Of these, Proctor-Silex suffered some losses in eliminating its percolator business because it had introduced new percolator products during the endgame; it was relatively slow in responding to the challenge of the automatic drip coffee-makers.

Corning Glass Works also exited early. Its percolator products were made of pyroceramic and glass, also. But Corning's losses from its percolator coffee-maker business were not solely due to endgame. They were also due to percolator product defects which the company had sought to remedy. Sunbeam and West Bend discontinued their percolator production but they continued to merchandise their percolators from inventory.

Firms Which Discontinued Production, but Continued to Merchandise Percolator Coffee-Makers. Wide-line appliance firms were not expected to exit completely from the percolator business; rather, such firms were expected to mothball their assets after producing percolators for inventory or to source percolators from the remaining producers. The firms which continued their participation in the percolator business but discontinued regular manufacturing operations—Sunbeam Appliance and West Bend—held percolator inventories in case a retail customer requested these products, and offered them in their catalogs, but they did not push these products.

"Shrink Selectively"

Proctor-Silex. Proctor-Silex experienced relatively high levels of disruption when it tried to exit from its percolator investment because (1) it was slow to recognize the impact of the automatic drip coffee-maker upon percolators; (2) it had introduced new percolator products even after the ADC was introduced; and (3) its percolators were shut out of retail outlets at a rate which Proctor-Silex could not control. Proctor-Silex manufactured one of the least expensive percolator coffee-makers and it used price-dealing and heavy advertising to support its percolator coffee-maker products. It should have done well in endgame, but Proctor-Silex's glass percolator products were eased off retailers' shelves by the glass-carafed automatic drip coffee-makers which acted as almost perfect substitutes in some retailers' perceptions. Proctor-Silex also met stiffer competition as its market was invaded from above by heavily discounted medium-priced specular aluminum percolator coffee-makers which were being squeezed out of the middle markets by the price reductions of automatic drip coffee-makers. Thus, in the lower-priced market where Proctor-Silex had competed, additional aluminum percolator firms challenged the polypropylene and glass percolator firms which were already competing vigorously there.

Given the market it served (glass percolators) and the competitors (plastic and inexpensive aluminum) which Proctor-Silex encountered in endgame, the most responsible strategy which Proctor-Silex could follow was to close the Baltimore plant and to limit its losses. Proctor-Silex was not constrained in doing this by strategic barriers because retailers had precipitated this decision; the discount channels which carried many Proctor-Silex percolators had already decided not to carry them as demand for them declined.

"Milk the Investment"

Corning Glass Works. Corning sold many percolator models made of glass and pyroceramics which were priced at medium and high levels and were sold primarily through department-store channels. Its products were targeted to the group of consumers which preferred high-quality products, which was also the group most likely to experiment with the new, high-priced automatic drip coffee-makers when they were introduced. During endgame, Corning Ware percolator demand was eroded in the medium-priced market by glass-carafed ADCs and the top-of-the-line Electromatic was discontinued after the Corning product recall created bad publicity for the Corning Ware lines.

Corning was not predominantly an appliance company, as were General Electric or Sunbeam Appliance, and thus it did not face strategic exit barriers to retain a "token" percolator, as did these other firms. Therefore, Corning would be more likely to phase out percolator production without retaining supporting inventories than would Sunbeam Appliances or other small appliance firms.

"Shrink Selectively"

West Bend. Because West Bend was a major percolator coffee-maker company, it would have been expected to encounter some strategic exit barriers if it had tried to discontinue its percolator line. West Bend had spent substantial sums on percolator advertising in order to develop customer goodwill and had designed percolators which were distinctive to the company's image, which identified it as a coffee-maker firm. West Bend had manufactured colored aluminum and polished-surface percolators which were the categories of percolator products which had been most thoroughly cannibalized by the automatic drip coffee-makers. As aluminum prices increased, aluminum percolators became more costly relative to polypropylene percolators, the substitute product whose market aluminum percolators had tried to penetrate.

When much of the demand for West Bend's aluminum percolators had been eroded, it produced percolators for inventory and dismantled its production line. West Bend's wide percolator product line had enabled it to phase out its percolator models while bringing its supply in line with demand.

Sunbeam Appliance. Sunbeam Appliance Company also faced strategic exit barriers because it was a well-known "appliance company" that was obliged to continue to offer at least one percolator coffee-maker during the endgame. Sunbeam's percolator products were also targeted to a medium-priced market and most of them were made from aluminum. Because Sunbeam did not engage in much price-cutting behavior, its percolator products were not as well positioned in the retail outlets which endured during the endgame. The most popular percolators in endgame were either higher-quality and higher-priced than most of Sunbeam's line or lower-quality (plastic) and lower-priced than Sunbeam's usual product offerings. Sunbeam was among the first firms to recognize that it could stockpile percolators and use its percolator plant for other production purposes. Sunbeam discontinued regular production and stockpiled percolators by shrinking down from a wide product line.

Sunbeam Appliance began the percolator endgame with five basic percolator bodies plus variations—one of the widest percolator lines among the appliance firms—but it discontinued the percolator designs which were not as popular with remaining customers, retaining a position in only the more lucrative markets. Sunbeam was not expected to retain a position in the lower-priced coffee-maker market because it had not been a firm which used price-dealing, "baker's dozen" deals, or other forms of price-cutting to obtain market share initially. Sunbeam's strengths in the percolator coffee-maker endgame were not in price-competition or in discounting distribution channels which were the salient strengths for successful performance in most of the percolator coffee-maker endgame when the ADC captured approximately 90 percent of the 1978 coffee-maker sales volume.

Firms Which Continued to Produce Percolator Coffee-Makers. The percolator firms which were well positioned in niches where demand continued to be healthy or which were obliged to produce percolators for strategic reasons continued to manufacture percolators. Firms such as Regal Ware, Inc., were particularly successful in the (plastic) percolators endgame because they could offer the demanded percolator product at the lowest prices using the most comprehensive distribution systems.

"Milk the Investment"

Mirro Aluminum. Mirro Aluminum was expected to retain a position in the percolator coffee-maker endgame because its aluminum percolators, which were one of its oldest aluminum products, constituted a type of strategic exit barrier for Mirro; it was well identified with aluminum coffee-makers. Yet Mirro Aluminum was not expected to reinvest in the endgame because aluminum became less popular among consumers and more costly for use in manufacturing during the endgame.

Mirro Aluminum had not redesigned its percolator dies since 1976. This omission and others may be interpreted to suggest that cash was being extracted from the percolator business rather than reinvested. Mirro was expected to produce a large inventory and to dismantle its production line sooner than many percolator manufacturers because although aluminum percolators were an important product for Mirro Aluminum—both economically and strategically—the sales volume Mirro Aluminum enjoyed in endgame did not justify keeping the Mirro percolator production line in operation.

S.W. Farber. S.W. Farber was expected to be a major hold-out in the face of the deteriorated demand for percolators because it had manufactured relatively high-quality percolator coffee-makers which were merchandised in department stores using company sales representatives to assist store clerks, and Farber was heavily invested in securing the percolator's survival. S.W. Farber was expected to continue to manufacture percolator coffee-makers because the Farberware percolator coffee-maker line was the center-piece of the company's high-quality aluminum-clad stainless-steel cookware line, and also because the firm faced strategic exit barriers which deterred it from exiting.

Farberware's failure to invest in new dies for percolator designs may be interpreted to be an indication that, in 1976, S.W. Farber was milking its percolator coffee-maker investment. Also, Farberware percolators appeared in some discount houses in 1976, and this marketing decision would tend to suggest that S.W. Farber was interested in increasing the potential cash flows which could be earned from its percolator operations. The less selective distribution policy meant relatively higher sales volumes, which also gave Farber the break-even volume necessary for economical production runs of percolators. Because S.W. Farber's strategic exit barriers were high, Farber would be expected to be more likely to produce and sell its unique type of percolator products in endgame, rather than merely merchandise the percolators.

General Electric. General Electric was expected to continue to manufacture and merchandise percolator coffee-makers during the endgame because it was the major percolator coffee-maker company within several market niches, it had invested in advertising and product quality in order to enable it to compete in both the high-quality markets and the heavy discounting of the lower-priced markets successfully, and it was likely to continue to manufacture percolators because it faced a potential strategic exit barrier which prevented General Electric from making a smooth exit even if it wished to do so. The bodies for one of the percolator coffee-makers still sold in the United States were rolled by a subsidiary in the United Kingdom whose local markets alone no longer provided adequate sales volumes to justify its continuing operations. British environmental factors may not have permitted shutdowns to occur with the relative ease possible in the United States and discontinuation of regular percolator production would mean closing down the U.S. subsidiary plant. Hence General Electric faced a strategic barrier to exit, even after it had pruned its product offerings and milked as much of its value from the percolator business as seemed to be possible.

General Electric had developed an image of quality and reliability which made its percolators very desirable for discounting by the high-volume, lower-priced market, and General Electric enjoyed a demand for its percolator coffee-makers that was adequate to justify running percolators in its factory during most weeks. When its volume tapered to a level which did not justify allocating plant space to percolators, General Electric could stockpile percolators as well because GE had previously competed in the lower-priced outlets by using price dealing and had developed the use of this marketing tool to yield acceptable returns for the company. Accordingly, General Electric was well positioned to continue to use these outlets in the endgame by offering both high-priced stainless-steel percolators for the department-store markets and aluminum percolators for the lower-priced markets.

Regal Ware, Inc.. Regal Ware would be expected to enjoy a profitable endgame because it was the leading manufacturer of polypropylene (plastic) percolator coffee-makers, the least-expensive type of coffee-maker unit, a type of percolator coffee-maker which sold very well in the lower-priced percolator markets. Discounters and catalog showrooms used the Regal Ware poly perc as an important traffic-building device by cutting its price below $10 in 1978, near or below its cost.

Regal Ware, Inc., was expected to remain in the percolator coffee-maker endgame because the polypropylene percolator was an important product for Regal Ware, and the poly perc was one of the lowest-priced percolators in the market. Moreover, it was not heavily advertised, making Regal Ware's investment position quite flexible because the blow-molding assets used to form percolators could be transferred readily from percolator production to other plastic products, and there were few goodwill barriers to overcome.

Regal Ware was serving the largest-volume market for percolators in 1978. The dies for its percolator designs were amortized, and all other blow-molding equipment could be used to produce other polypropylene appliances. Overall, Regal Ware was enjoying a successful endgame performance and low exit barriers in the event that it no longer wished to produce or merchandise percolator coffee-makers.

The Endgame in the Cigar Industry

A cigar is a compact roll of tobacco leaves for smoking. Historically, many small firms had produced cigars. Over 15,000 cigar factories were operated in 1915. But the once-fragmented industry's sales volume became increasingly concenrated among six cigar producers in endgame (their sales represented 85 percent of the unit volume). Historically, the industry had experienced a vast number of exits, until less than 500 cigar factories remained in 1964. In 1964, a near-historic peak in cigar consumption, the Surgeon General announced that cigarette-smoking was carcinogenic. In response to this announcement, thousands of cigarette smokers tried cigars, as they searched for an acceptable substitute for cigarettes. Due to the Surgeon General's announcement, demand for cigars soared to an historic high of 8,514 million withdrawals.

A Description of the Cigar Industry

The Product

Cigars were composed of three parts: the "filler," the "binder," and the "wrapper leaf." The filler was of tobacco leaves which provided the cigar with its distinctive taste and aroma. It had once been composed of whole tobacco leaves (long filler), but some cigars were reformulated to permit the use of scraps of tobacco and pieces of perfectly good tobacco leaf to be a part of the filler (short filler) in less expensive cigars. The binder was a leaf that held together the bunch of filler leaves. The best-quality cigars continued to use whole tobacco leaf binders, but by 1964 such cigars had become relatively rare. Binders were usually made from reconstituted tobacco leaf, called homogenized tobacco leaf (HTL). The wrapper represented 50 percent of the cost of a cigar and 4 percent of its weight. It was the external tobacco leaf which (1) covered the binder, (2) complemented the flavors of the tobacco leaves, and (3) gave high-quality cigars their distinctive appearance.

There were literally countless types of cigar products which could be produced and sold. Each brand name was produced in several lengths, shapes, and colors of wrapper tobacco. Because cigar consumption was determined by personal taste preferences, there could be room in the market for an almost infinite variety of products limited only by available retailer shelf space.

Classifications of Cigars. Cigars could be differentiated by their shapes, their materials (types of components), and their price. A single cigar brand could have as many as forty variations in these characteristics and most major cigar producers promoted more than one cigar brand in its many variations. There were "large cigars" (ten pounds or more per thousand finished weight), "small cigars" (more than three pounds but less than ten pounds per thousand finished weight), and "little cigars" (less than three pounds per thousand finished weight). A "perfecto" was a cigar of a standard shape which was thick in the center and tapered to a point at each end, sometimes called a "stogie." A "panatela" was a cigar of a long, slender shape; a "palmas" was the longest size of a slender cigar, like a panatela; and a "cigarillo" was the smallest cigar size. (A cigarillo could be "tipped" with a plastic mouthpiece or "untipped.") A "corona" was longer and larger than a cigarillo.

With the commercial perfection of homogenized tobacco leaf, cigars were also classified depending upon whether they were made of 100 percent natural ingredients or not. The ingredients used in making a cigar determined its quality. Quality in cigars could be used to justify higher prices. The high-volume, lower-priced cigars (up to a price point of 5 to 6 cents per cigar) were represented by products such as Swisher's King Edward cigar; Consolidated Cigar Company's Muriel 6-cent cigar; or Culbro's Robert Burns. This category of cigars corresponded roughly to IRS categories A to C in 1964. The medium-priced cigars (retail priced up to 15 cents per cigar) corresponded to IRS classes D and E. Examples of these cigars included Culbro's White Owl, Consolidated Cigar Company's Dutch Masters, and American's Roi-Tan. Upper-end cigars priced at over 15 cents to 40 cents per cigar corresponded to IRS classes F to H. These cigars included Consolidated Cigar Company's El Producto, American's Antonio Y Cleopatra, and Universal Cigar's Optimo.

Premium quality cigars were sold at prices which ranged from 50 cents each to $2.00 each. These cigars contained 100 percent natural tobacco ingredients (no homogenized ingredients). Premium cigars could be hand-rolled, or perhaps (in the lower end of the premium price range) machine-bunched and machine-rolled. Premium cigars included the Monte Cruz, Macanudo, and Partagas brands. Although the hand-bunched, hand-rolled market was very small, it could potentially offer a lucrative performance because these cigars frequently sold to the price-insensitive ($1.50 per cigar) market. In general, the class F to H cigars, when they could be sold in volumes which made plant utilization efficient, could be the most profitable cigars.

The best profit margins in 1964 were earned on cigars which were produced using high-speed machinery and using the homogenized binder and wrapper (short filler) typical of some of the cigarillo-sized cigars (explained below). But this was true only if the necessary sales volume was available and demand for cigars was inexpansible and quite price sensitive. Smokers were willing to spend a finite amount on cigars, which limited the absolute number of cigars consumed. If the price of cigars went up, smokers purchased fewer cigars. (An industry motto declared, "Raise your price one cent, close a cigar plant!") Most cigar manufacturers had few alternatives other than to change the formulation of their cigars in order to make them less costly to produce. Cigar prices in 1964 were approximately the same as they had been in 1945, but the cigar product's quality had been changed to offset rising costs. The major physical changes in the cigar product were a shortened filler, a homogenized binder, and a homogenized wrapper leaf. A change from long-filler to short-filler components enabled cigarmakers to purchase parts of the tobacco leaf rather than the more expensive whole tobacco leaf (which had to be stemmed before use in long filler cigars), and thereby reduced labor costs incurred in preparing the whole leaf for production as well.

Homogenized binder leaf (HTL) was a reformulation of pulverized cigar tobacco leaf which was produced in thin rolls, like paper. The HTL rolls were suitable for mounting on high-speed, automatic cigar-forming machines. The concept of recomposing tobacco particles into continuous or homogenized sheets was a common concept that had been commercialized by General Cigar (Culbro) in the 1950s. Use of rolls of homogenized binder leaf led to greater efficiency in operations and greater utilization of the ingredients used to make cigars (less wasted tobacco-leaf scraps). Homogenized wrapper leaf, like homogenized binder, was made from real cigar tobacco that was recomposed into continuous sheets for greater handling efficiency and automation. The less expensive homogenized wrapper was used for cigars in the lower price categories where price increases could not be sustained when natural ingredient production costs were rising.

The use of both homogenized wrapper and short filler affected the combustion and taste characteristics of the cigar more severely than using one of these components alone because the smell of burning homogenized binder was less pleasant than that of whole tobacco leaf binder. Where cigar smokers tasted their smoke, changes in the smell or in the combustion characteristics of their cigars influenced their perceptions concerning the satisfaction obtained from these "changed" cigar products. As raw-materials costs increased, the quality of some cigar brands was changed in small, insignificant stages which, when added together, resulted in deteriorated product quality.

Demand peaked sharply in 1964 in response to the Surgeon General's announcement concerning cigarettes. The most substantial response to the announcement, the switching of cigarette smokers to cigars, occurred in the A to C classes which were the 2.5-to-6-cents-per-cigar categories. When smokers did not find satisfaction with these homogenized tobaccos, they did not trade upward to better quality in more expensive cigars. They stopped smoking altogether or they returned to cigarettes and reduced their cigar consumption.

Cigar consumption had plateaued following the huge consumption of cigars in 1920 and, the Surgeon General's announcement revitalized demand for cigars again in 1964. Consumption of Cuban cigars had been declining before the embargo was imposed in 1963. Both imports from Cuba and withdrawals from bonded warehouses had declined 46 percent and 25 percent, respectively, from 1959 to 1961, and during that same period, imports from Puerto Rico and other locations increased by 140 percent and 73 percent, respectively.

Markets

The ultimate consumers of cigars tended to be males beyond the age of thirty-five who purchased their cigars from convenient retail outlets (lower-priced, such as drug stores, supermarkets, and discount stores) or specialty tobacco stores (higher-quality cigars). Because chain stores possessed the greatest economies in sales call results, the larger cigar companies which sold inexpensive cigars emphasized sales to chains. Distribution companies were also an important channel for distributing lower-priced cigars because they acted as wholesalers as well as manufacturers' representatives. In general, cigar-company sales representatives and distribution companies tried to place cigars anywhere that customers might see them and be motivated to purchase them on an impulse.

Premium-priced cigars were sold through limited distribution channels, such as tobacconists, and were less price sensitive. Other outlets where premium cigar products were sold included fine restaurants, theaters, or private clubs. In some cases, tobacconists ordered the desired stock of these cigars from specialty wholesalers who offered overnight delivery to ensure fresh cigars for customers. After the Cuban embargo, the U.S. cigar market was flooded by imported Caribbean cigars which were sold at inexpensive prices in bundles. The 100 percent natural cigars hand-rolled by cigar-makers in Honduras were effective substitutes for cigars manufactured and sold by U.S. companies at higher prices. Cigarettes were not considered substitutes for cigars because smokers consumed both cigars and cigarettes for different occasions. Cigars were smoked when relaxing. Nevertheless, both smoking products could be sold in the same channels to the same markets.

Marketing

Because cigars were purchased on impulse, cigar companies which possessed favorable distribution contacts, effective salesforces, or a captive distribution company possessed a crucial competitive advantage. Although advertising was effective for selling some cigar brands, physical distribution was more important. Some cigarmakers acquired regional distribution companies to ensure that their cigars reached the retail channels or granted exclusive distribution rights to wholesalers within geographic territories to ensure that vigorous promotional efforts would be undertaken to place their cigars on retailers' shelves. Because shelf space was quite valuable, retailers were powerful, and large cigar companies who could absorb the financial cost of returned merchandise possessed an advantage over smaller competitors because retailers returned substantial amounts of cigars unsold.

A cigar manufacturer offered several brands of cigars and several different sizes and variations of each brand in order to absorb shelf space which competitors might otherwise occupy. Each cigar company tried to ensure that if a competitor's cigars were also carried in a particular rack arrangement, they would be relegated to the bottom row where they would not be noticed or would be inaccessible. In a large rack of cigars, perhaps 15 to 20 percent of the cigars carried were brands which were popular and which turned over rapidly. The success of cigars in 1964 had encouraged firms to increase the width of their product offerings to try to lock out competitors' brands.

In urban markets, such as New York City, access to shelf space was controlled by a few distribution companies. In markets such as these, penetration by a new cigar company could be costly. Access was obtained through different "deals" (package deals, price promotions, free goods, or other distributor and retailer incentives). By contrast, in markets where distribution companies were not as strong, entry into retail outlets was easier and distribution (shelf space) was relatively easier to obtain and hold. There were over 200 such distribution companies serving various geographical regions. They were essential links to the small, independent retailers. Major cigar companies employed an in-house salesforce in addition to employing distribution companies to service retail outlets. Tobacconists and other specialty outlets were serviced by wholesalers who could provide overnight delivery of most high-quality, imported, or domestic cigar brands. Manufacturers' representatives frequently visited these outlets to service cigar displays, to sell new displays, and to oversee the distribution activities.

Whenever cigar sales slowed, distributors asked for more attention from cigar manufacturers' in-house sales representatives and retailers demanded more free goods in order to promote the slowly moving cigar brands. The industry had become even more deal-oriented, particularly in the northeastern states. Because there were many cigar companies who could afford to buy shelf space in 1964 retailers could not afford to allocate shelf space to cigars unless the return they received through sales margins and incentives made it worthwhile to do so.

Cigar prices were a confusing patchwork of historical compromises which reflected some of the rivalries of competitors within the cigar industry. Deeply entrenched traditions of noncooperation among the different cigar companies made price followership unlikely when a company tried to raise its prices. Pricing was also confusing in the cigar business due to pressures from the IRS tax system, from the various states which taxed cigars, and from the many high-volume cigar customers who wanted special price breaks.

Suppliers' Behavior

The tobacco-growing industry was fragmented; the cigar-forming machinery industry was highly concentrated. In order to control the quality of their cigar tobacco, many cigar firms were backward-integrated into tobacco-leaf plantations. When a cigar company grew its own wrapper tobacco leaf, it locked up its cash. Cigar companies could speed up their working capital turnover only by purchasing and pledging their inventories. When cigar quality became less critical, due to the rise of homogenized tobacco sheet, several hard-pressed backward-integrated companies divested their tobacco plantations or reduced the scale of their farming operations.

The best sources of cigar filler leaves were Havana, the Canary Islands, Honduras, and Mexico. The best cigar wrapper leaves came from the Connecticut Valley where they were "shade grown." When the Cuban embargo was imposed, refugees from Cuba smuggled the seeds of the Havana tobacco plant to other countries whose soils were also suitable for tobacco growing. Business customs in some of these new supplier locations made backward integration necessary in order for high quality to be maintained. Many cigarmakers, particularly the Tampa cigarmakers, owned a few thousand acres of land in Florida or New England to grow cigar wrapper leaves, to age tobaccos, and to process (stem) tobacco filler leaf, as well. The cigars' wrapper leaves were very expensive because they were hand-picked by youth labor which was paid the U.S. minimum wage. It was possible also for cigarmakers to buy their cigar tobacco from the worldwide markets. Most companies cured their own tobacco since the marrying of the filler leaves created a cigar's unique taste characteristics. Generally, more than a year's inventory of tobacco was held. Wrapper-tobacco inventories were also retained. The estimated cost of the fragile wrapper-leaf inventory was $4 per thousand cigars produced.

Because natural leaf wrapper tobacco was hard to handle whether it was used to hand-roll cigars or on machines, production times were slow. By contrast, homogenized leaf could be used on high-speed machines. The companies which produced cigar-forming machinery frequently manufactured and sold homogenized tobacco binder and wrapper leaf, as well as the forming machinery. The American Machine and Foundry Company (AMF) was the major U.S. supplier of cigar-forming machines. AMF required that lessors pay a large, up-front "installment fee" for the use of the machines in addition to royalties on each cigar produced using the machinery. The installment fee was usually capitalized and depreciated over a prolonged period of operations. The machines usually lasted more than thirty years. Hence, the machines were usually slowly depreciated. Culbro created and manufactured its own cost-reducing cigar machinery. One of its innovations was the creation of HTL binder, a homogenized cigar-wrapper tobacco. Later, Culbro created Ultra Star homogenized cigar-wrapper tobacco, which was also produced on rolls for use on its efficient cigar-forming machines.

Manufacturing Technology of the Cigar Industry

An integrated cigar plant contained the following operations: (1) steaming and sorting the tobacco leaves; (2) blending and storing the tobacco leaves in piles to cause them to blend; (3) stemming (that is, the removal of the major stem in the center of the leaf); (4) the actual production of the cigar on either hand-placement, automated, or hand-rolled technologies; and (5) the packaging operation. Cigars were made *on* machines, not by machines. The technologies used to make cigars ranged from a very labor-intensive hand-rolled technology to a completely automated plant, such as the new, fully automated plant at Philipsburg, Pennsylvania, operated by the Culbro Corporation. As cigarmaking automated in the 1950s and 1960s, it became an increasingly capital-intensive process.

Three types of technologies were used to produce cigars: (1) hand-rolled; (2) hand-rolled, automated using natural ingredients; and (3) automated using homogenized tobacco ingredients. The physical assets required for these operations varied and the size of the investment required varied. Cigarmaking using the hand-rolled process involved two steps: bunching the filler tobacco, and rolling on the binder and the wrapper leaf completely by hand. The physical assets were primarily carved dies for the bunching operation and knives to finish the ends after hand-rolling. The automated natural leaf operations used hand placements to position the binder and wrapper leaf. Four laborers were needed to operate AMF Corporation's hand placement machines. Leaves were transferred from operation to operation by a vacuum, after a tobacco leaf was placed on the platen.

The automated process using homogenized tobacco bunched scrap filler from a hopper. The binder looked like paper on a spool and was mechanically fed, using a similar vacuum-feed technology. The manufacturing process was almost completely automated. One supervisor was required to monitor the production process.

The physical production process of making cigars was different from that of making cigarettes. Cigarettes could be electronically monitored. The technology was almost peopleless compared with the technology used to produce cigars. Even the most automated process for cigar manufacturing used much labor and used natural products. Making a cigar required much inspection, substantial human inputs, and could be costly.

Economic Exit Barriers in the Cigar Industry. Cigar-forming machines cost approximately $4 million per unit but they could be leased from AMF for slightly less. The cost of leasing such machines represented approximately 40 percent of the asset investment required to manufacture cigars. The assets used to produce cigars which could be sold in a used-machinery market included general-purpose equipment such as conveyors, packaging machines, ovens, compressors, heaters, air conditioners, humidifiers, generators, and forklifts. The cigarmaking machines themselves would be returned to AMF in most cases. (AMF might lease the machines again if they were still relatively serviceable.)

The most process-specific assets used in cigarmaking included the stripping machines and the threshing machines used to make short filler. These assets and the natural tobacco cigar-forming machines, themselves, could only be used in order to produce cigars. There was virtually no resale market for cigar-forming machines which had been purchased rather than leased if the market for cigars was declining. The buildings and land used in cigar production could have been sold or the cigar company could have developed the tobacco plantation through real-estate operations. But because much of the farmland was not prime commerical land, there would have been few uses for the farm machinery assets (the tractors, trucks, and farm implements) other than in farming operations. The tobacco industry could be liquidated; receivables could be collected. (Raw materials represented about half of the cost of goods sold.)

The significant economic exit barriers in the cigar industry were the machines, which could not be used for purposes other than cigar manufacturing. If a firm introduced a new generation of cigar-forming machinery, it was locked into continued participation in the cigar industry until the value of the new capital investments had been retrieved. For example, if leased cigar-forming machinery were operated for fifteen years (until the "installment fee" had been amortized), a firm would face relatively low economic exit barriers. When the automated homogenized cigar-binding technology was commercialized by contrast, investment in it locked a competitor into another decade or more of participation in the cigar industry (because it had a longer economic life). Similarly, investment in the new homogenized cigar wrapper-leaf technology delineated a minimum time when competitors would have to continue to produce and market cigars until the value of their investment was recovered or face losses upon exit. Firms using a hand-rolled cigar technology faced the lowest exit barriers of all because their inventories were usually salable, their receivables were collectible, and their capital intensity was very low.

If a firm acquired a cigar company in 1964, the recapitalized book value of an acquisition would create a higher basis for subsequent depreciation. The capitalized goodwill incorporated in the acquisition price of a promising cigar company could constitute a large economic value which might deter an acquiring firm from exiting.

A Historic Overview of the Cigar Industry

The history of the cigar industry was shaped by the technological changes in the industry. Until the 1920s, cigarmaking had used the same type of hand-rolling operations which the Indians, who were smoking cigars when Christopher Columbus landed, had used.

Cigar-Rolling Machines. The introduction of cigar-rolling machines in the 1920s reduced the number of cigar factories in the United States. In 1910 approximately 22,500 factories had produced hand-rolled cigars; by 1964, widespread mechanization and other technological innovations had led to a consolidation and reduction of cigar factories to less than 400.

Automated Cigar-Forming Machinery. The new AMF machines were intricate gadgets with over 500 moving parts which laid the filler, applied the binder and wrapper, and finally automatically sealed the tip with a dab of special, invisible, and tasteless vegetable paste. Output per worker using such automated techniques had been doubled, from 85,000 units annually before World War II to approximately 172,000 units per worker per year in the late 1950s. The older AMF machines had produced 3,500 to 6,000 cigars per day in the late 1950s. The fully automated machines which used homogenous tobacco produced 43,000 to 48,000 cigars per day. The effects of these changes in the cigar business were to take cigarmaking out of the "craftsman" business by automating operations and lowering costs, and to make competition considerably more precarious for the smaller cigar companies.

Two other changes which influenced the cigar business severely in the early 1960s, as these cost-reducing innovations were adopted by leading firms were (1) the Organization of American States embargo of Cuban products, notably, in this case, of Havana tobaccos, and (2) the 1964 U.S. Surgeon General's announcement concerning the carcinogenic (cancer-causing) effects of cigarette-smoking.

It became increasingly difficult for a small cigar firm to operate in an industry which required increasingly large capital investments in addition to the tremendous inventories of raw tobacco (a one-and-one-half to two-year supply) which must be held. Since it could take up to two years to cure the leaf, cigar manufacturers had to bear costly inventorying expenses. Previously, prior to the introduction of automated cigar-forming machines, this investment had been the cigar industry's principal capital requirement. Before AMF and Culbro (General Cigar) commercialized their high-speed machines, cigarmakers had been caught in a cycle of limited capital, highly leveraged inventories, lagging consumption, and, consequently, poor profits. Although the scientific growing and tobacco-handling methods freed producers from this cycle, they squeezed out marginal producers who could not afford the large sums required to invest in these money-saving process improvements. (In 1964, for example, General Cigar's capital outlays totaled more than $12 million.)

Cigar firms had spent considerable amounts of their 1963 budgets to attract a new market. Advertising outlays had increased 275 percent over the 1953 industry expenditures of $8 million. The new packaging and wider variety of sizes and shapes introduced also increased captial requirements for this business.

Given these technological improvements, capacity outdistanced demand in most years until 1964 when the announcement of the carcinogenic effects of cigarettes increased cigar demand by 40 percent. Then demand outstripped capacity; cigar manufacturers could not add capacity quickly enough to accommodate the new cigar smokers' eagerness to try their cigar products.

Competition in the Cigar Industry in 1964

In 1964 the high-volume, mass-merchandised cigar markets were served by several wide-line, nationally distributed cigar companies and a few specialized companies which catered to regional or ethnic tastes. The largest number of competitors produced the higher-quality all-natural-ingredients (or mixed-ingredients) cigars in relatively small volumes. Although 351 companies produced the cigars in 1964, the sales of the leading four producers of cigars comprised approximately 71 percent of the sales volume of large cigars and sales of the eight leading cigarmakers comprised approximately 86 percent of the sales volume of large cigars.

Cigars were sold in regional markets; few brands were nationally distributed. For example Jno. H. Swisher's King Edward brand was the largest-selling cigar brand. Yet it was *not* available in New York City, Ohio, Illinois, or most urban centers. It was distributed predominantly in the South and Southwest. Because different brands were more popular in different regions of the United States, the leading brands of the West Coast differed from the leading sellers on the East Coast. Many of the cigar companies were single-business firms or were diversified into other, closely related tobacco production or distributing businesses.

Consolidated Cigar Company. In 1964 Consolidated Cigar and its divisions manufactured and sold cigars at nine points which were located in Berwick, Lancaster, Philadelphia, West Pittston, and Wilkes-Barre, Pennsylvania; Poughkeepsie, New York; Camden, New Jersey; Richmond, Virginia; Cayey and Caguas, Puerto Rico. It also operated two leaf-processing plants (Glastonbury, Connecticut, and Lancaster); a cigar-box manufacturing plant (Quakertown, Pennsylvania); a plastics-products manufacturing plant and a machine manufacturing plant. Consolidated Cigar owned or leased twenty tobacco warehouses, and eight farms in Connecticut and Massachusetts. In 1964, Consolidated Cigar Corporation's sales volume had been $158.5 million.

Consolidated Cigar was "the General Motors of Cigars" in 1964. It produced cigars in each price category and led the industry in advertising expenditures and new product introductions. Consolidated Cigar brands included Dutch Masters, Muriels, and El Producto, among others. Many of Consolidated Cigar Company's brands had been obtained through acquisitions. By 1963 Consolidated Cigar had moved 35 percent of its manufacturing operations to Puerto Rico and closed some of the plants it had acquired in an earlier time.

Consolidated Cigar Company and Culbro (General Cigar) retained an historic rivalry for the leadership of the cigar industry. Consolidated Cigar had surpassed Culbro in unit volume around 1945. Culbro had established itself as the industry's technological leader. Consolidated Cigar chose to emphasize marketing skills instead of imitating Culbro's technological tactics. Consolidated Cigar invested heavily in advertising campaigns on television and in its salesforce and distribution network, giving particular emphasis to selling to national chain stores. Consolidated created highly effective point-of-purchase display racks and convenience merchandising packages for its cigars. It dominated the distribution channels by focusing its efforts on drug stores, supermarkets, and discount stores. Although Consolidated had the larger market share, it was not omnipotent in influencing the industry. When, in 1964, Consolidated tried to raise its prices on some of its products, Culbro would not follow its lead.

Culbro (General Cigar). In 1964 the Culbro Company was General Cigar, and manufactured cigars at eight plants which were located as follows: Kingston, Mahanoy City, Nitacoke, and Philipsburg, Pennsylvania; Kingston, Jamaica; Utiado, Puerto Rico; and Tampa, Florida. The Leaf Tobacco Division's plants were located at Lancaster, Pennsylvania, Prairie du Chien, Wisconsin, and Caguas, Puerto Rico. Tobacco processing plants were located at Lancaster, Kingston, and Ephrata, Pennsylvania, and Caguas, Puerto Rico. The Homogenized Tobacco Division was housed at Mahanoy City, Pennsylvania. The Culbro Tobacco Divisions were located in West Hartford, Connecticut, and Greensboro, Florida. The corporate research laboratories and Ultra Star wrapper plant were located in Lancaster, Pennsylvania. Corporate sales in 1964 were $193.0 million.

Culbro had diversified into the premium cigar market by acquiring Gradiaz, Annis and Co., a well-known Tampa cigarmaker, in 1963. This acquisition gave Culbro an entree into the premium-priced, prestige cigars (Gold Label) then made from Havana tobacco. Culbro's leading domestic brands were Robert Burns Tiparillos, White Owl, and William Penn, among others.

In order to appeal to the increasing numbers of ex-cigarette smokers who sought a substitute smoking product, but who considered regular cigars to be too strong, Culbro introduced a new line of mild, small cigars called Tiparillos. The product was inexpensive because it used Ultra Star homogenized wrapper and a plastic mouthpiece (because early versions of the homogenized wrapper dissolved in the smoker's mouth).

In 1964, following the Surgeon General's announcement, Culbro was in the best position to capitalize on the rising demand for cigars because it possessed the technology and the capacity to produce the largest number of cigars. As the most technologically advanced, lowest-cost competitor, Culbro could enjoy the biggest windfalls of all because its plants had ample capacity to fill the demand for cigars.

American Brands (American Cigar). American Brands' principal business in 1964 was the manufacture and sale of cigarettes, cigars, and smoking tobacco. The company was also diversified into businesses such as biscuits, liquors, applesauce, and snack foods. Corporate sales in 1964 were $1,203.4 million. The American Cigar Corporation, which had specialized in 100 percent Havana tobacco cigars, produced a brand, La Corona, which once had been the epitome of a fine quality cigar. American Cigar had simulated the climatic environment of Cuba in a cigar plant in Trenton, New Jersey, to produce these hand-rolled cigars.

American Cigar tried to maintain a quality image for its products by using high-quality tobacco leaf whenever it was economic to do so. As the cost of raw materials and labor increased, this strategy became more difficult to execute. Although the cigar division emphasized cost control and efficiency by keeping its plant and equipment modern, and by engaging in research activities to improve its products, American Cigar's market share was slipping in 1964.

American Cigar's principal brands were Roi-Tan and Antonio Y Cleopatra, a grenadier-shaped cigar. Roi-Tan was one of the most popular 10-cent cigars; Antonio Y Cleopatra, a medium-priced cigar, was American Cigar's second-largest-selling brand. It featured a dark Cameroons leaf wrapper and a uniquely designed package. Antonio Y Cleopatra and Roi-Tan were distributed in channels which also frequently carried Consolidated Cigar Company products.

In 1964, American Cigar produced cigars at Charleston, South Carolina; Owensboro, Kentucky; Philadelphia, Wilkes-Barre, and Mountaintop, Pennsylvania. Research facilities were located at the tobacco operations headquarters in Richmond.

Jno. H. Swisher & Son. The most popular cigar brand in America (King Edward) was produced by Jno. H. Swisher & Son in Waycross, Georgia, Cullman, Alabama, and at its headquarters in Jacksonville, Florida. Swisher grew some tobacco on a plantation in Florida, but it also purchased tobacco. Swisher's principal brand, King Edward, had possessed the largest market share since the 1930s. It featured a natural wrapper leaf and sold for 8 cents or less. Smokers recognized that it was an excellent value.

Swisher used its ability to produce a high-quality cigar sold at a low price to keep other competitors out of its market niche. Swisher was able to accept a lower gross margin than other cigar manufacturers because Swisher did not advertise heavily. Instead Swisher relied upon an extensive distribution system of over seventy representatives who coordinated their activities with over 200 distributors who carried Swisher cigar products. Of these, a competitor, Havatampa Cigar Corporation (itself a manufacturer of lower-priced cigars), was an important contributor to Swisher's success by virtue of its distribution services. King Edward and other Swisher cigar products were sold in rural markets throughout the South, Southwest, and Midwest by firms like Havatampa. Consolidated Cigar Company and Culbro could not penetrate these markets due to the strong selling relationships Swisher sales representative and distribution companies had developed.

Swisher produced no high-priced cigars in 1964. All of its U.S. products retailed for under 11 cents per cigar. Swisher operated no premium-brand West Indies affiliate as did companies like Culbro. Instead, Swisher's U.S. products appealed to a mass market and were mass merchandised because Jno. H. Swisher produced the clasical curved-shaped cigars (which were sometimes called "stogies") which many cigar producers had discontinued, fearing it would label them irretrievably with the "graybeard" market.

Swisher produced and sold a substantial volume of this old-fashioned cigar design to its southern customers.

Havatampa Cigar Corporation. Havatampa was a distributing organization which sold cigars, cigarettes, tobacco, candy, chewing gum, paper goods, fountain supplies, and other related items such as razor blades, pipes, lighters, and matches. The company also operated a tobacco farm, two tobacco packing houses, a cigar factory, an insurance agency, and nine cigarette-vending operations. Havatampa manufactured its own cigars in a cigar plant at its headquarters in Tampa, Florida. Its principal brands were Hav-A-Tampa, Tampa Nugget, Tampa Straight, and Don CeSar. Havatampa's distribution unit promoted these and the cigars of other producers for whom Havatampa was a sales representative.

Havatampa Cigar Corporation promoted these inexpensive cigars with other low-priced cigar brands such as Jno. H. Swisher's King Edward cigars in eight southern states. Havatampa provided inventorying and promotional services to dealers through fifty-four distribution divisions. It was a very important and effective distribution channel in the southern states, particularly in C and D counties (rural counties). Havatampa Cigar operated a chain of Havatampa Houses, which were retail outlets for selling cigars. These outlets were used successfully to promote the various lines of lower-priced cigars Havatampa Cigar represented. Havatampa Cigar was recognized as being one of the most effective distribution companies in the market. Its cigars, by contrast, were not of high quality. They were consumed in large numbers nevertheless because they were inexpensive.

The Tampa Cigarmakers. The Tampa cigarmakers were represented by a particular kind of cigar product. Typically, a Tampa cigar was a class G or H cigar, which was the highest tax bracket classification. Tampa cigars have long filler, a natural-leaf binder, and a natural-leaf wrapper. Historically, the Tampa cigar industry had used Havana tobacco to manufacture its cigars. When the embargo eliminated this competitive advantage, the Tampa cigarmakers developed tobacco-growing operations in other locations such as Honduras, Nicaragua, Mexico, Santo Domingo, and occasionally in Brazil or Jamaica.

The economy of Tampa had been highly dependent upon cigarmaking, historically. Over 100 cigar companies were located in Tampa in the 1920s, employing 44 percent of the city's population. The Cuban embargo was the most devastating influence on the structure of the Tampa cigar industry because after the embargo many major cigar manufacturers sold out to larger, wide-line cigar companies or merged with each other. For example, the Morgan Cigar Company was sold to Gradias, Annas, which in turn was sold to Culbro (General Cigar). Garcia Y. Vega was sold to Bayuk Cigar. Their plants were later shut down.

Only five major Tampa cigarmakers continued to operate factories in Tampa in 1964. They were Corral, Wodiska Y Ca.; M & N Cigar; Perfecto Garcia; Villazon & Co.; and Arturo Fuente Cigar Co. (Havatampa Cigar was also located in Tampa, Florida. It did not produce premium-quality cigars, however.) The Tampa cigarmakers had operated as "bonded factories" until the Cuban embargo. This meant that their warehouses contained only Cuban tobacco and that the federal government controlled access to these warehouses as custom houses which were bonded and taxed as the tobacco was withdrawn from bond. These companies were usually privately held.

The Tampa cigarmakers would not compromise the integrity of their cigars by using homogenized ingredients or inferior tobaccos. Some companies, such as Corral, Wodiska Y Ca., owned their own plantations to produce the necessary tobaccos. The entrepreneurs who comprised the Tampa cigarmakers were known in the cigar industry as "epicures" because they supervised personally the progress of their crops and the marrying of their tobaccos. When the Tampa cigarmakers advertised, their messages made appeals on the basis of quality.

In addition to the major Tampa cigarmakers, there were many, many smaller shops called "buckeyes" which were in fact small shopfronts which also manufactured cigars in their back rooms. Their output was usually sold to regional cigar shops and retailers.

The Tampa cigarmakers were successful for several reasons such as their attention to purchasing good tobaccos and their low-overhead operations. Because they were not parts of larger corporations which possessed high earnings targets or which carried corporate overhead burdens, the cash flows generated by the Tampa cigarmakers were more than ample to keep their founders satisfied. Moreover, a low showing of profits would minimize the tax obligations these privately held companies might face. Therefore, the true probability of the Tampa cigarmakers is not documented.

Bayuk Cigars. Bayuk Cigars Incorporated was a closely held, independent cigarmaker whose principal brand, Phillies, provided the greater part of its sales. Bayuk's other businesses included candy, a premium company, and a machinery company which manuactured, sold, and leased machinery relating to tobacco processing and cigar manufacturing. Corporate sales in 1964 were $58.0 million, or 12 percent of the large cigar market.

Phillies retailed from 5 cents per cigar to two for 25 cents. It was one of the most widely sold cigar brands in the industry and had rivaled King Edward as the sales-volume leader. Bayuk's other major brand, Garcia Y Vega, was a Tampa cigar brand acquired when the Cuban embargo was imposed. Garcia Y Vega held a large inventory of Havana tobacco which Bayuk sold for cash-flow purposes. Bayuk had carried over ten cigar brands during the 1950s, and it had been necessary to weed out the less successful brands. The brands which Bayuk retained were heavily advertised until the mid-sixties when the affects of the saturation advertising campaign it pursued had built up Bayuk's market share, but the costs of continuing to advertise against Consolidated Cigar and Culbro became increasingly high. In 1964 Bayuk gave greater emphasis to its premiums program. Bandwagon U.S.A. was a marketing company specializing in premiums which were offered in monthly "bonus gift magazines." The premiums Bandwagon U.S.A. offered to exchange for Bayuk cigar wrappers were intended to enhance Bayuk's other sales efforts. Bandwagon did not distribute cigars.

Bayuk cigars grew some of its own wrapper tobacco in Florida and Puerto Rico. Bayuk did not have a West Indies cigar affiliate which enabled it to participate in the development of prestige brand cigars. Bayuk Cigar produced cigars in factories located in Philadelphia and York, Pennsylvania; Selma, Alabama; Long Island; and Tampa, Florida. Its ten tobacco warehouses were located in Massachusetts, Connecticut, Pennsylvania, and Puerto Rico.

Corporate Strategy Exit Barriers. Managerial exit barriers could have been operative in the cigar industry where firms tried to retain their cigar operations, even when losses were being incurred, because it had been a "family" business or for other sentimental reasons. The Tampa cigarmakers, American Brands, and Culbro Corporation (the Cullmans of Culbro were an old-line tobacco farming dynasty) are examples of cigar companies where managerial exit barriers might have made exit difficult, even if alternative investments had seemed more attractive because they were single-business companies for whom cigarmaking had been a family occupation for several generations. This meant that exit from the cigar industry would be a difficult decision for many cigar companies to execute.

Since many of the family-operated single-business cigar companies would likely redouble their efforts to compete for regional shelf space rather than end their cigarmaking operations, the cigar plants of many of the smaller cigar companies tended to be more fully utilized than were the plants of the larger nationally distributed cigar firms. Their lower earnings requirements (price deals) were an operating advantage the small firms possessed which, when exploited, resulted in more volatile competition because these small cigar companies faced strategic exit barriers and exhibited a willingness to deal in price breaks at the retailer level. Because the capital-intensive firms which mass-merchandised and advertised their cigar brands nationally had faced higher exit barriers as well as the opportunity to spread their costs by selling more units in new markets, their commitment to remaining in the endgame was also high.

Summary of Competitors in the Cigar Industry

In summary, the major brands of cigar available in various distribution outlets in 1964 were produced by companies which varied in their strategic postures along the following dimensions: (1) the different market niches they served; (2) the capital intensity of their cigar-forming technology; (3) the ways in which firms differentiated and promoted their cigar brands; (4) the extent of their forward and backward integration; (5) the number of brands (and variations within a brand name) they carried; and (6) the importance of the cigar business to the company which owned the cigarmaking assets. For example, the 8-cent cigar of Swisher and the 12-cent cigar of Consolidated Cigar were virtually identical. Consolidated Cigar had been advertising its cigars more intensely than Swisher and charged higher prices for them.

Many of the competitors described above were somewhat backward-integrated; few were forward-integrated. Tobacco-leaf farming made most cigar firms at least taper-integrated. Some firms also made their own cigar boxes, plastic tips, and cigar-forming machinery.

The cigar competitors varied in the number of brands they produced and in the importance of their cigarmaking operations to the total corporation. Some firms were essentially single-business companies. Many cigar companies, including some of the major firms, were managed by members of "cigar families." It was not unusual in these venerable firms for the chairman of the board, the president, and the executive vice-president of the cigar company to bear the same surnames.

Some of the cigarmakers were quite capital-intensive. The firms who produced lower-priced, short filler cigars made from homogenized binder and wrapper were well suited for automation. By contrast, most higher-quality cigar companies rolled cigars by hand. But by 1964, there was substantial diversity even among the leading cigar companies in the industry with respect to their cigar-forming technologies.

*A Mapping of Strategic Groups in the
Cigar Industry*

This section attempts to cluster the competitors along discriminating dimensions which will describe the differences in these firms' strategic postures. Using the dimensions described and discussed above, one can anlayze where the competitors in the cigar industry might differ in ways which constituted relative competitive advantages.

Within the cigar industry, one way of classifying the competitors would be according to whether their cigar products were predominantly high quality (this usually implied natural ingredients) or predominantly low quality (this usually implied homogenized ingredients or other cost-cutting operations). There could be firms, like Culbro, which owned a subsidiary which made very prestigious cigars, perhaps under a famous label. These premium cigar operations were not integrated into other corporate activities; such firms were merely held by the larger cigar company as a diversification from its generally lower-quality, homogenized cigar products.

The strategic groupings of the cigar firms could also discriminate between the types of manufacturing technologies in use by categorizing them according to relative capital intensity. Thus the competitors in the cigar industry could be grouped in the following manner.

	Not Capital-Intensive Technology	Relatively Capital-Intensive Technology
Relatively High Product Quality	(Culbro) Tampa Cigarmakers	
	————————— Consolidated Cigar —————————	
Relatively Low Product Quality	American Cigar Bayuk Cigar	Culbro Corporation Jno. H. Swisher Havatampa Cigar

Along these axes, the firms committed to a particular characteristic are positioned at the relative extremes of this "strategic space." For example, Culbro was highly automated and produced homogenized tobacco products for the mass markets, good-quality cigars for the traditional markets, and premium-quality cigars for the prestige market. The premium cigars were hand-rolled. The Tampa cigarmakers also produced cigars of notably high quality using low-technology processes or hand-rolling. There were no firms whose technologies enabled them to produce high-quality cigars on highly automated production lines. A substantial amount of labor was required to handle the fragile natural leaf.

There were variations in the geographic markets where particular brands of cigars were most popular. For example, American Cigar's Roi-Tan was quite popular on the West Coast, as was Consolidated Cigar Corp.'s Dutch Masters. Consolidated Cigar's Harvester brand was popular only in the northern Midwest. Kind Edward was most popular in the South.

Despite differences in their geographic distribution patterns, their capital intensity, and the relative importance of cigars to the total corporate enterprise, the cigar industry was volatile because (1) competitors overexpanded in 1964 by misjudging the duration of the increased demand for cigars; (2) there were too many cigar brands and variations of brands; (3) large competitors began to invade new market segments to sell their excess capacity; and (4) cigar competitors were busily stealing market share from each other instead of from other tobacco products as total cigar consumption peaked in 1964, and then declined. One of the problems of the cigar industry had been that, as a group, they had been very conservative and tradition-bound. The cigar companies had not produced the products which consumers wanted in many cases. (The introduction of the mild Tiparillo, in 1964, is an exception to this.) There was no marketing response to declining cigar demand (market-research studies, attribute-analysis studies, and so on) which yielded a successful new product after 1964. The major cigar firms were "producton-oriented." Rather than adapting to the environment of declining demand, many cigar firms continued to use the same tactics they had used in the past.

The Endgame in the Cigar Industry

Demand for cigars declined slowly from the 1964 peak and at unequal rates for different classes of cigars. There had been precedents for predicting consumer responses to the cigarette-smoking hazard, but cigar companies apparently preferred to believe that cigar demand would remain high. Instead, under new IRC classifications, the lower-priced cigars (classes A to C) fell in consumption most sharply, while demand increased for premium cigars (classes F to H).

Several forces lessened the public's acceptance of cigar-smoking, including changing social values, a ban on television advertising of small cigars, and improved technology which exacerbated the excess capacity problem by making it possible to produce cigars at a faster rate.

Competition in the cigar industry became more difficult as re-investments in advertising and promotional campaigns, new machinery, or new plants became necessary. Competition became more cutthroat at the wholesaler and retailer level, eroding cigarmakers' margins severely. Expenditures for television advertising continued to rise because cigarmakers could not overcome their rivalries and decrease the magnitude of these expenditures cooperatively. They were trying to steal market share from each other intensely in 1975. After 1975, competition was on the basis of "dealing"—to the ultimate cigar consumers in addition to dealing to the wholesalers and retailers. More free goods and price reduction were employed in this campaign. Advertising expenditures of the major cigar companies increased significantly in 1973 over 1964. This was the year in which cigarette advertisements were banned from radio and television, an event which some cigar firms hoped might enhance cigar consumption by creating for them a competitive advantage over cigarettes. If any such advantage did exist, it was shortlived because cigarette companies quickly learned how to promote their products effectively without using the air waves.

One of the major changes in the cigar industry made competition more intense for the Tampa cigarmakers who had differentiated their high-quality cigars from those using homogenized components. So successful were the Tampa cigarmakers that the major cigar firms imitated them by acquiring premium cigar labels or reformulating their clear Havana brands using other high-quality tobaccos. By 1978 the famous luxury-class Cuban brands of the Menendez and Garcia families such as H. Upmann were reintroduced successfully through the cooperation of major cigar firms such as Consolidated Cigar or the Culbro Corporation.

A Chronological Description of the Endgame in the Cigar Industry

1965

Culbro (General Cigar). The booming demand for cigars created by the cigarette scare increased, benefiting firms such as General Cigar (Culbro) which possessed excess capacity and had created several high-volume production techniques. During 1964 and 1965 Culbro had invested $23 million for plant modernizations in order to increase its capacity. In 1965, an efficient cigar-manufacturing machine would have cost approximately $4 million per unit, but Culbro manufactured its own cigar-machine designs to lower costs, instead.

Also in 1965, Culbro acquired the Metropolitan Tobacco Co., a New York and New Jersey distributor of tobacco and sundries, to intensify coverage in the prime New York City market and expanded its markets by boosting its advertising budget by 40 percent and strengthening the sales staff. Culbro also purchased the tobacco acreage of American Sumatra Tobacco Corporation, including Sumatra's landscape nursery operations, in 1965.

1966

Jno. H. Swisher. In 1966 American Maize-Products Company acquired the Jno. H. Swisher & Son Company for approximately $18 million. American Maize-Products manufactured corn syrups by the wet-milling process, corn syrup solids, corn sugars, corn germ, proteins from corn, modified and special starches, dextrines, and various chemicals. In 1966 its sales were $63.0 million.

Bayuk Cigar. In 1966 Bayuk Cigar reported a loss of $172,000 on the disposal of one of its cigar plants, net of taxes.

1967

Culbro. In 1967 Culbro acquired the 100-year-old Jamaican-based cigar firm Temple Hall, Ltd., and renamed it Gradiaz, Annis of Jamaica, Ltd. Temple Hall, Ltd., was acquired by General Cigar because it manufactured the legendary, hand-made luxury line of Macanudo cigars, which were generally ranked by some European smokers as being just below genuine Havanas.

DWG Cigar. In 1967 the cigar business of DWG Corporation, which had represented 4 percent of the market, was terminated. Assets were sold for $4.7 million (to Universal Cigar), which resulted in an after-tax loss of $1.5 million. An additional parcel of assets valued at $1.2 million was not yet sold at the end of 1967. The DWG Cigar Corporation was severely overextended in 1964 because it managed fourteen different cigar brands, many of which were acquired with plants containing outmoded, slow cigar-forming machines. The company was severely undercapitalized. DWG management had tried to make DWG Cigar a national cigar company by advertising its brands on national television. DWG funded these aggressive programs by selling its large inventory of Havana tobacco to other cigar companies. As the sales of DWG increased, however, the company's profitability plummeted. When DWG tried to raise the prices of its cigars, no competitors followed its lead and its profits had turned to losses and the company was liquidated.

1968

Consolidated Cigar. On January 1, 1968, Gulf + Western Industries acquired Consolidated Cigar Company, which formed the foundation of Gulf + Western's new Consumer Products Group. In 1967, prior to the acquisition, Consolidated Cigar's net physical plant and equipment had been valued at $29,856,000 and the tobacco inventories were valued at $68,301,000, representing 23 and 54 percent of total corporate assets, respectively. Gulf + Western Industries was a diversified holding company with operations in eight major groups as follows: manufacturing (E.W. Bliss Company and others); metals and chemicals; distribution; agricultural products; leisure-time activities; consumer products; financial services; and real estate. Sales in 1968 were $1,313.9 million.

Gulf + Western Industries monitored the performance of the companies in its operating groups on the basis of their performance in terms of cash flow, net operating income, sales, inventories, receivables, working capital turnover, fixed asset turnover, and return on investment, but it did not intervene in the operating groups' affairs unless they asked for assistance or major performance problems arose. Under Gulf + Western Industries, Consolidated Cigar produced and sold cigars in the United States and in Canada and the Netherlands, through subsidiaries.

Culbro. In 1968 Culbro purchased distribution companies in Albany, New York, and Pittsfield, Massachusetts, to form a network of distributors. Although the company had achieved technological virtuosity, Culbro did not yet possess a distribution network equal to that of Consolidated Cigar Company.

Culbro consolidated cigar operations by purchasing distribution companies and through aggressive dealing activities at the wholesaler and retailer levels, by purchasing premium cigar brands, and by increasing advertising and promotion budgets.

1969

Culbro. In 1969 Culbro commenced a nontobacco diversification which included purchasing controlling interest of Ex-lax, Inc., Bachman Foods (snack foods), a molded plastics business, and snuff and chewing-tobacco lines (Helme Products, Inc.). These were all products which could be distributed through Culbro's Metropolitan Tobacco Distribution Company and the other distribution organizations Culbro had recently purchased. Then, in June 1969, Culbro raised its retail prices by 3 to 5 percent on most of its national branded cigars.

American Cigar. As a part of its campaign to retain its slipping market share, American Cigar expanded its cigar salesforce in 1969. In response to Culbro's price increase, American Cigar raised only the price of its Roi-Tan products because although the cigarmakers recognized the need to raise their prices, they feared that price increases would precipitate widespread consumer rejections of cigars.

Consolidated Cigar Company. Consolidated Cigar followed the price increases of Culbro and American Cigar selectively by increasing the prices of some, but not all, of its cigar products. Consolidated Cigar also launched a fourth flavor, blueberry, in its Muriel Tipalits line of flavored cigars. In 1969 Consolidated Cigar opened cigar-research facilities at the Glastonbury, Connecticut, facility and an automated cigar-tobacco sheet-manufacturing plant in McAdoo, Pennsylvania. Overseas, Consolidated Cigar expanded five of its cigar manufacturing facilities in Holland and in Belgium.

Bayuk Cigar. Instead of reinvesting cigar product earnings in the cigar business, Bayuk Cigar invested its cash in a portfolio of securities. Apparently Bayuk possessed more confidence in the stock market than in its own management potential or in the future of cigars. Its portfolio held only 8 percent of its stocks in tobacco products.

1970

American Cigar. In 1970 American Cigar again expanded its cigar salesforce and emphasized point-of-purchase display materials in its promotional campaigns to sell cigars.

Culbro. In 1970 Culbro substantially increased its advertising expenditures for its Robert Burns Tiparillo and its White Owl cigars. Culbro also introduced a new product, a "little" cigar which was produced on cigarette-forming machinery, called Tijuana Smalls. General Cigar backed the little cigar product with a million-dollar advertising campaign, and Tijuana Smalls were popular immediately.

Consolidated Cigar Company. Following Culbro's successful introduction of a little cigar, Consolidated Cigar launched Dutch Treats. By year end, both of the little cigars had attained substantial popularity. They were promoted using entertaining television advertisements and were packaged in hard packs, like cigarettes. It was fortunate that "little" cigars appeared to be a growth area for cigars as demand for large cigars deteriorated, because retailers reduced the shelf space they allotted to cigar products.

1971

Culbro. In 1971 Culbro expanded its Philipsburg, Pennsylvania, plant by installing the latest automated cigar-forming equipment. Culbro also constructed a new tobacco warehouse to accommodate its anticipated increased production needs, and increased the prices of its other 10-cent cigars by a penny. When competitors did not follow immediately, price controls trapped Culbro at these higher prices. Until competitors matched Culbro's price increases, it lost substantial market share. When the adjustments finally came, Culbro had been reduced to its pre-1964 sales volume.

American Cigar. Culbro's price increase was followed by American Cigar, which raised prices on some of its 10-cent cigars by a penny in 1971, later in the year.

Consolidated Cigar. Consolidated Cigar also increased the prices of some of its 10-cent cigars by a penny in 1971, later in the year.

Havatampa Cigar. In 1971 Havatampa Cigar allocated $5.5 million to build a new cigar-manufacturing facility to replace its three-building complex. The new building was an integrated plant which would make extensive use of automated handling equipment and an $800,000 climate-control unit.

Bayuk Cigar. Bayuk Cigar did not expand or modernize its cigarmaking capacity in 1971 at all. Instead, it began to seek buyers for some of its cigarmaking assets, and repurchased approximately $200,000 of its capital stock.

1972

R.J. Reynolds and the "Little Cigars" Fad. When a ban was imposed upon *all* radio and television advertising of cigarettes in January 1971, R.J. Reynolds introduced Winchester little cigars using network television messages which looked very similar to its "Marlboro Man" advertisements. The R.J. Reynolds campaign, costing almost $6 million, captured 64 percent of the little-cigar market, but when several smokers who had given up cigarettes began to smoke again (allegedly due to the powerful effects of R.J. Reynolds advertisements), congressional clamor over the little-cigar advertisements pressured R.J. Reynolds to remove its Winchester TV ads and banned all little-cigar advertisements from the national airwaves. Although the ban on the "Winchester Man" hurt R.J. Reynolds, the ban on little-cigar advertisements hurt the cigar companies even more severely.

Culbro's Wilkes-Barre cigar plant was flooded by Hurricane Agnes in 1972, causing a severe labor-shortage problem. The Culbro cigarmaking machinery had to be transferred to another plant not directly affected by the flood and the Wilkes-Barre plant was shut down. Also in 1972, General Cigar closed its Perth Amboy cigar factory, warehouse, and shipping facility, and consolidated cigar operations in the Kingston, Pennsylvania, facility which had been constructed in 1961.

American Cigar. In 1972 American Cigar closed its Connecticut Valley growing facility because growing its own tobacco wrapper leaf was no longer economical.

Consolidated Cigar Company. In 1972 Consolidated Cigar purchased a controlling interest in the Dominican Republic operations of a Cuban manufacturer, Menendez y Garcia, giving Consolidated Cigar the premium brands, H. Upmann, Por Larranaga, and Monte Cristo. This acquisition may have been motivated by the success Culbro had enjoyed in its acquisition of the Gradiaz, Annis Company and of Macanudo-brand cigars.

1973

American Cigar. In 1973 American Cigar closed its Charleston, South Carolina, cigar plant because its operations were no longer economic. Also, American Cigar had sold its Connecticut Valley farms and closed the South Carolina plant. In 1973, American Cigar introduced Deringer's little cigars, with a $500,000 advertising campaign. Little-cigar TV advertisements were banned shortly after the product's introduction.

Consolidated Cigar. In 1973 Gulf + Western Industries acquired Campania Insular Tabacalera, S.A., a producer of premium cigar products. Refugees from Cuba had formed Campania Insular Tabacalera, S.A., in the Canary Islands to manufacture the legendary special high-quality brands Don Diego, Monte Cruz, and Flamenco using smuggled Cuban tobacco seed.

Jno. H. Swisher. In 1973 Jno. H. Swisher converted its lower-priced King Edward cigars to homogenized sheet tobacco ingredients.

1974

Bayuk Cigar. In 1974 Bayuk Cigar ceased its wrapper tobacco growing operations because it had suffered extraordinary operating expenses which increased management's desire to remove more of the company's assets from cigars to invest in the stock market. Bayuk had tried to consolidate its operations by offering some of its cigar plants for sale. It had reduced its inventories, and tried to lower its aggregate plant capacities and working capital requirements as demand for its cigars dwindled. Finally, in 1974, Bayuk Cigar terminated Bandwagon U.S.A., Bayuk's premium company, because it allegedly did not enhance Bayuk Cigar's sales efforts as it had in earlier years.

Culbro. In 1974 the Jamaican operations of Gradiaz, Annis, Ltd., were expanded as Gold Label, Culbro's Tampa cigar brand, introduced new cigar styles. Production of them began in Jamaica as Culbro prepared to phase out the relatively more costly operations within the Florida Gold Label factory.

Consolidated Cigar. In 1974 Consolidated Cigar commercialized its new, highly successful brand, Capitan de Tueros. The cigar was a slender, dark grenadier cigar similar to American Cigar's Antonio y Cleopatra, one of the most widely purchased medium-priced cigars.

American Cigar. In 1974 American Cigar test-marketed a new cigar designed to reduce the disagreeable odors associated with cigar-smoking, which was wrapped in charcoal-impregnated, homogenized leaf. Unfortunately, a cigar that had no smoke had no taste and the new cigar was a failure.

Jno. H. Swisher. In 1974 Swisher suffered a seven-and-one-half-week strike at two of its three cigar plants which caused shortages of King Edward cigars and resulted in many lost sales. Where previously Swisher sales had represented 32 to 40 percent of American Maize-Products' sales volume and 60 to 75 percent of its operating profits, the cigar company represented 22 percent of corporate sales volume and 15 percent of corporate operating profits in 1974. This dramatic change was due in part to lower profits in the cigar operations.

1975

Some changes in merchandising cigars were occurring in 1975 as retail outlets which carried the lower-priced cigars demanded more and more costly incentives to carry these cigars and allocated a shrinking amount of shelf space to them. Tobacconist shops became less important as cigar sales outlets as the major cigar companies enjoyed success in selling cigars through convenience channels. In 1975 cigar distribution companies introduced some premium cigars into the convenience channels accompanied by substantial dealer incentives, and a shelf-space war began in earnest. This time, rather than advertise heavily to counter shrinking demand, cigar-makers began to consolidate their operations in order to become more profitable.

Bayuk Cigar. In 1975 Bayuk Cigar lost a significant amount of money on its securities portfolio investment and offered again to sell some of its cigar plants. The diminished profit margins Bayuk reported were due to high relocating and closing costs resulting from shifting its production between factories and phasing out activities such as growing wrapper tobacco in order to restructure its remaining operations and to be less capital intensive.

Bayuk Cigar reduced its properties from fourteen plants and warehouses in 1968 to five properties in 1975, and donated one of its cigar plants to the city of Philadelphia, thereby lowering the firm's inventorying costs and its break-even point. These changes made operations at Bayuk Cigar slightly more profitable.

Culbro Corporation. By 1975 the former General Cigar Company had diversified into snack foods, proprietary medicines, plastics, other tobacco products, and real-estate investments. Because cigars now comprised only 20 percent of General Cigar's sales by 1975, it changed the corporation's name to the Culbro Corporation. In 1975 Culbro closed the Tampa, Florida, plant of Gradiaz, Annis, Inc., where Gold Label and the legendary handmade luxury line of Macanudo cigars had been produced. Operations were expanded in Jamaica as Macanudo was enthusiastically welcomed by connoisseurs.

In 1975 Culbro acquired the Partagas brand, another high-quality premium cigar name owned by Cuban refugees operating in the West Indies. This acquisition expanded Culbro's participation in the expanding segment of the luxury cigar market. It raised the prices of Robert Burns, White Owl, and other medium-priced brands in popular styles and sizes. Culbro's share of this market had fallen to 19 percent while Consolidated Cigar's share had grown to 24 percent of the cigar units consumed in 1975.

Consolidated Cigar. In 1975 Consolidated Cigar reevaluated its apparent strategy of market-share dominance, reevaluated its cigars investment, and began to consolidate its operations including (1) phasing out unprofitable manufacturing operations while consolidating others; (2) phasing out branch offices to streamline the distribution network; (3) redesigning jobs to make better use of manpower; (4) making some selective price increases; and (5) selling its Canadian subsidiary, H. Simon, to Quebec's McDonald Tobacco Company. Consolidated Cigar also reduced its advertising expenditures and moved out some of its managerial resources as it closed some of its plants and cut back on the investments it had to make in the cigar business. The Scranton, West Pittston, and Philadelphia, Pennsylvania, plants were among those which had been closed.

1976

Jno. H. Swisher. In 1976 Swisher installed new machinery to improve its productivity using homogenized tobacco sheet to produce the higher-priced King Edward cigars. Swisher also inaugurated a new sensory laboratory to enable it to test new products using cigar taste-panel research teams.

Consolidated Cigar. In 1976 Consolidated Cigar Company continued its program of closing marginal plants and distribution centers, introducing improved farming methods and manufacturing processes, and increasing productivity. Marketing funding increased in 1976, as Consolidated Cigar introduced Susan Anton, its new, curvaceous spokesperson for the Muriel cigar brand. The previous spokesperson had been Edie Adams (widow of the well-known cigar afficionado Ernie Kovacs).

American Cigar. In 1976 the American Cigar Company reformulated its Roi-Tan product by changing the Connecticut tobacco wrapper to one from Ecuador. This change and others altered the taste unfavorably and the revision was judged a failure as Roi-Tan began losing its market share.

Bayuk Cigar. In 1976 Bayuk Cigar lost money on both its securities investments and its cigar operations. To cope with these losses, Bayuk Cigar wrote off obsolete equipment and retired idle facilities. It ceased all agricultural operations and reduced tobacco inventories. In 1976 Bayuk leased new, high-speed, homogenized, tobacco-fed cigar-forming machines. Bayuk reformulated its Phillies line to use all homogenized ingredients, yet it raised the price of these cigars successfully, as well. Considerable "dealing" margins encouraged retailers to promote this brand heavily. Bayuk Cigar's maneuver was successful and the Phillies market share increased. Bayuk put the profits it earned on this promotion back into its marketing budget.

1977

Bayuk Cigar. Bayuk continued to dispose of excess assets in 1977 by consolidating cigar manufacture in its Selma and Dothan, Alabama, plants and closing all of its other cigar plants, and Bayuk Cigar also raised the prices of some of its cigar sizes after it had tried, unsuccessfully, to sell its premium Garcia Y Vega brand to U.S. Tobacco Company.

Consolidated Cigar. In 1977 Consolidated Cigar closed its Caguas, Puerto Rico, cigar factory and consolidated operations in its Cayey, Puerto Rico, plant.

Culbro Corporation. The figures released in the 1977 10-K report of the Culbro Corporation implied that $2 to $3 million may have been lost in its General Cigar Company operations in that year, although it reported that its cigar operations were profitable.

Jno. H. Swisher. Swisher Cigar plants were again paralyzed by labor strikes in 1977, but the strikes were settled more quickly this time. In 1977 Jno. H. Swisher and Sons discontinued its farming and tobacco leaf handling operations in West Florida because use of homogenized tobacco wrappers enabled Swisher to dispose of nonessential leaf-growing lands and handling facilities.

1978

Havatampa Cigar. In April 1978, 25 percent of the assets of the Havatampa Cigar Corporation were acquired by Culbro Corporation through a brokerage firm. Havatampa Cigar had manufactured and distributed lower-priced cigars in the southern markets extending to Texas and had been a principal distributor for Jno. H. Swisher and Sons' King Edward-brand cigars. The acquisition of Havatampa by Culbro appeared to be a direct market challenge to Jno. H. Swisher. Culbro was ordered by an antitrust decree to sell the cigar manufacturing arm of the Havatampa Cigar Company but it was permitted to retain the distribution company. In 1978 the former president of the Metropolitan Cigar Company assumed the presidency of the Havatampa Cigar Corporation to apply his fifteen years of marketing experience at Metropolitan Tobacco Company to improve Havatampa Cigar's performance. Havatampa Cigar had promoted the brands of its clients through occasional campaigns. Following the acquisition by Culbro of an interest in Havatampa, it is likely that General Cigar brands would at last be able to penetrate southern markets successfully. Promotional programs following this acquisition were expected to favor General Cigar brands rather than Swisher's brands.

Although cigar sales had been 5 percent lower in 1978 than they were in 1977, cigar producers were optimistic in 1979 about the future of the cigar industry because the postwar baby boom generation was approaching the traditional cigar-smoking age of thirty-five. As these children had reached high-school and college age in the 1970s, beer sales had increased significantly. As this generation aged, it was hoped that demand for cigars would be revitalized by this demographic change.

Analysis of the Cigar Endgame

The Surgeon General's announcements concerning cigarettes and cancer drove 10 million new smokers to try cigars in 1964, but there was great uncertainty regarding how long this new demand would endure. Strategic responses to the new, increased demand for cigars were complicated by the Cuban embargo of the previous year because without Havana tobacco leaf most firms which offered quality cigars would be obliged to make substantial reinvestments in R&D if they wished to remain in the cigar business. In 1964 most firms were investing in new cigar-forming machinery, homogenized-leaf technologies, and new cigar-tobacco reformulations, but industry behavior seemed confused because (1) there were many pockets of demand for cigar products in this industry and (2) producers did not know which market niches would be most successful. Firms were uncertain of consumers' preferences for cigars as they tried to forecast future demand for various cigar products, and consequently firms made very wide product offerings, hoping to blanket demand for cigars.

In this endgame, many small firms which had served only regional markets were squeezed off retailers' shelves, but, because demand declined slowly, there was usually adequate time for firms to arrange nondisruptive exits that paralleled the average life (twenty years) of cigar-machine leasing arrangements.

By 1978, aggregate cigar consumption (including imports) was approaching this century's nadir of 4.6 billion cigars (consumed in 1933). Customers were quite price-sensitive and demand was again inexpansible. Because raw-materials prices have been rising faster than cigar prices, the endgame environment does *not* appear to be favorable in 1978, although some niches within the industry have proved to be favorable for continued competition.

Because different firms served numerous parts of the market within several niches—geographically and in terms of quality—there was no agreement concerning which firms should exit or shut down their excess capacity for various types of cigars. This was particularly so when the major cigar companies were seeking to maximize their market shares instead of profitability. Consequently, the timing of exits was erratic. Also, there were high emotional barriers associated with cigar products for some firms. Even where a cigarmaker may have been able to recover a good proportion of its undepreciated value from a cigar investment, it was reluctant to do so. Conditions in 1964 made exit barriers difficult to surmount in this endgame.

Characteristics

Demand. Cigars were a luxury good and demand for them was price-sensitive, but they were not addictive like cigarettes, hence, their purchase could be postponed.

Product Differentiation. Cigars were available in different sizes, shapes, blends, and brands. Their images were developed through advertisements appealing to quality, enjoyment, or the smoker's sophistication, and product differentiation was very effective.

Markets. In 1964 cigars were mass-marketed through convenience outlets and places of entertainment. Higher-quality cigars were marketed through tobacconists' shops where a larger amount of the service offering came from personal attention and product knowledge than from convenience.

Substitutes. Imported cigars (sold near cost) were direct substitutes for domestically produced cigars. Cigarettes, pipes, or other tobacco products were indirect substitutes for cigar-smoking. Preference among these products was a matter of price and personal taste.

Customer Industries. Cigars were distributed through wholesaling companies which specialized in selling tobacco and candy products to convenience outlets which usually possessed exclusive "regional franchises." There were many such companies dealing with cigar companies.

Supplier Industries. In 1964 most of the major cigarmakers were backward-integrated to produce tobacco leaf, but filler and wrapper leaf could also be purchased in world tobacco markets. Cigar-forming machinery was supplied by one company, but several major cigar companies produced their own machines and developed their own process innovations to supplement their machines.

Manufacturing Technology. There were three processes in use to produce cigars in 1964. The degree of automation involved in each process varied from hand-rolled cigars to relatively fully automated production.

Technological Innovation. Frequently, new products were introduced. An important process change during endgame involved the increasing use of homogenized tobacco leaf for lower-priced products whose costs were rising faster than their prices.

Capital Intensity. Depending upon which technology was to be used, the capital costs of a cigarmaker would be high (fully automated) or quite low (hand-rolled). The automated natural leaf machine had cost $400,000 per unit, but the new generation of fully automated, homogenized leaf machines were ten times more costly, and during the endgame more cigarmakers reformulated cigars to include some homogenized leaf and thereby increased their capital outlays and operating overhead.

Competitive Structure. There were many cigarmakers, but a core of six of them grew to represent over 70 percent of the total market. Each regional market contained several local competitors in addition to twenty or more of the largest national cigar firms. Imported cigars also competed in this market.

Competition was for shelf space, not on the basis of retail price wars. (Dealing activities at the wholesale level were tantamount to price wars.) Advertising was used to compete for ultimate smokers' patronage.

Analysis of Declining Demand for Cigars

Cigarmakers made reinvestments in the cigar industry because they believed that demand for cigars would endure at an improved level. Cigarmakers wanted to believe that demographics would support the demand which the Surgeon General's announcement had already created. The cigar industry also believed that when the baby-boom generation reached the age of thirty-five (around 1983), the consumption of cigars would increase again, (like the earlier revitalization of beer), but the industry overlooked several other reasons why demand for cigars was more likely to recede from the 1964 level to settle at a lower level of consumption. Cigars were, in fact, losing (or never really gained) smokers because (1) life-styles had become more active; by contrast, cigars were traditionally consumed while relaxing; (2) cigars possessed an old-fashioned image; by contrast, cigarettes were associated with youthful "sex-appeal" images in the media; (3) women were historically opposed to smelly cigars whose smoke permeated a house or apartment through the ventilation system, and they loathed the sight of chewed cigar butts in their ashtrays; (4) nonsmokers grew increasingly militant about their comfort in close working quarters and public places; and (5) for health reasons, ex-smokers feared that, even though cigars were not inhaled, they might, with time, also be found to be detrimental to one's health. The baby-boom generation which the cigar industry's assumptions rely upon has been more active and interested in physical fitness than the previous generations had been. Hence, they may not be as interested in cultivating the cigar habit. Also the baby-boom females (52 percent of those babies were female) were less reluctant to restrain their male companions from smoking in their homes, their automobiles, or in public places. Also, the "baby boom's effect on beer" argument, which likened the coming revitalization of the declining cigar industry when this demographic group becomes thirty-five years old to the historic revitalization of the beer industry when they became seventeen to nineteen years of age, overlooked the female consumption of beer which contributed to beer's turnaround. Fewer females may be expected to cultivate the cigar habit.

Two of these reasons were particularly devastating to cigars. The chance that cigar smoking may be found to be carcinogenic looms as a threat over the entire cigar industry. An increasing amount of legislation aimed at limiting the freedoms of smokers in public places—for example, Proposition 5 of California—also reduced the consumption of cigars. No effective means of countering these objections had been found in 1978.

It would be expected that relative uncertainty among the competitors regarding the rate and extent of obsolescence of an endgame product would result in some reinvestments, an erratic pattern in the timing of exits, and general confusion in the industry regarding whether firms should remain invested if so, and how they should participate in the endgame. It was found that although several exits did occur, (1) firms still reinvested in physical assets, advertising, and R&D during the endgame; (2) some firms (like Bayuk) appeared to be both liquidating and reinvesting simultaneously; (3) competition was volatile at the wholesaler level; and (4) cigar companies talked of increasing confidence in the industry's future while they retired their plants and consolidated operations.

It would be expected that price increases would be difficult to sustain in a market where customers were extremely price-sensitive as they were in the lower-priced cigar market. In this endgame small (one-cent) price increases were possible very infrequently and some of the deteriorated demand for cigars may have been in response to price increases after 1970. Even the expensive, high-quality (but lesser-known) cigar brands faced some stickiness in raising prices because bundled, hand-rolled, all-natural cigars readily available from the West Indies or Latin America were almost perfect substitutes for these products if cigars were demanded.

It had been forecast that the presence of pockets of enduring demand within the endgame would encourage firms to remain invested in it. There were such niches in the cases of higher-quality cigars—classes F, G, and H—for which demand increased during the endgame. These niches of the market were heavily populated with small cigar firms, and entry into them was relatively easy in terms of productive assets or regional marketing. Therefore, in the cigars endgame, major cigar firms sought to reposition themselves in order to offer such higher-priced products (if they did not already do so). Hence, although demand for cigars in product classes F, G, and H was growing, and the firms which had produced these products historically remained invested in this business in 1978, it is expected that some of these firms will be squeezed out of the industry by structural changes precipitated by the larger cigar firms.

Analysis of Endgame Industry Traits

It had been predicted that if the endgame environment seemed "favorable," some competitors might reinvest in their businesses in order to serve the niches of enduring demand, to try to revitalize demand for their products (if potential for that were present), and to enjoy good profits. The cigars endgame seemed favorable because there were some niches within the cigar industry and firms believed that demand for cigars would revitalize due to demographic changes in the 1980s.

Product Traits

The cigar was a highly differentiable product. This meant that a competitor could justify offering its cigars in a higher-priced bracket than the product of another firm. It would be expected that there could be room in the cigar market for an almost infinite variety of products because consumption of cigars was determined by personal taste preferences and image maintenance (fashion) considerations. In this endgame the physical constraint upon the number of cigar products which could be offered in a single outlet would be shelf-space limits and inventorying costs. Firms acted as if there were some advantage to maintaining the cigars' differentiated character.

There were several different niches a firm might serve. These niches endured and declined with different speeds. (In some, demand increased.) The endgame was unequally profitable for firms, depending upon which pocket of demand they served.

Customer Traits. It had been expected that in an industry where access to distribution channels was crucial, customer industries would have substantial bargaining power to extract lower prices, promotional supports, or other dealer-incentive devices. In this endgame, both the distribution companies and the retailers extracted such rents from the cigarmakers in exchange for access to shelf space or shelf position. These dealing activities became even more intense when demand for cigars slowed dramatically in the late 1970s. It would also be expected that where access to shelf space is a crucial competitive advantage, firms would integrate downstream to capture this advantage. In this endgame, distribution companies were so important to the cigarmakers that Culbro Corporation acquired Metropolitan Tobacco Company (New York City), two distributors for its New England territories (New York and Massachusetts), and the Havatampa Cigar Corporation (the South) in order to ensure that its products could be given good distribution in its various important retail markets.

It would be expected that when the cigar companies emphasized dealing activities, less market growth could occur. Cigar competitors' expenditures were diverted into price promotions to their wholesalers and retailers in the mid-seventies in this endgame, and expenditures for advertising or other demand creating activities did not occur as frequently as before.

Customer industries of the cigarmakers were not expected to help them to endure in this endgame because wholesalers and retailers were not dependent upon any particular manufacturer for a supply of cigars, and did not find cigars to be high-margin products. Indeed, it was found that retail outlets preferred to minimize their cigar volume if that were possible because they could merchandise alternative products (perhaps with higher turnovers) in the shelf space given to cigar products and generate higher returns by doing so. It would be expected that price increases would be difficult to sustain where customer industries would encounter difficulties in passing on price increases to their customers. Because cigar customers were highly price-sensitive in the lower-priced markets, cigar companies encountered difficulties in keeping their prices at their increased levels after price increases, particularly when greater volumes of cigar merchandise were returned from their retailing customers as being stale and unsalable.

In summary, in this endgame, shelf space wars grew more heated where fewer cigars were being smoked but more cigar products were offered nevertheless. Turnovers on cigar inventories slowed and larger numbers of cigars were returned as being unsalable. (This increased the relative cost of competing against the larger firms.) Retailers and distributors demanded more incentives to perform the same services they had performed in the past.

Supplier Traits. It had been expected that where a good-quality supply of tobacco leaf would be important for the production of high-quality cigars, cigarmakers would backward-integrate into the production of tobacco to ensure that a good supply would be available. Some cigar companies had operated their own tobacco farms during the early part of endgame. However, the use of homogenized tobacco components in making cigars of medium-priced quality and the availability through the tobacco commodities market of acceptable tobaccos which could be obtained without incurring the high overhead charges associated with tobacco plantations discouraged firms from continuing their tobacco farming activities if they served only lower-priced markets.

Technological Characteristics

If a cigarmaker were serving the lower-priced cigar market, the cost of its cigar products would be an important determinant of the firm's profitability because prices for cigars were generally fixed (but subject to some dealing to buy shelf space). Consequently, firms which used more automated manufacturing technologies tended to possess lower operating costs if they could produce at an economic volume. Firms which used these capital-intensive technologies were frequently locked into long-term leases or other obligations which constituted economic exit barriers. For them, the presence of these barriers would inhibit flexibility in responding to declining demand for their cigars.

It had been expected that the labor-intensive (less-automated) cigar technologies would create greater strategic flexibility in this endgame because they would be less difficult to retire. Smaller firms which exited used less labor-intensive assets and possessed equipment leases which expired. The firms which invested in high-speed equipment in the mid-sixties faced relatively higher exit barriers. These were also firms which competed in the lower-priced markets. In order to operate these capital-intensive plants at an economic volume, dealing activities were necessary, thus reinforcing the need to use potentially volatile and unprofitable competitive tactics.

Competitive Characteristics

The inherent differentiability of the physical cigar product enabled many different types of firms to compete in the cigar industry, serving several asymmetrical types of market segments. The segment of the market which was growing (high-quality) was small and had been served by the little firms which had narrow product lines, low-volume requirements, low overhead expenses, and high potential flexibility to maneuver tactically. By contrast, the declining market segments (the high-volume, lower-priced cigars) were characterized by shelf space wars, requiring product proliferation and investments in new technology to lower prices. It was not surprising that high-volume cigar producers switched some of their resources into the high-quality cigars market.

The entry barriers in that market were not high. But once these new competitors had entered, some of the tactics in the high-quality market were changed. The mass-merchandising firms were accustomed to taking high volumes of returns and providing their distributors with incentives for handling a particular cigar brand. Introducing these practices into new outlets had the effect of "raising the stakes of competition" for the smaller firms and it eroded the profit margins of all of the competitors.

Given these asymmetries in cost structure and other strategic posture differences, it is not surprising that wholesaler price levels and retailer prices were volatile, even where prices to the consumer seemed to be steady throughout the endgame. Shelf-space wars grew more heated as cigar product turnovers slowed and higher amounts of cigars were returned as being unsalable in order to finance customers who provided access to shelf space. In this way the environment grew increasingly unfavorable for capital intensive competitors.

Analysis of the Corporate-wide Strategic
Needs of the Cigar Firms

It had been predicted that firms might retain an "important" endgame business longer than a mere economic analysis might suggest was advisable. Hence, the presence of "strategic exit barriers" might influence the timing of firms' exits or the timing of the implementation of tactics designed to reduce firms' investments in the endgame industry. Strategic exit barriers did retard the retirement of some cigar firms' plants and deterred the exit of Bayuk Cigar in this endgame.

Subsequent to the base year of 1964, Consolidated Cigar Company and Jno. H. Swisher & Son were acquired by firms which expected that the demand for cigars would continue to rise or, at worst, might plateau at a higher level of demand. These firms acted as if they expected to acquire cigar companies for the cash-generation powers they seemed to promise. Their lease obligations and goodwill assets were captialized, creating a potential strategic exit barrier for firms concerned about recognizing losses because the cost of exiting soon after this acquisition would be large. In this endgame, an economic exit barrier was created when the book value of a cigar company was recapitalized upon acquisition, which, as had been expected, meant that the depreciation schedule on the higher book valuation began again for the new owner of the business assets and the presence of these undepreciated assets constituted a strategic barrier to exit.

It had been expected that vertical integration linkages could create strategic exit barriers for cigar firms which owned distribution companies specializing in cigar products, or which owned tobacco plantations. As the endgame progressed, however, tobacco farming (backward integration) became less important to some competitors and very frequently was abandoned as being too costly. Cigar distribution companies were operated independently of their cigar suppliers. The effect of these developments was to lower the expected heights of this potential strategic exit barrier with time.

It had been expected that corporations whose names were identified with cigars (American Cigar, Consolidated Cigar Company, Bayuk Cigar, Havatampa Cigar, for example) would face strategic exit barriers. In some cases, the barriers might have been more of a managerial (sentimental) nature than a truly strategic nature because their cigar businesses were no longer a substantial portion of their earnings. But for small firms, strategic exit barriers in this endgame were substantial, and, even for a large company such as Consolidated Cigar Company, the spin-off of the cigar business could be difficult to accomplish if the business were suffering from poor performance.

Strategic exit barriers seemed to be important to most of the other cigar companies because they were essentially single-business companies, and even in the cases of Consolidated Cigar, General Cigar Company, and Jno. H. Swisher, which were owned by large, diversified parent companies, the cigar business was the primary business of their divisions. These firms persisted in believing that demand for cigars would endure and even increase significantly.

Analysis of Endgaming-Firms'
Competitive Strengths

It had been expected that firms which possessed the appropriate competitive strengths would be better-suited to pursue some of the more aggressive strategy options in coping with declining demand. A comparison of the strategic postures of firms in the cigars endgame indicated that different strengths were important in order to serve the varying cigar market segments well. When demand for some types of cigars dwindled, large firms which had served these markets focused their financial strengths, underutilized plants, and other resources upon new markets and competed against each other as well as against the original members of the new strategic group of cigarmakers they invaded by emphasizing some new strengths.

The lower-priced cigarmakers needed production strengths to provide good cigar quality at the lowest acceptable prices such as absolute cost advantages including proprietary processes and machinery designs. Jno. H. Swisher, Consolidated Cigar, and Culbro Corp. possessed resources and strengths in their strategic postures which enabled them to become the most efficient producers of lower-priced cigars. Jno. H. Swisher also possessed the important competitive advantage of effective selling relationships with its distribution channels, which made Swisher's cigars the most widely distributed cigars within their sales territories, although they were not the most widely advertised cigar brands.

Although shelf-space exposure was important in selling large quantities of lower-priced cigars, the procurement of that shelf space could not be considered to be an advantage if the cost of obtaining it were high. For example, after losing money on its portfolio of securities for several years, the Bayuk Cigar Company invested heavily in a packaging deal whereby it gave discounts to retailers for bundling and selling packages of Phillies. Although the packaging deal garnered a 15 percent increase in sales volume, Bayuk Cigar allegedly enjoyed neither high profits nor healthy cash flows from this tactic.

Low labor costs were important in the medium-priced cigar market where natural leaf placements were used for some cigar products because natural leaf was quite fragile to handle. Quality was a more critical consideration in the middle-priced market than in the lower-priced one because customers' expectations were higher. In addition to labor-force skills, access to sources of better tobaccos was important in this market. Distribution channels continued to be important in the medium-priced cigar market because some of the better medium-priced cigars could be sold in both mass markets and selective outlets. Contacts with a wide variety of different types of channels, particularly convenience channels which would handle cigars, became an important advantage.

The most important competitive advantage a firm could possess in serving a premium cigar market was a well-known brand name which carried a recognized reputation of quality. Cigar craftsmen in the tobacco fields and warehouses who purchased, blended, and aged the natural tobaccos used to produce high-priced cigars were another important strength if a cigar firm were to deliver the quality consumers expected.

In summary, production strengths were important in the lower-priced markets, but brand names and product quality were most important in the premium-priced markets. Cigar companies which were supported in their research by corporate parents were in the best position to resuscitate former Cuban brands and to reformulate them in a manner which would retain their reputations of high quality. All of the cigar markets also required production specialists and a good distribution system in order for a firm to be successful.

The lower-priced cigar market where the largest percentage smokers were giving up smoking was not an attractive business, although it represented 49 percent of total cigar consumption in 1977. The companies which performed best in this market segment were companies which could produce an acceptable quality cigar at a low price while still earning their required profit margins and cash flows. Quite frequently, doing this meant investing in very efficient production plants (which might be more risky to erect) or an aggressive marketing program, both tactics which could create high risks if the demand for lower-priced cigars did not endure.

Analysis of Firm's Performances in
the Cigar Endgame

Given the relatively "unfavorable" industry structural traits in most segments of the cigar industry, few reinvestments were expected in this endgame. Given the relatively high percentage of total corporate asset values the cigar business represented for many smaller firms, some competitors were expected to encounter difficulty in overcoming their strategic and emotional exit barriers in eliminating their cigar-production activities. (Despite the relatively high recovery values available for the assets most cigarmakers utilized, the noneconomic exit barriers were stronger and kept many smaller firms in this industry.) Given the differences in firms' strategic postures in this confusing endgame, some firms were expected to exit in an orderly fashion, while others remained to their economic detriment. Some firms in promising market niches would even make reinvestments in order to serve these markets because for them the endgame environment was relatively favorable.

DWG Cigar was the only firm in the cigar business which exited completely from the cigar industry. It is cited as an example of a cigar company (1) whose strategy was not well formulated or well focused and (2) which incurred significant losses when it tried to divest its cigar business. Many smaller, regional firms also exited, but they incurred fewer losses than did the DWG Cigar Corporation. DWG Cigar's strategy was poorly chosen for the particular needs of the firm. DWG Cigar possessed a fragmented distirubtion system, poor advertising economics, and operating diseconomies during the endgame because its plants were not efficient or modern in design. Consequently, DWG Cigar was actually poorly equipped to cope with its investment situation. Although it should have exited from some cigarmaking activities sooner rather than later, DWG was poorly managed and unable to analyze the condition of its cigars investment.

Continued Investment. In general, the large wide-line firms such as Consolidated Cigar or Culbro Corporation were able to close out plants and to discontinue cigar brands which were not performing adequately. They were also able to acquire high-quality cigar brands and to support them with appropriate advertising and promotional attentions.

"Milk the Investment"

Bayuk Cigar. Bayuk Cigar was not expected to perform well during the cigar endgame because its timing seemed to be inappropriate. When other cigar companies were reinvesting in high-speed equipment to produce more cigars, Bayuk's cigar-producing facilities were allowed to become obsolete. When Bayuk did invest in homogenized tobacco-handling equipment, other lower-priced cigar companies had concluded that this market was a disaster. Bayuk stopped its heavy cigar advertising when the other firms increased their advertising budgets, and Bayuk did not update the corporation's plants when work-method improvements were needed to lower costs. Bayuk allegedly tried to sell its only premium cigar brand—the major salvation of the firm's otherwise bleak financial performance—to liquidate its shareholders' investments in the cigar business.

Jno. H. Swisher & Son. Jno. H. Swisher & Son could be predicted to make strong contributions to its parents' corporate requirements because Swisher had established itself successfully in a market which few other firms could serve as well. Jno. H. Swisher made inexpensive but high-quality cigars that were recognized to be good values. Swisher's principal competitive strengths were its selling and distribution contract advantages, its relative operating efficiencies, and the goodwill generated by its popular King Edward cigar. Swisher also possessed operating economies associated with a specialized product line. King Edward, Swisher Sweets, and the other cigars sold by Jno. H. Swisher comprised only eleven varieties of cigars, and enabled the company to limit its inventory costs. Returns were a smaller percentage of sales since the product line was so narrow.

The Swisher strategy was somewhat risky because the cigar firm was not in the medium- or higher-priced cigar markets. It had recently reinvested in some homogenized tobacco-leaf equipment in order to lower operating costs. This recent investment could have constituted an economic exit barrier that would keep the firm in cigar production for several years longer. The Swisher strategy was also risky because it was heavily dependent upon good trade relations with firms like Havatampa Cigar. The effect of the Culbro Corporation's acquisition of Havatampa Cigar Corporation upon Jno. H. Swisher was not clear. The Culbro brands had not achieved intensive coverage in the South as had the Swisher brands. With this change in ownership policy, the strength of the Swisher franchise may have been eroded for the future and its future profitability may have been eroded.

"Hold the Investment Level"

The Tampa Cigarmakers. The Tampa cigarmakers would be expected to perform well in the endgame because they produced the most popular cigars of the late endgame—the high-quality, 100 percent natural ingredient cigars, but few of the Tampa cigarmakers possessed the distribution contacts which would have been needed to cover a national territory (an asset the major cigar firms did possess). Yet while the Tampa premium-cigar manufacturers could not compete against the wholesale distribution channels of the large cigar companies, they earned acceptable returns because they could offer local tobacconists in their regional markets higher margins by dealing directly with them.

The larger, better-known Tampa cigar firms competed with increasing frequency with the higher-quality cigars of Consolidated Cigar, American Cigar, and the Culbro Corporation, among others. Although these Tampa cigar companies were required to take a relatively large number of returns, their lower profit aspirations and other lower performance requirements (due to lower overhead requirements) enabled them to endure and to prosper in a market where the larger, publicly traded companies had to struggle in order to be as profitable.

Havatampa Cigar. The financial performance of Havatampa Cigar Corporation had satisfied the cigar company and several other regional cigar companies (like Jno. H. Swisher & Son) which relied upon Havatampa Cigar for distribution. It is not clear what will become of the cigarmaking assets of two Havatampa cigar brands—Nuggets and Jewels—which were low-priced, mass-produced cigars which were slightly less expensive and of slightly lower quality than King Edward cigars. The past successes in selling these cigars were the result of the aggressive efforts of the Havatampa Cigar distribution company's salesforce. Without a continuing close relationship with that company, the Hav-A-Tampa cigar brand may be less successful in obtaining shelf space.

"Shrink Selectively"

American Cigar. Because American Cigar was a part of the American Tobacco Company, it was a substantial competitor on a national level. American Cigar's reformulated Roi-Tan and LaCorona grenadiers were an unquestioned success. Other American Cigar brands were moving slowly, however.

American Cigar may have retained some of its brands for reasons of sentimentality rather than economics, however. The tobacco products of American Brands represented only 25.9 percent of domestic corporate sales (twenty-two cigarette brands, ten smoking tobaccos, and five cigar brands) and cigars were in fact, a very small portion of this sales volume. The losses incurred by subsidizing these brands may be insubstantial, but although its products were popular, if cigar profits deteriorated more severely after 1978, American Brands could no longer afford to retain some of these brands merely to retain customer goodwill.

Consolidated Cigar Company. Consolidated Cigar Company would be expected to perform well in this endgame because it had repositioned itself earlier, shutting down eight obsolete facilities and adding several new ones dedicated to the production of high-quality, famous-brand cigars to pursue aggressively this lucrative niche. This was important for Consolidated Cigar when operating economies were impossible to achieve using homogenized tobacco technologies in the lower-priced cigar market.

Consolidated Cigar was highly automated and its machinery was newer (less depreciated), making its operating costs lower than those of most other cigar firms which were automated. If improvements in cigar products occurred, they were expected to emanate from Consolidated Cigar because the firm was believed to be enjoying the best performance in the industry.

Consolidated Cigar had consistently spent more on advertising per sales dollar than the industry average. Consolidated Cigar's salesforce, by contrast, was proportionate with its sales volumes, but both were highly efficient. The distribution companies serving Consolidated Cigar emphasized chains in their sales calls to obtain sales-promotion economies.

Consolidated Cigar Company was multinational and it owned foreign subsidiaries which produced premium cigars for the parent firm. In endgame, Consolidated Cigar Company continued to pursue a profitable wideline product strategy while it eliminated unprofitable cigar-related investments and streamlined its cigar operations.

Culbro Corporation. Culbro Corporation experienced some unevenness in its performance because some of its tactics were acts of desperation. Like Consolidated Cigar, Culbro's Cigars covered the entire gamut of product offerings. Culbro had closed as many facilities, purchased similar types of cigar brands, and matched Consolidated Cigar Company in technology improvements and investments in distribution tactics. Culbro had led the invasion into premium cigar brands with the acquisition of the Partagas and later the Macanudo brands.

Culbro was able effectively to lock out many of its competitors from its New York City markets, where its Metropolitan Cigar Company was the dominant distribution company. It built upon this strategy by acquiring an interest in the most effective southern distribution company, Havatampa Cigar. Neither Culbro nor Consolidated Cigar Company had previously been able to penetrate the southern markets effectively. (King Edward enjoyed the largest sales volume of any cigar brand. Jno. H. Swisher had been the dominant cigar company in these southern markets. Its distributor had been Havatampa Cigar Company in the South.) Participation in the ownership of Havatampa Cigar Corporation is expected to help Culbro to achieve better coverage of a growing market where its brands were underrepresented.

The Endgame in the Rayon Industry

"Rayon" is the chemical name for cellulosic (made from wood pulp) fibers. Rayon (viscose process) is also the name of cellulosic fibers which were used for tire-cord fabric; acetate filament, which has less tensile strength, was used only as the woof in weaving textiles. Rayon is used in textile applications, such as apparel and home furnishings, and in nonwoven applications, such as sanitary products. Consumption of rayon has declined in some of these applications due to (1) substitutions by other natural and synthetic fibers and (2) competition from imported fibers. In 1968, the year of the largest volume of shipments in the cellulosic fibers industry, 1,688 million pounds of rayon and acetate were consumed in the United States (including imports).

A Description of the Rayon Industry

The Product

Rayon is a chemically based cellulose fiber whose primary advantage in comparison with natural fibers has been in the uniformity and standardization of the finished product which can be achieved through manufacturing control and self-imposed industry quality standards.

Filament. Rayon can be extruded in long, continuous strands, which can be produced in many different deniers or degrees of fineness, with varying numbers and sizes of filaments, and different degrees of luster and twist. (Denier is a way of expressing comparative weights per common lengths of filament or staple. It is a measure of strand density.)

Filament fiber can be "made to measure" with respect to chemical composition, diameter, length, luster, dye affinity, strength, and extensibility, depending upon the specific application requirement needed. Its quality is determined by the number of knots on a spool of filament yarn and the number of strands is determined by the number of holes in the spinnerette (the device which extrudes the viscose).

High-tenacity Rayon Filament. Industrial-grade rayon filament was particularly strong and was frequently produced in deniers as high as 4,400. (Fine cuprammonium yarns were produced in deniers as low as forty.)

Staple. Rayon staple was composed of short fibers, usually one to eight inches in length, depending on the applications needs. It may be especially prepared for efficient spinning on either the cotton or wool textile systems, and, like filament, staple characteristics could be controlled through the manufacturing process.

High Wet Modulus Rayon Staple. High wet modulus describes the tenacity (strength) and extensibility (stretchability) of a wet piece of rayon fiber. Older rayon had a *low* wet modulus, which means it would rip and shrink when scrubbed or washed. The high wet modulus improvement made rayon staple more like cotton, giving high wet modulus rayon staples high wet strength, low breaking elongation, and high elastic recovery. They also displayed low water absorption properties, good dimensional stability, and could be used for wash-and-wear applications.

Tow. Tow is the coarse and broken fibers of rayon before they are spun into filament or cut into staple for processing. Tow was produced for fabrication into flocking or for cigarette filters using assets which also produced staple.

There were differences between the filament and staple fiber made using the (1) viscose process, (2) acetate process, and (3) cuprammonium process for creating cellulosic fibers which affected the characteristics of the fibers created and determined which markets for man-made fibers a firm might serve. The viscose process yielded a rayon which had chemical properties similar to cotton and was noteworthy for its strength and creping characteristics. Acetate was notable for its softness in feel and superior draping characteristics, and it absorbed less water than rayon yarns produced from the viscose or cuprammonium processes. Cuprammonium rayon looked like viscose rayon; however, finer denier fabrics could be made from cuprammonium rayon because the holes in the spinnerettes used in this process were smaller.

High-tenacity rayon filament consumption peaked in 1949 at 485.0 million pounds and regular rayon filament consumption peaked in 1951 at 270.9 million pounds. Rayon staple was at its highest sales volume in 1968, at 720.0 million pounds.

Markets

Rayon was used in apparel markets, in home furnishings, and in several industrial applications. Rayon staple was used like cotton to weave textiles for apparel including athletic uniforms, children's and women's garments, fake furs, lingerie and underwear, linings, rainwear, robes, sportswear, suits, ties, and work garments. Home furnishings usually had consumed as much as 40 percent of the staple produced in a particular year, and other uses for staple included air hoses, filters, medical products, military uses, non-wovens, stuffed toys, teabags, tents, and sanitary products.

Tow was used for cigarette filters. In nonwoven applications, staple competed against cotton and other man-made fibers. In cigarette filtration, tow competed against paper and tobacco-leaf filters.

Rayon filament was used as textile yarn. Heavy denier, high-tenacity rayon filament was used for tire cord. The principal markets for rayon textile yarn and monofilament in 1968 included apparel (27 percent); linings (14 percent); home furnishings (25 percent); narrow wovens and braided trims (12.5 percent); and other uses (13 percent). Exports consumed 0.8 percent of shipments, while imports comprised 8 percent of rayon yarns consumption.

Historically, the major use for rayon filament had been for tire cord and industrial belting because acetate filament had not proven to be strong enough or well suited to tire-fabric uses. The estimated market for such tire fabric was a substantial amount of the existing rayon-extruding capacity as late as 1964, when the estimated rayon tire-cord consumption of the Big Five original-equipment tire-cord manufacturers had been 220 million pounds per year. The original-equipment market for tire cord represented 150 million pounds; total high-tenacity rayon cord capacity that year was 275 million pounds. But, in 1968, when the Chevrolet automobile division of General Motors Corporation used nylon tires on its new models instead of rayon, the decline of high-tenacity rayon filament production began in earnest. Although tire construction uses of rayon had peaked around 1949 at 485 million pounds, the rayon tire-cord market had been able to make technical advances at the same rate as other tire-cord manufacturers. Removing rayon tires from original-equipment applications would have had the effect of reducing rayon's future expected market for replacement tires as well.

Natural fibers, such as cotton and wool, and noncellulosic fibers, such as nylon and polyester, all competed against rayon but the cellulosic fibers were less expensive and their producers gave fabric companies assistance in running cellulosic fibers on cotton-based assets. In 1968 rayon possessed a 5-to 7-cent price differential advantage over cotton and was at least 25 cents per pound less expensive than polyester in 1968. One of the most significant substitutes for U.S. rayon was competition from overseas plants which possessed lower costs than did the U.S. plants because many American rayon plants had been erected when cellulosic-fibers technology was still embryonic. At that time, engineers guessed what size plant would be most efficient, but Courtaulds, Ltd., of the United Kingdom had erected rayon plants throughout the globe since it first built the American Viscose plants in the 1910s and it had determined that the minimum efficient scale of a rayon plant was about three times larger than the average-sized U.S. rayon plants. Thus foreign competitors' plants were built at these larger scales which gave them a better cost structure even in light of U.S. tariff barriers.

Marketing

Yarn customers, whose needs were routine and steady, sought to exert their bargaining power over rayon producers more frequently than customers in other customer groups because they were purchasing a commodity fiber which they fabricated into quasi-commodity textiles or other woven or knitted products for resale to other manufacturers. These ultimate fashion-apparel customers were least loyal to a particular fabric and could be most responsive to advertising programs designed to increase household demand for a particular fiber or company's fiber. Accordingly, all fiber producers spent some funds on corporate-identity advertising to gain recognition among household customers served by this market. It had been necessary to create new products to catch the next phase of growth in the dynamic fashion business, where products like rayon could not be sold on the basis of price alone. An estimated $15 to $20 million were reinvested annually in such product-development activities by the largest cellulosic fiber companies (approximately 5 percent of sales which had developed products such as Avril® and Tyrex®, which were merchandised under registered trade names.

Fiber was shipped to order from rayon plants as quickly as was possible, from sales offices in New York City (fashion-oriented) or in Ohio (tires oriented). Plants were located near their customers rather than near their raw-materials suppliers in order to provide prompt delivery, and production was usually booked in advance of shipments, although producers maintained emergency stocks to fill some orders immediately. Only when rayon stocks were tight and production was booked several months in advance of delivery could prices be increased.

Historically, rayon producers had offered technical assistance to textile mills to persuade weavers and knitters to convert their looms from cotton, silk, or wool to rayon. Knitting mills were risk averse. They would not produce textiles made from materials such as rayon which they did not understand or accept. Consequently, the companies who hoped to serve the apparel market had to forward integrate to perform all of the fabrication tasks, including selling finished garments to households, if necessary, in order to prove that garments using these fibers *would* be successful.

Although the basic product patents for making rayon had expired long ago, entry into rayon production was infrequent because of the other barriers to entry: high financing obligations to hold inventory for customers rather than producing to order; a quasi-contractual buyer-seller relationship for the nonfashion textile applications; and high R&D investment requirements for the fashion-oriented applications. The R&D entry barriers could be high and improvements upon the basic rayon fiber formulations could be protected by patents and licensed by their creators. The cost of selling rayon to customers in the textile industry was substantially higher than selling rayon yarn to one of the Big Five tire companies. Although the rayon producers could influence many physical attributes of their fibers, such as ease of care, solution-dyes, luster, and tenacity, their customers, the textile mills, were also important in differentiating rayon end products.

Suppliers to the Rayon Industry

The raw materials used to produce rayon were cellulose (high alpha, dissolving wood pulp); caustic soda; carbon disulphide; and sulphuric acid. Some rayon companies were backward-integrated to provide wood pulp; others possessed quasi-contractual arrangements with dissolving-wood-pulp companies. (ITT Rayonier, which was one of the major high-alpha, dissolving-wood-pulp companies, sold pulp on a global basis from several pulp mill locations). The chemicals needed to produce rayon were relatively common and were readily available for use at several locations.

In 1968 only Avtex possessed a captive cellulose supplier (Ketchikan Pulp). The other major domestic producers of high-alpha dissolving pulp for cellulose acetate production were ITT Rayonier, International Paper, Buckeye Cellulose, and Weyhaeuser Company.

The Manufacturing Technology of Rayon

Plant sites were influenced by (1) proximity to an abundant supply of flowing water for effluents; (2) availability of large parcels of land to be used as drainage areas for the acidic effluents from the production process and for the large, sprawling lay-out of the rayon-extrusion plant; (3) proximity to a supply of cheap electricity; (4) availability of a railroad siding, an ample labor force, and favorable freight rates on coal; and (5) relative nearness to rayon markets. The assets used in the intricate cellulosic fiber extrusion processes were capital-intensive and highly specific to cellulosic fiber production. Some interchangeability among staple, tow, and filament equipment was possible.

To produce rayon by the viscose process, purified wood pulp was steeped in a strong caustic-soda solution to convert it to alkali-cellulose, then pressed, shredded into "crumb," and placed in closed containers to age at a constant temperature for about two days. The aged alkali-cellulose was treated with carbon disulphide to form cellulose xanthate, a yellow-orange crumblike substance, which was dissolved in a weak caustic solution which rendred it into a viscous, honey-colored liquid called "viscose," and was filtered several times and ripened for two days under controlled temperatures. During this critical period, timing and temperature limits could not be exceeded because crucial chemical changes occurred in the xanthate. When the desired condition was reached, the solution had to be pumped to the spinning machines and spun, by forcing the viscose solution through fine openings in a nozzle (spinnerette), usually made of a gold-platinum alloy or other precious metal sufficiently resistant to both the xanthate spinning solution and the acid spinning bath. As the strands flowed from the spinnerette, which was submerged in a bath containing sulphuric acid and other chemicals, they coagulated into cellulose filaments.

The strands were wound up as yarn on bobbins or collected as cakes, spun into small centrifugal pots, and purified by washing, desulphurizing, bleaching, and rinsing. Then it was dried, twisted, conditioned, oiled, and wound into cones or skeins for shipment. Viscose staple fiber was made by collecting the continuous filaments and feeding them to a cutter which cut them into fibers of the desired staple length. They were then purified, washed, opened, and baled for shipment.

Capital Costs. The size of the original rayon and acetate plants, which were erected in the 1910s and 1920s, were experimental, but by 1968 it was recognized that a very large rayon plant was needed to enjoy the lowest operating costs, requiring an outlay of from $40 million to over $100 million in the early 1950s. The cost of building a rayon staple plant in the early 1950s was approximately $.040 per annual pound. Thus a 110-million-pound rayon plant would have cost $43 to $44 million. A rayon tire-yarn plant of the same size could have been built for approximately $87 to $88 million, ($0.80 per pound). A rayon textile filament plant would have required $2.00 per annual pound, an investment of $220 million. Substantial advertising and R&D expenditures would have been required to generate the volume needed to keep a rayon plant operating at these economic capacities. Entry into the rayon business with an economically efficient-sized staple plant in 1978 would have required an investment of $165 million, ($1.50 per annual pound), as contrasted with $44 million in the early 1950s.

The assets used to produce textile yarn were not necessarily the same as the assets used to produce tire-cord yarn, and the costs of a filament plant were higher than those of a staple plant because filament plants were more labor-intensive, and the laborers in such yarn plants achieved only relatively low productivities. For example, industry sources estimated that 4,500 people would have been needed to operate a rayon filament plant producing a mixture of 125 million pounds a year. By contrast, a rayon staple plant that could produce 110 million pounds per year would have required only 500 people.

Many rayon plants were smaller than the size which was subsequently found to be a rayon plant's minimum efficient scale of 100 million pounds per year, but by 1968 the rayon plants would have been physically well-depreciated, and the relevant operating costs were those incurred by laborers' wages, chemicals and wood-pulp prices, fuel costs, and pollution-control costs. Rayon plants were both very polluting and energy-intensive, and high wet modulus rayon staple was the most costly in these terms.

In old filament plants, the winding, washing, skeining, and packaging steps of the production had to be done by hand, but newer filament plants were automated. Some rayon plants produced both filament and staple, but on different lines. Rayon extrusion assets could be converted from the production of filament to staple without incurring high switching costs, but the plant would be operating uneconomically, relative to competitors, after conversion. By contrast, capacity which was designed to produce high wet modulus rayon staple could be converted to regular staple production incurring only slightly higher operating costs. Regular staple facilities could be converted to high wet modulus capacity, but to do so was both costly and uneconomical to operate.

Rayon producers of filament moored their lines in concrete slabs which left holes eight feet deep and fourteen feet in diameter. There were few outlets in which to dispose of the assets employed to produce an obsolete rayon product, other than the junkyard. A substantial portion of the value of a rayon plant was in the lead-lined plumbing which connected the many acres of the plant. It was necessary to line with lead all pipes through which the corrosive cellulose xanthate flowed. All transfers of the viscose substance were accomplished by pipeline within the plant. These lead pipes would have had to be torn out from the floor or broken out with a blowtorch in order to recover their value.

A Historical Overview of the U.S. Rayon Industry

Rayon fibers had been "glamour" products in their early years of manufacture. The original rayon company (the American Viscose Company) had increased the value of its stock by 590 percent in its first sixteen years of operation, (approximately 72 percent compounded growth per year) and had achieved aggregate net earnings in the first twenty-four years of operation of 38,000 percent of the original investment (approximately 55 percent compounded growth per year). The original technology employed to produce rayon and acetate was imported from Europe. The first rayon plant was built in Marcus Hook, Pennsylvania, in 1911, by a subsidiary of Courtaulds, Ltd., of London, the American Viscose Company, which constructed seven plants to produce rayon between 1911 and 1940.

E.I. duPont de Nemours, the second-largest early producer of celluosic fibers, imported its rayon technology from the Comptoir des textiles Artificiels of France for a plant operated in 1921 at Buffalo, New York, and from Alsa Societe Anonyme of France for a plant operated in 1929 at Richmond, Virginia.

Industrial Rayon Corporation (IRC) was founded in a joint venture with a subsidiary of Snia Viscosa of Italy in 1920. American Enka was formed as a subsidiary of N.V. Nederlandsche Kunstzijdefabriek "enka" of the Netherlands in 1929.

Beaunit Mills, Inc., merged the interests of American Bemberg (1926), North American Rayon Corp. (1928), and Skenandoa Rayon (1926) into one rayon company in 1949. In 1941 Courtaulds, Ltd., sold its interest in American Viscose and reentered the American market in 1951 by building a large, high-technology rayon staple plant in Alabama.

In 1961 Midland-Ross Corp. purchased Industrial Rayon Corporation (IRC) as a diversification to enter the polyester business. In 1963 the American Viscose Corporation (Avtex) entered into an agreement with FMC Corporation which provided for the sale by American Viscose of all its properties, assets, and business. The reported purchase price of $116 million gave FMC a company whose main products were rayon, acetate, and cellophane. (Avtex assets represented 45.5 percent of FMC's total equity in 1963 after this acquisition.) Rather than enter the consumer chemicals field cold, FMC had sought a partner which possessed the technical know-how to enter synthetic fiber chemicals markets, especially polyester ventures. In 1967 the El Paso Company acquired Beaunit Corp. to enter the polyester industry. By this time Beaunit operated six fiber plants (including polyester and nylon) and twelve fabric mills. In 1963 E.I. duPont de Nemours closed its last rayon tire-cord plant, in Richmond, Virginia, ending duPont's participation in all forms of rayon, but duPont still produced acetate filament in Waynesboro. In 1968 the major remaining producers were Avtex (FMC), American Enka, Courtaulds N.A., Beaunit, and Industrial Rayon Corporation.

Competition in the Rayon Industry

The strategies of the competitors which produced rayon in 1968 differed substantially depending upon whether they were predominantly "chemicals"-oriented or "fibers"-oriented. Although producers of fibers were also chemicals companies, there was a difference in firms' perceptions of the textile industry which suggested whether they essentially viewed their fibers business as a commoditylike product like many other chemical products they produced. The differences between these outlooks contributed to some of the pricing conflicts and misunderstandings which exacerbated competitive rivalry in this industry. For example, the fibers-oriented firms would have been accustomed to lowering prices during an economic or industry downturn in order to fill their plants, but the chemicals-oriented companies would have been more accustomed to (1) posting a general price level which changed infrequently; or (2) raising prices to pass on increases in operating costs, not recognizing competition from other fibers or the need to keep a fiber "in style." Thus FMC Corporation tried first to raise rayon filament prices at a time when a price increase was infeasible, then later to eliminate rayon products which did not behave like chemical, commoditylike products.

Avtex Fibers. In 1968 Avtex Fibers was the American Viscose Division of FMC Corporation, a conglomerate whose principal businesses included machinery, chemicals, and defense plants. FMC's machinery group included equipment for airline service; agricultural and automotive operations; canning and frozen-food processing; packing and packaging machinery; petroleum, water systems, bulk materials handling equipment; and railroad freight cars. FMC's chemicals group included both organic and inorganic chemicals divisions; agricultural insecticides; and the American Viscose Division (45 percent of rayon industry capacity and approximately 31 percent of FMC's corporate assets in 1968), which manufactured rayon filament and staple fiber; acetate yarns; vinyon staple; rayon tire yarn and fabric; cord strappings; cellophane; and microcrystalline cellulose. The FMC chemicals division produced carbon disulfide, caustic soda, and natural soda ash, which were used in the processing of cellulose into rayon and acetate. FMC Corporation also held a 50 percent interest with Georgia-Pacific Corp. in Ketchikan Pulp Co., producer of dissolving wood pulp, and produced the spinnerettes needed for its rayon operations in a plant in Aston, Pennsylvania. Although FMC Corporation was primarily a machinery and chemicals company, Avtex was a significant part of its assets (31 percent) and represented one-third of its sales volume for many years. In 1968 Avtex sales were approximately $413 million of total corporate sales of $1,376.2 million.

Avtex was the original Viscose Company founded by Courtaulds, Ltd., whose patent protection had enabled it to earn profits in excess of its parent's investment in several of its early years of operation. Stock in Avtex was purchased by American investors in 1941 when Courtaulds, Ltd., was forced to sell its subsidiary in order to raise funds for the British war effort. The American Viscose Company did not sell knitted or woven acetate fabrics on a commercial basis, as did Celanese Corp.; however, experimental knitting and weaving of rayon and acetate fabrics were an important part of its R&D activities. Before being acquired by FMC, Avtex had been among the leaders in rayon research and had been a major factor in nylon production (Chemstrand) as a duPont licensee. Avtex had established the brand names Avril and Fibers 40 & 43 for its rayon, and it had achieved customer loyalties by advertising its rayon fibers heavily in the past.

When Avtex Fibers was acquired by FMC Corporation, much of the research which it had done in rayon technology was discontinued in preference for research in other man-made fibers such as polyester. The unit was a poor fit with the other businesses in FMC's chemicals-oriented portfolio because of differing market time perspectives.

When it was a privately held corporation, Avtex's strategy had been (1) technical research to improve manufacturing processes and to reduce production costs; (2) product research to develop new products and to improve existing ones; (3) emphasis on merchandising through a national advertising program and promotion of brand names through retail stores; and (4) furnishing engineering assistance to textile manufacturers with respect to knitting, weaving, finishing, and dyeing rayon and acetate fabrics. American Viscose had also developed several machines for the processing of cellulosic fibers to increase their manufacturing efficiency. Avtex had also been one of the pioneers in developing nonwoven uses for rayon staple. Other major markets included the home-furnishings market and apparel-textiles market. Avtex was also one of the major producers of rayon tire cord in 1968. Its major proprietary product was a fashion fiber called Avril, which was a high wet modulus staple fiber.

Avtex was the largest producer of rayon yarn and monofilament, with 29 percent of industry yarn capacity, and the largest producer of rayon staple, with 51.5 percent of industry staple capacity. Overall, it represented 38 percent of combined fibers capacity. Rayon was produced by Avtex at Lewiston and Meadville, Pennsylvania; Front Royal, Virginia; and Nitro and Parkersburg, West Virginia. Rayon yarn was produced at Lewiston, and staple was manufactured at Nitro. The other rayon plants produced a mixture of yarn and staple products.

American Enka. American Enka had been the founding company for Akzona, a diversified chemicals manufacturer. American Enka was still partially owned (65 percent) by AKZO N.V. of Arnhem, Netherlands, previously Algemene Kunstzijde Unie (AKU), in 1968, and manufactured rayon, nylon, and polyester yarns and fibers for textile and industrial uses. Its major diversification at that time, the Brand-Rex Division, manufactured plastic-coated wire and cables, high-frequency insulation material, and extruded plastic for communications and electronics industries. Corporate sales in 1968 were $238.6 million.

Man-made fibers were American Enka's primary business. Rayon filament was manufactured in plants in Enka, North Carolina, and Lowland, Tennessee, and rayon staple was produced in the Lowland plant. In 1961 American Enka had acquired the Hartford Rayon Company, whose plant in Rocky Hill, Connecticut, produced regular staple rayon and had built additional capacity to produce the fiber in Lowland, Tennessee. Later, it closed the Connecticut plant because it was uneconomic to operate. American Enka's rayon extrusion capacity represented 26 percent of yarn and monofilament industry capacity and 15 percent of staple capacity. Since its entry into staple production in 1955, American Enka had advertised its rayon staple's use in women's apparel as it had advertised the use of Enka rayon tire cord. Although American Enka conducted its own research activities, its affiliation with AKZO N.V. gave it the advantage of research findings from laboratories larger than the small firm could afford alone. American Enka's strategy for rayon fibers was one of high quality, reinforced by advertising which featured each of the different types of fabrics which American Enka manufactured, a policy industry sources suggested emanated from policies of its European parent, AKZO N.V. Rather than lose its high-quality image, it was suggested, AKZO would discontinue a fiber product which was becoming uneconomic to produce.

Courtaulds, Ltd. Courtaulds, Ltd., was a multinational manufacturer of man-made fibers, textiles, plastics, chemicals, steel cords, packaging films, wood pulp, paints, packaging containers, and specialized machinery engineering whose corporate sales in 1968 were 394.3 million pounds sterling.

Courtaulds, Ltd., the dominant man-made cellulosic fibers producer in the United Kingdom, produced rayon staple in a plant in Le Moyne, Alabama, within the Courtaulds North America subsidiary. Since Courtaulds operated 300 plants in the United Kingdom and seventy factories overseas, the rayon plant in Alabama was important not so much for its economic performance as for its strategic position within the large U.S. market. Courtaulds, Ltd., was backward-integrated to the production of chemicals and wood pulp and downstream to the production of textiles.

The Courtaulds North America rayon staple plant, which was constructed in 1952, represented 26 percent of U.S. rayon staple capacity and incorporated technology improvements developed since the Courtaulds group had constructed the original Viscose Company plants in Pennsylvania, in 1910 and 1917. These improvements made Courtaulds the lowest-cost producer of rayon staple in the United States. Moreover, its multinational marketing linkages enabled it to face the market for its rayon staple differently than did the other U.S. rayon firms. Courtaulds, Ltd., was a centralized operating company which coordinated the activities of its many factories on a global scale. It had operated textile mills and garment factories in order to create markets for its fibers; it grew spruce trees to provide the high-alpha dissolving wood pulp needed to produce cellulosic fibers, and applied technological improvements in its works method and new plant sites.

There did not seem to be many reasons in 1968 for Courtaulds to wish to exit from rayon production in the United States. Courtaulds produced only rayon staple, not tire cord. It had installed capacity for high wet modulus staple production, its fuel contracts were favorable, and its plant was energy efficient. The United States was a vast, lucrative market for cellulosic fibers, and operating in Alabama put Courtaulds behind the tariff walls of the United States. Its plants could be operated full out because its cost efficiency enabled Courtaulds to price approximately 5 percent below American Enka, when necessary, without damaging its performance goals.

Beaunit Corporation. In 1968 Beaunit was a part of the El Paso Company, a conglomerate whose subsidiaries had businesses in petrochemicals, plastics, fibers, textiles, agricultural chemicals, wire fabrication, oil and gas production, mining, and the utilization of nuclear explosives for industrial purposes. Rayon tire yarn and textile filament were produced in the Beaunit subsidiary of the El Paso Company, which had been acquired in 1967 for 34.4 percent of Beaunit's stock value at approximately $27.6 million. This investment was approximately 7.8 percent of the El Paso Company's total interests. Total corporate sales were $821.0 million in 1968.

The Beaunit Company's business in 1968 consisted principally of the Fibers Division, which produced rayon, polyester, and nylon at six plants, and the Textile Division, which produced fabrics for clothing, home furnishings, and industrial products, at twelve plant locations. Many of Beaunit's plants had been the assets of defunct rayon companies; consequently, Beaunit Corporation possessed no particular operating cost advantages. It did not perform a notable amount of product or process research, and it marketed its fibers as if they were commodities.

Beaunit produced rayon tire cord and tow at Childersburg, Alabama, and Elizabethton, Tennessee. The Childersburg rayon plant also possessed capacity to produce 20 million pounds of wet modulus rayon staple. Beaunit produced regular tenacity rayon filament at Utica, New York, and at the American Bemberg plant in Elizabethton, Tennessee. (The Bemberg plant was the only U.S. rayon plant which used the very expensive cuprammonium process to produce fine, silklike fabrics.) In addition to Beaugrip tire cord, Beaunit produced nylon and polyester tire cord, and also polypropylene fibers which were used for upholstery in automobiles in 1968. Beaunit's position in the home-furnishings and apparel markets was not as strong as other rayon producers who emphasized those markets, and Beaunit's small high wet modulus rayon staple output limited its power as a significant staple producer.

Midland-Ross Corporation (Industrial Rayon Corporation). Midland-Ross was a Cleveland-based manufacturing concern whose most important product lines were power-brake systems for trucks, buses, and automobiles; industrial furnaces and heat-treating equipment; automobile, truck, and bus frames; and rayon and polyester tire yarn, cord, and fabric. Corporate sales in 1968 were $323.7 million, of which the Industrial Rayon Company represented 30 percent.

Industrial Rayon Company (IRC) was one of the four major U.S. manufacturers of Tyrex rayon tire yarn; its yarn capacity was 17 percent of industry capacity. Although IRC had operated three rayon plants during the 1930s, it operated only one plant, located in Painesville, Ohio, which produced rayon yarn, monofilament, and high wet modulus rayon staple in 1968.

Although IRC maintained a rayon research facility in Cleveland after merging with the Midland-Ross Company, it was acquired as an entree into the production of polyester. IRC had devoted 57 percent of its plant capacity to high-tenacity tire yarn, cord, and cord fabric. Its mechanized, continuous process technology had been well suited to the manufacture of tire yarn, and because IRC had been one of the first rayon producers to develop an integrated system for twisting, processing, and weaving cord into tire fabric, IRC's operating costs had been low. The Industrial Rayon Company had been quite profitable when rayon filament was an important product for producing tire carcasses. But IRC had been the most conservative member in the adoption of Tyrex tire cord products, and its addition of high wet modulus staple capacity was viewed by some observers as being an effort by IRC, a firm which never marketed regular staple, to avoid being too late in participating in the next profitable rayon product.

Corporate Strategy Exit Barriers

Strategic exit barriers would be highest for firms which had acquired rayon operations relatively recently before their investments went sour. Given the higher bases at which these firms would have valued their cellulosic fibers investment, failure to recover a substantial percentage of recent book values would constitute a reporting loss which could seem devastating on firms' financial statements, particularly where the cellulosic fibers business' sales had been large in proportion to other categories of corporate sales. New acquired cellulosic fiber subsidiaries were frequently valued at a higher accounting value than the book values they had previously carried in many of the acquisitions reported above. Unless firms' fiber subsidiaries could be spun off intact to new owners who would value these fiber businesses for their earnings potential, there could be exit barriers caused by firms' reporting goals when these firms failed to recover the book value of their investments when they tried to divest their endgame business unit.

For some companies which were backward- or forward-integrated divestiture of their rayon business would not be economically advisable even where they have earned low rates of return because their cellulosic fibers business provided them with an internal market for chemicals or wood pulp. In order to dis-integrate these operations, time would be needed to cultivate strong external alternative markets before changes in the status of a firm's cellulosic fibers business could occur. Thus, strategic linkages whereby business units inside a company interacted in a buyer-seller relationship could influence the timing of a divestiture decision or could constitute a substantial reporting loss on disposal of the cellulosic fibers investment. Hence, these cellulosic businesses were more likely to be retained rather than eliminated.

Where the U.S. cellulosics business was a part of a global network of fibers investments, or was a part of vertically integrated system, it would be expected that strategic exit barriers would also be substantial. In the situation where a rayon plant has linked operations on several continents, the benefit of having these linkages may perhaps offset the below-average performance of the cellulosic fibers unit when measured alone. Multinational linkages could keep a firm invested in the United States (and keep foreign subsidiaries operating) longer than an independent economic analysis might suggest. For example, if overseas units relied upon a U.S. subsidiary to act as a market for its output, an exit barrier might be created, hindering a firm from spinning off or shutting down its cellulosic operations. Thus multinational linkages could act as strategic exit barriers rather than as inducements to exit.

Summary of Competitors' Profiles

Cellulosic fiber producers, in general, produced both staple and filament. All of the cellulosic-fibers producers also manufactured some substitute fibers, usually nylon or polyester. Some companies offered substitute fibers which directly cannibalized their rayon fiber sales. Few companies advertised their rayon fibers separately from their other fiber products.

There was no strong pattern regarding upstream or downstream integration, except that highly vertically integrated companies also tended to invest relatively larger amounts in product or process research. Rayon companies could be backward- and forward-integrated. Some producers of rayon were not vertically integrated at all.

The age of the rayon plant provided an estimate regarding the relative cost position of a particular competitor. Where a cellulosic fiber plant was old and little R&D had been devoted to process improvements, the plant was more likely to have relatively high operating costs than if the plant were new and the firm's policies devoted research investments to process improvements in cellulosic fibers operations. Some old plants had been kept efficient through renovations and new, automated handling systems. The patented or trade-named fibers were more likely to justify higher prices which made them more profitable to their respective firms.

In 1968 Courtaulds relied more heavily on its woven textile markets than on markets for knitted textiles. Other firms, such as American Enka (37 percent), Beaunit (40 percent), or Industrial Rayon Corporation 57 percent), carried a substantial proportion of their capacity in high-tenacity rayon tire-cord yarn. Tire cord appeared to be the fiber form that was most severely declining.

A Mapping of Strategic Groups in the Rayon Industry

Important dimensions of the strategic postures of firms in the rayon industry were (1) the type of markets they served; (2) the relative amount of R&D devoted to cellulosic fibers; (3) the relative importance of the cellulosic fibers business to the firm; (4) the extent to which a firm was backward- or forward-integrated; and (5) whether the firm produced staple or filament fibers. Competitors could be grouped according to these dimensions in order to isolate strategic differences within the industry.

	Industrial Markets	Textile (Commodity Traits)	Textile (Fashion Apparel)
Cellulosic Fibers Relatively Important in Corporate Product Mix	(American Enka) Industrial Rayon Corporation (Tire Cord)	Avtex Fibers (Wide Product) Coutaulds (Staple Only)	American Enka (Rayon Only)
Cellulosic Fibers Relatively Unimportant in Corporate Product Mix		Beaunit (Tire Cord and Textile Filament)	

Along these axes, the firms most strongly identified with a particular characteristic are positioned at the extremes of the "strategic space" shown above. For example, Industrial Rayon Corp. (tire cord) was most strongly identified with industrial markets. Although Avtex Fibers competed with all other firms in some markets, competitors of Avtex did not serve exactly the same markets as did Avtex. For example, American Enka served the higher-quality market for staple. Beaunit served high-quality textile markets which sought cuprammonium denier (fine) filaments. But as the demand for different types of fibers declined, the remaining competitors were forced to compete with new rivals within the rayon markets.

Firms differed in terms of the importance to them of their cellulosic fiber businesses. The missions these businesses were to accomplish for different firms were not alike. Cellulosic fibers were considered glamorous or were "pet" projects in some companies. They were being treated like cash sources in other firms. Frequently, firms acquired cellulosic fibers businesses in order to enter other synthetic fibers businesses. Their strategic outlooks for cellulosic fibers were not necessarily long term. These firms competed in endgame against the other group of firms for whom cellulosic fibers were important.

In summary, there was strong competition to rayon fibers from substitute, noncellulosic fibers which tended to erode the potential benefits of the existing competitive structure. The five rayon firms each tried to create niches where they could satisfy pockets of demand without encountering volatile competition. The competitors' own cost structures, their asymmetric perceptions of this industry, and the ease with which substitute fibers replaced cellulosic fibers militated against success for them with respect to their nonaggressive strategic posturing tactics.

The Endgame in the Rayon Industry

The most important competition to cellulosic fibers after 1968 came from polyester fibers. Frequent quality improvements in fiber durability and washability made polyester a better value than rayon for some uses. Table 9-1 details shipments of rayon from 1955 to 1978.

As consumption declined, the most important changes in rayon products included (1) new improved performance high wet modulus rayons, particularly with respect to high degrees of crimp and twist; (2) more versatile acetylated rayons; (3) cross-linked rayons with better retention of strength, abrasion resistance, and enhanced launderability; and (4) ultra high strength modulus rayons with better toughness and adhesion for tire cord. Firms also created trade names for their high wet modulus rayon fibers, which enabled them to avoid the head-to-head competition which was typical of the commoditylike fibers. The ability to impart physical differences to their rayon products enabled these firms to charge slightly higher prices for some of their proprietary rayon products in the years which followed.

A Chronological Description of the Rayon Endgame

1969

Industrial Rayon Corporation. In October 1969 American Cyanamid purchased the assets of Industrial Rayon Corporation from Midland-Ross Corporation because American Cyanamid was reportedly interested in expanding its capacity to manufacture industrial fibers, such as polyester.

Courtaulds N.A. FMC had earned a return of more than double its investment since it had acquired Avtex in 1963. But in 1969 FMC Corporation lost money on its Avtex Fibers business for the first time. In an effort to turn around the Avtex Fibers Division, FMC announced that it would expand its rayon staple capacity at three staple plants: by 30 million pounds at Nitro, W. Virginia; 50 million pounds at Parkersburg, Virginia; and 50 million pounds at Front Royal, Virginia. But FMC also raised the price of its rayon fiber by 2 cents per pound.

American Enka. In October 1969 American Enka and Industrial Rayon Corporation also raised their rayon prices (2 cents a pound), citing rising wood-pulp and chemical prices as reasons for the increase.

1970

New Bedford Rayon Yarn Company. In September 1970 the New Bedford Rayon Yarn Company, a producer of 6 million pounds a year of regular-tenacity rayon filament, went out of business because it was too small to be economic in competing against larger rayon firms and other filament companies.

Beaunit Corporation. In December 1970 Beaunit Corporation announced the suspension of operations at Beaunit's unprofitable American Bemberg rayon plant in Elizabethton, Tennessee, which produced 35 million pounds a year of rayon using the cuprammonium process. The write-down totaled $2,591,000 even after the assets were sold to an entrepreneur, and other shutdown-related costs totaled $2,818,000.

Table 9-1
Manufacturers' Capacities and Shipments of Rayon Fibers
(millions of pounds)

| Year | Yarn and Monofilament | | | | Staple and Tow | | | Total Rayon Consumption (Including Imports) |
	High Tenacity	Regular Tenacity	Acetate	Imports	All Rayon	Acetate	Imports	
Manufacturers' Shipments of Rayon								
1955	429.6	205.3	220.5	2.3	332.0	57.4	172.0	1251.1
1956	357.5	183.3	184.6	1.6	329.5	52.5	91.8	1200.8
1957	324.0	157.6	203.1	1.1	354.4	53.2	83.6	1177.0
1958	266.2	155.9	220.7	0.7	328.3	72.0	83.4	1127.4
1959	322.5	177.2	220.7	1.8	348.1	67.0	115.1	1252.4
1960	258.7	143.1	220.6	2.5	314.4	57.0	59.1	1055.4
1961	235.9	149.3	240.8	1.8	411.8	51.4	37.0	1128.0
1962	242.7	141.9	281.7	2.6	499.2	44.4	50.9	1263.4
1963	229.7	151.0	305.0	1.7	578.8	57.5	116.5	1440.2
1964	247.1	152.5	363.8	5.2	575.7	57.5	114.5	1516.3
1965	242.6	166.7	366.4	6.8	636.3	54.4	77.2	1550.4
1966	224.5	165.1	387.5	3.7	636.5	59.0	114.8	1591.1
1967	163.3	147.8	421.0	7.7	625.9	49.5	85.0	1500.2
1968	188.6	164.9	426.4	14.6	720.0	48.5	125.0	1688.0
1969	—[a]	294.7	444.7	4.1	737.9	42.3	91.2	1614.9
1970	—[a]	251.1	444.8	3.7	599.9	34.3	80.6	1414.4
1971	—[a]	297.0	432.3	5.2	643.6	26.2	81.3	1485.6
1972	—[a]	246.9	385.9	10.8	690.7	27.7	51.3	1413.3
1973	—[a]	197.6	392.3	18.1	709.5	25.0	25.0	1389.9
1974	—[a]	153.1	320.3	9.2	569.5	19.7	38.7	1110.5
1975	—[a]	74.9	293.7	9.2	373.4	12.0	37.9	801.1
1976	—[a]	65.1	249.4	25.1	461.0	11.0	43.2	854.8
1977	—[a]	68.1	259.4	23.9	444.9	8.0	57.9	862.2

Table 9-1 *(continued)*

Manufacturers' Capacities

1961	314.0	160.0	n.a.	n.a.	538.0	n.a.
1962	314.0	165.0	n.a.	n.a.	557.0	n.a.
1963	251.0	178.0	n.a.	n.a.	635.0	n.a.
1965	271.0	174.0	n.a.	n.a.	800.0	n.a.
1966	274.0	174.0	n.a.	n.a.	815.0	n.a.
1975	—[a]	100.0	384.0	n.a.	737.0	28.0
1976	—[a]	85.0	399.0	n.a.	691.0	18.0
1977	—[a]	85.0	315.0	n.a.	655.0	8.0
1978	—[a]	85.0	318.0	n.a.	650.0	8.0

Source: Annual statistics reported in *Textile Organon*, (New York: Textile Economics Bureau, 1977). Reprinted with permission.

[a]High-tenacity yarn production reported with regular-tenacity rayon monofiliment)

1971

Beaunit Corporation. In March 1971 Beaunit announced that the Utica, New York, rayon plant which produced 15 million pounds a year of regular-tenacity yarn would be shut down. Beaunit took a write-down on Utica of $15,615,000 (less a deferred tax credit of $7,827,000) which represented a charge of $7,788,000 after taxes. El Paso Company, Beaunit's parent, was able to sell the building for other industrial purposes. The productive assets were hauled away by a junk dealer for the value of the equipment. The total estimated costs of closing down the Utica and Elizabethton plants were estimated to be $10.2 million.

In June 1971 Beaunit closed its 54 million pounds a year rayon plant in Childersburg, Alabama, which had produced regular and high-tenacity filament, high wet modulus staple, and tow. The Childersburg rayon plant assets were appraised by several potential buyers, but nobody purchased them. Among the companies who considered operating this plant was ITT Rayonier (a pulp supplier) which had hoped to be able to reassure customers of rayon by keeping rayon capacity in operation.

Avtex. In June 1971 Avtex raised the price of rayon staple (2 cents a pound) and filament (3 cents a pound), and the price increases were matched by competitors. In that same year, "significant sums" were appropriated by FMC to correct air and pollution problems at the older Avtex rayon plants where the effluent was highly corrosive and the smell was quite unpleasant.

Courtaulds. In March 1971 the production of rayon staple at the 230 million pounds a year Courtaulds N.A. Le Moynes, Alabama, plant was disrupted due to a major fire. The cost of the fire was not disclosed.

1972

Industrial Rayon Corporation. In July 1972 American Cyanamid announced that it would discontinue the production of rayon filament and staple at its Painesville, Ohio, plant. The shutdown left three producers of rayon tire cord to serve an annual demand of 125 million pounds a year. The costs associated with discontinuing the IRC rayon investment were reported as being "minor" by American Cyanamid. FMC bought the rayon staple-producing assets of IRC when American Cyanamid closed down its rayon business because IRC had installed capacity to produce 20 million pounds a year of high wet modulus rayon staple. But Avtex found IRC's "modernized" equipment to be in very bad shape and less valuable than Avtex had expected it to be.

Avtex (FMC Corporation). In 1971 Avtex closed its 45 million pounds a year Lewiston, Pennsylvania, rayon filament plant due to damage from tropical storm Agnes by donating the rayon plant to the community and taking a tax write-off against this donation, the amount of which is not known due to its combination with other credits. The shutdown of Lewiston's tire-yarn capacity alarmed some manufacturers of rayon-belted tires who negotiated take-or-pay contracts containing cost escalator clauses to ensure that adequate tire-yarn rayon would remain available to them. Avtex Fibers raised rayon staple prices by 1 cent a pound and tow prices by 1.5 cents a pound. At this time, the cost of cotton, a substitute for rayon staple, had increased substantially.

1973

Avtex (FMC Corporation). In March 1973 Avtex announced that it would increase the rayon staple capacity of its Front Royal, Virginia plant by 28 million pounds a year. In 1973 the 160 million pounds a year Front Royal facility produced rayon staple and tire yarn, Avlin polyester, and a preblended polyester-rayon staple mixture.

In 1973 FMC again allocated expenditures for pollution-control equipment to Avtex to meet the more stringent air- and water-pollution requirements of federal and state agencies. Over $81 million was spent for pollution control at Nitro, West Virginia, to meet pollution-control requirements and to return the staple line there to a viable and profitable position.

Beaunit Corporation. In 1973 Beaunit Corporation began a modest expansion of capacity at its remaining rayon filament plant in Elizabethton, Tennessee. Work stoppages in May 1974 and raw materials shortages prevented Beaunit from producing a new industrial yarn, Beaugrip II, in the quantity demanded.

1974

Avtex (FMC Corporation). In February 1974, Avtex Fibers increased the price of its rayon staple products by 7 cents a pound.

American Enka. In February 1974 Ameican Enka raised the prices of its regular rayon staple (7 cents a pound) and its high wet modulus staple (also 7 cents a pound). In July American Enka raised its rayon staple prices again (3 cents a pound). Staple prices increased successfully because the nonwoven market for rayon staple was competing with the apparel market for rayon fibers.

Avtex (FMC Corporation). In July 1974 Avtex discontinued the production of rayon textile filament and decreased its production of rayon tire cord. This move left major firms such as Burlington House, which had been using millions of pounds of filament a year, without a vendor. In July 1974 FMC phased out production of rayon filament at its Parkersburg, West Virginia, plant. This reduction represented 25 percent of U.S. rayon industry capacity, approximately 20 million pounds a year of potential rayon yarn production capacity, resulting in a charge of approximately $5,450,000 ($2,834,000 after tax).

Avtex held take-or-pay contracts with tire manufacturers which it had negotiated earlier. In order to execute these contracts after the Parkersburg filament line was shut down, Avtex produced more rayon filament at the Front Royal, Virginia, plant. This expansion required a $3.5 million zinc recovery system and a wastewater treatment facility. In October 1974 the Parkersburg, West Virginia, rayon plant of the American Viscose Division of FMC was closed completely. Although Avtex had announced in July 1974 a phase-out of only the rayon filament production there, the 1974 fiber recession and high reinvestment costs, which appeared to be unjustified, hastened its decision to close Avtex's oldest and least efficient rayon staple operation. Seventy-five percent of the Parkersburg output had been rayon staple.

American Enka. In July 1974 American Enka announced a phase-out of filament production at its Lowland, Tennessee, rayon plant and a 10 million pounds a year expansion of filament capacity to a total of 60 million pounds a year at its Enka, North Carolina, plant. Although reserves had been established by American Enka in the 1940s for the contingency that the rayon filament plant would have to be shut down, they still reported a writedown of $4.6 million in converting the plant and compensating employees.

After FMC had closed the Parkersburg plant, American Enka announced that it would convert filament capacity at Lowland, Tennessee, to staple production instead. By mid-1976 Enka predicted that its staple-producing capacity would be 140 million pounds a year at the Lowland plant.

Beaunit Corporation. In 1974 Beaunit introduced a new rayon matte jersey made from Beaunit rayon yarn and Chinon, a Japanese protein fiber with silk qualities, for which Beaunit was the sole U.S. distributor. The new specialty textile was well received by the fashion-apparel market.

1975

American Enka. In March 1975 American Enka announced the closing of its forty-six-year-old Enka, North Carolina, rayon filament plant, the first plant ever operated in the United States by American Enka. Modernization efforts to improve its efficiency had been underway; however, increases in costs of raw materials and energy resulted in rayon filament being priced out of the market. (The Enka plant had a pretax loss of $4 million in 1974 and was reported to be losing about $900,000 per month in 1975.) It was anticipated that pretax charges of $10.5 million would be required for American Enka to write off the remaining fixed assets and cover other costs associated with this shutdown. American Enka would have been required to spend between $8 and $10 million over the next two years to bring the plant into compliance with state and federal pollution-control requirements.

Avtex Fibers (FMC). By mid-1975 it was becoming evident that optimism regarding the future of rayon which had prompted many firms to invest in pollution-control devices and new product investments was unfounded. FMC lost a total of $45 million before taxes and corporate overhead in 1974 and 1975 on sales of $853 million in its Avtex Fiber Division and announced that it would sell the Fiber Division (book value $120 million) as a part of its continuing program to redeploy its assets to more attractive business areas, and to improve its financial position. At this time, Avtex's capacity represented 55 percent of the rayon staple market and its book value represented 14.5 percent of FMC Corporation's total equity.

Courtaulds N.A. and American Enka. Customers which had been using rayon fibers panicked at the FMC Corporation announcement. If no purchaser's for the huge rayon company could be found, over half of the U.S. industry's rayon staple capacity would be eliminated. That abandonment would probably erode much of the remaining confidence customers had in using rayon fibers.

Following FMC's announcement, Courtaulds North America and the American Enka Company indicated that they would consider increasing their production of rayon staple to maintain customer confidence in the future of rayon and to stave off customer switches to other fibers. At this time, American Enka's capacity was 100 million pounds a year. Courtauld's capacity was 225 million pounds a year. Both firms also offered to buy pieces of the Avtex rayon assets.

Avtex. FMC Corporation was determined to sell the Avtex unit in one piece, as an operating unit, rather than break the company into several plants. Avtex's annual sales volume was over $300 million and industry observers believed a quick sale of such a large unit would be unlikely. Nevertheless, personnel changes and preparations for a sale proceeded.

1976

The market for rayon was very poor in early 1976. Rayon plants operated at less than 45 percent of capacity for several months because the cost of cotton and polyester had fallen very low while rayon prices had continued to rise.

Avtex (FMC Corporation). In April 1976 Avtex announced the results of its product research, a new fiber called Avril II. The new rayon staple was a variation of Avril I, but it was not intended to replace the original high wet modulus fiber. The two fibers were priced identically and used for different types of apparel. Two months later, FMC Corporation sold Avtex to a group of former employees of the Avtex Division. Loans were secured by the division's plants and equipment. Its receivables were factored and trade credit was extended from suppliers. Aetna Business Credit, Inc., provided a ten-year, $15 million loan on Avtex's physical assets, at five points above the prime rate. Walter Heller & Co. agreed to advance up to $25 million against receivables, and ITT Rayonier, Inc., offered Avtex Fibers extended credit for purchase of high-alpha dissolving wood pulp. The sale price was $47 million (on FMC Corporation's book valuation of $120 million), and FMC Corporation recognized a write-off loss of $47.5 million ($25 million after tax). Avtex plants were operating at less than 50 percent capacity when the company was sold.

FMC sold its captive supplier of wood pulp, Ketchikan Pulp Company, separately. Its sales were badly eroded by a depressed housing industry, a steep decline in the high-alpha dissolving wood pulp demanded by U.S. and Latin American rayon and cellophane producers, and due to the $32 million waste-water facilities required by the Environmental Protection Agency for the Alaska plant. The net loss from these discontinued operations was reported at $34.3 million, but the sale generated $105 million in cash.

Beaunit Corporation. The El Paso Company was required by the EPA to install $1.8 million in additional pollution-control equipment at its Elizabethton, Tennessee, rayon filament plant by spring 1977. But late in 1976 the El Paso Company announced that it had entered into an agreement to sell the Beaunit Corporation to members of Beaunit's top management team. The sale resulted in a onetime after-tax charge of $53.7 million (a pretax loss of $92.6 million). Beaunit had lost money for six of the eight years it had been operated and the investments for pollution control were only one of several expenditures El Paso Company had made to turn it around. Consequently it sold Beaunit for $35 million, of which $13 million was in subordinated notes and the balance was payable primarily through the assumption of Beaunit's liabilities by the new corporation.

The condition of the 1928-vintage Beaunit plant was not encouraging because in addition to a strong labor union which was adverse to layoffs due to higher productivity, the Beaunit rayon plant possessed productivity problems. Despite investments in time-motion methods studies, incentive programs, and consultants, productivity had not been increased significantly.

1977

The sales of Avtex and Beaunit alarmed rayon customers who had relied upon these firms for their rayon needs, and American Enka and Courtaulds N.A. received a substantial portion of the patronage of these customers, some of whom remained with their new vendors, even after the spun off companies survived their initial months of divestiture.

Avtex Fibers. By March 1977 Avtex Fibers announced that it had regained approximately 56 percent of the U.S. rayon staple market (particularly important to Avtex were sales of high wet modulus rayon staple) and that its plants were operating at 85 percent of capacity. Among the customers who had helped Avtex during this crucial period were Proctor & Gamble, Johnson & Johnson, Playtex, Scott, and Kendall in the nonwovens market; B.F. Goodrich and Gates Rubber in the industrial filament market; and J.P. Stevens and M. Loewenstein & Sons in the textiles market. Some of these customers placed more orders with Avtex Fibers than they had done previously while other firms worked with Avtex's research laboratory to develop proprietary products which used rayon.

Previously, rayon companies had been willing to hold fiber inventories in order to give customers rapid delivery services, but Avtex Fibers now refused to carry more than a minimum of fiber inventories. (In effect, it declined to finance its customers.) The reluctance of Avtex Fibers to carry inventory for its customers hurt it during its crucial transition period. By March 1977 its reliance upon the volatile fashion-apparel market had increased, but it also announced that it had increased the price of its rayon staple again by 3 cents a pound and would not raise prices higher than that level for six months to give its customers price stability.

American Enka. Shortly after the Avtex Fibers price increase, American Enka announced that it was also raising the prices of its rayons by 3 cents a pound.

ITT Rayonier. In April 1977 ITT Rayonier, which operated a 250,000 ton a year high-alpha dissolving-wood-pulp plant in Jessup, Georgia, announced a new technology for cellulose solvents used in making rayon, and offered to license users of this process. Use of this new technology could enable rayon-spinners to impart any characteristics desired to the rayon fiber and could radically change the production process of rayons, making a new rayon plant potentially more profitable than a depreciated one.

Also in 1977, ITT Rayonier launched a $250,000 print-ad and sales-promotion campaign for the benefit of the rayon staple producers (particularly for high wet modulus staple producers) in response to a marketing and research arm, called Cotton, Inc., of cotton growers, created to promote the use of cotton in textiles and nonwovens after the cotton marketing association lost some markets to rayon and other fibers after 1970.

FMC Corporation. In May 1977 the 25 million pounds a year Fredericksburg, Virginia, rayon tow flocking plant of Avtex Fibers was shut down. (The rayon tow plant had not been acquired by new Avtex management when Avtex Fibers was spun off from FMC.) The Fredericksburg plant had supplied 50 to 75 percent of the flocking industry's needs. Beaunit Corporation refused to expand its capacity and Courtaulds N.A. imported rayon tow from its parent corporation's plants in the United Kingdom to serve this demand. Imports of rayon tow also increased.

Avtex Fibers. In July 1977 the Federal Energy Administration ordered Avtex Fibers to convert from oil and natural gas fuel to the more costly coal as its main energy source. The price of coal energy had risen geometrically. Given the depressed demand for rayon, it was difficult to pass on this cost increase to customers. Particularly damaging to Avtex were the imported rayon fibers which continued to undercut the prices of U.S. producers because their technologies were newer, hence more efficient. Avtex filed dumping complaints with the U.S. Treasury to combat the increasing number of European rayon companies which were allegedly "undercutting" the United States price of rayon, causing U.S. rayon plants to run at an uneconomic 70 percent of capacity. Avtex complained against Chemiefaeser Lenzing of Austria; Fabelta of Belgium; Svenska Rayon of Sweden; Kemira Sateri of Finland; Rhone-Poulenc Textile of France; and Snia Viscosa of Italy, and won preliminary decisions against Chemiefaeser Lenzing and Fabelta in 1977. Chemiefaeser Lenzing acquired one of the defunct cellophane plants FMC had retired to jump into the U.S. market behind the tarriff wall and produce rayon after this lawsuit.

Beaunit Corporation. In late December 1977 Beaunit Corporation increased its rayon yarn prices by 5 cents a pound, its rayon tow for flocking by 3 cents a pound, and its industrial yarn by 3.5 to 14 percent depending upon the yarn denier and end-use category. Beaunit was the sole U.S. producer of rayon textile filament and rayon tow at this time.

1978

ITT Rayonier. In 1978 ITT Rayonier launched a massive $28 million advertising and promotional campaign to promote rayon and paid commissions to some of New York City's leading haute couture designers to showcase rayon in their collections. ITT Rayonier's campaign, which featured these designers and their collections on primetime television advertisements and in trade and consumer newspapers and magazines, retold the well-known facts about the advantages of rayon over cotton. The campaign specifically helped Avtex Fibers.

Beaunit Corporation. In April 1978 Beaunit Corporation raised the price of rayon filament textile yarns by 12 cents a pound, but many gray-goods weavers and converters which produced men's better suit fabrics did *not* switch to acetate lining filament following this price increase because acetate substitutes had less abrasion resistance and would be unsuitable for use in high-quality garments.

Avtex Fibers. In 1978 Avtex Fibers continued its legal battle against the European rayon companies which, it alleged, were dumping their fibers in U.S. markets at uncompetitive prices by appealing to the Treasury to reexamine the national economic policies of the governments of these producers in a well-publicized media campaign. After finishing a profitable first year of independent operations Avtex Fibers incurred a loss in its second year as earnings were hurt by heavy imports of rayon fiber, the long coal strike of 1977-1978, and the heavy costs of maintaining its old machinery.

Beaunit Corporation. In August 1978 Beaunit Corporation completed negotiations with SNIACE, a Spanish producer licensed to produce high wet modulus rayon staple, who purchased the rayon staple assets of Beaunit's Childersburg, Alabama, plant to produce rayon at Torrelavega, Spain. The assets, from one of four rayon lines formerly produced at Childersburg, which had been mothballed since the plant's shutdown in 1971, were sold to SNIACE for $250,000 and would cost another estimated $250,000 to transport to Spain.

Avtex Fibers. In October 1978 Avtex raised the prices of its high wet modulus rayon staple by 2 cents a pound.

American Enka. In October 1978 American Enka raised the prices of its regular rayon staple yarn by 3 cents a pound and its high wet modulus rayon staple by 2 cents a pound.

M. Loewenstein & Sons. In August 1978 M. Loewenstein & Sons, one of the largest U.S. producers of print cloth, announced that it was substituting rayon staple for cotton in one plant in its polyester-blend printed-cloth operations. It was a small change, but it signaled the beginning of a move away from cotton in favor of rayon due to OSHA's cotton dust standard which was intended to curb the incidence of bysinosis, a type of "brown lung" disease.

In 1978 rayon textile yarn (filament) was used for two high-quality markets which represented a stable, slowly growing demand: men's suit lining and casket velvets, where rayon was the best material. By 1978 only one U.S. firm continued to produce this type of textile rayon. In tire cords, rayon belts provided a comfortable ride, but the tires did not wear durably. Even Michelin's new U.S. factory used steel belting fibers for durability rather than rayon filament for comfort. In rayon staple, the outlook was improving at the cost of cotton's disuse due to bysinosis. As of the end of 1978, however, there had been no new investment in rayon plants and no new rayon production technologies had been introduced.

Demand for rayon will likely continue as long as some producer is willing to produce and sell these fibers at a low price. The worldwide cellulosic fibers producing capacity has been increasing, not decreasing, during the U.S. rayon endgame. This would suggest that when the return on invested capital on cellulosic fiber production becomes unacceptable in the U.S., demand will be satisfied by imports.

Analysis of the Rayon Endgame

There was great uncertainty among the rayon competitors regarding future demand for their fiber products because demand for rayon filament, staple, and tow was declining at uneven rates. In some years rayon staple, for example, was particularly profitable and demand was so great imported fibers were used to supplement domestic production. In other years, the volume of cellulosic fibers which were consumed utilized only 50 percent of the industry's capacity as import substitution allegedly caused by dumping eroded the lessened demand for cellulosic fibers. Such transitory revivals revitalized competitors' hopes that demand for some of the cellulosic fibers would pleateau and become more profitable and kept firms in the endgame.

Firms which served the rayon tire filament market recognized that nylon and polyester tire filaments had replaced rayon tire filament, but firms which produced rayon staple had expected demand for these fibers to remain viable even when it fell dramatically instead. Consequently, there was great uncertainty among many firms regarding the level at which demand for the various fiber forms would stabilize. Because hope lingered, orderly retirements of fiber extruding capacity were slow or did not occur. Firms divested the firms they had acquired abruptly and incurred substantial write-off losses in doing so. Firms' cost structures made them use price-cutting tactics when excess capacity occurred in order to try to obtain the sales volumes needed to fill their continuous-process rayon plants. This painful condition worsened when imported cellulosic fibers or other domestic synthetic substitute fibers were utilized heavily by customer industries.

A ready supply of imported fibers and synthetic substitute fibers for rayon made this an unprofitable endgame where it was difficult to sustain price increases in line with rising costs. Customer industries were price-sensitive for most uses of rayon and therefore the environment was *not* generally "favorable" for reinvestment in this declining business.

Competition in this industry was not profitable because the nature of the fibers industry, in general, was highly price-competitive. In addition to competing with each other, the cellulosic fibers producers were required to monitor and match the maneuvers of producers of substitute products and profits were restricted to the barest of margins during periods of industry depression. The principal factors which made competition difficult in this endgame were the cyclicality of demand for cellulosic fibers and the reinvestment requirements mandated by pollution-control laws. Firms which made these reinvestments were locked into continued competition at unprofitable returns when demand fell very low, but the alternative to suffering operating losses during these periods of low demand was to face a substantial write-off on the recapitalized value of the rayon firm or on the capitalized value of the pollution recovery investment. A brief summary of industry traits in 1968 follows.

Characteristics

Demand. Demand for cellulosic fibers was price elastic because of the high availability of substitute products, such as polyester, which offered genuinely superior characteristics.

Product Differentiation. Both specialty fibers and commodity-grade rayons were available in 1968. Cellulosic fibers could be differentiated by texture, denier, luster, color, tenacity, and other physical traits.

Markets Where Sold. Cellulosic fibers were sold by the bale or by skeins to mills which produced fabrics for firms which produced apparel, home furnishings, industrial products, tire cord, or nonwoven products. Sales to these markets could be achieved through direct negotiation between buyer and seller.

Substitutes. Rayon could be used in applications which did not require durability. Cotton, nylon, polyester, and other synthetic fibers were also substitutes. In the tire-cord market, steel wires were substituted for rayon by 1968.

Structure of Customer Industries. The tire companies who used rayon filament were concentrated. The textile mills were fragmented. Some of the producers of cellulosic fibers had been vertically integrated and knit rayon textiles.

Structure of Supplier Industries. The wood-pulp mills were relatively fragmented and were dependent upon rayon for their sales. Chemicals manufacturers were relatively concentrated and did not have a substantial stake in the welfare of the cellulosic fibers industry. Some of the rayon firms were backward-integrated into either wood pulp or chemicals or both.

Manufacturing Technology. Cellulosic fiber production was a continuous process using old assets which were not only industry-specific, but also processor or even *product*-specific. Although the original assets were well depreciated, those firms which reinvested in high-technology or pollution-control equipment still had value locked into the assets in the industry during 1968.

Technological Innovation. There were a few firms who made significant improvements in the basic cellulosic spinning technology. Product innovations were more frequent.

Capital Intensity. Although the capital costs were high in this industry, many old plants were relatively labor-intensive. A large plant was needed to achieve economies of scale and it had to be operated near capacity to achieve the lowest unit costs.

Competitive Structure. In 1968 there were five major firms, one of which held a major share of the capacity to produce rayon. All producers of cellulosic fibers produced other synthetic fibers, as well.

Analysis of Declining Demand for Rayon

Demand for rayon declined due to strong substitution from newer, and in some cases better or less expensive, fibers. Where other fibers were technologically superior and were less expensive, they replaced cellulosic fibers. Firms in the rayon business did not all recognize that the major competitive strength of rayon would be its cheapness; instead some firms expected that rayon would continue to be a "glamour" product and they acted accordingly.

Pockets of demand for rayon did endure. There were price-insensitive niches such as rayon textile filament (used for men's high-quality suit-lining fabrics) but only a few firms were able to serve these niches of demand because other firms could not afford to scale their mobility barriers in order to reposition themselves to serve these markets. Also, demand for these uses was insufficient to sustain more than a few firms' capacities. The most enduring category of demand for rayon was for applications where these fibers were least expensive and their cost advantage relative to other fibers vacillated.

In 1968 environmental pollution standards were tightening. Rayon extrusion was highly polluting to air and water and the investments required to keep rayon plants in compliance raised its costs to a level where, in some cases, it was priced out of particular markets.

In 1971 a significant new market was developed for rayon staple in nonwoven applications and rayon staple producers sometimes reduced their staple output available for apparel textile manufacturers in order to gain entry in this new market for rayon because they believed it would be less volatile than the fashion industry. In 1978 nonwovens represented over 30 percent of the uses for rayon staple.

It had been predicted that relative uncertainty among the competitors regarding the rate of obsolescence and deterioration of demand in various market segments would result in chaotic exit or shutdown patterns as well as the incurrence of major write-off losses or disruptions to other corporate activities. In most cases, this uncertainty affected the endgame behavior, as had been expected. Firms which had correctly identified the enduring market niches and had moved decisively to supply those customers groups were able to retain good cash flows during the worst years of declining demand for rayon and acetate. Other firms suffered losses.

It had been expected that where demand for the endgame product is price elastic and a superior product competes with and becomes more cost competitive with the endgame product due to technological improvements, superior marketing programs, or some other superior differentiating characteristic, the outlook for strong or growing demand for a product such as rayon would become residual demand and sales volumes would usually be gained at the expense of profit margins.

The timing of substitute fiber capacity expansions could have been used to predict when exit might be necessary for rayon firms. Firms shut down plants or exited when their profits were endangered by their introduction of fiber substitutes or when the costs of competitors' substitute fibers declined to levels where their prices made them sustantial threats to rayon products.

Polyester, for example, was not mature until 1972, and steel-belted tire technology was not widely used until after polyester had been adopted by most tire-makers. Thus, exits from rayon tire cord were not numerous until 1972 or later.

It would be expected that price increases would be difficult to accomplish where customers' switching costs to the substitute fibers were low. As the prices of substitutes came closer to the price of rayon, customers switched readily to polyesters, nylons, or other fibers. Prices could be raised for rayon textile filament only where no other fibers were acceptable.

Analysis of Endgame Industry Traits

It was expected that an "unfavorable" endgame environment would not encourage firms to undertake reinvestments and in general, this was an unfavorable industry environment because even where the product could be differentiated, there were few pockets of demand which could be exploited. The easy substitutability of nylon, cotton, or polyester for rayon and acetate made it difficult for a rayon producer to keep the loyalties of its customers. Price-cutting was endemic because there was overcapacity in the aggregate synthetic-fibers industry.

It was difficult for firms to exit from this industry due to economic exit barriers but competition was volatile. Rayon producers were loath to exit because of recent economic investments in R&D, pollution control, or residual goodwill. The synthetic fibers industry was overcrowded and this condition invariably resulted in price-cutting when demand for synthetic fibers became weak.

Product Characteristics

Although producers of rayon staple had invested in substantial sums to prevent their products from developing commoditylike traits, customer industries treated rayon fibers as if they were commodities. It would be expected that where a product had developed commoditylike traits, prices higher than those of substitute products would be difficult to justify and where firms tried to prevent products from developing commoditylike traits, the endgame would be more costly for them because of the reinvestments they would have to make.

It would be expected that prices could be increased if pockets of demand for the endgame product existed. It was possible for the producers of rayon industrial-grade and textile-grade filament to charge higher prices in the latter part of the endgame after several producers had shut down their filament plants because the men's high-quality suit-lining textiles market and the comfort-oriented tire-cord market provided small but lucrative pockets of demand. But in general, it was fruitless to spend money on differentiating a product whose overall demand was falling rapidly in this endgame.

Customer Characteristics

It would be expected that prices would be depressed for rayon throughout much of the endgame because of the ready availability of substitute products and because customer industries provided value-adding services which enhanced their bargaining power. It would also be expected that price increases would be difficult to sustain where customer industries were price sensitive and exercised their bargaining power to resist higher prices. The textiles industry (and apparel industry) was highly competitive and highly price-sensitive.

Supplier Characteristics

It would be expected that where a supplier industry would suffer from the retirement of its customers' plants and where sales to those customers were important to suppliers, they might be willing to help important customers. In this endgame, ITT Rayonier helped Avtex Fibers and the rayon staple industry to survive because the high-alpha dissolving-wood-pulp industry could be substantially damaged by the retirement of several rayon plants. ITT Rayonier used institutional advertising to reassert the advantages of certain physical characteristics of the rayon fiber when used in fashion apparel. ITT Rayonier also extended supplier credit to Avtex Fibers in order to provide some of the financing which was necessary in order for the large rayon firm to survive. This was necessary because Avtex had become a linchpin for the rayon industry. Courtaulds N.A. could not act in a fashion that would save the U.S. rayon industry. American Enka, despite its research and marketing strengths, was too small to reassure customers of the viability of rayon alone. Therefore, this intervention by a supplier to the industry did help to rebuild confidence for the fiber after Avtex's spin-off and near demise.

In summary, profit margins on rayon were usually thin because prices could scarcely be raised above costs for major parts of the endgame. Customers who were not locked into using cellulosic fibers switched fibers readily.

Technological Characteristics

Because the major competitive advantage which cellulosic fibers possessed over other fibers was their low cost to customer industries, rayon firms which had invested in process R&D to make their plants more productive or more energy efficient were in a position of relative pricing advantage when competing in the endgame. But in some cases these firms also faced economic exit barriers where abandoning these improvements would be costly.

Capital Requirements. It would be expected that the high cash reinvestments required to service a fashion-oriented fibers market could create economic exit barriers if the value of product or process improvements were not recovered at the time of contemplated exit. It was necessary to invest in new product development if a firm sought to achieve lower operating costs or to control the direction of the fashion-oriented markets for cellulosic fibers. Such a tactic, which was expensive but necessary, increased the height of firms' economic exit barriers while it protected firms' fabric designs from immediate imitation. Competition by R&D discoveries was an effective short-term form of differentiating fibers and producers in the fashion-oriented rayon industry; however, few firms could afford to pursue such tactics. Entry into rayon production was costly and the bulky size of the entry investment made the number of cellulosic plants few and the likelihood that many additional or replacement plants would be built poor.

It would be expected that the required pollution-control investments could encourage rapid exits from the industry. Rayon effluents were quite polluting to the air and water, and the cost of remedying these conditions was high. Most of the rayon plants had been built before pollution of the environment became an important consideration, and the capital requirements of remedying a pollution problem acted as an inducement to exit from the cellulosic fibers industry rather than to reform the rayon plant.

It would be expected that price-cutting would be frequent in an endgame industry where scale economies were realized only at high levels of capacity utilization in large plants. The minimum efficient scale in rayon production was, for example, 100 million pounds a year. This large-scale requirement exacerbated the potential pricing volatility of this endgame. Demand for rayon was cyclical because customer industries themselves suffered from cycles of demand and the presence of large, unutilized lumps of capital in the fibers industry allowed textile customers to bargain for lower rayon prices.

Asset Specificity. It would be expected that a thin market for endgame business assets would retard the timing of a firm's exit from endgame where the value of its assets was relatively undepreciated and write-off losses could be effective deterrences to exit. But where some cash flows could be realized by junking unmarketable endgame assets, such an opportunity might encourage a more timely exit from the cellulosic fibers industry. Although the assets used to manufacture rayon were highly specific to the cellulosic fibers industry, buyers for those assets (other firms within the industry, or customer or supplier firms) were sometimes interested in purchasing these plants because mothballed rayon lines could be revised and sold to new entrants overseas, pieces of an old cellulosic fibers plant could be salvaged for use in other plants; elsewhere, lead and other metals used in rayon production could be salvaged and sold to metals merchants, and junk dealers were even willing to haul away remaining obsolete cellulosic fibers equipment for the value of the equipment. Because a small recovery value (perhaps 25 percent of book value) may have been retrieved by selling production assets in the outlets listed above rayon producers frequently balked at accepting bids for their plants which they regarded as being too low. Disposal of these assets as an ongoing plant was preferable to disposal of the physical assets of rayon plants in pieces because firms hoped to recover the substantial goodwill they had accumulated.

Economic Exit Barriers. It would be expected that economic exit barriers could be created when the book value of a cellulosic fibers firm was recapitalized upon acquisition. The depreciation schedule on the new possibly higher book valuation would begin again for the new owner of the business assets (including some capitalization of goodwill) and firms would be loath to lose that value. In the rayon endgame, undepreciated asset values did delay some exits from the endgame; however, the rising costs of pollution-control compliance and of shutting down rayon plants encouraged rather than discouraged relatively early shutdowns. Judging from the sizable write-downs some firms endured upon exits, it may be inferred that these losses were preferable to the damage which retaining the rayon plant could have created to the profit and loss statement for firms such as FMC, American Cyanamid, or the El Paso Company in the future.

Competitive Characteristics

It could be predicted that price-cutting would be used in competing in an industry where the product was essentially a commodity and the competitors' viewpoints regarding the endgame were asymmetric, although the industry structure itself was concentrated. In the rayon endgame, differences in the attitudes of the "fibers-" and "chemicals-"oriented firms exacerbated the price-cutting pressures of excess capacity suffered in this capital-intensive industry and the firms which acted as if they were selling commoditylike products suffered from unstable price levels very similar to commodity price fluctuations.

Competition was volatile in this industry because some firms kept their rayon plants operating near an efficient capacity by undercutting competitors' prices. These pricing fluctuations forced competitors to follow the price leaders "all over the ball park." The signaling of price changes in the rayon business was not effective due to the diversity of physical forms of rayon which some firms tried to manage, due to the diverse industry outlooks held by each of the competitors and due to the firms' varying cost structures. It would be expected that a lack of consensus among firms in a concentrated industry would create a perilous endgame environment. The lack of agreement among competitors regarding the importance, mission, and means of executing their strategies in rayon made a more volatile, less desirable competitive endgame environment.

In summary, the low switching costs incurred by users of cellulosic fibers made substitution by other fibers a continuing problem in the rayon and acetate industry. Only the competitors which could create some loyalties for their products could sustain good price levels during the endgame. Competitors' physical cost structures and differences regarding their outlooks for the fibers' missions made this industry a volatile environment for endgame.

Analysis of the Corporate-wide Strategic Needs of the Competitors

It had been expected that firms might retain an "important" endgame business longer than economic analysis might suggest was advisable because they were deterred by "strategic exit barriers." In the cellulosic fibers business, the firms which valued their rayon investments in this manner tended to be fibers-oriented, while the chemicals-oriented companies were not deterred by these types of exit barriers. It would be expected that firms which had acquired an endgame business unit in a merger while in the process of acquiring other, more desirable businesses would be among the first participants to exit from a bad endgame situation, and in the rayon endgame, Midland-Ross, which had acquired the Industrial Rayon Corporation (IRC) for its potential tire yarn capabilities, did sell its rayon business to American Cyanamid when it became clear that the company was encountering difficulties. American Cyanamid retired the rayon plant because it desired to obtain tire-cord manufacturing knowledge from IRC; it had not acquired IRC to be in the rayon business. Similarly, FMC Corporation acquired Avtex Fibers and the El Paso Company acquired Beaunit Corporation for their other, noncellulosic fibers businesses. Because cellulosic fibers were relativley important to the acquired business units, but not to their parent firms, both FMC Corporation and the El Paso Company spun off these business units to their employees (at considerable write-downs) during the depressed years of the endgame.

Vertical Integration Constraints. It had been expected that firms which were strategically linked upstream (to wood-pulp production) or downstream (to textile production) would be less willing to exit from rayon or acetate production than would be firms which were not vertically integrated. But in this particlar endgame the firms which owned wood-pulp companies did not retain their rayon operations as customers to these businesses, nor did textile firms try to help their rayon businesses. Firms which also wove or knit textiles used whichever fibers were demanded by apparel companies in producing their fabrics and would not subsidize their cellulosic fibers units. Some firms, such as Beaunit, intentionally avoided a regular buyer-seller relationship internally in order to divest operations which were performing inadequately.

Cash-Flow Characteristics. It had been expected that firms which had acquired or retained their rayon operations because they were good generators of cash would be more likely to shut down plants or to exit if these cash-flow patterns were disrupted by reinvestment requirements. In endgame, pollution-control requirements increased while cash flows decreased due to declining demand for rayon, and firms such as FMC-Avtex or El Paso-Beaunit retired plants rather than make these reinvestments.

Diversification Considerations. It had been expected that where the firm's broad corporate strategy placed it in the substitute synthetic fibers business, as well as in rayon, firms which were successful in nylon or polyester would be more likely to retain their cellulosic fibers business in order to offer customers a wider array of fibers. In the rayon endgame, FMC-Avtex (which had been most dependent on rayon sales) spun off its cellulosic fibers business, as did El Paso-Beaunit. Firms such as American Enka (nylon) or Courtaulds (many synthetic fibers), which were more dependent upon other successful fibers' sales volumes, retained their cellulosic fibers operations. These firms did not suffer from the downturns in rayon demand as severely as did firms whose diversifications into alternative fabrics had been less successful, and hence whose dependence upon cellulosic fibers seemed to be greater.

Strategic Exit Barriers. It had been expected that exit would be deterred where the write-off losses which would be incurred would be all or a significant portion of the firm's total reported profits. Firms such as FMC Corporation and the El Paso Company encountered high barriers due to recent reinvestments in pollution-control devices and because the firms had recently recapitalized their rayon acquisitions. When they divested, these firms did incur large write-offs (and very likely they carried other unrecognized losses in the form of notes to their spun-off subsidiaries when they divested them). Moreover it is likely that the size of the write-off loss associated with exit would affect the timing of the firms' exits as well as the form of their exits. For example, Avtex's plants, which represented almost one half of the rayon industry's productive capacity, could not simply be closed down because the remaining rayon fiber suppliers would not be considered adequate or reliable sources of fiber for applications which might have used rayons. Therefore, the FMC-Avtex divestiture was constrained in its strategic flexibility because of the future industry consequences if its capacity were retired.

In summary, some of the firms which might have wished to exit or to retire capacity could not do so. American Cyanamid closed down obsolete rayon tire-cord filament capacity without difficulty because the investment-value was minor. American Enka had to overcome some adversity to recognzing write-offs in conjunction with shutting down poorly performing cellulosic fibers units. Avtex and Beaunit encountered the greatest difficulties in divestiture.

Analysis of Endgaming-Firms'
Competitive Strengths

It had been predicted that firms possessing relative competitive strengths would be better suited to pursue some of the more aggressive strategy options appropriate for coping with declining demand. The firms whose postures were most advantageous were those firms whose technologies enabled them to enjoy lower production costs or whose product development investments had yielded marketable fibers which were perceived as being differentiated. Avtex marketed Avril I, Avril II, and Avril III aggressively to try to persuade users that rayon fiber was "flexible," that it could be engineered to possess several different, desirable characteristics. In 1978 Beaunit was the most important firm providing rayon textile filament because all other firms which had produced this filament denier had retired their assets when they shut down their tire-cord filament plants. Therefore, Beaunit's advantageous position was gained by default.

Marketing and Selling Skills. It had been expected that firms which possessed multinational marketing linkages, trademarked fibers, or a wide range of fiber offerings would possess strengths in the rayon endgames. Linkages to overseas production of rayon or acetate was a strength when shortages in fibers developed during the cyclic decline of these fibers and firms such as Courtaulds also used these subsidiaries as alternative markets for their rayon production to help them endure through the depressed periods in this endgame.

Production Advantages. It would be expected that firms which possessed the best operating economies or most efficient work methods, materials-handling systems, or other cost-cutting devices would possess an advantage in an endgame where competition was waged on the basis of price-cutting. Courtaulds possessed the greatest technological advantages because it possessed the most efficient-sized plant (210 million pounds a year) and had implemented cost-saving techniques and plant features when it constructed this most modern rayon plant (1951). It also possessed the most favorable fuel contracts and had designed its plant to be highly energy-efficient.

Locational advantages could also be important strengths. Some firms like Avtex Fibers were located in regions that required costly, non-remunerative pollution-control investments while other firms like American Enka operated plants at locations where the bodies of water into which they dumped their effluents did not reach levels considered to be polluting as rapidly. Thus some competitors in the rayon business were able to enjoy a delay in the need to invest in this equipment.

In summary, the most significant internal strengths possessed by firms competing in the endgame were (1) efficient plant technologies and efficacious R&D product and process investments; (2) multinational subsidiaries which served as safety valves for marketing cellulosic fibers; and (3) effectively differentiated products. The notable failures in the cellulosic fibers industry were firms whose (1) markets were obsoleted; (2) plants were inefficient; and (3) plant locations were highly polluting.

Analysis of Firms' Performance in the
Rayon Endgame

Given the unfavorable industry traits and the widespread uncertainty concerning the duration of demand for rayon few substantial reinvestments were expected in this endgame. Yet firms which served the fashion markets were reinvesting at least $2 million per year in product research and development, and Courtaulds expanded its physical plants.

Firms which had acquired rayon companies in order to gain entree into other fibers such as polyester divested these firms. The chemicals-oriented companies—American Cyanamid, FMC Corporation, and the El Paso Company in particular—could have been predicted to be less willing to struggle through the "feast-or-famine" cycles of the fashion industry. By contrast, it could be foreseen that the fibers-oriented firms—Courtaulds and American Enka—would be more likely to consolidate their operations and to strengthen them rather than to divest their cellulosic fibers when environmental conditions became difficult. The firms which remained in endgame were the firms which had captured niches of demand successfully, the lowest-cost competitors, and the competitors which were best-known as fibers-oriented companies. These companies were able to plan their end-game activities and to execute their tactics successfully because they understood the nature of the cellulosic fibers endgame better than the chemicals-oriented competitors.

FMC-Avtex Fibers closed two plants and spun off the rayon business in a sale to its employees. El Paso Company-Beaunit closed three plants and spun off its rayon business in a sale to its employees. American Enka closed costly plants where demand for its products was flagging. Most firms which did shut down plants recognized some write-off losses upon disposal. The spun-off Avtex and Beaunit units appeared to be failing in the months following divestiture from their parents.

Firms Which Exited Early. The most important factors in determining which firms would remain in the endgame were the firms' cost structures and the duration of demand for the market niche each respective firm serviced. Rayon filament plants closed around 1973. The major divestitures of staple occurred after the depressed market conditions of 1975.

Early Exit: "Milk the Investment"

Industrial Rayon Corporation. The assets of Industrial Rayon Corporation were among the most likely rayon plants to be shut down when nylon and polyester tire cord became more effective as substitute for rayon tire-cord filament because American Cyanamid which had acquired IRC was not interested in its rayon tire-cord technology; rather it sought to learn more about tire-construction techniques. Because IRC was heavily invested in rayon filament, it was quite vulnerable to the effect of substitute products upon its rayon tire-cord sales.

Industrial Rayon Corporation had suffered some disadvantages in the past because its timing was slow when it introduced product improvements such as Tyrex yarn. It added only 20 million pounds a year of high wet modulus after the new staple formulation was introduced (an inefficient capacity level) and did not seem to be very innovative in developing other rayon products after demand for rayon tire cord had peaked in 1951. Although Industrial Rayon Corporation had been very profitable from its founding in 1916 until the 1950s, IRC's dominant product had been high tenacity rayon filament, the product which was most clearly obsoleted in this endgame. IRC could not switch to textile-grade filament when tire filament declined because the market for textile-grade rayon filament at that time was not large enough to absorb all of the productive capacity IRC would be converting from tire cord, given the capacities of other firms which then supplied the textile market.

Midland-Ross had recovered some of the value of its investment in IRC, but American Cyanamid tried to milk the investment without much success. (American Cyanamid was depreciating IRC from a recently recapitalized asset base.) Avtex bought the IRC high wet modulus staple line when American Cyanamid shut down. (It had to junk the high wet modulus assets because they were in poor condition.) Because the massive tire-cord assets were scrapped, American Cyanamid could recover only a small amount of the rayon fibers investment's remaining value.

Continued Presences in the Endgame. Among the firms which shut down plants or repositioned themselves to remain as producers of cellulosic fibers in the endgame, Courtaulds North America seemed to be in the most advantageous position. It was well entrenched in its particular niche of demand, and due to competitive strengths did not encounter damaging competition. Courtaulds sold only regular rayon staple (to nonwoven markets principally) with great success due to its lowest cost position.

"Shrink Selectively"

Beaunit Corporation. Because Beaunit Corporation was obliged by a court order to reinvest in pollution-control devices for its remaining rayon filament plant, Beaunit was not expected to remain in the endgame beyond 1978. Beaunit was serving a stagnant but enduring demand for textile-grade rayon filament alone at that time. Nevertheless, its position did not seem to be promising because it did not appear to be able to comply with the court order regarding effluent controls. Beaunit operated several old, mixed-technology plants and none of the plants was particularly efficient because they were all too small. Beaunit had been the only U.S. producer of cuprammonium rayon, a very high denier filament which was in great demand in 1978, seven years after depressed price levels had forced Beaunit to close that plant. Beaunit spun off three other rayon plants during endgame because it could not afford to operate these plants given the prevailing prices of substitute products.

Because its capacity was small and its markets were selective, few other firms competed against Beaunit Corporation. It occupied a quasi-monopoly position as the only U.S. producer of rayon textile filament, a fiber which the higher-quality men's suit-lining market must continue to use while its price is reasonable, because rayon is the best material for this application.

Beaunit was reported to be in a highly liquid position which would enable it to divest its industrial and textile rayon filament plant without difficulty if it were necessary to do so. Since its divestiture from the El Paso Company, Beaunit's ailing rayon operations had been fully utilized, but its prices had been squeezed to an almost unprofitable level by imports. Because the market for textile filament had been tight, Beaunit had recently raised its prices for rayon filament successfully while Beaunit divested unprofitable rayon operations. Because it had suffered large losses when it retired these assets in the past, Beaunit was not considered to be a successful endgame participant.

Avtex Fibers. Because of its tenuous existence and history of losses in the rayon business, Avtex Fibers was expected to perform poorly in the late endgame and to suffer significant disruptions to business activities and profitability if it tried to close down portions of its assets. Avtex had recently reinvested substantial sums in the spun-off FMC rayon business to try to keep it and the entire U.S. rayon industry viable, but Avtex's recent reinvestments had not been recovered by the end of 1978. Because the salvage value of the assets Avtex employed would likely be low, Avtex faced a thin resale market for them, and a substantial exit barrier if it wished to exit from the rayon industry.

Avtex Fibers had been the highest-cost producer because its plants were the oldest, it was required to make the largest investments in pollution-control equipment, and Avtex was required to change to coal, a more costly form of energy whose prices had risen four-fold in as many years. This fuel change may prove to be devastating to Avtex because its principal endgame product, high wet modulus rayon staple, used a very energy-intensive production process. Avtex profits were lower in its second year of postdivestiture activity, Avtex's profits were lower and it was renegotiating the maturities on some of its financing instruments. Its future, and hence the future of the U.S. rayon industry, did not look particularly promising because an exit by Avtex could create a major disruption in the rayon industry.

Avtex had tried to shrink the rayon investment by closing plants which seemed to be uneconomic, retiring its textile-grade filament capacity, as well as a portion of its high-tenacity tire-cord capacity. When it did so, Avtex had negotiated take-or-pay contracts with its remaining tire-cord customers which constituted contractual exit barriers for Avtex.

American Enka. American Enka would be expected to remain invested in the rayon endgame because American Enka was a fiber company that had been founded on rayon. Although its orientation had been broadened to nylon and other synthetic fibers and several acquisitions had changed its risk profile, American Enka was still researching a superior rayon staple technology with its parent company AKZO N.V., which discontinued the production of its rayon staple in Europe rather than degrade its quality. American Enka had developed an image of quality through advertising its rayon and through frequent technology improvements. Its linkage with AKZO N.V., through a licensing agreement, expanded its research capacity and because its rayon staple was of a consistently high quality, Enka's plants were usually fully utilized.

American Enka would be in a relatively good position to exit without much disruption of other operations if the future demand for rayon plummeted. Enka's rayon staple was produced in a complex which manufactured other fiber products, where, if rayon capacity were vacated, the plant space could be leveled, excavated, and given to other fiber products. The Enka rayon investment had already been well depreciated and provisions were made for its retirement. Because its plant was in good condition (1948-vintage), there may even have been pieces of the rayon-producing equipment which Enka could salvage by selling them overseas.

Rather than enter into requirements contracts for its rayon filament tire cord with tire producers as Avtex did in 1973, American Enka phased out its production of filament and placed its heaviest emphasis upon regular rayon staple. Thus, American Enka shrank selectively to reposition itself in a product for which demand was declining at a slower rate. Although American Enka incurred write-off losses in closing its rayon filament plant, this reduction in earnings was matched by reserves which had been established for the purpose of cushioning the cost of retiring its rayon plants when they were constructed in the 1940s.

Courtaulds North America. Courtaulds would be expected to participate in the rayon staple endgame even if its Alabama plant lost money because its location constituted an important beachhead for its corporate parent, Courtaulds, Ltd., in the United Kingdom. In fact, although its profitability cannot be ascertained with certainty from its globally consolidated financial statements, the Courtaulds North American plant runs full out and is expected to be highly profitable. In addition to possessing strong multinational linkages, Courtaulds also was completely vertically integrated from forests to final garments because a South African tree farm provided its wood pulp, much of its rayon staple output could be sold to an affiliate fabricate company for processing, and, as a participant in the U.S. market, Courtaulds also sold rayon to outside fabric or apparel customers and marketed some fibers from affiliate companies in the Courtaulds family.

Courtaulds's large automated plant had been expanded during the endgame and always operated near efficient capacity. Pollution-control investments had already been made and the plant had been designed to incorporate energy-conserving principles and resource-recovery systems for wastes because it was built using the criteria of a European plant's design.

Courtaulds was well entrenched in the interlinked competitive niche it served and there did not seem to be any need to exit in 1978 because its return on investment was acceptable for Courtaulds, and it was in a relatively strong position in the rayon industry.

In summary, as the endgame progressed, imports became a more important means of satisfying short-term fluctuations in the demand for cellulosic fibers, but because the cost of entering rayon de novo was so expensive, there may be a time in the future when the U.S. market must be served predominantly by imported rayon, after most U.S. rayon plants have been shut down due to relative operating diseconomies and required re-investments. As the healthful handling properties of cotton come into question (due to the increase of bysinosis among textile workers), the long-term viability of rayon staple could become less questionable. But, if more rayon is needed, imports will likely be needed to supplement the limited productive capacity that will remain in operation after environmental laws and other depressing factors squeeze out some remaining firms. No new entries are anticipated.

10 The Endgame in the Acetylene Industry

Acetylene is an industrial gas which can be generated either from calcium carbide or from natural gas. Acetylene is used (1) as the raw material (feedstock) in the synthesis of many organic compounds; (2) for lighting, under certain circumstances; and (3) as a fuel with oxygen to produce a hot flame such as in a blowtorch. Approximately 10 billion cubic feet of acetylene were produced and sold on the open market in 1965, while a slightly smaller amount of acetylene, approximately 9 billion cubic feet, was consumed internally by integrated firms that produced it. This made 1965 the year of the largest volume of acetylene production ever recorded. However, there were signs that acetylene demand could not be maintained at the present levels given cost increases and the existence of some emerging substitute products.

A Description of the Acetylene Industry

The Product

Acetylene (HC $\equiv$ CH) is a colorless, poisonous, and highly flammable gas which is highly volatile and will explode, without the presence of oxygen, if handled incorrectly. Despite these undesirable physical attributes, acetylene was highly desirable for chemical synthesis and was unmatched as an inexpensive fuel for cutting metals.

Acetylene could be produced by making calcium chloride from lime, coal, and water. Acetylene was generated by dropping calcium carbide into water. Acetylene could also be produced in a multi-step process from petrochemicals—usually natural gas—using a partial oxidation process. Acetylene gas possessed the same chemical properties whether it was generated from carbide or from natural gas.

Markets

Acetylene was used in three principal ways. It was combined with oxygen to produce a very intense oxyacetylene torch for welding and cutting metals. It

I am indebted to Michael E. Porter for his assistance in editing this chapter.

could also be used for illumination in cases where electricity was not available or was dangerous to use, for example, for miners' helmets. Finally, acetylene could serve as a building block for chemical synthesis of many compounds.

Welding. There were literally thousands of firms involved in industrial welding with acetylene. Welders used a "torch" and associated welding tools which were designed specifically for using acetylene. In 1965 nearly all welders had acetylene equipment. For most welders, the cost of the welding gas was a relatively small part of their costs.

There were a number of substitute gases available for welding in 1965, however. Using these gases required investing in new welding equipment. Acetylene was the most cost-effective welding gas relative to these substitutes, in applications where heavy cutting was required, such as salvage work.

There were over 200 welding-supply wholesalers who supplied the welding market. The larger firms were full-time industrial gas producers like Union Carbide and Airco, and these firms produced their own calcium carbide. The many smaller, regional welding-supply firms usually generated their own acetylene but used calcium carbide purchased from a larger firm.

Calcium carbide-based acetylene could be bottled at a central site or it could be generated at the work site using purchased portable generating apparatus, since the carbide solids were easily transported. Small quantities of natural gas-based acetylene could also be tapped from a natural gas-based plant's pipelines and bottled under compression for sale in the welding market.

Welding supply wholesalers tried to sell welding use customers on (1) the idea of a captive, carbide-based acetylene source, or (2) a close relationship with the acetylene firm whereby compressed acetylene tanks or carbide for portable generators would be repurchased with regularity. These two approaches to distributing acetylene were in competition with each other. Firms tried to differentiate their acetylene offerings on the basis of (1) services, (2) variety of other industrial gas products offered, (3) corporate reputation, or (4) delivery schedules.

Welding-supply wholesaler companies sometimes cannibalized their acetylene sales by selling new welding systems which did not use acetylene gas. They were motivated to do this because the margins on other welding gases could be higher than margins on acetylene.

Chemical Synthesis. The greatest usage of acetylene in 1965 was as a "building block" to create a variety of plastics and other organic compounds. The growth of acetylene consumed for this purpose had more than tripled the cubic feet of acetylene produced in the previous decade. About

88 percent of U.S. acetylene produced in 1965 was used for chemical synthesis applications in 1965. Acetylene was used to produce the following products.

Vinyl Chloride Monomer. Vinyl chloride monomer (VCM) is a colorless gas used to make polyvinyl chloride (PVC), which was calendered (32 percent); extruded (26 percent); and used in coating, bonding, or adhesives (15 percent) in 1965. VCM was the largest single outlet for acetylene in 1965.

Vinyl Acetate Monomer. Vinyl acetate monomer is a compound of acetic acid which was polymerized to form resins or plastics for a variety of industrial products. There were two principal methods (or "routes") to producing vinyl acetate in 1965, one using acetylene and another using ethylene, which was derived from oil.

Acrylonitrile. Acrylonitrile is a colorless liquid used in synthetic polymerization and in making acrylic fibers, synthetic rubber and plastics, resins, and soil conditioners. In 1965 synthetic-fibers production consumed 48 percent of U.S.-produced acrylonitrile; exports, 22 percent; nitrile rubber, 7 percent; resins, 14 percent; and other miscellaneous uses, 9 percent. Acrylonitrile could also be produced using alternate routes besides acetylene. By 1965, it had become evident that the propylene-ammonia route was a lower-cost way to produce acrylonitrile than the acetylene route, and new acrylonitrile plants were being constructed with propylene-based technologies.

Neoprene. Neoprene is a synthetic rubber product developed by duPont which resisted heat, sunlight, many chemicals, and oil and gasoline. Until Tenneco Chemicals's Petro-Tex Corp. decided to erect a neoprene plant under a duPont license, duPont had been the only U.S. producer of neoprene. DuPont made neoprene from acetylene at Louisville, Kentucky, and Montague, Michigan. However, there was also a butadiene-based route to producing neoprene, and the new Tenneco neoprene plant planned to consume butadiene instead of acetylene, even though Tenneco Chemicals was a producer of acetylene.

Trichloroethylene. Trichloroethylene is a toxic, colorless liquid used as a solvent for fats, oils, and waxes. It is also used in dry-cleaning compounds. In 1965, 75 percent of the trichloroethylene capacity had been based upon acetylene feedstock; however, there had been a gradual shift from acetylene to ethylene as the feedstock.

Acrylates. Acrylates are transparent thermoplastic resins, such as Lucite®, formed by polymerizing esters of acrylic acid. Acrylates are used mainly in protective coatings. Although several processes existed for making acrylates, those starting from acetylene accounted for over 50 percent of the total capacity in 1965.

Marketing

Many firms produced some or all of their acetylene internally. Acetylene is a very volatile gas which could not be transported in an easy manner because of the gas's highly explosive characteristics. As a result, acetylene-producing capacity (in-house or otherwise) was located in close proximity to users, and acetylene was shipped continuously by pipeline. Facilities were also closely integrated, and the user's production process was often tailored to the particular acetylene technology of the supplier. Firms who wanted to sell acetylene to chemical users competed to entice a chemical user to construct a plant near their acetylene plants and interconnect to it. In chemical synthesis using acetylene, plant and equipment were designed specifically for the acetylene-based routes. Changing the route required scrapping or drastically overhauling the existing synthesis facilities.

Sales of acetylene for chemical synthesis were made under binding long-term contracts of up to twenty years at an agreed-upon price. Sometimes the pass-through of raw material costs in producing acetylene were part of such contracts, and often the depreciation period of the acetylene-generating facilities was tied to the length of the contracts.

Engineering expertise, reliability of operating processes, and the availability of raw material feedstocks at favorable prices (in cost pass through contracts) were important to competing in the chemical synthesis markets. Most acetylene produced for this purpose was produced using natural gas-based acetylene. A few firms produced acetylene for chemical synthesis using calcium carbide as a feedstock for generating acetylene.

Acetylene plants which transported the gas pipeline to chemical customers could divert some of that gas into compressed tanks from which it could be sold for welding uses. The acetylene firms supplying the needs of a particular chemical customer could also hold a "merchant position," whereby they sold excess acetylene to other customers. They could also lay a pipeline to a new customer and divert any excess acetylene to an additional user in that manner. When a price was negotiated by natural gas-based acetylene producers for a onetime sale of excess acetylene to marginal users (not contractual customers), market pressures might force firms to sell at prices lower (or higher) than their long-term contract prices.

Suppliers to the Acetylene Industry

Carbide Process. Calcium carbide consumed substantial amounts of energy and was costly to transport to the worksite. Most calcium-carbide plants were located near large hydroelectric installations.

Natural-Gas Process. Acetylene plants were located near natural gas or naptha sources, and acetylene-consuming plants were also nearby to minimize the need to transport the volatile gas. Natural-gas producers frequently used acetylene products to convert regulated gas into profitable, nonregulated chemicals.

Acetylene Production

Acetylene could be produced using two basic methods, carbide or natural gas.

Carbide Process. Acetylene could be produced by first producing calcium carbide and then using it to generate acetylene. Calcium-carbide production required facilities to crush limestone and coal, high-temperature electric furnaces, facilities to cool the molten product (chill pots), as well as crushing and screening equipment. To produce acetylene, a generating station where finely ground carbide was reacted with water was necessary. Producing calcium carbide consumed large amounts of energy and water (effluents were recycled), required handling of large quantities of solid materials, and was quite capital intensive. While 100 percent of the acetylene produced had once come from carbide, few calcium-carbide plants were being built in 1965 and only 50 percent of acetylene production still came from this source. There were some alternative uses for calcium carbide besides acetylene production.

If a firm did not smelt calcium carbide, the investment required to generate acetylene from purchased carbide was low. The capital investment in a large carbide plant was $115 million, and few acetylene customers required the quantities of calcium carbide which would make such a smelter cost-efficient.

Natural-Gas Process. Acetylene could also be produced by decomposing natural gas (or closely related "oil gas"), using a variety of continuous process methods. This method of producing acetylene was newer, and was subject to much greater technological uncertainty than the carbide process. A great deal of chemical-engineering expertise was required, as well as spending on R&D to perfect the process.

Natural gas-based processes had relatively high minimum efficient scales (30 million pounds or more of acetylene per year) but had lower unit costs at full capacity than carbide-based processes on the same scale in 1965. Capital requirements were on the order of $10 million, and the facilities were highly specialized. Most of the cost of facilities (75 percent) was in fixed "plumbing" and storage tanks. Annual maintenance expenditures on the order of $1 million were required to keep the cracking facilities operating. Partial oxydization can be volatile and very sooty. If the gas is not quenched in time, soot (carbon) results. Efficiency is poor in these processes (only 31 percent) relative to chemical reactions which have little waste. Much natural gas is not converted in these processes and escapes. If the reaction is not timed correctly, an explosion results.

Several commercial natural gas-based processes for making acetylene had been developed in 1965. These alternative, natural gas-based processes are explained below.

BASF Process. The most widely used natural gas-based acetylene process is the one-stage BASF flame process which partially oxidizes natural gas. In this process, the feedstock is heated to 2,700° C very quickly and then cooled as quickly as possible to prevent the natural gas from decomposing into its elements. The reacting gases are cooled quickly by spraying either water or thermally stable oil into the gas stream as it leaves the reaction chamber. The resulting gas is compressed and acetylene is recovered from it by selective absorption in a solvent under pressure. The solvent is then desorbed and stripped of the acetylene product.

The firms using the BASF process in 1965 included American Cyanamid, Rohm & Haas, Monochem, and Monsanto.

Montecatini and SBA Kellogg Processes. The Montecatini one-step flame process differed from the BASF partial-combustion process in that it operated at a higher pressure and used water to quench the partial chemical reaction of combustion. Diamond Shamrock modified this process for its acetylene plant in Deer Park, Texas. The Diamond Shamrock/Montecatini acetylene plant cost $10 million to erect. It required $3.4 million in the first year of operation (1963) to correct operating flaws, and an additional $3.2 million the following year. Its technology was experimental and required extensive reinvestments to make it operable. The related Kellogg-SBA process used an all-metal, water-cooled burner. Although the overall process is similar to the BASF process, the solvent used for the recovery of acetylene differed. Tenneco Chemical Company modified the SBA process for use in its acetylene plant located in Houston, Texas.

The Electric-Arc Process. The duPont electric-arc process was patterned on the German Hüels process and had lower operating costs, in theory, than any other process. In it, the heat necessary for the conversion of natural gas to acetylene was supplied by an electric current. DuPont's electric-arc process acetylene plant in Montague, Michigan, used an electric arc instead of the usual burners of the partial oxidation process.

The Wulff Regeneration Process. The regeneration processes used heat exchange between the feedstock and a hot refractory to provide the heat needed for acetylene formation. Both ethylene and acetylene are produced in this process, and the ethylene-acetylene ratio could be adjusted to any ratio between 100 percent acetylene produce and 100 percent ethylene. Acetylene is usually produced in small quantities as a by-product in ethylene-cracking operations. (For example, Monsanto's Chocolate Bayou ethylene plant probably produced some acetylene by-product). The by-product acetylene formed in ethylene plants is used internally in these plants as feedstock to produce other specialized chemicals. Ethylene itself can be produced inexpensively as a by-product in the process of cracking petrochemicals. Hence, very small quantities of acetylene are normally produced in routine cracking operations.

Union Carbide operated the only commercial Wulff U.S. acetylene plants, though the Wulff process was used extensively in other countries. The cost structure (fixed and variable cost relationships) in the Wulff process was very similar to that of the partial-oxidation processes. (The economics of the cracking process depended upon the costs of raw material. There were many alternative uses for natural gas and its price was rising in 1965.) A typical non-Wulff partial-oxidation plant would cost $11.5 million if natural gas were used as the feedstock; $9.0 million if LPG (liquified petroleum gas) were used as feedstock. The capital costs of a Wulff plant would be $6.5 million compared with $11 million for other natural gas-based acetylene processes. In all acetylene plants there was the danger of explosion, which could do damage costing millions of dollars.

Substitute Products

It was becoming apparent by 1965 that ethylene might be even more economical than natural gas-based acetylene for use in many of the chemical-synthesis markets for acetylene. Ethylene used oil as a raw material, and its unit costs were lower than either the natural-gas or the carbide processes for making acetylene, as is shown in table 10-1. Natural-gas acetylene had been overtaken by ethylene as a result of the rising price of natural gas. However, there was uncertainty in 1965 over the timing as well as the inevitability of the substitute ethylene technology as well as over the other potential substitutes for acetylene described above when the markets for acetylene were discussed.

Table 10-1

Cost Comparison of Production of Vinyl-Chloride Monomer Using Acetylene versus Ethylene Feedstocks

(basis: 200 million pounds of VCM per year)

	Acetylene	*Ethylene*
Capital costs	$3.4 million	$4.7 million
Offsite capital	$1.0 million	$1.4 million
Working capital	$2.0 million	$2.0 million
Plant operating costs	0.8¢/pound	0.9¢/pound
Sales and administrative overhead	0.3¢/pound	0.3¢/pound
Raw Materials		
Acetylene at 8¢/pound; ethylene at 4¢/pound	3.4	1.9[a]
HCL at $35/ton; chlorine at $50/ton	1.0	1.7
Plant operating costs	0.8	0.9
Controllable sales and administrative overhead	0.2	0.2
Out-of-pocket costs	5.4	4.7
Depreciation at 10 percent	0.2	0.2
Noncontrollable sales and administrative overhead	0.1	0.1
Break-even costs	5.7	5.0
Return on investment at 20 percent	0.6	0.8
Minimum required selling price	6.3	5.8

Source: Robert B. Stobaugh, Jr., *Petrochemical Manufacturing and Marketing Guide* Volume 2. Copyright © 1968 by Gulf Publishing Company, Houston, Texas. All rights reserved. Used with permission.

[a]All figures are in cents per pound of VCM.

Economic Exit Barriers. When a natural gas-based acetylene plant must be shut down, a chemical company could not resell its assets. Only 5 percent of the asset value was represented by the buildings, which were control rooms and rooms for maintenance crews and equipment. Much of the asset value was in plumbing and barrels; the plant looked like a refinery. The cost of removing it would likely exceed the salvage value of the machinery. Firms which generated acetylene using carbide needed only a delivery system if they did not smelt their own carbide. Economic exit barriers would be high for calcium-carbide plant assets.

In summary, in the acetylene business capital requirements and asset specificity were high and economies of scale were important in operating cost efficiencies. Large investments and large write-offs of technological failures (processes that did not work) were commonplace in the chemicals industry, however.

Strategic Exit Barriers. The need to have reliable captive sources of acetylene could act as a strategic barrier to exit for an acetylene company if no other chemical firm nearby could supply the needed capacity of feedstock acetylene. "Switching costs" were high, further deterring an exit from using acetylene. Even if an acetylene-generating firm had extricated itself from its internal needs for acetylene, exit could still be deterred if contractual relationships to supply acetylene to customers existed until the firm wishing to exit from acetylene found a producer to continue its plant's operations. Contracts typically ran twenty years or longer.

A Historical Overview of the Acetylene Industry

Acetylene was discovered in 1836 and synthesized successfully in 1860. The commercial method of making acetylene from calcium carbide was discovered in 1892. The discovery that acetylene could be generated by combining the elements of carbon and hydrogen by means of the electric arc is considered to be the beginning of the synthetic carbon-based chemical industry.

The first commercial U.S. calcium-carbide plant went into operation at Niagara Falls, New York, in 1896. This company was to become the Union Carbide Corporation. In about 1906, the Prest-O-Lite Company of Indianapolis compressed acetylene and pumped it into cylinders packed with porous materials saturated with acetone to produce a torch with a very hot flame. This was the beginning of the acetylene welding and cutting industry. Prest-O-Lite also became a part of the Union Carbide Corporation.

During World War I, acetylene-based processes were developed to produce a number of other products. German chemists, in particular, were interested in developing synthetic rubber using an acetylene process. In 1915 the first electric-arc process acetylene using a petroleum feedstock was developed, the Hüels process. This discovery was particularly significant for the U.S. chemical industry because of its abundant natural-gas reserves.

The versatility of acetylene enabled scientists to synthesize many new or special chemicals. In the 1930s Reppe and a large number of German scientists and engineers commercialized high-pressure, high-temperature methods to synthesize chemicals by using acetylene, named "Reppe chemicals." The new German carbon-based chemistry industry in Europe relied upon abundant coal supplies. The combination of knowledge of Reppe chemistry and an abundant, low-priced supply of natural gas and petroleum in the United States enabled U.S. chemical producers to develop shorter and cheaper processes to achieve these same ends. The U.S. acetylene-generating business had initially been comprised of firms generating acetylene from carbide, mostly for welding purposes. Many of the carbide-based plants were in operation before 1950. The large acetylene plants, near calcium-carbide producers, may have furnished acetylene for chemical uses as well prior to 1950. (Allied Chemical, for example, used carbide-based acetylene to produce vinyl chloride monomer prior to 1950.)

Acetylene production capacity was enlarged significantly in the 1950s through the building of fully integrated plastics plants which used acetylene as a feedstock. There were significant savings to be enjoyed in using a natural-gas route to acetylene if a user's volume requirements could justify a large investment. Airco and Tenneco were the largest "merchant" acetylene producers. These operations' livelihoods depended upon continued sales of large quantities of acetylene to outside consumers since their acetylene plants generated a larger output than they could consume internally. When their users found alternate ways to produce their end products, ways without using acetylene, it would leave these producers with large excess capacities. Hence the positions of vendors of acetylene were becoming more risky as cheaper substitute materials were being discovered.

Competition

Chemical Synthesis Markets. Because of the contractual nature of acetylene sales, and because a large part of the acetylene produced was used internally, price competition did not occur in what could have been a very volatile environment.

Welding Markets. Welding gas-supply firms sold acetylene as a part of a full product line in addition to the substitute gases which were replacing acetylene. Price competition could be important to them.

Overview of the Acetylene Firms

The Census of Manufacturers indicated that over 200 producers generated acetylene in 1965. Many of these firms were welding-supply firms generating acetylene using carbide which they purchased from larger producers of calcium carbide. However, 48 percent of the acetylene-generating capacity estimated to be available in 1965 was represented by the capacities of the four largest producers and 70 percent of the capacity was represented by the largest eight producers of acetylene. Firms tended to supply primarily either the chemical market or the welding market, but rarely both. Except for Union Carbide, those acetylene firms who sold into the welding market sold acetylene to welding-supply firms and not to end customers. The major competitors in acetylene are profiled below.

Union Carbide Corporation. Union Carbide was the oldest and the best-known acetylene producer. The principal businesses of the Union Carbide Corporation were carbon products, chemical products, consumer products, industrial gases and equipment, metals and minerals, nuclear products, plastics, and textile materials. Union Carbide operated 280 plants in the United States and Canada in 1965 and total corporate sales were $2,664 million. Sales of industrial gases to outside customers represented approximately 5 percent of Union Carbide's worldwide corporate sales.

In 1965 Union Carbide Corporation produced acetylene in two divisions, the Linde Division and the Olefins Division, and consumed it in several other divisions in the production of vinyl-chloride monomer, vinyl-acetate monomer, and industrial welding gas. The Linde Division was charged with the sale of a full line of industrial gases, including acetylene. The Olefins Division produced acetylene and other organic chemicals for sale and for use in other divisions. Union Carbide had been producing acetylene from calcium carbide since the company's founding in 1917. Union Carbide maintained an active research program in production technologies for both carbide- and hydrocarbon-based acetylene.

Calcium carbide was produced at Sheffield, Alabama; Woodstock, Tennessee; Niagara Falls, New York; Ashtabula, Ohio; and Portland, Oregon. Union Carbide generated acetylene from carbide for chemical synthesis and welding at these locations. Acetylene using the partial oxidation and Wulff processes was produced at Texas City, Texas, and at South Charleston and Institute, West Virginia. Union Carbide also recovered acetylene as a by-product of ethylene generation at its Seadrift, Texas, facility. It used naptha and gas oil instead of natural gas as the raw material for producing its hydrocarbon acetylene.

Union Carbide consumed approximately 60 percent of its acetylene for chemical synthesis purposes internally. Union Carbide produced vinyl-chloride monomer at South Charleston, West Virginia, and Texas City, Texas; acrylonitrile at Institute, West Virginia; vinyl-acetate monomer at South Charleston and Texas City; and acetylene black at Ashtabula, Ohio. Customers used at least a portion of Union Carbide's acetylene capacity at most major plants, but Union Carbide was losing some customers in 1965 to alternative raw-materials technologies. The customers who still consumed large amounts of Union Carbide's acetylene included chemical firms such as National Starch, General Aniline and Film, and Hooker Chemical. Union Carbide also had substantial acetylene sales to the welding market.

Airco, Inc. Airco, Inc. (Air Reduction Company, Inc.), was one of the leading producers of oxygen and acetylene gases used in metals-welding and cutting operations. Airco, Inc., was also the leading producer of carbon dioxide (liquid and solid). Airco produced cryogenic, industrial, and medical gases such as nitrogen, hydrogen, neon, krypton, xenon, argon, helium, and rare gas mixtures as well. It also produced a wide line of welding equipment to service its acetylene-gas customers and a wide line of medical equipment to complement its medical gases. Total corporate sales in 1965 were $376.8 million, of which its sales of acetylene represented 12.9 percent or $48.6 million.

Airco, Inc.'s, Ferroalloys Division produced calcium carbide which was used in its acetylene business. Airco, Inc., serviced several industries with acetylene products nationwide using a widespread, geographic distribution system. Airco's Calvert City, Kentucky, complex was the largest plant in the United States. The Calvert City plant produced carbide, generated acetylene for internal uses, and serviced several customers who had built plants at Calvert City to use acetylene as a raw material. Airco, Inc., did not produce any acetylene made from natural gas.

Airco, Inc.'s, physically integrated customers in 1965 included B.F. Goodrich Chemicals (vinyl chloride—$6 million in sales; (acrylonitrile—24 million pounds per year), Airco Chemical (vinyl acetate—30 million pounds per year), and General Aniline and Film (high-pressure acetylene derivates—$6 million in sales.) In addition to the Calvert City plant, Airco acetylene was produced at Louisville, Kentucky, and at about thirty other plants—for "bottled" merchandising.

Airco sold bottled acetylene chiefly to the steel and railroad industries, but sales were also made to the marine, automobile, oil, utility, and building industries. Airco sold 55 percent of its acetylene to outside firms.

Chemetron Corporation. Chemetron produced industrial gases, medical gases, welding and cutting equipment, and a diversified group of other industrial products. Industrial and medical gases and other chemical products accounted for about two-thirds of sales of $208.5 million and three-fourths of earnings of $14 million in 1965.

Chemetron's National Cylinder Gas division produced or sold high-purity oxygen, hydrogen, acetylene, nitrogen, and argon in liquid forms. It also sold oxy-acetylene and electric arc-welding and flame-cutting equipment. Chemetron's position in the industry was one of offering more technical services than many of the other industrial gas welding apparatus firms. The division also produced or sold medical testing equipment and other industrial devices. Chemetron's affiliate, Midwest Carbide Corporation (jointly owned with Shawnigan Products Corp.), owned and operated calcium-carbide plants in Keokuk, Iowa, and Pryor, Oklahoma. Acetylene was produced from calcium carbide by Chemetron at thirty-six National Cylinder Gas locations. Chemetron produced no hydrocarbon-based acetylene.

Chemetron was one of the leading suppliers of welding apparatus and gases in 1965. Unlike some of the other industrial-gas producers, Chemetron's National Cylinder Division did not equip a customer with a plant to generate the desired gases. Chemetron sold bottled acetylene mostly for welding, and supported it with a wide line of welding equipment and supplies.

Monsanto Company. The Monsanto Company manufactured a widely diversified line of chemical products which were sold to many different industries. Its largest products groups included chemical fibers, plastics, and synthetic resins; phosphate products and detergents; chemical intermediates and plasticizers; chemical yarns and fibers; and agricultural chemicals. Monsanto also produced ethylene, butadiene, and other substitutes for acetylene.

Monsanto used acetylene to produce acrylonitrile, vinyl acetate, and vinyl-chloride monomer. It supplied its acetylene operations in Texas City with natural gas which it produced in its Hydro-carbon Division. All acetylene produced by Monsanto was consumed internally.

An acetylene plant came on stream at Monsanto's Texas City chemical complex in 1952 to supply an acrylonitrile plant. The start-up of the acrylonitrile plant at Texas City was the largest single research project Monsanto had undertaken prior to 1952. The riskiness of this venture had been compounded by the use of the then-new BASF natural gas-based process for making acetylene, an even more costly venture. As the first of their kind, the downstream acrylonitrile and vinyl-chloride monomer plants were particularly customized for the use of the new hydrocarbon-based acetylene. Monsanto built its organic chemical program around acetylene, and the company increased the productive capacity of its acetylene plant through process improvements. The year in which the process improvements were completed, 1962, was also the year in which the Monsanto Company's Chocolate Bayou, Texas, chemicals plant came on line. The new plant, first announced in 1960, produced several feedstock chemicals which Monsanto required for internal consumption, including ethylene, which could be substituted for acetylene in the production of vinyl-chloride monomer. The new ethylene complex had a capacity of 500 million pounds per year. By 1963 Monsanto had built a second acrylonitrile plant. The second plant was located in Chocolate Bayou and used the propylene-ammonia route to producing acrylonitrile rather than acetylene.

Monochem, Inc. Borden Chemical and UniRoyal built an acetylene plant in a joint venture called Monochem, Inc., in 1962. The acetylene plant supplied feedstock to Borden Chemical's vinyl-chloride monomer plant and UniRoyal's vinyl-acetate and acetylenic-chemicals plant. Each of the partners to the joint venture erected plants next to the Monochem, Inc., acetylene plant in Geismar, Louisiana, for these purposes.

Borden was a holding company with interests in chemicals, dairy foods, processed foods, cosmetics, and bakery goods. Chemicals represented approximately 10 percent of its sales, which were $1,385.5 million in 1965. UniRoyal was a manufacturer of synthetic fibers, dyestuffs, and adhesives. UniRoyal produced and sold synthetic rubber produced in a joint venture with Texaco. The UniRoyal Chemical Division, which shared in the

Monochem plants output, produced synthetic elastomers, rubber chemicals, fungicides, and plastics materials. UniRoyals's worldwide chemical sales represented approximately 20 percent of corporate sales.

The Monochem venture had an initial capacity of 80 million pounds of acetylene per year, which was increased to 120 million pounds in 1964. When this capacity came on line, Monochem would represent 8 percent of 1965 total industry acetylene capacity.

There were several reasons why the Monochem, Inc., venture had been profitable. All of Monochem's sales were internal. The Monochem acetylene plant used the BASF process which at that time had the lowest unit costs for a plant of large capacity. Natural gas had been secured on a long-term contract at a low, fixed rate which would expire in 1981. The plant was running at full capacity in 1965 and had been so utilized by Borden and UniRoyal since its construction.

E.I. duPont de Nemours & Company. DuPont was the world's leading producer of chemical products in 1965. Its twelve industrial-product departments included elastomer chemicals, electro-chemicals, explosives, fabrics and finishes, film, industrial and biochemicals, organic chemicals, pigments, and plastics, as well as others. Total sales in 1965 were $2,999 million.

Acetylene was used by duPont to produce several products within several departments. However, in most of these cases, duPont was a *customer* for merchant acetylene rather than a consumer of internally generated acetylene. It was the largest consumer of acetylene in 1965.

DuPont's Elastomer Chemicals Department produced neoprene, a major patented synthetic-rubber product. Neoprene used acetylene as a feedstock. The Elastomer Chemicals Department, which represented 4 percent of corporate sales, constructed an acetylene plant in Montague, Michigan, in 1961 to supply its neoprene operations. The Montague plant used a natural-gas feedstock and an electric-arc technology which had been developed internally at duPont. This process gave duPont a cost structure which was significantly lower than that which any other acetylene producer enjoyed in 1965.

DuPont had an acetylene contract with Airco, Inc., for its Louisville, Kentucky, neoprene plant. At its other plants for producing polyvinyl acetate at Memphis and Niagara Falls, duPont purchased its needed supplies from the Union Carbide Corporation.

Diamond Shamrock. Diamond Shamrock was the combination of Diamond Alkali Company and the Shamrock Oil Company. It manufactured a large number of inorganic basic chemicals, such as soda ash, as well as a few organic chemicals within its Chemical Group. Diamond Shamrock also produced oil and gas and petrochemical products. Its Industrial Chemicals Division (sales of $170 million) had twice the volume of sales of its Plastics Division ($75 million). Corporate sales were $208.6 million in 1965.

In addition to providing its own natural gas, Diamond Shamrock was also forward-integrated to consume the acetylene it produced in the Plastics Division. Diamond Shamrock produced vinyl-chloride monomer in a plant linked to its Deer Park, Texas, acetylene plant.

When Diamond Shamrock had doubled its original vinyl-chloride monomer capacity in 1957, a captive acetylene plant was not yet justified by the monomer plant's raw materials needs. Diamond Shamrock purchased acetylene from a nearby source, instead, until demand for monomer necessitated construction of an acetylene plant. In 1960 the construction of an acetylene plant was considered to be necessary in order to strengthen Diamond Shamrock's raw-materials position. Chlorine, the other chemical required in order to produce vinyl-chloride monomer, had already been produced by Diamond Shamrock for several years.

The Diamond Shamrock acetylene plant came on line in 1962. Initially, all of the acetylene was consumed internally. The plant cost $10 million. Diamond Shamrock had purchased the Montecatini process for generating acetylene. The process was later discovered to possess several problems which reduced the plant's engineered efficiency and made it more expensive than the already-known BASF acetylene process. Diamond Shamrock spent almost $7 million more to remedy flaws found to exist in the Montecatini process.

Tenneco Corporation. The Tenneco Corporation was a holding company which controlled subsidiaries engaged in oil production and processing, chemical manufacturing; producing paperboard and packaging; and real estate, banking, and insurance. Corporate sales were $621 million in 1965. Tenneco's Chemical Division sales represented approximately 10 percent of corporate sales.

Tenneco Chemicals Division was formed through several acquisitions in the 1960s. Its major products in 1965 included organic chemical intermediates; industrial gases; vinyl-chloride monomer for consumption by the plastics division; and paints, resins, and petrochemicals. Tenneco Corporation tried to upgrade its profit margins by using some of its natural-gas production to produce nonregulated, higher-margin chemicals such as polyvinyl chloride, produced from vinyl-chloride monomer using acetylene as its feedstock. Tenneco's natural gas was price-regulated in its pipeline operations; PVC was not.

Tenneco Chemical's Houston acetylene plant was constructed in 1964. The new plant tried to exploit acetylene scale economies by using a new technology in order to produce at a capacity of 100 million pounds per year.

The plant's cost was estimated at $40 million, which meant a capital cost of 20 percent higher per pound than a smaller 30 million pounds a year acetylene plant. Although its capital costs were higher, however, its operating costs were expected to be the lowest in the industry.

The large new Tenneco Chemicals acetylene plant was designed to use the SBA-Kellogg process which, it was hoped, would be more efficient than the known BASF process. Tenneco began the start-up of its acetylene plant in early 1963. Because the plant failed to operate at designed levels of production and efficiency, numerous modifications and additions were made. Their cost is not known. By the end of 1963 the plant was operating at approximately 70 percent of designed capacity. During 1964 additional modifications were made, but the plant had still not reached design efficiency and capacity at year end. Additional alterations were made in 1965.

Tenneco sold acetylene to outside customers, as well as consuming it internally. Tenneco Chemicals, Inc., held a long-term marketing contract with a customer, Cary Chemicals, Inc., of New Jersey, who was waiting for Tenneco's acetylene and vinyl-chloride monomer capacity to come on line. Cary Chemicals used polyvinyl chloride to produce plastic floor and wall tiles, phonograph records, coatings for electric wire and other plastic products used in the home and by industry. In 1965 Tenneco had acquired Cary Chemicals. Tenneco Chemicals also supplied acetylene to Rohm & Haas and to duPont. The former used acetylene to produce acrylates; the latter, for the production of tetrahydrofuran.

American Cyanamid Company. American Cyanamid was a producer of cyanamid which, through acquisition or merger, diversified into the following product groups: pharmaceuticals, surgical specialities, synthesized building materials, Formica®, plastics and resins, fibers, industrial chemicals, organic chemicals, pigments, agricultural products and consumer shampoos and cleaning products. Total corporate sales were $863 million in 1965.

American Cyanamid had constructed an acetylene plant in 1954, in Fortier, Louisiana, as a part of its acrylonitrile plant complex. The Fortier complex had been built to replace an older, relatively obsolete acetylene complex in Warners, New Jersey. The Fortier complex had a large acetylene plant (100 million pounds per year) representing 6 percent of 1965 acetylene industry capacity. It had grown to this size after American Cyanamid had doubled its capacity (from 50 million pounds per year) in 1958 in order to accommodate the American Cyanamid acrylonitrile plant's growing demand for acetylene.

In 1965, American Cyanamid Company announced the opening of a new acrylonitrile facility at its Fortier site. The new plant would use ammonia and propylene to produce its acrylonitrile rather than use acetylene and oxygen. The company announced that some parts of the existing acrylonitrile unit at Fortier which had utilized the relatively low-cost BASF acetylene-based process would continue to operate as long as their output was needed. The cost of this BASF-process facility had been substantially depreciated, American Cyanamid reported.

Rohm & Haas Company. The Rohm & Haas company produced a diversified line of chemicals in 1965. Its major products included plastics, including Plexiglas® acrylic sheet, resinous products used in coatings, leather chemicals, textile and paper chemicals, and many other agricultural and sanitary chemicals. Rohm & Haas also operated a laboratory at the Redstone Arsenal under U.S. Army contract for basic research and development in rockets and propellants. Sales in 1965 totaled $347.5 million. For several decades the firm had prospered under the leadership of the founding Haas family.

Rohm & Haas Company produced acetylene which was all consumed internally in the production of acrylate monomers. Until 1959 the acetylene was generated from calcium carbide. In 1959 a BASF natural gas-process acetylene plant of 35 million pounds per year was added to supply acrylics production. Its cost was $10 million. Subsequent expansions of acrylic capacity were accomplished by purchasing acetylene from firms which had excess capacity in their acetylene plants and were located near the Rohm & Haas Company in Houston. Thus, although the Rohm & Haas Company's nameplate capacity was 2 percent of total 1965 industry capacity, Rohm & Haas Company actually consumed more acetylene than this. By 1965 the acetylene industry recognized that the BASF acetylene technology in which Rohm & Haas had invested was the lowest-cost acetylene process.

Air Products & Chemicals, Inc. Air Products & Chemicals, Inc., was a producer and distributor of industrial gases, catalysts, and chemicals. Its products included oxygen, hydrogen, argon, nitrogen, helium, anhydrous ammonia, acetylene fluorine, oxoalcohols, urethanes, and imidazoles. It manufactured and sold equipment for the production and distribution of chemicals. Although the industrial-gases business was important, Air Products and Chemicals was distinguished for its industrial-engineering and plant-engineering study services. Air Products also produced and sold cryogenic and welding equipment. Sales for 1965 were $121 million, of which 73 percent were from sales of industrial gases and related cutting and welding apparatus.

Although Air Products & Chemicals listed acetylene among the gases it produced and sold, it did not smelt calcium carbide but bought it from the Union Carbide, Airco, and others. Air Products & Chemicals served its acetylene customers from company-owned equipment located on customers' premises. It produced specialty gases for welding and cutting equipment which it had designed, of which acetylene was one. Air Products & Chemicals was the largest of a group of firms purchasing calcium carbide to generate acetylene for welding purposes, packaging the gas under compression to increase its value to customers.

Dow Chemical Company. Dow Chemical Company manufactured a diversified line of organic and inorganic chemicals, plastics, bio-products, and metals in 1965. Corporate sales were $1,176 million in that year. Dow Chemical Company's plastic products included polyvinyl chloride, acrylonitrile, and polyethylene. This product group comprised 36 percent of corporate-wide sales in 1965.

Dow Chemical Company's acetylene plant was supplied with raw materials from the company's Brazos Oil & Gas Company Division, which produced natural gas. Brazos Oil & Gas Company supplied a substantial portion of Dow Chemical Company's requirements in 1965.

Dow Chemical Company used the acetylene it produced to make acrylonitrile in the Dow Chemical Texas Division located in Freeport, Texas. Dow Chemical's acetylene plant was completed in 1958. The interconnected acrylonitrile plant came on line in 1959. At that time, acetylene and acrylonitrile were new products for Dow Chemical. Dow did not sell any acetylene in 1965.

Dow Chemical developed its own technological route in producing acetylene from hydrocarbons. Hence, no direct cost comparisons with other natural gas-based processes can be made here. However, there were economies of scale in producing acetylene when a plant exceeded 30 million pounds per year. Since the Dow Chemical plant was small its costs were probably higher than others' costs.

Summary of Competitive Environment. Only a fully loaded natural gas-based acetylene plant could achieve engineered operating economies, acetylene customers' switching costs to a new feedstock technology were high, and precedents had been established for customers to file suit for the termination of the chemical-supply contracts they had negotiated.

Acetylene producers pursued one of two product strategies for acetylene: (1) they produced acetylene for resale to industrial users either for chemical synthesis or for welding, or (2) they produced acetylene for internal consumption. The "merchant" acetylene firms frequently sold welding equipment, industrial gas delivery systems, and other products or services as well, for which acetylene was a complementary product.

In 1965 some producers of acetylene relied upon large customers to take a large portion of their acetylene capacity, and they would be most encumbered if, when they wished to exit, their large customers wanted to continue to use acetylene as a feedstock.

A Mapping of Strategic Groups
in the Acetylene Industry

Within the acetylene industry there were two major strategic dimensions along which the competitors could be arrayed: (1) degree of merchant sales compared with internal consumptions, and (2) hydrocarbon-based processes compared with calcium carbide-based processes. Within these classifications the firms could be grouped into strategic clusters as follows:

	Acetylene Produced Using a Natural-Gas or Hydrocarbon Process	Acetylene Produced Using a Calcium-Carbide Process
Primarily Merchant and Internal Consumption	Tenneco Chemical	Air Products & Chemicals Chemetron
	— Union Carbide Corp. —	
Primarily Internally Consumed	Monsanto American Cyanamid duPont Diamond Dow Chemical	Airco, Inc.
	Rohm & Haas Company	(Allied Chemical)

Along these axes, the firms most committed to a particular characteristic are positioned at the extremes of this "strategic space." For example, Rohm & Haas held a merchant position in acetylene only briefly in 1963; during most of the endgame, it purchased extra acetylene from the others. Although Tenneco constructed an acetylene plant for its own use, it also sold acetylene to others. Union Carbide straddled all categories. With its six major chemical-acetylene plants and many smaller welding-acetylene plants, Union Carbide had the broadest product strategy for acetylene.

In summary, the companies who produced acetylene had plants of significantly different sizes. They used their output in significantly different ways—for internal consumption or for external sales. They provided acetylene to customers for different end-uses—for chemical synthesis or for welding gas uses. Hence, the competitive structure was asymmetrical. The strategic group which provided acetylene for internal consumption for chemical synthesis uses was concentrated in structure. The structure of the strategic group who generated acetylene to sell to external customers was not concentrated. The competitors in the acetylene industry differed in other ways as well.

All firms did *not* produce products which could have been substituted for acetylene (such as ethylene or propylene). Firms differed across the industry in the strategic mission acetylene was intended to execute; missions were similar within the strategic groups, however. Nevertheless, despite these asymmetries in strategic diversity, in missions, and in ways in which firms satisfied the demand for acetylene, the largely contractual nature of buyer-seller relationships in this industry did *not* create a volatile competitive environment.

The Endgame in the Acetylene Industry

While relative costs of using acetylene as a feedstock versus ethylene, propylene, butadiene, and some other feedstock had been debated as early as 1962, by the middle to late 1960s it had been generally recognized that acetylene was no longer the optimal feedstock for several of its user markets in chemical synthesis. This conclusion was increasingly reinforced as natural-gas prices rose much more rapidly than the price of petroleum. By 1974 consumption of acetylene had decreased markedly for several chemical synthesis uses and had been eliminated completely from others. However, though acetylene sales were down sharply acetylene consumption for a few chemical synthesis uses had been increased by 1974.

Demand for welding acetylene had plateaued and was declining as more sophisticated welding and cutting devices using electricity or other gases besides acetylene were being aggressively commercialized. The relatively low price of acetylene torches allowed acetylene to retain salvage and heavy metal-cutting applications. Well-established, full-line welding-gas firms had been helped by the excess capacity of natural gas-based acetylene firms. Their excessive acetylene was compressed into welding cannisters and cost less than acetylene generated from carbide. This arrangement put some smaller welding-supply firms at a disadvantage if they had no such source for lower-cost acetylene. Table 10-2 summarizes the production and shipments of acetylene through 1977.

A Chronological Description of the Acetylene Endgame

1966

American Cyanamid. In 1966 the new acrylonitrile manufacturing unit at American Cyanamid's Fortier, Louisiana, complex began producing. It did *not* use acetylene as a feedstock. The older, acetylene-based facility at the same location was phased out of operation in the latter part of 1966.

Table 10-2
Production and Shipments of Acetylene

Year	Estimated Capacity (millions of pounds/year)	Production		Shipments		Value of Shipments ($1,000)	Average Value of Shipments (¢/lb.)
		(billions of cubic feet)	(millions of pounds/year)	(billions of cubic feet)	(millions of pounds/year)		
1977	950	5.91	408	n.a.	n.a.	n.a.	n.a.
1976	950	7.11	490	4.41	304	$133,984	.44
1975	1,049	6.70	462	4.14	286	129,100	.45
1974	1,049	7.81	538	4.80	331	99,844	.30
1973	1,079	8.28	571	5.06	349	78,864	.23
1972	1,079	11.46	790	7.21	497	93,876	.27
1971	1,369	12.35	852	7.72	532	102,001	.19
1970	1,383	14.83	1,023	8.92	615	98,952	.16
1969	1,482	15.82	1,091	9.37	646	98,542	.15
1968	1,482	15.07	1,039	8.15	562	89,025	.16
1967	1,485	14.27	984	8.18	564	87,147	.16
1966	1,485	16.60	1,145	9.55	659	97,532	.15
1965	1,585	16.66	1,149	9.69	668	98,000	.15

Sources: Bureau of the Census, Department of Commerce; *Chemical Economics Handbook* (Fairfield, N.J.: Charles Kling & Company, 1978).

Tenneco Chemical. In 1966 Tenneco announced an expansion of the facilities using acetylene feedstock. The Tenneco vinyl-chloride monomer plant (255 million pounds a year) and an oxygen air separation plant, both a part of the integrated acetylene-based complex, were expanded.

Chemetron Corporation. In 1966 Chemetron Corporation acquired a Hawaii-based producer of industrial gases, welding, and industrial products. Its product line included oxygen, nitrogen, argon, acetylene, and carbon dioxide.

1967

Rohm & Haas. Since 1964 Rohm & Haas Company invested more than $200 million in a new acrylate-monomer plant in Houston, Texas. This massive expansion included the construction of more acetylene-generating capacity. Although propylene had been suggested as being a less costly route than acetylene to acrylate production, Rohm & Haas did not invest in propylene assets in 1967.

Diamond Shamrock. In 1967 Diamond Shamrock's vinyl-chloride monomer operation at Deer Park, Texas, interrupted production to repair damage resulting from an acetylene-handling explosion. Damages from the blast exceeded $1 million and two employees were injured. Diamond Shamrock kept its polyvinyl-chloride operations running by purchasing vinyl-chloride monomer from other producers. It soon became clear that it was cheaper to buy vinyl-chloride monomer than to produce it using an acetylene-based process.

1968

Airco, Inc. In 1968 Airco, Inc., expanded its own vinyl-acetate monomer operations which consumed acetylene at Calvert City, Kentucky, to double its previous capacity. However, Airco's plastics group also sold two vinyl-fabrics plants in 1968, which had consumed some of the chemical intermediates produced from acetylene. Many of Airco, Inc.'s, chemical-synthesis customers for acetylene had switched to other feedstock technologies or closed down their plants. Consequently Airco, Inc., had to reposition its uses of acetylene to consume more of its own acetylene internally.

Dow Chemical. In 1968 the acetylene requirements of the Dow-Badische plant which used the gas to produce acrylate had increased. Dow Chemical expanded its acetylene capacity by 7 million pounds per year to meet these needs, increasing its acetylene capacity to 15 million pounds per year.

E.I. duPont de Nemours Company. Apparently the Hüels-technology acetylene plant duPont had erected was not as cost-efficient as duPont had boasted it would be. In 1968 a duPont Company spokesperson indicated that it might decide to close its Montague, Michigan, acetylene plant. Industry sources suggested that the 50 million pounds per year plant would be closed when a new internal-consumption contract for acetylene could be negotiated. The actual shutdown was announced in May 1968. DuPont's 70 million pounds per year neoprene operation continued to be fed by acetylene generated from calcium carbide by Union Carbide nearby. This was the same calcium carbide-based acetylene generating plant which Union Carbide had used earlier to supply duPont's needs for acetylene. It had been operating when the neoprene plant was built but it had been idled when duPont built its Hüels-technology plant. DuPont bought the plant from Union Carbide and, apparently, renegotiated a contract for a supply of calcium carbide to run it. In 1968 duPont produced neoprene (using acetylene) at Louisville, Kentucky, Deep Water, New Jersey, and Beaumont, Texas, as well.

Monsanto Company. In 1968 Monsanto Company closed its 150 million pounds a year vinyl-chloride monomer plant at Texas City, Texas, and reduced acetylene capacity by 25 million pounds a year. This shutdown was in accordance with the plan which was formulated in 1960. Since 1962 Monsanto Company had successfully run a process for producing vinyl-chloride monomer from ethylene. However, it did not have a strong position in chlorine, the other raw material needed in this process. Hence in 1968 Monsanto Company quit producing monomer completely and purchased it from an outside vendor at a lower cost. There were no write-off losses attributed to the acetylene investment from this decision (the Monsanto plant had been built in 1952). The closing of the vinyl-chloride monomer plant drastically changed the economics of Monsanto's Texas City acetylene-based plants. Acetylene was used only for acrylonitrile productions, and the days of Monsanto's remaining acetylene operations were numbered because the acrylonitrile plant was scheduled to be shut down.

Union Carbide. In 1968 construction for a new Wulff-process acetylene-ethylene plant commenced at Taft, Louisiana. The new plant had the capacity to produce 18 million pounds of acetylene per year. Union Carbide probably erected the plant for the ethylene capacity, however.

Monochem, Inc. In 1968 the Borden Chemical Company, one of the owners of Monochem, doubled its vinyl-acetate monomer capacity at Geismer, Louisiana, while continuing to use acetylene as a feedstock. The acetylene-generating capacity of Monochem, Inc., was expanded to 165 million pounds per year to accommodate this expansion. Monochem purchased its natural-gas requirements under a very favorable fixed-price contract. Hence it was not as vulnerable as most other firms to the changing economics of natural gas and ethylene.

Borden's reaffirmation of dependence upon acetylene came at a time when several foreign producers had renovated their vinyl-acetate monomer capacity, substituting acetylene plants with plants using an ethylene-based process. In 1968 *Chemical and Engineering News* reported that duPont, Monsanto, and Airco were all considering new plants for vinyl-acetate monomer expansions that would use ethylene rather than acetylene.

1969

Airco, Inc. The carbide segment of Airco, Inc.'s, Alloys & Carbide Division did not attain the level of profitability which the firm had anticipated in 1969. Several factors were cited as contributing to this poor performance. Sales of acetylene had declined and labor and raw-materials price increases offset increased revenues gained from selling price increases. A major maintenance problem on the furnace at Calvert City, Kentucky, also penalized Airco's 1969 performance. Greater than anticipated start-up costs were suffered in the installation of a new 50,000-kilowatt furnace at the Louisville, Kentucky, carbide-acetylene plant.

Rohm & Haas Company. In its 1969 annual report, which detailed construction expenditures, the Rohm & Haas Company announced the construction of an acrylate-monomer plant using a propylene-oxidation process instead of acetylene. This unit would be Rohm & Haas's first use of the propylene process. Acrylate monomers were still being produced using acetylene in 1969; however, the new technology was expected to be available by 1972 and would eventually replace the acetylene-based process.

In 1969 the U.S. Department of the Interior's Office of Coal Research sponsored research by Avco Corporation to develop an inexpensive way to pyrolyze coal to produce acetylene. Coal had been the foundation of the European carbon-based chemicals industry. Avco researchers expected to be able to produce acetylene from coal at a delivered cost of 4 to 5 cents per pound (in 1969 the delivered price of Gulf Coast acetylene was approximately 10 cents per pound). A commercial acetylene plant was expected to be operating in 1978.

1970

Monsanto Company. In 1970 Monsanto shut down its multi-million-dollar, 100 million pounds a year acetylene plant, 130 million pounds a year acrylonitrile plant, and 80 million pounds a year vinyl-acetate monomer plant. Monsanto abandoned acetylene completely and switched to ethylene and synthetic-gas feedstock. The Texas City site was leveled. Since the acetylene-related assets were well depreciated by 1970 there was relatively little write-off. There is always some write-off loss associated with this type of shutdown because of the annual reinvestments which must be made in the acetylene plant to keep it operative. Acetylene produced in a cracking plant produces some soot which clogs its apertures, the openings where raw materials and by-products flowed. It must be cleaned out, using a jackhammer in some cases.

Chemetron. Construction on a new 12 million cubic feet per year (0.8 million pounds a year) calcium-carbide acetylene plant in South Haven, Mississippi was begun by Chemetron in 1970. A Chemetron plant for producing welding consumables in Costa Rica was completed. Chemetron was also expanding its sphere of operations by investing to become a major supplier of welding products throughout the world. Growth in industrial-gases consumption was most rapid in overseas markets, Chemetron had found. It was also experiencing great success in its welding supply business in the United States.

Airco, Inc. In 1970 Airco, Inc., sold its chemicals and plastics businesses. Some of the products produced by these businesses had consumed acetylene produced at its Calvert City and Louisville, Kentucky, plants. Many of Airco's other acetylene customers had shut down their interconnected plants as well.

E.I. duPont de Nemours Company. In 1970 the duPont Company announced the construction of neoprene plants in LaPlace, Louisiana, and Victoria, Texas, which would utilize a superior new chemical process based on butadiene as the basic raw material instead of acetylene.

In 1970, 218 establishments reported the production of acetylene. Of these, 204 generated acetylene from calcium carbide.

1971

The Rohm & Haas Company. Although Rohm & Haas was expanding its acrylate-monomer capacity, it had not started construction of the propylene plant which it had proposed as the new feedstock to its acrylate operations in 1969. In 1971 the Rohm & Haas Company again announced an expansion of its acrylate capacity in Houston. The acrylate expansion meant that either more acetylene would be needed or the new propylene plant would have to be built and the accompanying technical changes would have to occur. Rohm & Haas delayed the capital expansion through a short-term acetylene sourcing agreement with Tenneco Chemicals.

For a very brief time in 1963, Rohm & Haas had sold some of its excess acetylene capacity to Diamond Shamrock, whose plant was giving it trouble and who used acetylene to produce vinyl-chloride monomer. As it became more economical to purchase the vinyl-chloride monomer, Diamond Shamrock reduced its use of internally produced acetylene in 1969 and sold its excess acetylene capacity to Rohm & Haas, who by 1969 needed more acetylene for its acrylates production. This arrangement enabled Rohm & Haas to expand its acrylate-monomer capacity without adding another acetylene plant and without building the proposed propylene plant.

Airco, Inc. Airco, Inc., reported adverse performance in both the sales and earnings of its acetylene and calcium-carbide businesses in 1971. The sharp decline in industry sales of these products was attributed to a generally soft economy. However, the exodus of many of Airco, Inc.'s, acetylene customers might have had an influence upon Airco's performance problems. Airco's acetylene plant was severely underutilized.

In 1971 a small company (Flamex Systems, Inc.) introduced a substitute welding gas, Flamex, which gave a hotter flame than acetylene but which was less toxic than American Cyanamid's popular synthetic fuel gas, Cyanogen. This and other synthetic welding fuels were considered to be superior substitutes for acetylene. In addition to competition from these synthetic gases, acetylene welding fuels also faced competition from electric welding technologies as these technologies also improved. Acetylene welding fuel was relegated to a few unglamorous uses such as cutting apart wreckages or salvage work by 1971. Acetylene was preferred only in cases where the cost of welding or cutting was important. Acetylene was less expensive than many of the new welding gases.

Chemetron. The National Cylinder Division of Chemetron was reorganized in 1971 to expand Chemetron's line of welding products and services. Chemetron sold the older oxyacetylene torches as well as the newer super welding gases. The reorganization gave National Cylinder responsibility for replacement sales of acetylene canisters.

Tenneco. By 1971 Tenneco had discovered that it was cheaper to purchase vinyl-chloride monomer than to produce it using an acetylene-based technology. As Tenneco Chemicals tried to back out of vinyl-chloride monomer production, it obtained a sales contract to supply acetylene to the duPont Company, who used it to produce tetrahydrofuran. When, in 1972, the Diamond Shamrock acetylene plant was shut down, the Tenneco Corporation also undertook Diamond Shamrock's sales contract to the Rohm & Haas Company. This meant that Rohm & Haas Company, which was already purchasing some acetylene from Tenneco Corporation, expanded its purchases from Tenneco.

Although Tenneco was backing out of its own vinyl-chloride monomer investment, it still had sales contracts to provide customers with polyvinyl chloride. Tenneco closed its own vinyl-chloride monomer plant, but continued to service the other customers. The monomer used to produce polyvinyl chloride was purchased on the market. Tenneco's vinyl-chloride monomer plant was a smaller capital investment than was its massive and relatively new acetylene-generating plant. Hence, Tenneco shut down the monomer plant first.

By 1971 there was some demand for technical assistance in building acetylene plants in Middle Eastern countries rich in natural gas which had decided to produce acetylene-based chemicals. Tenneco and Diamond Shamrock both participated in such technical-assistance contracts.

1972

Diamond Shamrock. In 1972 Diamond Shamrock shut down the Deer Park acetylene plant. The total write-off was $2 million ($1 million after tax). Diamond Shamrock no longer consumed its acetylene output internally. When Diamond Shamrock discovered that it was cheaper to buy vinyl-chloride monomer than produce it, it had sold its acetylene output to the Rohm & Haas Company.

Airco, Inc. In its 1972 annual report, Airco, Inc., made an extraordinary charge to income of $16 million, net of related tax benefits of $14.7 million, to provide for losses which totaled $30.7 million before tax related to the discontinuation of its carbide-acetylene business at Calvert City, Kentucky. Airco had hoped to be able to convert many of its large carbide furnaces there to the manufacture of ferroalloys. However, large increases in the cost of power and the substantial cost of installing and operating effective air-pollution controls forced Airco to abandon this asset-recovery plan. Airco, Inc., continued to operate the Louisville carbide facilities until contractual commitments had been fulfilled. Although Airco, Inc., continued to sell acetylene as a part of its full-line strategy for industrial gases, the company purchased this acetylene and resold it to its customers as needed when the Louisville output was not available.

Monochem, Inc. In 1972 the Monochem acetylene-plant capacity was again expanded to a new capacity of 180 million pounds a year. Because Monochem, Inc., was protected from natural-gas price increases by its long-term supply contract, it was able to benefit from the operating economics of a larger plant and the most efficient acetylene process, the BASF technology.

1973

The American Chemical Society found that 70 percent of the 750,000 tons of calcium carbide made in the United States in 1973 were used in the chemical-synthesis markets. Another 25 percent of the calcium carbide was used to make acetylene for oxyacetylene welding, cutting, and scarfing. The iron and steel industry used the other 5 percent for nonacetylene-related uses. Nevertheless, 80 percent of the acetylene produced in 1973 came from hydrocarbon-based processes.

Rohm & Haas. In 1973 the Rohm & Haas Company again announced the start of construction upon a new 400 million pounds a year acrylate-monomer plant at Houston. The new facility would use the propylene-oxidation process. It was scheduled for start-up in early 1976. Rohm & Haas's acrylic sales had been growing so successfully that it had become evident that there would not be adequate acetylene nearby to satisfy its needs. Building another acetylene plant was not economic in light of higher natural-gas prices and greater operating efficiencies from other feedstock gases.

In 1973, 212 establishments reported the production of acetylene. Six exits had occurred since 1970.

1974

The *Chemicals Handbook* reported the consumption of 507 million pounds of acetylene in 1974. Seventy percent of this was derived from hydrocarbons. Welding and metal cutting accounted for 21 percent of the acetylene consumed in 1974. This meant that much excess acetylene produced from natural gas was being bottled for sale in the welding market.

During the period 1967 to 1974, twenty-three chemical plants using acetylene were closed down, retiring an aggregate capacity of 1,030 million pounds a year. Few firms which produced and consumed acetylene internally still retained their plants for captive consumption in 1975.

Union Carbide no longer produced vinyl-chloride monomer using acetylene at South Charleston, West Virginia, or at Texas City, Texas.

Monsanto, Diamond Shamrock, Allied Chemical, and Airco had also ceased to produce vinyl-chloride monomer from their own acetylene feedstocks by 1975. American Cyanamid and Monsanto ceased producing acrylonitrile from captive acetylene. Airco, Monsanto, and Union Carbide no longer produced vinyl-acetate monomer from internally produced acetylene. The firms which had used acetylene as a feedstock had shut down their uneconomic plants, leaving only a few vertically integrated producers of acetylene for chemical-synthesis uses. Most of the firms which still generated chemical-synthesis acetylene did so in fulfillment of customers' contractual obligations.

As the price of natural gas increased, acetylene prices had to be increased. When natural gas was priced at 30 cents per thousand cubic feet (MCF), acetylene cost 12 to 14 cents per pound (on average) to manufacture. When natural gas was priced at 50 cents per MCF, acetylene would cost 14 to 16 cents per pound (on average). During endgame, the price of natural gas rose to $2.00 per MCF. Acetylene costs were estimated at 29 to 32 cents per pound. In 1975 calcium carbide-based acetylene had cost 20 cents per pound as the price of calcium carbide had risen more slowly than the price of natural gas. Prices (cents per pound) for acetylene shipments during endgame were as follows:

Year	Pipeline	Compression
1971	13.7	41.8
1972	13.2	40.7
1973	14.3	40.9
1974	20.4	49.9
1975	33.8	66.6

Source: *Current Industrial Reports*, Series M28C. U.S. Dept. of Commerce, Bureau of the Census.

In 1975 almost 70 percent of the acetylene-generating capacity was held by the four largest firms (Airco, Union Carbide, Monochem, and Tenneco) and 88 percent of industry capacity was held by the eight largest firms. Although the percentage of acetylene used for welding-gas purposes had doubled (to 24 percent) by 1976, most acetylene generated was still used in chemical synthesis.

Tenneco. In late 1974 a new Tenneco polyvinyl chloride facility had been completed and was in operation. It used a purchased supply of vinyl-chloride monomer. Although Tenneco no longer needed the acetylene plant for captive production of vinyl-chloride monomer, the plant could not be shut down because Tenneco was bound by contract to provide acetylene to both Rohm & Haas and duPont.

1976

Rohm & Haas Company. A major new plant was completed at Houston, Texas, by the Rohm & Haas Company for the production of acrylate monomers via the propylene-oxidation process in 1976. The plant gave Rohm & Haas added acrylate monomer capacity of 100 million pounds per year. Although Rohm & Haas intended to shut down both its acetylene plant and its acetylene-based acrylates plant, the company kept both plants on line during 1977 as a precaution against process difficulties in the new acrylate monomer plant. If the new process did not work, the old integrated complex would have to be revived. The cost of the acetylene plant which came on line in 1959 was estimated at $10 million. It had not been written off in 1977, although it appeared to have been mothballed. The acetylene plant represented the largest part of the total cost of the acrylates facility.

Tenneco. The impending shutdown of Rohm & Haas Company's acetylene-based acrylate monomer operations reduced the amount of acetylene which could be sold in that market. Although a contract with du-Pont had been negotiated in anticipation of a great demand for acetylene used in producing tetrahydrofuran, the demand did not materialize. Tenneco's acetylene plant was operating at a very low level of capacity utilization in 1976 after Rohm & Haas closed its acetylene-based plant and ceased consumption of Tenneco's acetylene.

Union Carbide Corporation. The November 1976 profile of acetylene production in *Chemical Marketing Reporter* showed four changes in the acetylene-producing activities of Union Carbide's natural gas-based acetylene plants. The Texas City, Texas, plant was reduced from 80 to 25 million pounds a year; the Taft, Louisiana, plant was reduced from 18 to 12 million pounds a year; the Seadrift, Texas, plant was increased from 15 to 20 million pounds a year; and a new ethylene plant which produced 12 million pounds a year of acetylene coproduct came on line in Ponce, Puerto Rico. These changes were easily executed since Union Carbide Wulff-technology plants produced both ethylene and acetylene in controllable proportions.

Much of Union Carbide's acetylene by-product was bottled and sold for welding purposes. General Aniline and Film consumed some of the by-product acetylene produced by Union Carbide in making Reppe chemicals.

In 1976, 202 establishments reported production of acetylene.

1977

The profitability of acetylene was squeezed in 1977 by a combination of rising natural gas ($2.00 per MCF) and energy prices and falling acetylene prices (a 3.5 percent annual decline in prices). The latter was an abrupt change from the pattern of increases previously shown. As the price of natural gas rose, long-term acetylene requirements contracts were being reassessed and some firms decided to phase out acetylene in 1977.

1978

Although Tenneco Chemical had terminated internal uses of acetylene, its acetylene plant (which was the costliest part of the chemicals complex) was still bound by contract to supply duPont. Tenneco negotiated a contract whereby Rohm & Haas Company restarted its acetylene plant which had been mothballed and was held as a precaution in case the new propylene technology did not work. Under a cost-plus management contract, Rohm & Haas Company started supplying duPont with acetylene in autumn 1978. Tenneco's 100 million pounds a year acetylene plant, which had been operating inefficiently at 50-percent capacity, was scrapped. Little recovery of asset values was possible. The write-off loss for closing this Houston plant was approximately $2 million. The cost-plus contract gave Rohm & Haas Company a guaranteed profit margin for the sale of acetylene regardless of how high the costs of its natural-gas feedstock rose. Rohm & Haas no longer had any asset exposure in this business and the plant was operated as if it were duPont's own plant.

In 1978 the following firms were still producing significant amounts of acetylene: Dow Chemical, Monochem, the Rohm & Haas plant, Chemetron, Air Products and Chemicals, and Union Carbide (at more than five plants).

In 1981, industry sources estimate, the cost of operating the Monochem plant will quintuple when the natural-gas contract expires. At that time, the plant will be fully depreciated, and in all likelihood will be terminated.

Industry sources indicated that Monochem sells its excess acetylene to Union Carbide, who bottles it to resell for welding purposes. The Monochem acetylene is significantly less expensive than is the calcium route to making acetylene used by Union Carbide.

Analysis of the Acetylene Endgame

Exits from the welding acetylene markets were orderly and did not create major write-off losses. Because the price of calcium carbide increased slowly, most firms which sold acetylene generated from calcium in this form had adequate time to discontinue their product offerings and the price of their acetylene rose slowly, without difficulty, until 1975. Because the welding firms were well diversified, they encountered few emotional barriers in replacing acetylene with a more expensive synthetic gas or with an electric welding product. Although there were so many regional firms operating in this part of the acetylene endgame that there appeared to be little advantage in being among the last firms in the industry, firms like Chemetron and Air Products appeared to perform satisfactorily in this endgame. Chemetron in particular expanded the level of its investment in the acetylene business.

The pattern of exits from the chemical-synthesis part of the acetylene industry was not uniform. Although some firms were able to plan orderly exits and incurred few write-off losses or disruptions to other corporate activities, other firms which wanted to exit were locked into unprofitable customer contracts which made their exits haphazard, incurring substantial write-off losses because their timing was poor. The differences in the experiences of firms in the chemical-synthesis portion of the acetylene endgame may have been due to the different amounts of uncertainty firms held regarding the speed of and extent to which other feedstocks would become less expensive than acetylene. Because downstream sales were contractual, there was no advantage to being the last firm in this part of the industry because one did not gain abandoned customers in doing so. (The exception here is the Rohm & Haas experience: the firm experienced an unexpected windfall return for the use of its acetylene-generating assets to serve another firm's customers.) There was not much opportunity for chemical synthesis firms which had not previously sold a portion of their excess acetylene to the welding market to be able to enter this market later in the endgame due to strengths of previously established marketing relationships.

The only significant reinvestments in the chemical synthesis acetylene endgame were (1) some new Wulff ethylene-acetylene plants which replaced older, obsolete, or experimental plants and (2) some expenses incurred in clearing away the sites where obsoleted acetylene plants had previously been operated. Each remaining producer incurred annual reinvestment requirements in order to maintain its acetylene plants, as it had in the past. The firms which enjoyed the best performances in the chemical-synthesis markets were those firms which used acetylene internally. Firms which were locked into the industry through outside customer contracts were less flexible in their asset deployment, and did not enjoy successful performances as frequently as did firms which controlled acetylene consumption by being vertically integrated. A summary of industry conditions in 1965 follows.

Characteristics

Demand. Acetylene was supplied on a contractual basis in most cases in 1965. Although demand was price sensitive, switching to another product as a feedstock represented a major change in a firm's production technology and investment base.

Product Differentiation. The industrial gas, acetylene, was a commodity which meant the services accompanying the providing of acetylene could be differentiated, but the physical product itself offered little potential for differentiation.

Markets. In 1965, 88 percent of the acetylene produced was used for chemical synthesis of plastics and synthetic fibers. Acetylene was also used in welding activities.

Substitutes. Other feedstocks (for chemical uses) became less costly than acetylene. Other welding gases were better suited for specialty applications, but they were not necessarily less expensive than acetylene in 1965.

Customer Industries. Users of acetylene had much bargaining power if their needs were supplied under a contract with the acetylene-generating firm and if they were interconnected. Many chemical users were backward-integrated into acetylene in 1965. Welding gas users of acetylene had relatively less bargaining power over suppliers.

Supplier Industries. Producers of carbide were usually forward-integrated into acetylene. Some natural gas producers were forward-integrated into acetylene. Equal amounts of carbide or natural-gas raw materials were consumed to make acetylene in the base year.

Manufacturing Technology. The carbide-and-water bottled process was quite old. Hydrocarbon continuous-cracking processes to produce acetylene were relatively newer and lower in cost. The natural-gas processes required sophisticated chemical engineering skills due to the gas's volatility.

Technological Innovation. Many firms developed their own processes to generate acetylene. Each firm's process innovation hoped to lower the unit cost of the acetylene generated.

Capital Intensity. If a firm purchased calcium carbide to generate its acetylene, capital costs were relatively low. Where larger amounts of acetylene were required, and either a hydrocarbon-cracking plant or a carbide-smelting plant were used, capital costs were very high. The hydrocarbon-based plants which were relatively new in 1965 were highly specific to acetylene production in addition to being durable. In 1965 carbide-smelting furnaces could have been used elsewhere (but by 1970 environmental-quality standards limited their transferability to other uses).

Competitive Structure. When 88 percent of the acetylene produced was consumed internally or by contractual customers, the twenty firms which generated acetylene did not compete with each other. The welding-supply firms (over 185 companies which comprised the other 12 percent of total consumption) did compete as a part of selling their welding tools and services.

Analysis of Declining Demand

Demand for acetylene in the welding markets declined slowly, allowing firms which wished to discontinue acetylene-welding supplies ample time in which to do so. All uses of acetylene for welding did not disappear, as acetylene continued to be used for repair work or other, less specialized applications. Because demand declined slowly, and uncertainty was low, significant losses did not occur in this market.

Demand for acetylene in the chemical-synthesis markets was affected by the timing of development and the costs of substitute feedstocks as well as by the ease with which users could switch to these substitutes. For example, ethylene and butadiene processes were perfected relatively early, but the propylene process did not reach a condition of economic attractiveness until later in the endgame. Firms which monitored the R&D investments of the plastics and synthetic fibers industry could have planned their acetylene investments to accommodate these technological improvements. It would be expected that where a chemical process such as the partial oxydation of acetylene has been acknowledged to be physically inefficient relative to that of other substitute feedstocks and where doubt regarding the viability of the product is clarified through increases in the prices of the process's raw materials (in this case, natural gas), participants would recognize these conditions and exit if it were appropriate to do so. Five of the chemical-synthesis firms producing acetylene exited completely and two more of these firms closed down at least one of several acetylene plants during the endgame. The exits occurred as soon as substitute feedstocks were identified and acetylene-generating assets could be retired smoothly in the cases of Monsanto, American Cyanamid, duPont, and Rohm & Haas. Airco, Diamond Shamrock, and Tenneco Chemical exited despite large write-off losses when a smooth exit from their respective acetylene investments was difficult to execute. In general, firms in the chemical-synthesis acetylene market understood the inevitability of the decline of acetylene when substitutes became cheaper but they could not respond promptly to the timing of declining demand for acetylene (despite their rapidly rising operating costs) because they had invested in acetylene assets in a particularly inflexible manner due to an earlier misreading of the duration of demand.

In summary, demand for acetylene in welding and metal-cutting applications is expected to continue since some customers must have acetylene-cutting tools and supplies. Firms which were in an advantageous position to serve this petrified demand (Chemetron, Big Three Industries, and others) would be expected to remain in the endgame. But demand for chemical-synthesis acetylene is not expected to remain viable or to revitalize given natural gas costs and the costs of utilizing acetylene-process chemical plants. Reinvestments in this technology would be unusual unless (1) the relative costs of other chemical feedstocks increased significantly, or (2) if the coal-arc process developed by Avco Research were to offer very low costs per unit. However, such a new acetylene technology would very likely require new acetylene-generating plants and new receiving plants for use with the acetylene plant, and would offer little promise to a firm which would be reluctant to invest in the new process plants needed for generating and utilizing acetylene.

Analysis of Endgame Industry Traits

The acetylene industry did not possess favorable traits. The potential exit barriers were high and the manufacturing technology created undesirable cash-flow requirements. Moreover, the economic operating size of an acetylene plant frequently necessitated dependence upon outside customers to consume a firm's excess acetylene production, making the industry environment "unfavorable" for continued participation and reinvestments. Thus firms were not expected to reinvest in this endgame unless they possessed a unique competitive advantage or a compelling strategic need to remain an acetylene producer.

Product Characteristics

Although acetylene was a commodity, the engineering (handling) skills needed in avoiding explosions or other delivery services could be used to differentiate a particular firm's product offering, enabling particular firms to gain those niches of demand where industrial gas customers valued services, including technical counseling, in choosing a vendor or supplier or interconnected chemical-synthesis operations. Union Carbide served many interconnected customers at its several locations because it was perceived as being the best-qualified firm to provide many potential customers with acetylene.

Buyer Characteristics

Welding-gas users of acetylene which had recently purchased acetylene-based equipment tended to repurchase acetylene gas canisters even when more effective substitutes became available because they faced moderately high switching costs. Use of new gases would require the purchase of new welding equipment. Therefore suppliers' cost increases could be passed on to these customers in price increases and customers would not balk at these higher prices. Welding-supply vendors frequently discontinued their acetylene lines if they were not concerned with maintaining a full product line because the turnover of acetylene products slowed significantly. Moreover the margins on many substitute welding gases were substantially higher than that on acetylene. If customers were slightly price insensitive, they could frequently be switched to these higher-priced, higher-margin products which replaced the less-efficient acetylene tools.

Customers using acetylene for chemical synthesis were not expected to switch to other feedstocks as easily because for them the cost of using another chemical for monomer production was usually the cost of a new plant. Unless customers (1) incurred heavy opportunity costs by not switching to a lower-cost raw material or (2) had already operated the acetylene-based receiving plant long enough to recapture much of the value of their plants, switches to other feedstocks were infrequent. Vertical integration provided an acetylene-generating firms with greater flexibility in managing their asset investment because when the cost grew too high to continue supplying acetylene to downstream (captive) users, the whole package of assets was evaluated in the exit decision to avoid opportunity costs incurred in acetylene generation for the sake of marginally profitable monomer-production activities.

Supplier Characteristics

Because there were other lucrative uses for calcium carbide and natural gas as raw materials, integrated suppliers were not expected to continue generating acetylene when demand declined. Companies like Tenneco and Diamond Shamrock which had previously upgraded natural gas to acetylene to obtain higher nonregulated prices for their products in interstate commerce could achieve that benefit in other ways after their prices increased and substitute products had eroded the demand for acetylene and had freed them of their supply contracts to outside firms.

Technological Characteristics

The most important product trait in this endgame was the cost of raw materials and of production. Although large, capital-intensive plants possessed the lowest operating costs when fully loaded, economic exit barriers also kept other firms operating in this industry which were not able to enjoy good cash flows or a high degree of asset retrieval upon exit because of the technological problems inherent in their acetylene plants.

Economic Exit Barriers. There were two types of exit barriers which reflected the costliness of exiting from the chemical synthesis acetylene market. The shutdown of an acetylene plant would incur substantial removal costs due to the capital intensity of the partial-oxidation process. The write-off loss which may have been incurred could also act as a substantial deterrent. Acetylene generation for chemical-synthesis markets was highly risky because the capital investment required to enter this business was high ($10 million minimum for a partial oxidation plant) and annual maintenance expenses (which were as high as $1 million per year) were required. The physical assets were highly specific to acetylene generation and the downstream receiving plant for producing chemical monomers was also highly inflexible in its uses. Given these high exit barriers, firms which had recently erected acetylene plants might be expected to remain in this endgame even after it became uneconomic to do so because firms like Diamond Shamrock, Tenneco, and Airco still faced recognition of write-off losses on the highly undepreciated values of their acetylene plants in 1965. (When Diamond Shamrock and Tenneco made significant reinvestments in their technologically flawed processes, these reinvestments did not correct their technological problems, but rather they raised the height of the economic exit barriers these firms faced because the cost of exiting became even higher.) Some integrated acetylene firms continued to operate their plants even after it became clear that they could have purchased vinyl-chloride monomer or vinyl-acetate monomer more cheaply than they could produce it because their acetylene plants were still too undepreciated and the consequent write-off loss would be too large to abandon them.

Although acetylene plants were highly specific and would have little resale value when abandoned, some firms did shut them down early rather than continue to operate inefficient plants. E.I. duPont de Nemours, for example, ignored the sunk costs of its acetylene plant, concluding that an unacceptable opportunity cost was being incurred by operating its Hüels electric-arc acetylene plant when the differences in feedstock prices became significantly disadvantageous. Raw materials represented a large proportion of the cost of producing acetylene; for example, the price of natural gas (which was approximately 40 percent of the operating costs of a partial-oxidation acetylene plant) increased ten-fold during endgame.

Although it may be reasonable to assume that acetylene firms could recover some damages for supply contracts which were repudiated before their expiration, most transitions from acetylene to a rival technology occurred when supply contracts expired. The physical value of carbide-based acetylene-generation plants which had been built particularly for some of these customer needs was depreciated on a schedule to coincide with contract expirations. Carbide supply shipments could be stopped after advance notification had been given by their customers, and a carbide acetylene firm's exit from such an investment in plant and equipment could be relatively smooth. Similarly, some exits from chemical-synthesis production using natural gas could be executed cleanly.

Firms which did not smelt their own calcium carbide did not encounter substantial economic exit barriers because they could sell their inventories to another supply house if that were necessary in exiting, making it relatively easy to discontinue merchandising activities. Exit was more difficult if firms were obligated by servicing contracts as a part of their customer-supply contracts or if they did in fact smelt calcium carbide. Only a few calcium-carbide producers could exist in endgame because the capital costs and capacity requirements of an efficient-sized carbide plant were large (300 million pounds a year of acetylene-generating capacity) and exit would be more difficult for these firms given their high economic barriers. In particular, Airco (which was primarily using its calcium-carbide output to supply chemical-synthesis customers) encountered difficulties in exiting which resulted in substantial reported write-off before taxes of $30.7 million due to the high cost of its undepreciated acetylene plant for which a thin resale market prevailed.

Acetylene assets were lumpy packages of capital which could not be written off in a timely manner by many of the participating firms because they apparently believed that the write-off losses they might incur upon exit would be poorly evaluated by their shareholders. Consequently, exits and plant retirements did not proceed smoothly in line with demand for acetylene.

Competitive Characteristics

Competition was not volatile largely because (1) the chemical-synthesis acetylene producers did not sell to the welding-gas market on a regular basis (occasionally some excess capacity was bottled); (2) the welding-gas acetylene producers did not sell to the chemical-synthesis markets; (3) chemical-synthesis marketing relationships were contractual and long term (twenty years); and (4) welding-gas firms were diversified such that they did not percieve that price-cutting behavior was an important marketing tool for them in acetylene-welding supplies. Thus what would have been a volatile environment plagued by excess capacity did not become so. Acetylene prices were negotiated at the time of contract and firms did not use price competition to attract customers because reliability and technical proficiency were more important differentiating factors in competing for customers in chemical synthesis; service was important in welding gas markets.

In summary, although some of the structural traits of the acetylene endgame constituted the preconditions for what would have been a bitter endgame in some other industries, other structural characteristics helped ease the problem in this endgame. For example, acetylene firms rarely competed directly with each other, and there was little temptation for firms within one strategic group to invade another group's markets.

Analysis of the Corporate-wide
Strategic Needs of Competitors

Because an "important" business unit or one which is ensnared behind strategic exit barriers might be retained longer than economic analysis may suggest was advisable, the timing of firms' exits or of tactics designed to reduce the level of firms' commitments to the endgame industry might be influenced by these strategic considerations. Strategic exit barriers retarded the exit of at least two acetylene firms in the industry, preventing these firms from enjoying the profitability and ease of exit enjoyed by other industries.

Strategic Exit Barriers. Full-line welding supply firms would be expected to continue to offer acetylene torches and fuel as a part of their wide array of welding gases (but they might pass on to their customers the higher prices of acetylene which resulted from the higher energy prices in smelting carbide). In this endgame, many welding-supply firms continued to carry inventories of acetylene-welding products and some carbide-smelting firms actually increased their acetylene-generating capacities during the product's decline in order to fulfill supply contracts which were undertaken as a service that was consistent with their wide-line strategy. A continuing investment in acetylene was of relatively low risk for welding-gas firms because their excess acetylene could be sold to smaller "bottle-shop" welding supply firms which were not already served by contracts from other large acetylene firms.

As the price of acetylene rose and more effective welding technologies were developed, less acetylene was consumed, but as the consumption of acetylene for welding gas and metal-cutting declined, welding-gas merchandising firms reduced the amount of carbide they purchased and hence the amount of acetylene produced because they were not backward-integrated or (if they were backward-integrated) sought alternative markets for their carbide (thus cutting back on the amount of acetylene generated for welding-contract uses). Because the full-line strategies of welding-gas supplies obliged them to carry some acetylene, they faced a decision which influenced quantities, not whether to carry acetylene products.

Firms in the chemical-synthesis markets which were completely integrated—upstream and downstream—exercised the greatest control over their decision whether to remain invested in acetylene because (1) they could best evaluate whether alternative markets for their raw materials were more attractive; (2) they could best evaluate whether another less expensive means of providing chemical monomers to their customers existed; (3) they controlled the viability of their downstream consumer (the monomer plants); and (4) they were *not* constrained from exit by contracts with outside consumers obliging them to supply acetylene, perhaps at unremunerative prices. The presence of an outside, contractual customer frequently affected only the timing of firms' exits rather than their decision as to whether an exit from acetylene was imperative. If downstream customers using acetylene could have been easily converted to the use of some other, less expensive feedstock or another supplier, firms such as Tenneco or Airco could have terminated their acetylene plants sooner. Since many monomer plants were usable only with acetylene inputs, the entire complex was useless without acetylene. But where cheaper routes existed to produce the end product and more lucrative uses of the raw material existed, firms became increasingly eager to discontinue their acetylene operations, especially when it became cheaper to purchase monomer. In summary, vertical relationships were not as substantial a deterrent to exit in endgame as was the obligation to service outside customers. Only those firms which were locked in by contractual obligations to inefficient operating volumes tended to face high strategic exit barriers.

Analysis of Endgaming-Firms' Competitive Strengths

Firms which possessed internal strengths appropriate for profitable long-term participation in this endgame environment were better suited to pursue some of the more aggressive strategy options in coping with declining demand for acetylene. The most significant competitive advantages in the acetylene endgame were absolute cost advantages (having the lowest-cost technology, the most favorable raw materials contracts, or well-depreciated but servicable assets) and an established reputation for engineering skills in the chemical-synthesis market. The more significant competitive strengths in the welding-gas markets were marketing strengths (having a wide line of products, a strong system of support services, and a good welding-supplies distribution system). Multinational linkages were also a significant competitive strength.

Marketing and Selling Strengths. Within the chemical synthesis market, marketing strengths were not relevant because vendors and customers were interlinked, but in the welding-gas markets marketing strengths enabled firms which smelted carbide to locate new markets for their excess capacity. Access to multinational markets for acetylene products became an internal advantage because as the use of acetylene as welding gas declined in the United States, firms which possessed multinational selling channels, such as Chemetron, used these linkages to tap demand in overseas markets for welding supplies and gases where acetylene was still a relatively inexpensive welding gas, despite its cost increases.

Technological Advantages. One of the most important production advantages in the acetylene endgame proved to be favorable raw-materials contracts which did not pass on natural-gas price increases such as the Monochem, Inc., natural-gas contract or other similar contracts for carbide. Because the cost of transporting raw materials made carbide a more expensive raw material than natural gas for acetylene generation, Union Carbide, for example, purchased any excess acetylene Monochem generated because it could be resold at a profit for a price lower than carbide acetylene cost to produce. The other significant technological advantage needed was a low-cost plant design, such as the BASF or Wulff processes, because natural gas and oxygen represented as much as 40 percent of the operating costs of a partial-oxidation plant, but, in the less efficient plants, only 30 percent of the acetylene cracked might be recovered. Cost advantages could also be enjoyed from scale economies if an acetylene plant could be operated near the level of its engineered efficiency. The optimal size of a partial-oxidation plant was 100 million pounds per year and the optimal size of a carbide-based acetylene plant was 300 million pounds per year. Many large plants could not operate efficiently because there was not adequate acetylene consumption to run them full out. The acetylene industry offered few opportunities for product differentiation activities, its assets were highly specific, and long-term contracts to supply acetylene could lock a firm into the industry. Therefore the most important strength a firm could possess was a production-cost advantage.

Analysis of Firms' Performances
in the Acetylene Endgame

Few reinvestments in the acetylene endgame were expected given the relatively "unfavorable" structural traits of this industry, and several firms were expected to encounter difficulty in overcoming their exit barriers given the high cost of retiring an acetylene plant and the high, undepreciated values at which these plants were carried in 1965. The firms which had undertaken massive ($40 million) investments in allegedly improved acetylene technologies, in particular, were expected to encounter difficulties.

Firms Which Exited Early. Three firms exited relatively early from the acetylene business: American Cyanamid, Monsanto, and E.I. duPont de Nemours—of which only duPont was likely to incur losses because its plant was very new when it exited and the cost of removing it was likely very high because the technology was experimental (duPont had developed it from internal R&D activities). Monsanto had planned its exit ten years in advance to allow time to extract the value of its acetylene investment. (It announced the Chocolate Bayou project in 1960.) Few of the firms which exited relatively early in the endgame suffered major disruptions to profits, to their strategic well-being, or to managerial morale because the exits were carefully planned, their plants were old, and their customers were captive corporate units.

Firms Which Exited Late. The two firms which exited relatively late in endgame, Tenneco and Diamond Shamrock, both tried to milk their investments, and both firms suffered losses upon exit when they tried to remove the experimental acetylene technologies which they hoped would lower operating costs. (Their losses were $2 million each.) Rohm & Haas has exited, but its plant continues to operate in a special situation. It is holding its investment without significant risk, and its endgame may be considered a success.

Early Exit: "Milk the Investment"

Monsanto. Monsanto's experience in endgame would be expected to be among the most successful because the firm was able to extract the value of its investment from the acetylene plant on the timetable it had announced in 1960 and executed in the ten years which followed. Monsanto had been an early entrant (1952) into the use of acetylene and had purchased the most efficient acetylene process, the BASF technology, for use in producing several chemical intermediates which used acetylene internally. By 1970, when it exited, the Monsanto plant had been operated for eighteen years and there was virtually no write-off upon its disposal.

Because Monsanto had consumed all of its acetylene internally, and its plant had been fully depreciated at the time of contemplated exit, Monsanto was not expected to face substantial economic or strategic exit barriers. It had decided with the 1963 commercialization of Chocolate Bayou and the 1968 shutdown of its vinyl-chloride operations at Texas City that acetylene could be phased out successfully if it extracted the value of its investment carefully. Monsanto had entered acetylene at a propitious time and was able to replace it as a feedstock before acetylene became exceedingly uneconomic for Monsanto to use.

American Cyanamid. American Cyanamid would be expected to recover the value of its acetylene investment successfully because it possessed the lowest-cost technology (BASF) and it executed its exit before natural-gas prices had increased to a level which would have reduced operating profits to unacceptable levels. American Cyanamid, like Monsanto, had purchased the lowest-cost BASF technology in 1954 and was able to replace the plant on an orderly timetable after enjoying much of the value of the investment. Because it consumed its acetylene internally, American Cyanamid did not incur strategic exit barriers when it replaced its acetylene-based acrylonitrile plant.

Acrylonitrile was one of the first chemical intermediate products to use another, less expensive feedstock to produce acrylic fibers. American Cyanamid was able to perceive the changing technology of synthetic fibers and make an orderly transition to the substitute feedstock while maintaining its profitability.

Early Exit: "Divest Now!"

E.I. duPont de Nemours & Company. Although the abrupt shutdown of duPont's acetylene plant was unexpected, an analysis of the duPont Company would have suggested that it would be likely to rectify its investment errors in this manner. The company was known to be very cost-control oriented and willing to divest investments which did not meet expectations, hence duPont would have been expected to follow a conservative strategy in acetylene. Although the company was the largest consumer of acetylene, duPont built only one acetylene plant of its own when it tested the new electric-arc acetylene technology it had developed internally. (The costs of the plant were pooled with other R&D ventures and the new duPont acetylene plant was not as efficient when commercialized as it was hoped it would be. The size of the write-off is not known.)

DuPont was helped in its endgame by its technological strengths in developmental research. Also, in light of the difficulties which some of the other acetylene producers had encountered in timing their exit strategies, duPont's decision to purchase most of its raw-materials acetylene needs rather than to produce them also contributed to the ultimate success of du-Pont's experience in endgame. DuPont's losses could have been greater than those they actually wrote off in developmental expenses for the Montague electric-arc acetylene plant venture if it had operated several uneconomic acetylene plants.

DuPont suffered some disruptions upon exit, but not as much as Tenneco and Diamond Shamrock ultimately suffered. The duPont decision to "bite the bullet" early is consistent with its exit decision in the rayon endgame. Because duPont was producing acetylene only for itself, its relative strategic flexibility was *not* constrained by outside customers who might have refused to shut down their acetylene-consuming operations when duPont incurred losses from acetylene generation.

Late Exit: "Divest Now!"

Diamond Shamrock. When the failure of the Montecatini technology became apparent, Diamond Shamrock was expected to close down its acetylene plant, perhaps abruptly, despite the large investment the acetylene plant represented ($10 million was approximately 2 percent of Diamond Shamrock's assets in the base year). Regardless of the technological advantages the Montecatini technology had promised, Diamond Shamrock's position in the acetylene business was exposed as being unsound when several million dollars of total reinvestments were needed to remedy the initial technological flaws of the Montecatini design to make it perform near the efficiency of other types of partial-oxidation acetylene plant designs and an acetylene explosion caused over $1 million of damage in 1968. Diamond Shamrock also discovered that the routine maintenance of an acetylene plant could require reinvestments of $1 million per year, an unfavorable cash-flow pattern which also made the investment even more unattractive. Therefore, Diamond Shamrock management could perceive early after its commercialization that its acetylene plant would have to be retired.

Diamond Shamrock actually ran its acetylene plant for ten years before it was closed down. When, after 1968, Diamond Shamrock management discovered that they could purchase vinyl-chloride monomer more inexpensively than their acetylene plant could produce it, the plant was run to provide acetylene to a nearby chemical customer, Rohm & Haas. Without this outlet for its acetylene, Diamond Shamrock would have faced two other options: (1) produce vinyl-chloride monomer using a highly uncompetitive acetylene plant and lose money through operations (but recognize a smaller write-off later); or (2) shut down the flawed acetylene plant and recognize a relatively larger write-off loss sooner.

Tenneco Corporation. When its SBA-Kellogg acetylene technology proved to be flawed, Tenneco Chemical would have been expected to shut down its acetylene plant were it not for the high exit barriers it faced. Tenneco's Pasadena, Texas, plant was over three times larger than the Diamond Shamrock plant (100 million pounds per year) and had cost almost four times as much to construct. Tenneco sold its acetylene to outside customers (unlike Diamond Shamrock which was vertically integrated to PVC production) and, given its large size, needed a large customer to run at efficient capacity. Moreover, the flawed technology required more investments to make it operable, placing Tenneco in a very inflexible strategic position. In addition to economic barriers, Tenneco also faced strategic exit barriers due to its obligation to supply acetylene for duPont's tetrahydrofuran plant in Houston (until the Rohm & Haas Company alternative became available in 1978).

Tenneco's choice of plant size also placed it in a very inflexible oprating position because the supply contracts which Tenneco entered into to keep its acetylene plant operating at an efficient volume made Tenneco ultimately sacrifice its strategic autonomy in the timing of its exit.

Late Exit: "Hold the Investment Level"

Rohm & Haas. Rohm & Haas would be expected to find a means of minimizing any write-offs when it exited from acetylene because it had planned to retire the acetylene plant when it commercialized a new propylene-based acrylates plant (which would render obsolete its acetylene plant) and delayed construction of the newer technology until the economics of switching could be justified. Rohm & Haas possessed the lowest-cost BASF process and consumed as much acetylene as it could generate internally. Rohm & Haas was not backward-integrated and was very conservative in its operating policies.

The Rohm & Haas Company had enjoyed a spectacular success in acrylates and in acrylics production and had consumed acetylene voraciously as it produced acrylates. After expanding the capacity of its own acetylene plant, it purchased excess acetylene capacity from Diamond Shamrock and Tenneco. Like duPont, Rohm & Haas risked a limited amount of its own capital in acetylene capacity. Although Rohm & Haas was increasing its total consumption of acetylene, it merely "held" its own investment level in the acetylene endgame. The availability of other firms' undepreciated but usable acetylene assets enabled Rohm & Haas to expand its own acrylates production without building additional acetylene capacity or investing in a propylene-based technology before it was a proven success. The 1972 decision to scrap its acetylene-based acrylates process indicated that Rohm &

Haas would take a write-down if it were necessary to improve operating efficiency. The caution with which they implemented this decision worked to the advantage of Rohm & Haas because the 1978 Tenneco contract which leases the Rohm & Haas acetylene plant to Tenneco for duPont's tetrahydrofuran production limits Rohm & Haas Company's further risks in acetylene.

The Rohm & Haas Company had planned to scrap its acetylene plant when the propylene plant proved out. The Tenneco-duPont contract was a boon for Rohm & Haas Company; it pleased the duPont Company, which needed the acetylene supply for the tetrahydrofuran operation, and it allowed Tenneco to remove its oversized, underutilized acetylene plant from the industry. Tenneco actually saved money by leasing the Rohm & Haas acetylene plant because it was less expensive to operate than its own acetylene plant.

Continued Competition: "Milk the Investment"

Airco, In. Airco was expected to encounter difficulties in the acetylene endgame because it operated a large acetylene plant (300 million pounds per year) which supplied many outside customers whose capacity Airco would be unable to absorb when it disconnected from the acetylene plant.

Although some of the Calvert City, Kentucky, customers disconnected and terminated their acetylene contracts with Airco, other customers did not do so. Airco could no longer operate its carbide smelters there economically to fill the relatively small remaining demand after these customers departed, yet because it was bound by these contracts, Airco consolidated its carbide-smelting operations at its remaining Louisville plant and transported the heavy carbide back to Calvert City to generate acetylene for the remaining customers there (approximately 180 miles on a toll roadway).

Because Airco's acetylene plants were among the largest in the industry, they required operation at full capacity, otherwise they could not enjoy their engineered economies. Airco's experience in the acetylene endgame illustrates the difficulty of retrieving value from large, capital-intensive, and highly specific assets when the timing of one's endgame strategy is disrupted by an unforeseen event. The shutdown of Calvert City's furnaces made total operations less profitable, given the way the two acetylene-generating plants are being operated on a piecemeal basis.

Continued Participation: "Shrink Selectively"

Union Caride. Union Carbide (UCC) would be expected to maintain a favorable market position during this endgame and to control the closing of its acetylene plants as needed because (1) Union Carbide was the oldest and best-known acetylene producer, (2) there were many outside markets for its carbide, and (3) Union Carbide's Wulff-process plants produced ethylene as well as (or instead of) acetylene. Union Carbide's R&D staff had also developed a relatively low-cost partial-oxidation technology which permitted Union Carbide to test several different designs and to build its newer plants using the process which gave it flexibility in choices of feedstock (naptha or gas oil) and in proportions of ethylene and acetylene output. Because Union Carbide held the Wulff-process U.S. patent rights, no other firm could match its technology easily.

UCC was not the lowest-cost producer in 1965, but it chose its technologies with an eye to the future, when raw-materials costs could become a problem. When the cost of natural-gas feedstock rose, Union Carbide's Wulff-process plants enjoyed operating-cost advantages because they could use oil instead. Union Carbide's Seadrift and Texas City, Texas, plants were among the oldest successful hydrocarbon plants in the industry and permitted UCC to enjoy a relatively successful endgame experience. Union Carbide actually increased its investment in acetylene by opening a Wulff plant in Taft, Louisiana, by expanding acetylene operations at Ashtabula, Ohio, and by opening a new Wulff acetylene plant in Ponce, Puerto Rico. It also closed the Institute, West Virginia, acetylene operations in an effort to control its acetylene production volumes and to rearrange the locations where carbide acetylene was produced to suit customers' needs. Because Union Carbide had several plants in which to do this, it was able to execute the shrink-selectively endgame strategy, successfully while it continued to serve its many customer markets.

Union Carbide customers were using acetylene in the production of acetylenic chemicals, solvents, and other products which were expected to be growth markets and Union Carbide itself tested new products using acetylene in its R&D plant. Because Union Carbide was also the largest supplier of welding-gas users' needs, when many interconnected customers switched to other feedstocks adequate demand remained to keep Union Carbide's acetylene plants in production. In summary, Union Carbide apparently escaped some injuries because it had a diversified customer base. Also, although many of its plants were older, they were still efficient and the company had developed considerable recognition for its expertise in the safe handling of acetylene.

Continued Participation: "Hold the Investment Level"

Air Products and Chemicals. Air Products may anticipate some problems in acetylene because of the inflexibility of its strategic posture. Air Products and Chemicals used its unique marketing tool (it built onsite generating plants and sold the gas to its customers, as needed) to gain strong market coverage. Because of the unique marketing approach of this firm, it is not clear how many acetylene plants it is financing for customers at the present time. It would seem that its long-run performance in endgame will deteriorate if many of the acetylene plants it is financing are closed down prematurely. If acetylene use for welding declines faster than Air Products had forecasted, Air Products is inflexible to the extent that it must finance these assets. Fortunately, the firm was not backward-integrated to produce carbide, since this would have reduced its flexibility further, as it did for Airco, Inc.

Continued Participation: "Increase the Investment"

Chemetron. Chemetron is expected to perform well in the acetylene endgame because it was one of the top welding-gas acetylene producers, it produced acetylene in small plants but suffered no cost disadvantage in doing so because it resold the acetylene (at high markups) to the welding markets, and it possessed a strong distribution system to sell its acetylene and oxyacetylene torches. Also, Chemetron possessed multinational links to overseas markets which enabled it to enter markets of rising demand and faced low economic exit barriers if it wished to divest its acetylene operations because Chemetron's affiliate, Midwest Carbide, operated one of the older carbide-acetylene plants.

Chemetron increased its participation in the acetylene endgame by acquiring a Hawaiian industrial-gas firm and building an acetylene plant in Mississippi. When Chemetron's affiliate, Midwest Carbide, opened a new carbide plant in Oklahoma, Chemetron opened an acetylene plant next door. Chemetron strengthened its expanded base in welding equipment and supplies by opening company-owned stores. Chemetron did not serve the chemical-synthesis market, which had been responsible for the skyrocketing popularity of carbon-based chemical investments in the late 1950s. Hence, it did not participate in the rapid decline of that market. Instead, Chemetron served the slowly dwindling welding-gas needs of industrial users.

Dow Chemical. Dow Chemical is expected to perform well in this endgame because it was providing acetylene to customers in growth markets, it possessed favorable operating economics in its acetylene technology (until recently it operated an old, well-depreciated plant), and it was vertically integrated both upstream to natural gas and downstream to an internal customer. Its captive consumer—Dow-Badische (a joint venture with BASF)—was not cutting back on its acetylene consumption; hence, a market for Dow's output was virtually guaranteed. Although the details of the contracts are not disclosed, it would appear that Dow Chemical enjoyed some technological advantages from its joint venture with BASF which gave Dow Chemical access to subsequent improvements upon the BASF process. It is likely that Dow Chemical enjoyed favorable operating costs as a result of this liaison. When Hoffman LaRoche negotiated for a supply of 8 to 10 million pounds per year of acetylene. Dow Chemical may have increased the potential difficulty it would encounter from economic exit barriers were it to try to recover the value of its investment. Unless Dow Chemical holds a contract giving it favorable terms similar to those of Monochem, Inc., an expansion into the chemical-synthesis market by selling to an outside customer must be considered a risky tactic.

Monochem, Inc. The Monochem, Inc., venture is expected to be a success because the parent firms—Borden and UniRoyal—negotiated a favorable raw-materials contract (natural gas) which terminates when the Monochem plant is fully depreciated. The Monochem plant is fully utilized and highly efficient because Monochem uses the BASF technology which provides it with the operating efficiencies which had also been enjoyed by American Cyanamid (twelve years), Monsanto (eighteen years) and Rohm & Haas (eighteen years before initial shutdown). Monochem also enjoyed large potential plant-scale economies (180 million pounds per year) which it could exploit by full utilization of the plant. (Any excess acetylene generated is sold to UCC; it was probably the cheapest source of acetylene in the United States in 1978.) Monochem chose the right parents and customers and protected the plant against cost increases through the raw-materials contract, and against excess capacity through their requirements contracts. Assuming that Monochem can continue to run the BASF-process plant at its engineered capacity until 1981, without incurring any unbudgeted reinvestment requirements, it will enjoy a successful endgame.

11 Generalizations Concerning Strategies for Declining Industries

This chapter integrates the conclusions of the eight industry studies which have traced the behaviors of over sixty competitors in order to determine what generalizations concerning the formulation of endgame strategies can be made. By comparing the expectations of the endgame framework with the evidence from the sample of endgame performances, it can be suggested which industry structural traits were associated with the more profitable and less volatile endgames, and which of several strategies were most successful under various environmental conditions in declining industries.

This study has been based upon two key hypotheses concerning the formulation of strategies for declining industries. It is useful to restate these hypotheses in presenting the conclusions from the study.

First, it was hypothesized that declining industry environments differ; endgames are not homogeneous. Based upon the research studies which have explored orderly endgames, such as the receiving-tubes, acetylene, and synthetic soda-ash industries, as well as very volatile endgames such as the baby-foods industry, it can be concluded without question that endgames do differ significantly from industry to industry. Endgames can vary with regard to patterns of price levels, retirements of capacity, competitors' exits, and the presence of pockets of enduring demand, in addition to other salient industry factors which also determine the nature of endgame competition.

Second, it was hypothesized that there would be several business strategies which might be appropriate for coping with declining demand within a particular industry environment. This study looked at the different strategies of firms such as GTE Sylvania (receiving tubes), Gerber Products, and Dow Chemical (acetylene) which increased their investments in the endgame; at firms such as Mead, Johnson (baby food) which discontinued portions of their declining business investments but also reinvested in the more promising parts of their endgame businesses; and at firms such as duPont (acetylene and cellulosic fibers), Raytheon (receiving tubes), and American Cynamid (acetylene) which divested their endgame businesses early. Based on these research findings regarding competitors' behaviors, it can be concluded that there could be many different but appropriate business strategies for the endgame. Different firms within the same endgame industry could pursue different strategies for coping with the problem of declining demand successfully.

Moreover, within each industry examined, at least one firm performed relatively well and could be recognized ex ante as being in the best position to remain in the industry. This finding is significant because it suggests that it was possible for firms to perform well in a declining industry and that analysis of this strategic problem might have enabled some firms to assess their relative strengths and to deduce their positions in the industry more realistically, earlier.

This study also tested hypotheses concerning the industry characteristics which might influence the conditions of an endgame environment and the internal corporate characteristics which might influence certain types of competitors to choose a particular strategy. It is useful to restate these hypotheses in presenting the findings of this study.

It was hypothesized that the industry traits which defined the context of a particular endgame environment would influence the potential profitability of an endgame and thus could influence the range of strategies which might be appropriate for coping with declining demand within a particular industry. The specific findings associated with this hypothesis, and its cascade of subordinate hypotheses, are detailed, point by point, in the discussion below, where each of these industry traits is analyzed and findings regarding their effects on endgame strategies are summarized.

Also, the study hypothesized that differences among competitors' strategic needs and relative internal corporate strengths would make certain strategy options (as they were identified above) more appropriate for a particular firm operating within a specified industry environment than would other options. In particular, it was hypothesized that a firm's corporate strategic requirements may create strategic exit barriers which could deter the execution of a seemingly timely exit from the declining industry environment (which has been called "the endgame" in this study). The findings associated with the exit barrier hypotheses are discussed in the section following the analysis of industry traits.

The findings reported in this study are based upon observations of over fifty-one firms which competed within declining industries. The data were gathered from industry sites using interviews with chief executive officers, divisional presidents, or directors of marketing as well as from library-research and industry trade associations.

Nevertheless, in a study such as this, where there were many structural variables which interacted with each other and where there were substantial differences among the competitors' strategic postures and initial conditions, one must be conservative regarding the degree of confidence with which these conclusions can be asserted. The data do seem to indicate that the same factors recurred in different firms' endgame experiences and seemed to influence the outcome of their endgames. The presence (or absence) of these structural factors does seem to correlate with the competitive conditions which were forecast to result, and with behaviors which had been predicted to occur in the description of the endgame paradigm. Therefore, observations regarding the presence and absence of these factors are cautiously offered below and judgment on these factors is reserved until a subsequent chapter.

The previous chapters have presented the experiences of selected competitors within eight different declining industries which were chosen to isolate particular industry structural traits for study. In each example, the declining company examined represented a significant business unit for the particular parent corporation which was potentially of importance historically to the latter's images or to its overall strategic purposes.

In the endgame framework, it was expected that different competitors within the same declining industry would pursue different strategies because the competitors might possess differing strategic needs (for example, some firms faced exit barriers while others could apply their retrievable cash to other business investments easily), the competitors would be unequally equipped to respond to this challenge, particularly if their strategic postures differed significantly from the strengths which were most important for competition in a particular endgame. It was found that "strategic exit barriers" were quite important as a determinant of the timing of firms' exits and of their commitments to remaining in the endgame. Indeed, it was found that unpromising declining businesses (such as RCA's receiving-tube business and Bayuk Cigar's endgame business) were frequently retained or that exits were delayed where these barriers were present.

It was also found that successful participants which stayed in the endgame (such as GTE Sylvania in receiving tubes and Monochem, Inc., in acetylene) already possessed the relevant competitive strengths or they repositioned themselves early enough in the endgame to acquire those strengths which would be of the greatest relative advantage to them in serving the remaining niches of demand (if such niches existed) in a particular industry environment. Because these patterns of industry environments and firms' strategies seemed to vary in a predictable fashion, analysis of the influence of these determinants upon endgame conditions and strategy choices could yield useful insights for the corporate strategist facing this problem.

Endgame Environments

Favorable Endgame Environments

The more favorable industry environments examined included electronic receiving tubes, the high-quality automatic percolator coffee-maker market, the premium-cigar market, and the baby-foods market (after competitors had comprehended the demographic and cultural changes which had occurred with respect to the birth rate). Within the most favorable endgames examined (1) demand was somewhat price insensitive; (2) it was clear that replacement units would be needed for a predictable time into the future; (3) other environmental characteristics created pockets of demand in the market that were likely to endure indefinitely (albeit at a lower level than in the past). Most importantly, the competitors who enjoyed success in these industries understood which niches the demand patterns favored and repositioned themselves to serve those pockets of demand, or they were already producing products in the niches which sustained market demand.

Unfavorable Endgame Environments

The unfavorable industry environments examined were the synthetic soda-ash industry, the acetylene business, the rayon-filament business, the lower-priced cigars, and middle-priced percolators, as well as the baby-foods business (during the middle years of endgame). Although there were some relatively successful competitors within each of these industries, the structural traits of these industries per se did not create a hospitable environment for continued participation, particularly if a competitor were concerned with recovering a substantial portion of the value of its past investments in the declining industry.

Within the more unfavorable endgames examined (1) demand was highly price sensitive and competitive price-cutting became volatile; (2) demand for the endgame product plummeted abruptly, creating sizable write-off losses for firms which were forced to exit; (3) substantial reinvestment requirements forced competitors to exit prematurely; or (4) great uncertainty regarding the duration of demand induced other firms to reinvest in what was later revealed to be an unpromising industry environment. There was disorder in the patterns of investments and exits in these industries due, in part, to an inadequate understanding of the forces affecting demand for the product and also, in part, to an insufficient internal assessment regarding whether the firms involved were serving the most promising markets in endgame. The timing of effective repositioning and of exits proved to be quite delicate in the industries examined.

Sketches of Endgame Industry Environments

Receiving Tubes. The receiving-tubes industry endgame was a favorable one. Competitors shut down capacity as demand declined. Exits were relatively orderly. (RCA incurred unforeseen losses on disposal.) Prices rose over the endgame as foreign producers reduced their activities in the U.S. endgame and remaining manufacturers kept a stable control over costs and price increases.

Synthetic Soda Ash. Exits from the synthetic soda-ash endgame were forced retreats. In this industry, soda-ash prices were held down by producers of the substitute product. Supply was kept in line with demand during most of the endgame as synthetic soda-ash firms were squeezed out by natural soda-ash producers in a pattern which, upon ex ante examination, was predictable. Prices increased in this endgame only after it was clear that all of the synthetic soda-ash producers would eventually be forced to exit. Losses upon exit occurred for a few firms because they had not foreseen the catastrophic event which would force them out of the soda-ash industry prematurely.

Acetylene. Competition in the acetylene industry was not volatile. Exits occurred in an orderly pattern (according to firms' depreciation schedules, by which they recovered the economic values of their plants). Prices did not keep pace with increasing costs. Yet because of the industry's unique technology, price-cutting did not occur in either segment of the endgame (hydrocarbon and carbide routes). Acetylene was replaced for most applications by technologically superior substitutes (welding and cutting uses) or less costly substitutes (chemical-synthesis applications). There were some remaining pockets of demand, however, which some firms could service. A few firms expanded their acetylene plants during endgame.

Electric Percolator Coffee-Makers. The percolator coffee-makers endgame was not favorable for most firms' continued investment because the substitute product (automatic drip coffee-maker) was highly popular with many users. Prices rose slightly at retail but shelf-space battles were waged at the distributor level. Plant shutdowns occurred in an orderly pattern where firms possessed somewhat flexible or highly depreciated assets. Where the assets were inflexible, losses were incurred upon exit. Pockets of enduring demand for a few percolator models sustained the presence of only a small number of producers (in the high-quality and also in the very inexpensive percolator markets).

Cigars. The cigars endgame was characterized by intense shelf-space warfare at the distributor level. The decline in demand was slow and there was uncertainty regarding whether demand would revitalize. Hence, there were few exits by the major cigarmakers. Many small, family cigarmaker firms did exit. Prices at retail rose only 1 cent over fifteen years, but at the distribution level competition was volatile and operating losses were incurred. Some small pockets of demand (premium cigars) actually increased during the endgame. For lower-priced, high-volume products, the market was saturated.

Rayon. The rayon industry was not favorable for endgame because demand was cyclical in the fashion markets and virtually disappeared in the tire-cord market. The pockets of demand where consumption was stable (cigarette filters and nonwovens) were comoditylike markets. Pollution laws forced firms either to make large reinvestments to continue to operate their rayon plants or to incur substantial losses upon exiting. Excess capacity incited price-cutting. (Prices fluctuated during the endgame, but they increased overall.) Several rayon plants were shut down in disruptive patterns of exit. The substitute products were perfectly interchangeable and less costly for most applications. (In some markets, the substitutes were better than the cellulosic fibers.)

Baby Foods. The baby-foods endgame was highly disruptive because the competitors expected demand to increase while the birth rate continued to decline for almost twenty years. Hence, the major firms stayed in the industry and excess capacity there abounded. Price warfare continued for almost seven years at the distributor level, where total shelf-space allocations were shrinking. Assets were relatively new and exit barriers were high. Major changes in the product's formulation forced all of the firms to reinvest in this industry in order to remain competitive.

Industry Characteristics

Analysis of Demand Characteristics

Demand characteristics and competitors' expectations concerning demand proved to be quite important in determining the contours of an endgame environment. It was predicted that competitors' expectations concerning the duration of declining demand would affect the volatility of competition in the endgame. It was found that where there was relative certainty regarding (1) which pockets of demand would decline first, (2) how rapidly demand would decline for different products (or in different customers' markets), and (3) whether demand was likely to revitalize, the most orderly endgame experiences were also found. Where there was industry agreement concerning what would happen (as in the percolator coffee-makers, receiving tubes, and synthetic soda-ash businesses), the endgame proceeded without large foreseeable write-off losses for participants, and exits were not disruptive.

It was also found that where there had been substantial uncertainty concerning whether demand would revitalize, when, and who should exit while the industry waited for consumption to increase, chaos ensued. Few firms exited in environments of uncertainty (such as cigars or baby foods), thus creating great pressures upon prices due to excess capacity in the industry. Exits, when they occurred, were disruptive and costly.

It was found that the influence of competitors' expectations concerning the nature of future demand for their endgame products seemed to be quite important in creating a favorable (or unfavorable) environment for endgame activities. Uncertainty increased the likelihood that competitors would take actions which would disrupt the stability of an industry and make it an unfavorable arena for endgame competition because they did not understand the nature of the decline in consumption of their products. For example, if competitors were certain that demand would revitalize but they were uncertain *when* consumption would again increase (as in the baby-foods example), it was found that they continued to operate their plants, even at low-capacity levels for many years, rather than sell them, retire them, or use them for other purposes. It was found that the same type of behavior tended to occur—excess capacity was endemic—where there was clearly uncertainty regarding whether demand would revitalize.

It was expected that the rate of declining demand in industries which experienced technological changes (receiving tubes, percolator coffee-makers, synethetic soda ash, and acetylene) would be easier to forecast than the rate of declining demand due to demographic changes (baby foods), cultural changes (cigars), or fashion-related demand changes (rayon) because the progress of the substitute product could be monitored. It was expected that declining demand which was related to technological obsolescence could be assessed by producers with greater understanding of the likely future implications of these changes for revitalization of demand. Therefore, it was expected that there would be relatively greater certainty among producers within these declining industries regarding patterns of demand and of substitution. Relatively greater consensus among manufacturers regarding what should be done within these industries was expected if manufacturers produced the substitute product (transistors and solid-state devices, natural soda ash, or other synthetic fibers) as well.

It was found that the least volatile and relatively easiest endgames were experienced in the technologically obsolescent endgames where it was clear (1) whether any pockets of enduring demand still existed (such as receiving tubes, and also premium cigars), (2) how large the demand for obsolescent products was likely to be (how many producers it could sustain), and (3) how long demand within this pocket was likely to remain viable. The technological endgames like receiving tubes could be orderly because demand clearly would end by a horizon date; competitors could recognize and comprehend the need to plan for the transition to the new technology; and (because these factors were mutually recognized), there was less incentive to cut prices on the technologically obsolescent product.

The presence of pockets of demand in many endgames where the customers' switching costs were financially high (as in acetylene or receiving tubes) or were perceived as being high (as in rayon for men's suit linings and high-quality garments) seemed to be one of the most important determinants of whether an endgame industry could be favorable for continued endgame operations. Favorable endgame environments contained at least one pocket of enduring demand for the products.

Product Traits

It was expected that products which were differentiable would enable their producers to enjoy relative competitive staying power due to mobility barriers which firms (like Gerber Products or General Electric) may have erected. Differentiability would enable them to avoid head-to-head competition by serving customer niches which were distinct from these served by other competitors. Differentiated products would also be able to justify slightly higher prices for their baby foods, stainless-steel percolator coffee-makers, or premium-quality cigar brands, within those markets where customers valued these products' brand names or physically unique attributes.

It was found that loyal customers within the automatic percolator coffee-maker and cigars endgames did allow certain competitors to differentiate their products to enjoy the higher prices (and later, the higher staying power) possible from such products. By contrast, although baby food was also a differentiated product, and although it was found that Gerber Products could maintain a 10-percent price premium for its branded baby foods, study of that endgame did not indicate that the differentiation of these products was so complete that firms could erect mobility barriers high enough that competitors could not invade their markets by cutting the prices of competing products.

A distinction must be made between physical and perceived product differentiation traits. Fewer firms seemed to be able to retain their pricing control over branded products in endgame than over products which were physically different, such as high-quality percolators. Brand loyalties seemed to erode more rapidly than primary demand for physically different features.

Customer Traits

It was expected that firms whose customers were dependent upon a supply of the endgame product would help the producers by paying relatively high prices for it. But if customer industries possessed bargaining power over the producers of the endgame product instead, it was expected that customers (such as wholesalers, distribution companies or retailers) could exercise that power by demanding (and receiving) lower prices, free goods, or other forms of incentives, ostensibly to encourage them to continue to act as a conduit to the ultimate consumers of the declining product.

It was found that customer industries which did help the producers of endgame products by sustaining their price increases seemed to be those customer groups which were *not* sensitive to price increases because they could pass on price increases to their customers, in turn. (Examples of such customer industries included receiving-tube distributors and also retailers who sold high-quality percolator coffee-makers). Frequently these customer industries were partially financed by manufacturers of the endgame product or they received incentives for carrying a full line of the manufacturers' other non-declining products. Also, the endgame product may have been such a small portion of their raw-materials needs that they were insensitive to price increases.

By contrast, it was found that where the ultimate customers for the endgame product were price sensitive and the downstream (intermediate) customer industry was a retailer group that controlled access to shelf space used to reach the ultimate consumers, dealing with these customers tended to increase the costliness of the endgame. Although, for example, cigars, baby foods, and automatic percolator coffee-makers were differentiated, their potential profitability in endgame seemed to be reduced because producers had to compensate their downstream customer industries more for the slower turnover of their products which occupied retailers' scarce shelf space.

The fragmented customer groups (electronic-components distribution companies, users of welding torches, and ultimate groups of consumers) seemed to be relatively price insensitive and possessed little bargaining power. The concentrated customer groups (regional retailers, glass and detergent producers, and chemical-synthesis customers) seemed to be relatively more price sensitive. Their purchases of the endgame product were frequently larger, hence more important to the producer of the endgame product. Hence these types of customers groups seemed to possess greater bargaining power over endgame producers.

The least rewarding customers to service in an endgame environment were those who were themselves "sick" or those who pressed their bargaining power over producers of declining products in a manner which increased the costliness for those firms to continue to sell their products in endgame. The greatest control over customers occurred where totally forward-integrated producers of a declining product (like Rohm & Haas in acetylene) could decide when to shut down. Contractual external customers, by con-

trast, hindered the execution of timely exits from industries such as synthetic soda ash and acetylene. (The discussion of strategic exit barriers will
discuss this problem in greater detail.)

Supplier Behavior

It was expected that where the supplier industries had been relatively dependent upon their sales to the manufacturers of endgame products, these suppliers might try to help the endgaming firms to survive by financing them,
by advertising on their behalf, or by allowing them to take price discounts
because their sales to the endgaming industry had been significant to them.
It was found that few supplier industries were able to help producers of
declining products in this manner in the endgames studied. Although, for
example, the farmers and orchardists were in a relatively weak bargaining
position as suppliers to the baby-foods processors, they could be important
in upholding the quality standards of the raw materials used for baby food.
They could not help the baby-food processors, however, because they
themselves were too fragmented.

It was found that the only example of this expected helpful intervention
by a supplier industry to the endgame producers was in the example of a
large wood-pulp producer (ITT-Rayonier) which assisted the rayon producers (particularly the rayon staple firms) when FMC Corporation spun
off Avtex Fibers and half of the industry's capacity appeared to be failing.

In many of the endgames reviewed, suppliers were fragmented and the
endgame product did not consume a significant portion of most supplier
firms' sales. Hence, the validity of the helpfulness of this supplier-buyer
relationship in endgame has not been adequately established by this study.

Economic Exit Barriers

It was expected that economic exit barriers could deter the timely exit of
firms from the endgame because the value of their investments would be ir-
retrievable. It was found that such deterrences did exist and seemed to be
operative when firms were unable to close their plants, divest some of their
products, or otherwise reduce the extent of their investments within the endgame.

It was found that economic exit barriers deterred or delayed firms
within the acetylene industry, the cigars industry, the receiving-tubes industry, the rayon industry, and the synthetic soda-ash industry, for example. In each of these declining industries, reinvestments in physical, but in-

flexible assets had occurred near the time of the base year. These new and undepreciated asset values acted to lock in firms such as Diamond Shamrock, the Culbro Corporation, GTE Sylvania, Avtex Fibers, and PPG Industries, respectively, in their endgames.

In some of these examples, the economic exit barriers these firms faced constituted a form of staying power for them because they seemed to become particularly resolute in their intentions to remain in the declining industry until they had recaptured a satisfactory proportion of their asset values through depreciation. In other examples, particularly in the synthetic soda-ash industry, firms may have desired to recapture their investment values through operations, but they were forced out of the endgame industry by adverse, uncontrollable industry factors. These firms were forced to recognize sizable, unforeseeable losses due to the undepreciated balances of their recent physical and technological investments.

It was expected that highly specialized assets would be difficult to sell upon exit from the endgame, particularly after the declining demand conditions of the industry's markets had become widely recognized. It was also expected that firms which had invested in such highly specific assets enjoyed lower operating costs. Thus, there would have been an implicit trade-off between these advantages of flexibility and efficiency conditions in choosing a technology.

It was found that the highly specific machines and plant layouts did tend to be more efficient in most industries. But it was also found that technologies like those of the baby-foods producers were frequently (1) capital-intensive and that they required (2) high levels of utilization in order to attain their desired efficiency. This condition could be particularly unfavorable for endgame, it was found, because less capital-intensive competitors within, for example, the percolator coffee-maker industry and the offshore (handmade) cigar industry could actually operate less expensively at lower levels of capacity utilization and would accept lower prices than could the capital-intensive firms.

It was expected that the timing of firms' exits would be influenced by their abilities to recapture much of the economic value of the assets they had invested in endgame. This asset retrieval could be achieved through (1) operations or (2) by sale of the assets used in production and distribution of the product (or by salvage values obtained in junking the assets where no resale market existed).

It was found that economic operating factors and economic exit barriers deterred Avtex Fibers (cellulosic fibers), Diamond Shamrock (acetylene), Havatampa Cigar Corporation (cigars), and several percolator producers, for example, from exiting earlier. Instead they were locked into continued operations at low returns. Environmental regulations or intensified competitive expenditures made large reinvestments in the endgame business necessary. These expenses squeezed firms such as Olin Corporation (synthetic soda ash) and Swift & Company (baby foods) out of their respective industries because the increased costs of competition for them did not seem to be justified by the expected returns on their declining product investments.

The synthetic soda-ash industry, rayon industry, and cigars industry, for example, needed substantial infusions of cash in order to remain competitive shortly after the base years of their respective studies. It was expected that business units which consumed cash rather than threw off cash in a declining business environment would soon be divested.

There were several examples in the study of firms' endgames where the requirements for more cash investments were too high for firms to remain invested. It was found that (1) all but one firm had exited from the synthetic soda-ash business by 1978; (2) FMC Corporation, American Cyanamid, and the El Paso Company each spun off its rayon-extruding (and cash-consuming) business units; and (3) although many small cigar companies could not afford the cash investments required for the next wave of technological investments, none of the major firms traced through the endgame within the cigar industry had exited due to these new investment requirements by 1978.

Firms such as Esmark, Squibb, FMC Corporation, and the El Paso Company, for example, seemed to be able to overcome their strategic and economic exit barriers in order to divest unpromising endgame businesses. Most of these firms had acquired these businesses at a time when future demand for their declining products had seemed more promising and when the acquisitions had seemed to "fit" strategically for other reasons. It was found that many of the nonmerchant hydrocarbon-based acetylene producers, for example, delayed the shutdown of their plants due to economic exit barriers, and the timing of some firms' exits from declining businesses was indeed influenced by economic exit barrier considerations.

It was also expected that the new book values of acquired firms could constitute economic exit barriers if the acquisition soured later.

The acquisitions by Consolidated Cigar Company and Culbro Corporation did experience major increases in cigar demand during the endgame when demand for most cigars declined. Because there had been no divestiture of these premium cigar companies during the period covered in this study, it is not clear whether or not these assets which constituted mobility barriers will be salable when the acquiring firm seeks to divest them. (Industry sources had indicated that Bayuk Cigar was unable to sell its premium cigar brand when it wished to exit. However, additional information regarding the selling price Bayuk allegedly asked for the Garcia Y Vega brand was not available.)

Factors Influencing the Volatility of Rivalry

It was expected that the volatility of competition within an endgame environment would be influenced by factors such as (1) the number of significantly different strategic groups which served the same customers; (2) the relative height of the mobility barriers which protected a strategic group's loyal customer niche and the ease with which that niche could be invaded; and (3) whether competitors which served the same customers would use price competition against each other. It was expected that a volatile competitive environment would be less desirable than a stable one because it would erode the attainable earnings of firms which remained in the endgame. It was also expected that a relatively static membership of firms within the same product market (with well-known corporate strategic postures and a historic base of competitive experiences among these firms) would result in a less volatile competitive environment wherein the firms would have developed the ability to signal their competitive maneuver and thereby could avoid head-to-head competition.

The studies of the cigars and the percolator coffee-maker endgames, for example, indicated that the presence of several groups of firms, each possessing different strategic postures, which pursued the same customer groups could indeed make a volatile endgame environment.

It found that diverse strategic groups competed for the same shelf space within the cigar industry and the percolator coffee-maker business. The cigar industry was volatile at the distribution level and some channel invasion occurred. The percolator coffee-makers market was also pulling higher-quality percolators into lower-priced channels during the endgame. Here, too, dissimilar groups of competitors vied for the same customers. Performance was mediocre in these businesses, on the average, as well.

These examples confirmed prior expectations concerning "fragmented" and asymmetric competitive structures but there were also volatile endgames where the competitors were quite similar in their strategic postures and the industry was concentrated. (The baby-food producers, for example, were similar in the baby-foods market but dissimilar at the corporate level with respect to their patterns of diversification. These firms had competed against each other for thirty years in the same market niche. Nevertheless, the baby-food producers experienced a volatile endgame when demand declined severely.) The framework predicted that competitors in the same strategic groups (such as, for example, the synthetic soda-ash producers, the receiving-tube manufacturers, and the baby-food processors) would understand their markets and each other well. The baby-food processors' experiences in endgame indicate that perhaps other factors (in addition to competitive structure) were operative in this particular industry example and affected the volatility of competition.

For example, it was possible for economic exit barriers to influence the stability of price levels. In the baby-food endgame, excess capacity made price levels difficult to maintain. Firms such as Gerber Products continued to build new plants, warehouses, and other baby-food processing facilities even during the twenty-year period of falling birth rates. Strategic exit barriers seemed to deter these firms from using (for other food-processing purposes) these relatively new assets which economic exit barriers would not let them retire.

With so much underutilized capacity in the industry, a volatile price war plagued the baby-food firms for almost six years. Until a few plant retirements occurred, until other products were processed using some of the baby-food processing assets, and until temporary increases in the number of births occurred, competitors could not maintain a truce in their shelf-space war. Thus, in the baby-foods endgame, where substitute products were not a substantial challenge and where ultimate consumers were not highly price-sensitive, the deterrent effect of economic exit barriers upon the timing of plant-retirement decisions seemed to be strong. The excess capacity created by these economic exit barriers also appeared to influence pricing behavior among competitors.

The effect of excess capacity created by economic exit barriers upon the frequently depressed prices of products in the rayon industry, for example, is unclear. It is believed that exit barriers influenced these firms' pricing decisions. But it also appears that prices were low due to price pressures from substitute fiber products, and due to the bargaining power of cellulosic-fibers producers' customers, the fickle fashion industry, who infrequently featured rayon in the fabrics of a particular fashion season in order to extract lower prices from rayon producers.

Excess capacity seemed to affect price levels in other declining businesses, as well. Although hydrocarbon-based acetylene producers did not compete against each other (due to their physical interconnections to their primary customers), economic exit barriers created excess capacity which influenced spot prices for acetylene. When primary users consumed reduced amounts of acetylene, producers generated substantial excess volumes of the gas in their continuous-process plants nevertheless. Their excess acetylene was sold to outside, onetime customers on a negotiated price basis. As the excess capacity of acetylene producers increased while their relatively high economic asset values kept them temporarily locked into operations, this spot price provided increasingly lower margins to acetylene producers because increased costs could not be passed on. Had this been an industry where hydrocarbon-based acetylene producers competed against each other for customers, competition would have been volatile because

(1) some acetylene plants were less than five years old in the base year when industry-wide demand started to decline, and (2) these newest acetylene plants were among the largest ever used to generate acetylene. Therefore, excess capacity problems could have been severe.

Summary of the Influence of Industry Traits

In summary, an industry such as the baby-food endgame example illustrates the interactions of the most important industry traits which seemed to influence competitive conditions in an environment of declining demand. The baby-food firms acted as if they *believed* that the number of births would increase soon. Therefore, they competed aggressively despite their past experiences in this industry and despite their concentrated competitive structure. The baby-food firms built plants in anticipation of the large number of births they expected. When their new plants were underutilized, they were pressured into using price competition to try to fill their factories, despite their concentrated competitive structure. Customer industries controlled the important linkages to the ultimate consumer—shelf space. Despite the large expenditures these firms made to differentiate their particular brands of baby foods, customer industries (grocers) were able to extract a portion of the rents earned on this investment (and force the product to act like a commodity) by virtue of their power over the baby-food producers' access to customers.

Competitors' expectations regarding the likelihood of revitalization, the speed of declining demand, and the segments where demand will first fade seemed to be the most powerful predictors of what type of endgame environment would develop. The ways in which firms responded to their expectations regarding demand influenced (1) the products which were deleted in endgame; (2) the plants which were constructed (or shut down); and (3) which firms remained in the endgame for the most prolonged period of time. This finding would tend to suggest that if a firm could assess how the endgame environment would likely develop, it could prepare itself to exit early or to serve the market segments which it anticipated would decline most slowly. It might be able to obtain a timing advantage.

The presence of exit barriers and other factors which influenced the volatility of rivalry within the industry also seemed to influence the nature of the endgame environment. The influence of strategic exit barriers upon competitive volatility seemed to be particularly significant for analyzing how competitors might behave within an endgame environment. The findings from this study suggested that strategic reasons seemed to underlie many decisions by firms to remain invested in what appeared to be otherwise unpromising endgame environments.

Strategic Exit Barriers

It was expected that strategic exit barriers would deter a firm from retiring plants or entire businesses which were not achieving performance goals. It was found that strategic considerations did influence firms' behaviors with respect to declining businesses.

Corporate Image Barriers

It was expected that single-business firms or historical pioneers in an industry would be most strongly deterred by strategic exit barriers because they had been closely identified with the declining business in the past.

It was found that these types of strategic exit barriers seemed to deter the exits of (1) the smaller cigar manufacturers; (2) the baby-food processors; (3) the wide-line appliance firms which produced percolator coffeemakers; (4) the inorganic industrial-chemicals firms which had manufactured synthetic soda ash; and (5) the electronics firms which had been among the early (or largest) manufacturers of receiving tubes.

Strategic exit barriers due to corporate image considerations seemed to be relatively less important to (1) acetylene producers; (2) smaller appliance firms; (3) diversified synthetic-fibers producers; (4) widely diversified food processors or chemical firms; and (5) smaller electronics firms. Companies which had acquired declining businesses in the process of acquiring other businesses seemed to be among the least constrained divestors of declining businesses because the history of the industry had no strategic (or emotional) meaning for them. Therefore, although firms such as FMC Corporation, El Paso Company, and Squibb may have been deterred by economic exit barriers, it was not found that strategic exit barriers seemed to be operative with respect to these particular firms.

Customer Linkage Barriers

It was expected that where companies could overcome their corporate image barriers which might have deterred their exits, but where their external customers relied upon them for a supply of the declining product and also purchased other products from the companies, these strategic exit barriers might deter companies from divesting or retiring their declining products.

It was found that customer linkages seemed to be important strategic deterrents to exit in declining industries such as (1) synthetic soda ash and acetylene and (2) receiving tubes and rayon staple and filament (during a few years of shortages when demand and plant retirements were mismatched). The percolator coffee-makers continued to be offered as a service to retailers by leading, wide-line appliance companies but customer demand was scarcely dependent upon a supply of the product in the same fashion as were the contractual acetylene customers of firms such as Diamond Shamrock and Tenneco Chemical. In those particular examples it was found that operating losses were incurred while contractual obligations were satisfied by these acetylene producers. These contracts seemed to constitute an exit barrier.

Short-Term Reporting Goal Barriers

It was expected that firms which were aggressively acquiring or merging with other firms might avoid divesting their declining business units if they were of a significant size in order to avoid showing a short-term disruption in reported performances. Reporting goal considerations seemed to be important to many firms examined in this study which possessed endgame business with undepreciated assets which were not acquiring companies. Hence, it seemed that a combination of economic and strategic exit barriers could deter managers from divesting endgame business units in order to avoid showing erratic fluctuations in performance. (Managerial exit barriers of this nature sometimes seemed to coincide with the reporting goal deterrents, as in the example of the power-cable industry, which was not examined in this particular study.)

Vertical Integration Barriers

It was expected that the declining business unit would be retained if it were part of a vertically integrated structure only where the other part of the system (or integrated business unit) was more costly to retire or was profitable enough to justify retaining the endgame unit. If the endgame business were a relatively small proportion of a larger integrated business's economic value, it would be expected that it would continue to be operated even if it were not particularly profitable in itself.

Few of the firms in the seven sample industries studied were vertically integrated by 1978. Cigarmakers sold their tobacco farms. Few rayon producers owned wood-pulping plants or wove their own textiles by 1978. Receiving-tube producers sourced components for television receivers if they were less expensive, and monomer plants were usually shut down before acetylene plants were retired. In most of the experiences reviewed in this study, the endgame business unit was either of greater economic value than the assets of other links in the integrated operations or they were still viable as suppliers of replacement parts, even if the vertical relationship had been severed. Therefore, the industries in this sample did not provide examples of vertical integration exit barriers, and this hypothesis has not been adequately tested.

The Influence of Endgaming Firms' Relative Internal Strengths on Endgame Strategy Formulation

It was expected that the more successful firms which competed in an endgame environment would possess the relevant strengths for serving the remaining niches of demand. The firms which possessed these strengths would have either (1) made the appropriate investments in the past, or (2) invested in the assets required to serve the enduring niches of demand early in the endgame. Hence, it was expected that it should have been apparent relatively early in the endgame that some firms were laboring under competitive disadvantages.

It was found that a firm would not necessarily enjoy a satisfactory performance merely due to market share if the markets which a particular dominant firm served were not the "right" markets in an industry where several different market segments existed. In an industry where the product possessed commoditylike traits, market share seemed to be more frequently advantageous because of the economies of scale which size sometimes provided.

For each endgame industry which was examined, different competitive strengths seemed to be more relevant to firms' successes than others. The relevant internal strengths in an endgame seemed to be determined by the characteristics of the industry environment and by the competitive postures of the other firms in the industry. Whether a particular firm possessed or would acquire these relevant strengths seemed to be determined, in part, by the firm's expectations concerning continued demand for the products of the endgame industry. It would be expected that an analysis of the strengths of the competitors and their commitments to the endgame could have been made at the base year and the analysis of the endgame could have yielded predictions concerning firms' performances in endgame.

The competitive advantages which firms possessed in order to perform well in their respective endgames were those strengths which best enabled them to serve a viable pocket of demand better than their competitors could do. The important competitive strengths possessed by successful firms profiled in the industry were, to some large extent, advantages which had resulted form serving the right niches. Therefore, strengths which were important for serving a lucrative market in endgame may, in fact, have been a result of choosing the right customers.

Sketches of Competitive Performances in Endgame

Receiving Tubes

It could be expected that GTE Sylvania would perform well in the endgame because its plant was the most automated and it used offshore plants for preassembly operations. It could be expected that RCA would have incurred some operating losses because its plants were not efficient and RCA Corporation did not use automated equipment or offshore plants. The major strength which RCA possessed was its substantial distribution of RCA-tubed television receivers into the market.

Synthetic Soda Ash

It could be expected that Allied Chemical would perform well in the endgame because it was the only synthetic soda-ash producer to invest in natural soda-ash production. Also, it was located the greatest distance east of the natural soda-ash producers' plants. Hence, Allied Chemical was in the best relative position to serve the customers located in the far eastern and New England market for soda ash (the market which was the greatest distance from the natural-ash miner). Also, Allied Chemical's last synthetic soda-ash plant did not possess a pollution problem like Olin Corporation, whose effluents were dumped into a shallow river.

Acetylene

It could be expected that Monochem, Inc., would enjoy a profitable performance in endgame because it possessed favorable raw-materials contracts and the lowest-cost technology. It could be expected that Union Carbide would do well because it possessed numerous acetylene plants and a very flexible technology which enabled it to produce both acetylene and its substitute product, ethylene. It could be expected that the large acetylene plant of Tenneco Chemical would expose it to tremendous risks, as did its external customer contracts.

Rayon

It could be expected that Courtaulds, Ltd.'s, new, energy-efficient and relatively nonpolluting rayon plant would have given it lower operating costs than the old rayon plants of Avtex Fibers. In an industry such as the cellulosic fibers industry, where substitute synthetic fibers were readily available and were treated like commodities, it could have been predicted that the lowest-cost competitors would enjoy the greatest relative competitive advantages.

Baby Foods

It could be expected that the position of dominance which Gerber Products had established and the operating economies it enjoyed from its large market acceptance would have enabled Gerber to perform better than other firms in the baby-foods industry, even when it had misestimated demand due to declining birth rates. Gerber Products was also particularly strong (after 1973) because it had diversified its principal line of business to support its flagging revenues in its primary market, but its principal competitor, Beech-Nut Foods, had not done so. By contrast, Swift & Company was in the least competitive cost and product-line position because its product line was circumscribed by law and its plants produced baby meats to fill excess capacity only.

Electric Percolator Coffee-Makers

It could be expected that General Electric would continue to offer a percolator coffee-maker because it was a major, wide-line small electrical appliances company. It could be expected that the glass percolator coffee-maker product would have been among the first industry fatalities because a glass percolator would seem redundant to retailers; it looked too much like an automatic drip coffee-maker's carafe. Therefore, it could be predicted that Proctor-Silex would encounter some problems in the percolator coffee-maker industry.

Cigars

It could be expected that the firms which had obtained the best access to shelf space would perform the best in the endgame. Operating efficiencies were also important because the customers were relatively price-sensitive in the lower-priced, high-volume market. The merchandisers of the premium cigar brands may have enjoyed success, but the sales volume of classes G and H cigars was only a small fraction of the sales volume which large corporations like Culbro and the Consolidated Cigar Company were accustomed to servicing. Advertising goodwill was an important strength in the cigar market (as were strong distribution channels) because the larger firms depended upon high sales volumes to cover their advertising and distribution expenses.

Firms' Performances in Endgame

Performance was measured in the following manner. It was expected that the firms which performed well in endgame would have positioned themselves to serve the most promising remaining market segments or that they would be able to exit early in the endgame and thereby retrieve a reasonably large portion of the value of their past endgame investments. Firms which exited from the endgame early could be compared in terms of whether they could recover the value of their investments; whether their exits were timed to exploit the resale market benefits of being among the first firms to exit; and whether they retrieved additional benefits from operating experiences which could have been transferred to other related business activities. The firms which exited and seemed to achieve these benefits were American Cyanamid (acetylene) and Raytheon (receiving tubes). Each of these exited early.

Firms which continued to compete in the endgame throughout the industry study could be compared in terms of whether they are among the last industry competitors which appear to be prospering from price-insensitive demand or are well positioned to facilitate an easy exit when participation in the industry is no longer attractive. The firms which continued to compete and seemed to achieve these performances were Gerber Products (baby foods), GTE Sylvania (receiving tubes), Monochem, Inc. (acetylene), and Allied Chemical (synthetic soda ash). All of these increased their investment levels. There were other firms in the study which seemed to perform at better-than-average industry profitability rates. These firms were not highlighted above because their asset positions were not flexible with respect to value retrieval, their industry environments were not characterized by price-insensitive demand, and hence the rewards of remaining invested in their endgames were less than in other industries, and there were other barriers to exit associated with these otherwise successful firms' performances.

Firms which exited from their endgames early could be compared in terms of whether they lost substantial sums while operating and could not recover value of their investment upon exit, or otherwise suffered disruptions when they exited. The firms which exited early and seemed to suffer poor performances were Industrial Rayon Corporation (rayon), Diamond Shamrock (acetylene), RCA Corporation (receiving tubes), and Proctor-Silex (percolator coffee-makers). Most of these firms milked their investments until they could exit. There were other firms in the study which exited and which also suffered write-off losses on disposal of their assets that were not highlighted in the section above because their exits were somewhat precipitated by abrupt environmental requirements which were not foreseen. These firms included Olin Corporation, BASF Wyandotte, and PPG Industries. These firms had expected to continue to enjoy profitable participation in the synthetic soda-ash business because they had forecast that the substitute product, natural soda ash, would not be available in substantial quantities for several years into the future. (It is not clear whether the 1975 flurry of natural soda-ash plant construction would have occurred if, in 1970, the viability of synthetic soda-ash producers had not been severely reduced by environmental-control legislation.)

The following firms which were still participating in their endgames at the present time are expected to perform poorly because they were incurring operating losses or were feared to be in danger of possible failure because of previous tactics they had pursued. These firms were Bayuk Cigar ("milk"), Beech-Nut Foods (increased investment) as well as Beaunit Corporation (rayon) and Avtex Fibers (rayon). Both Beaunit and Avtex Fibers were created when their parent firms were forced to divest their endgame businesses.

It was expected that some reinvestments would occur in favorable environments so that competitors might serve the niches of enduring demand more efficiently. It was found that reinvestments were made by firms in market segments where demand was expected to endure. Firms reinvested in niches within the electronic receiving-tube industry (GTE Sylvania), the cigar industry (Consolidated Cigar Company), and the baby-foods industry (Gerber Products) with some degree of success.

It was found that reinvestments also occurred where there was confusion regarding the duration of demand for the declining product or where there was misjudgment concerning firms' abilities to serve that demand economically, given other uncontrollable industry factors. Specifically, it was found that reinvestments were made in industries even after there was evidence of problems in those industries. The investments in the synthetic soda-ash industry (Olin Corporation) and the rayon industry (Avtex Fibers-FMC and El Paso-Beaunit) resulted in write-off losses for the firms which had made them when they exited.

A Comparison of the Strategic Matrix's Predictions with Observed Performances

The strategy alternatives which were predicted to be appropriate for firms operating within various endgame environments differed according to the reinvestments a firm might be willing to make and according to how soon relative to competitors a firm exited after the base year. In agreement with the predictions of the strategy matrix developed in chapter 2, it was seen that many firms which were in favorable environments either exited quickly to "cash in" on the benefits of a strong position or made some reinvestments to improve their relative position in the endgame. The pattern of behaviors for less favorable environments was less clear and will be discussed at length in the section which follows. The framework has hypothesized that a firm which possessed strengths which were appropriate for its endgame in an environment where the industry traits were favorable would likely either increase the investment level to dominate the industry or hold the investment level if it harbored some uncertainty regarding the duration of declining demand for its products. As the firm maintained the productive potential of this business, it was also expected that it would seek to divest the declining business unit if it could arrange favorable terms for doing so. An exception to this expected behavior would likely occur if the firm faced high strategic exit barriers. It was expected that the presence of such exit barriers would affect the timing of divestitures, shutdowns, or the execution of other endgame tactics.

Industry Was Favorable—Firm Possessed Strengths

Where the business units were of relatively low strategic importance to a firm, the investment was milked or reduced in these examples even where the outlook for the strategic customer niche which the firm serviced seemed to be promising. The highly successful infant-formula producers pursued the most aggressive and optimistic strategies in our examples. Even there, Mead, Johnson divested its other baby foods which were consumed in the early stages of the feeding cycle to specialize in the formula product, exclusively. It had been forecast that strong competitors in favorable market niches should increase their investment levels or hold the investment level in endgame. Where the business was of relatively low strategic importance, this did not occur. Although firms in these circumstances performed well, they reduced their overall commitments to these businesses, instead.

Where the business units were of relatively high importance to a firm, their strategies more closely followed the predictions of the endgame strategy matrix. Most of the strong competitors in these relatively promising industries increased their investment levels or held investment levels without cutbacks. The exception to this, S.W. Farber, which produced percolator coffee-makers, suffered sales-volume reductions from its 1972 sales volume of at least 66 percent. Hence, it was less optimistic than the framework about the prospects of enduring demand for its high-quality line of percolators.

Industry Was Favorable—Firm Did Not Possess Strengths

Where the business units were of relatively low strategic importance to a firm, it was found that all of the competitors exited, thus clearing the industry for stronger competitors to continue to serve enduring demand. As the study had forecast, timely exits were executed after the investment values had been milked.

Where the business units were of relatively high strategic importance to a firm, firms did not perform as the framework would have anticipated on the basis of strengths alone. It was expected that the weaker firms in a favorable declining industry would do best by shrinking selectively or even by milking their investments. The companies sometimes expanded instead. The firms which pursued aggressive strategies were single-business firms in industries where demand was likely to plateau—baby foods and higher-quality cigars. Thus high strategic exit barriers and expectations that their industry would remain viable motivated these firms to become more committed to their declining industries rather than less committed. (These firms were also in industries where it is not certain whether their performances were successful.)

Industry Was Unfavorable—Firm Possessed Strengths

Where the business units were of relatively low strategic importance to a firm, it was expected that the competitors would shrink their positions to reduce their commitments to the industry or would milk their investments. Some firms, for whom this business was not important strategically, increased their investment levels, instead.

The examples of acetylene producers which increased their investment levels in an unfavorable endgame need additional clarification. Monochem, Inc.'s contracts were expected to terminate with the full depreciation of its plant in 1981. Dow Chemical's interconnected customer, Hoffman-LaRoche, was expected to bear the increased costs of using the acetylene route processes. Chemetron expanded its commitment to acetylene production to build a global distribution system for welding equipment and supplies. Thus these decisions were not the behaviors the framework would have predicted for firms formulating strategies for their declining acetylene plants. The behavior of Union Carbide Corporation, which did shrink selectively, conforms to the framework's predictions of endgame behavior.

Where the business units were of relatively high strategic importance to a firm—due to historic events, a wide-line product strategy, leadership in the industry, or because the business unit was a recently acquired, formerly entrepreneurial company—it was found that firms' behaviors were closer to the framework's expectations. It was expected that firms would shrink selectively or milk their investments if the market niches they serviced were unfavorable even when they possessed relative competitive advantages. Eighty-eight percent of the firms in this category did so. The exceptions were a percolator producer which dominated the poly-perc (plastic) market; a cigar producer and distributor which was the most successful lower-priced cigar house in the southeastern states; and a rayon producer whose plant possessed the lowest costs and whose century-old corporate success had been built upon rayon.

These firms had carved out positions of success within industries which were otherwise unfavorable. To the extent that these four examples represented favorable industry niches (and should be analyzed as such) the strategic matrix still provides a good description of the strategies which would yield the more successful performances because the strategies these firms pursued would be appropriate for competitors in the "favorable industry—firm has strengths" category when firms possessed some misgivings about the duration of demand for their products despite their immediate successes.

Industry Was Unfavorable—Firms Did Not Possess Strengths

Where the business units were of relatively low strategic importance to a firm, it was found that 75 percent of the firms had divested as the framework had predicted would occur. Of the firms which remained, American Cigar faced strategic (corporate image) barriers to exit and Airco faced economic exit barriers. Air Products could divest its acetylene product offerings relatively easily because it did not have a large amount of capital assets invested in this business.

Where the business units were of high strategic importance, but the industry environment was unfavorable and the firms did not possess competitive strengths, it was expected that firms would divest these businesses. It was found that (1) Olin had divested; (2) FMC Corporation had sold Avtex Fibers and El Paso Company had sold Beaunit Corporation, each to their respective managers; and (3) Bayuk Cigar was converting its earnings into a portfolio of securities and appeared to be liquidating itself. Thus, although firms remained in these endgames due to some form of exit barriers, the expected divestiture strategies had been pursued in many cases.

Table 11-1 presents maximum-likelihood estimates of the probability that exit will occur, given the presence of various industry structural factors described in the theoretical framework of chapter 2. The parenthetical figures shown below the coefficients of various specifications tested indicate the significance levels of the particular factors. The test considers whether the presence of a variable is positively or negatively correlated with a firm's decision to exit.

In the specifications of the exit decision, exit was less likely if (1) the niche a firm served possessed enduring demand traits; (2) manufacturing or

Table 11-1
Regression Analysis on Exit

R^2	High Strategic Importance	Favorable Industry Environment	Strong Customer Industry	Shared Facilities	High Qualty	Manufacturing Technology Barriers	Losses	Promo/ Advertising Barriers	Constant
.555		-.3209 (.0017)[a]	-.2374 (.0245)	-.3256 (.0015)	-.2623 (.0107)	-.3833 (.0007)	.3231 (.0022)		1.1629 (.0001)
.503		-.4008 (.0002)	-.1412 (.2019)	-.2501 (.0222)	-.2841 (.0088)	-.3736 (.0016)		-.1930 (.0620)	1.2744 (.0001)
.475	-.1101 (.3189)		-.2324 (.0451)	-.3109 (.0048)	-.2905 (.0116)	-.2955 (.0139)	.3964 (.0005)		.9883 (.0001)
.448		-.2584 (.0175)	-.3221 (.0050)	-.2262 (.0325)	-.2541 (.0241)		.3146 (.0063)		.8648 (.0001)
.401		-.3380 (.0024)	-.2246 (.0574)	-.1530 (.1741)	-.2754 (.0188)			-.1957 (.0812)	.9815 (.0001)
.367		-.3352 (.0030)	-.2685 (.0234)	-.2056 (.0647)	-.2775 (.0200)				.9624 (.0001)
.3421		-.4743 (.0001)		-.3001 (.0113)		-.4350 (.0007)			1.1063 (.0001)
.3127		-.3989 (.0005)	-.2645 (.0259)						.8594 (.0001)
.2935				-.2685 (.0274)	-.4256 (.0004)	-.3359 (.0090)		-.2428 (.0339)	.9618 (.0001)
.2679				-.3056 (.0144)		-.3809 (.0040)	.4045 (.0013)		.7299 (.0001)
.2542				-.1153 (.3384)	-.4090 (.0010)			-.2337 (.0524)	.7250 (.0001)
.2525			-.1668 (.1957)		-.3875 (.0024)	-.2058 (.1086)			.8007 (.0001)

Relative likelihood that exit occurred: 41 percent.

[a] Parenthetical figures represent levels of significance using a Student's t-test of the null hypothesis that the coefficient equals zero.

technological exit barriers were high; (3) customer-related (goodwill) barriers were high; or (4) customer industries were strong enough to exert bargaining power over producers of declining products. The incurrence of losses tended to increase the likelihood of exit.

From these limited statistical findings, it would appear that high manufacturing or technological exit barriers can influence a firm's performance adversely because then presence deters exits and incites price warfare. This finding would tend to suggest that firms should carefully consider investments in durable and specific assets in a mature industry if the likelihood of product obsolescence of that business seems credible.

From these results and the findings regarding the strategic matrix, some general conclusions about the strategic exit decision and other problems regarding declining demand can be offered which may be of interest to the business practitioner, the student of business administration, and public policymakers. Conclusions are contained in the chapter which follows.

12 The Policy Implications of the Endgame Study

The findings from this study have offered substantial evidence that the environment of declining demand differs across industries and that different strategies have been used successfully by firms to cope with the endgame. The discussion of these endgame strategies has indicated that firms possessing differing initial positions or pursuing different corporate strategies need not formulate the same types of responses to the endgame, and may, in fact, be able to influence their relative advantages in endgame by doing the analysis this study has suggested early—before endgame becomes a widely recognized problem.

The findings from this study have offered suggestions regarding how the presence (or absence) of certain industry traits may influence the conditions in an endgame environment. It is hoped that these findings would be of some value to managers in making informed strategy decisions for endgame. Since the characteristics of endgames do differ and since there have been different patterns of investment and exit across industries, it would seem that the analysis this thesis offers could offer important suggestions to managers when formulating their endgame strategies. In particular, the principal implications of the factual findings from the studies of declining industries suggest the need for attention in the following areas of analysis:

1. Managers may wish to devote more analytical attention to the behaviors of competitors in the endgame. The industry studies have indicated that, in conditions of declining demand, firms are thrust together which may be unaccustomed to competition against each other, as in the examples of electric percolator coffee-makers, and cigar industries, resulting in destructive price warfare and low profit margins (or losses) for all involved firms.
2. Misunderstandings of the nature of competition seem to have precipitated poorly timed exits, unremunerative asset disposals, and consequently disruptive performances in endgame, as the example of FMC's Avtex Fibers division would indicate. More attention to the strategic postures of competitors as they relate to the endgame may be appropriate in periods which precede declining demand.

Given the nature of the data gathered in the study of endgame environments and of different ways in which firms coped with declining demand, the study's findings must be subject to certain qualifications and limitations. For example, this study has focused on the patterns of activity in endgame, not upon the processes leading to the choice of a strategy. The forecasts of strategic conditions which emanate from this study must be modified in some cases (such as hydrocarbon-based acetylene) to accommodate some variations in strategy alternatives which may be explained by industry eccentricities. Wherever possible in the industry studies, proper recognition of firms' corporate policies regarding, for example, early divestitures (like the policy of duPont) or other considerations, such as their histories (for example, pioneers or single-business firms), which may have created dissimilarities in firms' perceptions of the same events, has been accorded to the firms in analyzing their endgame behaviors.

Since the studies are based on interviews and library research there are, of course, limitations to what can be learned about particular divestment or reinvestment decisions. Moreover, the behaviors of some of the fifty-one competitors were reconstructed from the reports of competitors and published information. These limitations of the study's conclusions and others are treated as they are encountered in the sections which follow.

Resource-allocation decisions made by firms within mature industries will influence firms' positions in the environment later when demand declines irrevocably. The problem is a dynamic one. The customer groups which may be overlooked in an active market could become the foundation of a profitable endgame in the future. If the firm could identify these customer groups and make reinvestments early to position itself to be these customers' major (perhaps only) supplier later, it could secure for itself a rewarding market opportunity in endgame.

The study's findings suggest that it may be possible for firms to analyze the characteristics of their customer groups while the industry is still mature in order to identify pockets of demand for the endgame product which are most likely to endure. The customer markets whose structural characteristics would make them attractive as customers in endgame may be an insignificant part of total market demand during the business's maturity.

This does not suggest that a firm should abandon its other existing customer groups prematurely. Rather, it suggests that the customers upon which competition is based in maturity may fade in endgame. The firm which is aware of these dynamics could deploy its resources and attentions to developing these alternative, potentially attractive markets which its analysis suggests will be the enduring customer groups in endgame.

There is more to the problem of endgame analysis than a mere economic calculation. The conclusions drawn from this study have relied heavily upon a preendgame analysis of industry traits and competitors' strategies. This would suggest that firms formulating strategies within an endgame could have taken preventive measures to avoid head-to-head competition when demand for their products deteriorated. The implications of these findings are explained below.

Implications for Business Strategists

Market Demand Traits

One of the most important findings regarding influences upon the nature of the competitive environment is that the power of the expectations of competitors (and of their customers) regarding future demand has not been fully recognized in the past. Customers can be driven away prematurely if they fear being stranded without a supplier. If firms' communications with their markets are unusually poor, as were those of the baby-foods producers or the cigarmakers, firms could develop inaccurate internal forecasts of expected future demand which they will act upon in the future even if the forecasts they have formulated are fallacious, and could invest erroneously in expected growth in demand when, in fact, their market segments are deteriorating rapidly. Some of the uncertainty which fired volatile price competition could be reduced if better information were utilized. The erratic competitive behavior of firms in the baby-foods, cigars and leather-tanning businesses suggests that the phenomenon of declining demand (and its underlying traits) was not well understood by firms within these endgames. Better analytical tools seem to be needed in order for firms to assess the potential evolutionary power of technological (or cultural and demographic) changes upon their industry's competitive structure. There may be some benefits to using scenario analysis and other qualitative forecasting tools which would help strategic managers to estimate (1) how quickly competitors are likely to exit, (2) which competitors would be most likely to remain invested, and (3) what types of competitors would be potential entrants (bringing a new technology to the industry, for example) when demand for a product declines.

Endgame Strengths

If a firm was not already producing the substitute products or was not already familiar with the economics of the alternative technology, strong arguments exist based upon the industry experiences presented that firms should do so in order to monitor the rate of commercialization of the new technology and to control the speed of transition of the firm's operations from the endgame product to its substitute. Firms which invested in substitute technologies were able to judge when substitution would be complete, where substitution would occur most slowly, and when to shut down their plant (or plants) and source the product rather than produce it internally (even if their entry was relatively late in the new technology's start-up).

This study's analysis of endgame suggests that if a firm is not the lowest-cost competitor in an industry where products are becoming commoditylike in nature, it will have to surrender market share during competition in the endgame. If the declining product is differentiable, new investments in the business may be justified in order to secure for oneself a more favorable position in endgame, but if the product does not service a demand which responds to differentiation—if the product is developing commoditylike traits which make customers increasingly price-sensitive— such reinvestments may not be justified because no true customer niche is likely to exist. Without the protection of the mobility barriers which product differentiation could provide, firms are vulnerable to market invasions by lower-cost competitors.

The study's findings suggest that if a firm possesses a large share of the market but does not possess the lowest operating costs, a strong distribution system, or a loyal niche of customers, it should try to overcome its exit barriers early to sell the endgame business to another competitor or a supplier, particularly if it possesses a large proportion of undepreciated assets. Without these particular strengths, it will be increasingly difficult to retrieve the value of the firm's investments as the endgame progresses. By contrast, if a firm possesses some strengths and if it believes that demand for the products of the industry will endure (making continued participation in some niches desirable), this study's findings suggest that a firm might purchase the assets of firms which serve such customer niches, particularly those of competitors which face high economic exit barriers or are indecisive regarding their expectations for demand in the endgame in order to reduce the presence of factors causing volatility in the endgame, particularly differing expectations concerning demand among competitors, and excess capacity which is locked in by economic exit barriers. Reducing the number of major competitors or plants in the endgame by helping them to retire their capacity from the market may ease a potentially volatile situation, and if customers are price-insensitive it may even become a lucrative strategy late in the endgame.

Industry Traits

This study's findings indicated that price levels stayed higher (and volatility was lower) where lower-cost, perfect substitutes did not exist; customer switching costs were high, making it difficult to replace the endgame product; customer industries did not extract pricing deals from producers of declining products; and excess productive capacity did not pressure firms to cut prices in order to fill plants to an economic level of their engineered capacity.

This study found that the presence of perfect substitute products (for example, other synthetic fibers for rayon, or natural soda ash for synthetic soda ash) or powerful wholesalers, distribution companies, or retailers reduced the attractiveness of continued participation in an endgame and the likelihood that price increases should be successful in such an environment. This suggests that if these factors are present in endgame, a firm should not make reinvestments in the industry or otherwise increase its commitment to the industry. This study found that competitors in a declining industry could keep their industry viable and profitable longer by retiring plant capacity in an orderly fashion to keep supply in line with demand but that the execution of such maneuvers would require weaker competitors to retire their plants in deference to more efficient competitors (or irrationally committed competitors) if price levels were to be maintained at a high level in the declining industry. Hence stronger firms should help weaker firms to exit.

An economic solution which this study suggests where excess capacity is increasing (but where strategic exit barriers also deter firms from exiting) is sourcing arrangements whereby the most efficient plants could (and in some endgames studied did) manufacture the declining product for several competitors to sell under their own corporate or brand names.

Firms were somewhat less likely to remain invested in industries where competition was volatile. The likelihood of a volatile endgame was amplified where switching costs were low and where price sensitivity, technological exit barriers, and brand loyalties were high. The finding that structural factors could predict the relative attractiveness of a declining industry for particular firms suggests that firms could develop contingency plans for exit when investing in an industry and could evaluate how long to remain in a declining industry after unit shipments have fallen to a criterion level in order to avoid the ravages of price warfare.

Competition within industries where there were a few strategic groups and high mobility barriers among each others' markets (for example, branded, premium cigars) was generally preferable to competition in industries where there were several strategic groups and low mobility barriers between them (as in lower-priced cigars). Competition in an industry where most competitors' capital assets were fully depreciated (as in synthetic soda ash or percolator coffee-makers) was generally preferable to competition in an industry where competitors which served the same market segments recently made substantial investments in physical assets—for example, baby foods or automated cigarmakers which invested in homogenized leaf technologies. (The firms in the latter examples were deterred from exiting by the plant-related economic exit barriers they created.) Where great uncertainty concerning the endgame existed—for example, against firms which were generally confused regarding (1) the outlook for industry demand, (2) who should exit, and (3) whose plants should be retired (and when their own retirement should occur)—competition was generally less desirable than in industries where firms were relatively certain of the nature of the endgame, recognized their interdependencies with competitors, and understood (as did the receiving-tube producers) when it was appropriate for their own exits to occur.

This study's findings indicated that certain external events could be particularly catastrophic for the vitality of a declining industry in the sense that investments may become necessary which were not likely to be recoverable. Events which tended to encourage exits included legislation concerning effluent standards, pollution controls, or other public-policy decisions which could accelerate the demise of an industry. Employee-health work rules, import traffics, and export quotas are other examples of public policies which affected the viability of the sample industries studied. (If a firm wished to ease others out of an endgame, it might make these investments in anticipation of such legislation and then encourage such laws to be enacted.)

These types of uncontrollable external events suggest that it might be appropriate to monitor governmental agencies closely and to prepare factual forecasts of the likely economic impact of such legislation upon communities where the firm operates in order to draw attention (if appropriate) to the loss of jobs, property-tax revenues, or other benefits currently associated with the presence of the business unit. Such an analysis would include a forecast of the cost of exit in order to facilitate informed decision-making by management. It may not be out of order for firms which have performed these analyses to provide a copy of their findings to the salient public policymakers and affected residents of the community.

Strategic Exit Barriers

The evidence from this study suggests that it is important to understand the corporate strategies of one's competitors in endgame and to understand how the endgame business unit fits into their corporate-wide plans. This study found that firms faced significant exit barriers which deterred their exits. Other competitors frequently wished that these marginal firms would exit from the endgame sooner because their presence exacerbated the low profitability of the industry, but these marginal competitors stayed and accepted returns that were lower than their corporate-wide opportunity costs of capital in order not to disturb strategic linkages or other relationships which they valued within the declining industry.

Therefore, the evidence of this study suggests that firms will not necessarily exit when economic analysis, such as an abandonment calculation, would suggest they will do so. In forecasting strategies and competition in the endgame it is necessary to recognize the patterns and extent of competitors' diversifications, their histories in the corporation (endgame businesses are sometimes the "mother" business unit), and the basis for firms' competitive postures in the declining industry. It will be necessary to look beyond the economics to the firms' strategies in order to understand their behaviors and likely responses to declining demand.

The Timing of Endgame Strategies

Although it is desirable to sell one's physical assets upon exit or to retire them without incurring any write-off losses, the example of E.I. duPont de Nemours (which retired from two declining industries in this study relatively early in their respective endgames) suggests that companies which will bite the bullet in divesting businesses when they first begin to sour and offer unacceptable returns are valued as being well managed. Although E.I. duPont de Nemours has divested several declining businesses and recognized write-off losses in doing so, duPont has not lost its aura of excellent management because it retired from its rayon, acetate, and acetylene production activities when its evaluation of their performances and future potential for earnings was judged by management to be inadequate.

This study has provided greater definition of the nature of the environment of declining demand than did earlier studies which may have merely touched upon this particular strategic challenge in the life of a business enterprise. From the findings of this study, it is clear that all endgame environments are not alike. Successful ways of coping with decline have also been dissimilar.

The Declining-Demand Research Study's Contribution to Academic Research

The findings from this study supplement previous works illuminating the nature of competition within an industry, particularly the literature which develops and amplifies the concept of competition within strategic groups. This study isolated strategic groups in seven industries and traced the dynamics of these groups through their respective endgames. It has found that the characteristics of firms' strategic postures—how they have developed their resources in order to serve customer markets—could be analyzed in light of other strategic groups in the industry to suggest a basis for determining which niches of a shrinking market a firm might be best suited to service and whether it should exit.

This study of firms' endgame strategies has explored the concept of exit barriers and has amplified upon published studies of their deterrent effects upon the implementation of corporate strategies. The study has explored the different types of influences economic exit barriers have had upon firms operating in environments which are already recognized as being in deterioration. This study has found that firms are unwilling to recognize write-off losses upon disposal even in such businesses. Thus the presence of economic exit barriers in an industry cannot be deemed a trivial problem because firms apparently weigh them as factors in timing their terminations or divestitures of declining business units.

This study found that strategic exit barriers were substantially important in timing exits from a declining business and that even where the book value of assets in a declining business had been recovered, firms were reluctant to exit from businesses which they considered to be important to their images or necessary to service important customers. Although strategic exit barriers are difficult to measure, their influence over the timing of firms' decisions to retire plants or to terminate their participation in a business is not insignificant. This is an area that might profit by additional research.

In presenting the data gathered in the field and library research, this study has used a standardized format for describing an industry according to the relevant variables which will define the competitive conditions of that environment. Use of such a common format facilitates comparisons of firms' behaviors and performances in cross-sectional studies of different industries. If these are the right variables to consider in comparing strategies and performances, this format could be a useful tool. It provides replicability of results and the opportunity for large sample studies which, in the past, have been difficult to obtain in corporate-strategy studies.

Areas for Further Research

The exploratory study of strategies for declining industries has mapped out the factors which influenced strategy-formulation decisions in the endgame. Further research of a diagnostic nature could investigate other predictive aspects of the nature of declining-demand characteristics. For example, this study has determined that demand in certain types of endgames has remained viable for longer durations than in other endgames. Further testing of the hypotheses concerning these demand traits could provide useful information which would assist strategists in their environmental forecasting and product portfolio management activities. Such a study could suggest which products possess the greatest likelihood of rapid obsolescence and could highlight product traits which could help strategists recognize these businesses in maturity. (It would be necessary to do so, then, in order to make preventive changes in the businesses' strategic postures.)

There are unanswered questions regarding the "gaming" or market signaling aspects of the endgame problem which may benefit from further research. In an environment like the endgame where competitors' attentions are being tightly focused upon the common problem of declining demand, it would be expected that signaling may have become well developed from historic competition. In an effort to maintain high price levels, firms operating in the same strategic group may be tempted to coordinate their plant retirements, capacity changes, and other competitive tactics in order to avoid destructive pricing warfare through *misunderstandings*. Public policy which is premised on a free-market economy would prefer the lower prices which accompany volatile competition (even if it meant that several plants would be operating at less than efficient capacities rather than a few plants operating at more fully loaded capacities). If, however, there were public-policy justifications for preserving several relatively inefficient firms in endgame (reasons such as a desire to protect the national industry against import competition or to avoid massive unemployment in depressed industrial regions), then perhaps further exploration of ways to facilitate orderly retirements of capacity while preserving the productive capabilities of remaining competitors (and attaining these other policy objectives) may be appropriate. Public-policy considerations may suggest a review (and possibly a reevaluation) of the law regarding market signaling as well.

The sizable losses which some firms reported upon disposal of their declining businesses suggest that research in the area of strategy-formulation models which could assist business firms in improving the timing of their exits from endgame may be beneficial and fitting. Such a model (which might use data gathered as in a process study) was not in the purview of this study. However, if several replications of the data used in financial analyses performed by firms to determine when to exit were available, the data from such a study could be tested against financial models of abandonment. Firms varied in their willingness to supply these data. But if they were available, such studies could suggest where practice could be improved and where the existing financial models need fine-tuning or revisions.

The research methodology employed in this study used a hybrid design comprised of library data, public source information (press releases, local newspaper announcements, trade-association publications, and so on), and field interviews with the actual participants in the sample endgame industries explored. The next step in testing the framework would be a statistical study that gathered the financial and qualitative data required to test the entire regression equation which has been described.

Implications for Public Policymakers

This research merely reports on the findings of the study and suggests what these results may mean. The researcher's task is to review the study's results;

it is not to recommend policy changes. However, the results of this endgame study would appear to suggest that some changes in policies regarding industry structure and market behavior seem to be necessary if it is deemed desirable to keep at least one manufacturer of the declining product in operation (for example, to supply needed components to costly machinery) at an efficient cost. The phenomenon of exit barriers can create uneconomic conditions of exess capacity while corporate investment criteria may create pressures for an early exit. The market forces may be circumvented only if the undesired outcome seems likely to occur.

From the business person's perspective, products which offer low returns on invested capital and which no longer generate adequate sales volumes to permit economic-sized production runs are candidates for divestiture or shutdown, but exit barriers can lock these firms temporarily into such low-return businesses, constraining their flexibility so severely that these declining businesses must endure uneconomic prices for their products (a condition which exacerbates their poor performances). If the need for at least one remaining supplier is great enough, perhaps measures are needed to ensure the survival of at least one viable and efficient manufacturer of the declining product.

The evidence from this study of the problem of declining demand and industry-wide exits could be interpreted to suggest that some form of tacit competitive coordination and pooling or sourcing arrangements among producers of the declining product might yield the most efficient production of the declining product, despite potential objections from some policymakers who would view declining business arenas in antitrust the same way they would view competition in growing a mature business. The potential anticompetitive costs of encouraging such a rationalization of production facilities to continue to make declining products available would have to be weighed against the expected benefits to some subset of consumers within the market which could be gratified by obtaining a continuing supply of the declining product.

The findings from this study highlight the discrepancy between a market-based rationalization of declining industry structures and a governmental solution based upon antitrust policies or other intervention. It would be expected that rational and orderly patterns of exits are preferable to business managers over the chaos or wastefully volatile price-cutting the antitrust laws foster which drives all producers out of the industry. In an industry suffering from excess capacity due to declining demand, an orderly retreat has greater intuitive appeal than the irrational dynamic conditions which actually occurred.

U.S. antitrust policy has no provision for a "failing industry," as does the spirit of European antitrust decisions. If the market mechanism does not in this instance permit rational decisions regarding who should exit and at what time, then perhaps U.S. antitrust policy might be modified in this one small respect to accommodate pooling activities in declining industries to attain the desired rational behavior.

The questions regarding equity in paying for this availability of the declining product are also in the bailiwick of the public policymaker. The evidence from this study suggests that higher prices would be needed to sustain production of many declining products. The need to encourage technological process does not necessarily mean older products are doomed to extinction, provided that the technological laggards or others who do not wish to convert to the substitute products will be willing to pay the higher rents which would be necessary to indemnify the producers or obsolescing products.

If consumers are willing to pay high prices for obsolescing products, the market will tend to provide them if the rents from them are adequate and if no more attractive use for the investment exists elsewhere, but findings from this study have indicated that these rents may be more frequently extracted by retailers (who are remunerated for slowly moving shelf-space allocations) than by the manufacturers themselves.

Public policymakers who wish to encourage the mobility of resources from low-return to high-return industries should recognize the stultifying impact of exit barriers upon the ease of resource movements. Governmental policies themselves may actually discourage timely exits. While it is possible that some government programs (such as compensation for import competition) could help the firm exit in an orderly fashion, other interventions could harm the profitability of the firm by keeping it in the industry longer than a free and unfettered market might encourage it to remain.

Several of the studies of endgame illustrated the implicit trade-offs of national employment goals versus quality of life. This study's industry chapters focus attention upon the enormous power of legislation (or even publicly supported programs) to shape or destroy an industry. Further research in this area appears to be needed.

Findings from this study could be interpreted to suggest that the accounting treatments of reporting the divestiture or shutdown of a declining business make timely exits inordinately difficult to execute. Rather than allow a company to switch to a more rapid form of depreciation to expedite the retirement of excess capacity (which may be continuing to operate in the industry for economic exit barrier reasons alone), reporting rules keep firms locked into their investment mistakes. The elimination of reserves (allocated in the past for the contingency of a need to shut down a capital-intensive business unit) will likely exacerbate this situation because continuing operation of unprofitable divestiture candidates to offset reporting write-offs will be necessary without the continuation of these reserves.

The evidence from this study of declining demand also supports the observations of business critics who have argued that the timing of major business divestitures or other investment activities is influenced heavily by taxes. This study indicated that some firms' divestitures of declining businesses were timed to minimize the recognition of other gains or to capture in full other types of incentives. If the tax code is so powerful as a tool for policymaking, greater investigation of it in rationalizing the structure of declining industries may be appropriate if such an objective is desirable from a public-policy perspective.

Bibliography

Chapters 1 and 2

Aguilar, Francis Joseph. *Scanning the Business Environment*. New York: Macmillan, 1967.

Alexander, R.S., "The Death and Burial of 'Sick' Products." *Journal of Marketing*, April 1964, pp. 1-7.

Ansoff, H. Igor. *Corporate Strategy*. New York: McGraw-Hill, 1965.

_____ . "Managing Strategic Surprise by Response to Weak Signals." *California Management Review* 18 (Winter 1975):21.

Bain, Joe S. *Industrial Organization*, Second Edition. New York: John Wiley & Sons, 1968.

Baumol, W.J. *Business Behavior, Value, and Growth*. New York: Harcourt, Brace, 1967.

Berenson, Conrad. "Pruning the Product Line." *Business Horizons* 6 (Summer 1963):63-70.

Berg, Thomas L., and Shuchman, Abe. *Product Strategy and Management*. New York: Holt, Rinehart, and Winston, Inc., 1963.

Bettauer, A. "Strategy for Divestment." *Harvard Business Review*, March-April 1967.

_____ . "New Strategy for Divestiture." *Harvard Business Review*, March-April 1969.

Boston Consulting Group. *Perspectives on Experience*. Boston: Boston Consulting Group, 1972.

Brien, John M. *Corporate Market Planning*. New York: John Wiley & Sons, Inc., 1967.

Buzzell, Robert D. "Competitive Behavior and Product Life Cycles." In *New Ideas for Successful Marketing*, edited by John S. Wright and Jac L. Goldstucker. Chicago: American Marketing Association, 1966, pp. 46-68.

Buzzell, Robert D.; Gale, Bradley T.; and Sultan, Ralph G.M. "Market Share—A Key to Profitability." *Harvard Business Review*, January-February 1975.

Carter, Eugene E., and Cohen, Kalman J. "Portfolio Aspects of Strategic Planning." *Journal of Business Policy* 4 (Summer 1972):8-30.

Catry, Bernard, and Chevalier, Michel. "Market Share Strategy and the Product Life Cycle." *Journal of Marketing*, October 1974, p. 29.

Caves, Richard E. *American Industry: Structure, Conduct and Performance*, Third Edition. Englewood Cliffs, N.J.: Prentice-Hall, 1972.

Caves, Richard E., and Porter, M.E. "Barriers to Exit." In *Essays on Industrial Organization in Honor of Joe S. Bain*, edited by Robert T. Masson and P. David Qualls. Cambridge, Mass.: Ballinger Publishing Company, 1976.

————. "From Entry Barriers to Mobility Barriers: Conjectural Decisions and Contrived Deference to New Competition." *Quarterly Journal of Economics*, (May 1977):241-261.

Clarkson, G.P.E., and Simon, H.E. "Simulation of Individual and Group Behavior." *American Economic Review* 50 (December 1960):920-932.

Clifford, Donald K., Jr. "Managing the Product Life Cycle." In *Corporate Strategy and Product Innovation*, ed. Robert R. Rothberg. New York: The Free Press, 1976, pp. 21-30.

Cohen, Kalman J., and Cyert, Richard M. "Strategy: Formulation, Implementation, and Monitoring," In *Corporate Strategy and Product Innovation*, ed. Robert R. Rothberg. New York: The Free Press, 1976, pp. 51-68.

————. *Theory of the Firm*. Englewood Cliffs, N.J.: Prentice-Hall, 1965.

Conley, Patrick. "Experience Curves as a Planning Tool." In *Corporate Strategy and Product Innovation*, ed. Robert R. Rothberg. New York: The Free Press, 1976, pp. 307-318.

Cowling, K. *Market Structure and Corporate Behavior*. London: Gray-Mills, 1972.

Cox, William E., Jr. "Product Life Cycles as Marketing Models." *Journal of Business*, October 1967, pp. 375-384.

Cyert, Richard M., and March, James G. *A Behavioral Theory of the Firm*. Englewood Cliffs, N.J.: Prentice-Hall, 1963.

Davis, J.W. "The Strategic Divestment Decision." *Long Range Planning*, February 1974.

Dhalla, Nariman K., and Yuspeh, Sonia. "Forget the Product Life Cycle Concept!" *Harvard Business Review*, January-February 1976.

"Disinvestment: Two Successful Cases." *Corporate Financing*, May-June 1970.

Fellner, William J. *Competition among the Few: Oligopoly and Similar Market Structures*. New York: Knopf, 1949.

Fox, Harold W. "A Framework for Functional Coordination." *Atlanta Economic Review* 23:6 (1973):8-11.

Galbraith, John Kenneth. *American Capitalism*. New York: Houghton-Mifflin, 1956.

Gilmour, Stuart Clark. "The Divestment Decision Process," Unpublished doctoral diss., Harvard Business School, 1973.

Gorlel, Peter, and Long, James. *Essentials of Product Planning*. New York: McGraw-Hill, 1973.

Grayson, C.J. *Decisions Under Uncertainty*. Cambridge, Mass.: Division of Research, Harvard Business School, 1960.

Hatten, K.J.; Schendel, Dan E.; and Cooper, Arnold C. "A Strategic Model of the U.S. Brewing Industry, 1952-1971." *Working Paper* (H.B.S. 76-24), Division of Research, Graduate School of Business Administration, Harvard University.

Hayes, R. "New Emphasis on Divestment Opportunities." *Harvard Business Review*, July-August 1972.

_____ . "Optimal Strategies for Divestiture." *Operations Research*, March-April 1969.

Henderson, Bruce D. "The Experience Curve—Reviewed." *Careers and the MBA*. Boston: Boston Consulting Group, 1975, pp. 47-57.

Hilton, P. "Divestiture: The Strategic Move on the Corporate Chessboard." *Management Review*, March 19, 1972.

Hise, Richard T., and McGinnis, Michael A. "Product Elimination: Practice Policies and Ethics." *Business Horizons*, June 1975, pp. 25-32.

Hofer, Charles W. "Toward a Contingency Theory of Business Strategy." *Academy of Management Journal*, December 1975.

Hutchinson, A.C. "Planned Euthanasia for Old Products." *Long Range Planning*, December 1971.

Johnson, Michael L. "End of the Line for Weak Products?" *Industry Week*, September 15, 1975, pp. 25-29.

_____ . "Pruning Products to Pad Profits." *Industry Week*, May 31, 1976, pp. 37-40.

Kaplan, A.D.H.; Dirlam, J.B.; and Lanzillotti, R.F. *Pricing in Big Business*. Washington, D.C.: Brookings, 1958.

Kelly, Eugene J. *Marketing Planning and Competitive Strategy*. Englewood Cliffs, N.J.: Prentice-Hall, 1972.

Kollat, David T.; Blackwell, Roger D.; and Robeson, James F. *Strategic Marketing*. New York: Holt, Rinehart, and Winston, 1972.

Kotler, Philip. *Marketing Decision Makng: A Model-Building Approach*. New York: Holt, Rinehart, and Winston, 1971.

_____ . *Marketing Management: Analysis, Planning, and Control*. Englewood Cliffs, N.J.: Prentice-Hall, 1972, chapter 12.

_____ . "Phasing Out Weak Products." *Harvard Business Review*, March-April 1965.

Kotler, Philip, and Bloom, Paul N. "Strategies for High Market-Share Companies." *Harvard Business Review*, November-December 1975.

Kotler, Philip, and Levy, Sidney J. "Demarketing, Yes, De-marketing." *Harvard Business Review*, November-December 1971.

Laflen, Milton L. "Product Life Cycle Analysis of the Semi-Conductor Industry." *Arizona Business Review*, May 1967, pp. 122-129.

Levitt, Theodore. "Exploit the Product Life Cycle." *Harvard Business Review*, November-December 1965.

————. *Marketing for Business Growth*. New York: McGraw-Hill Book Company, 1974.

Lovejoy, F.A. *Divestment for Profit*. New York: Financial Executive Research Foundation, 1971.

Luce, D., and Raiffa, H. *Games and Decisions*. New York: John Wiley, 1957.

Luck, David J. *Product Policy and Strategy*. Englewood Cliffs, N.J.: Prentice-Hall, 1977, chapter 7.

Markham, Jesse W. "An Alternative Approach to the Concept of Workable Competition." *American Economic Review*, June 1950, pp. 349-361.

Markham, Jesse W., and Papanek, Gustav F., eds. *Industrial Organization and Economic Development in Honor of E.S. Mason*. Boston: Houghton Mifflin, 1970.

Marvin, Philip. "Developing a Product Strategy. In *AMA Management Report No. 39*, Elizabeth Marting. New York: Management Association, 1959, pp. 11-34.

McDonald, John. *Strategy in Poker, Business, and War*. New York: W.W. Norton, 1950.

McGuire, J.W. *Theories of Business Behavior*. Englewood Cliffs, N.J.: Prentice-Hall, 1964.

Michel, George C. "Product Petrification: A New Stage in the Life Cycle Theory." *California Management Review*, Fall 1971, pp. 81-94.

Narver, John C., and Savitt, Ronald. *The Marketing Economy: An Analytical Approach*. New York: Holt, Rinehart, and Winston, 1971.

Nees, Danielle B. "Research Project on the Divestment Decision Process." Unpublished manuscript, Harvard University, April 1976.

Norton Company. "Strategic Planning for Diversified Business Operations." ICCH 1-377-044.

Patton, Arch. "Top Management's Stake in a Product's Life Cycle." *Management Review*. New York: American Management Association, June 1959, pp. 3-26.

Phillips, Almarin. *Market Structure, Organization, and Performance*. Cambridge, Mass.: Harvard University Press, 1962.

Polli, Rolando, and Cook, Victor. "Validity of the Product Life Cycle." *Journal of Business*, October 1969, pp. 385-400.

Porter, Michael E. "A Framework for Assessing Competitors." Unpublished manuscript, Harvard University, March 1977.

————. *Interbrand Choice, Strategy, and Bilateral Market Power*. Cambridge, Mass.: Harvard University Press, 1976.

————. "Note on the Structural Analysis of Industries." ICCH 4-376-054.

_____ . "Please Note Location of Nearest Exit: Exit Barriers and Strategic and Organizational Planning." *California Management Review* 19:2 (Winter 1976):21-33.

Raiffa, Howard. *Decision Analysis*. Reading, Mass.: Addison-Wesley Press, 1968.

Richards, Max D. "An Exploratory Study of Strategic Failure." *Academy of Management-Proceedings*. Boston: AMA, 1973.

Rodger, Leslie W., ed. *Marketing Concepts and Strategies in the Next Decade*. New York: John Wiley & Sons, 1973.

Rothe, James T. "The Product Elimination Decision." *MSU Business Topics* 18 (Autumn 1970):45-52.

Schelling, Thomas C. *The Strategy of Conflict*. London: Oxford University Press, 1960.

Scherer, Frederic M. *Industrial Market Structure and Economic Performance*. Chicago: Rand-McNally, 1970.

Schoeffler, Sidney; Buzzell, R.D.; and Heany, D.F. "Impact of Strategic Planning on Profit Performance." *Harvard Business Review*, March-April 1974.

Shubik, Martin. *Strategy and Market Structure*. New York: Wiley, 1959.

Smallwood, John E. "The Product Life Cycle: A Key to Strategic Marketing Planning." *MSU Business Topics* 21, (Winter 1973):29-35.

Speiser, M.M. "Corporate Divestitures: How to Sell Off a Subsidiary." *Management Review*, April 1969.

Staudt, Thomas; Taylor, Donald A.; and Bowersox, Donald. *A Management Introduction to Marketing*. Englewood Cliffs, N.J.: Prentice-Hall, 1976.

Steenbruner, J.D. *The Cybernetic Theory of Decision*. N.J.: Princeton University Press, 1974.

Steiner, George A. *Top Management Planning*, New York: Macmillan, 1969.

Stigler, George J. *Organization of Industry*, Homewood, Ill.: Irwin, 1968.

Stone, Merlin. *Product Planning: An Integrated Approach*. New York: John Wiley & Sons, 1976, chapter 4.

Talley, Walter J., Jr. "Profiting from Declining Product." *Business Horizons* 7 (Spring 1964):77-84.

Telser, Lester G. *Competition, Collusion, and Game Theory*. Chicago: Aldine/Atherton, 1972.

Thackray, J. "Disinvestment: How to Shrink and Profit." *European Business*, Spring 1976.

_____ . "Spin-off—A New Lease on Corporate Life." *European Business*, Winter 1972.

Tilles, Seymour. "How to Evaluate Corporate Strategy." *Harvard Business Review*, July-August 1963.

———— . "Strategies for Allocating Funds." *Harvard Business Review*, January-February 1966.

Udell, Jon G. *Successful Marketing Strategies*. Madison, Wis.: Mimir, 1972.

Vignola, Leonard, Jr. *Strategic Divestment*. New York: American Management Association, 1974.

Wallender, H.W. "A Planned Approach to Divestment." *Columbia Journal of World Business*, Spring 1973.

Wasson, Chester R. *Dynamic Competitive Strategy and Product Life Cycles*. St. Charles, Ill.: Challenge Books, 1974.

Webster, Frederick E., Jr. *Marketing for Managers*. New York: Harper & Row, 1974.

Chapter 4

The following sources were especially useful in preparing the analysis of the receiving-tube endgame.

Books

Pettingill. *Electronic Components: Production and Related Data*, U.S. Department of Commerce, 1959.

Marcus, Pettingill, and Stearns. *The U.S. Consumer Electronics Industry*. Office of Business Research and Analysis, Department of Commerce, 1976.

Periodicals

Business Week
Electronics
Electronic News
Fortune
Wall Street Journal

The following articles were especially useful:

"The Electronics Era." *Fortune*, July 1951, pp. 40-46.
"The Battle of the Components." *Fortune*, May 1957, pp. 136-138.
"Transistors Find Way into More Products." *Wall Street Journal*, November 11, 1962.

"The Coming Battle for Color TV." *Fortune*, January 1966, pp. 144-147.
"Shrinking TV Tube Sockets Plus Imports Jab U.S. Makers." *Electronic News*, June 23, 1969.
"Little Left of Receiving Tube Market." *Electronics*, August 5, 1976.

Corporate Annual Reports (of firms traced through endgame).

Corporate Interviews, five producers (or former producers of receiving tubes), two electronics components merchandisers, one television-repair person.

A special acknowledgement is due to the Reference Library staff of the Dewey Library, Sloan School, Massachusetts Institute of Technology, for their reference services and assistance in preparing this chapter.

Chapter 5

The following sources were especially useful in preparing the analysis of the synthetic soda-ash endgame.

Books

Noble and Innes. *Marketing Guide to the Chemical Industry*. Fairfield: N.J.: Charles Kline & Co., Inc., 1968.
Reuben and Burstall. *The Chemical Economy; A Guide to The Technology and Economics of the Chemical Industry*, London: Longman Press.

Periodicals

Business Week
Chemical and Engineering News
Chemical Marketing Reporter
Chemical Purchasing
Chemical Week
European Chemical News
Industry Week
Journal of Commerce
U.S. Industry Outlook
Wall Street Journal

"Chemical Briefs—Soda Ash." *Chemical Purchasing*, June 1976, pp. 42-47, 66.

"Back to Nature for Soda Ash." *Business Week*, July 19, 1976, p. 49.

"Time to Get Out!" *Chemical Purchasing*, July 1976, pp. 42-47.

"The Only Way Out at Saltville." *Chemical Week*, August 19, 1970, pp. 91-94.

"Synthetic Soda Ash Seen as an Endangered Species: Allied Closes Lousiana Plant." *Chemical Marketing Reporter*, May 5, 1975.

"Natural Product Leads Surge in Soda Ash." *Chemical and Engineering News*, November 24, 1975, pp. 10-12.

". . . And Then There Was One," *Chemical Week*, November 29, 1978, p. 41.

Chapter 6

The following sources were especially useful in preparing the analysis of the baby-foods endgame.

Periodicals

Advertising Age
Barrons'
Business Week
Class, Brand, YTD $
Consumer Reports
Dun's Review
Financial World
Fortune
New York Times
Product Marketing
Progressive Grocer
Wall Street Journal

The following articles were especially useful.

"The Lower Birthrate Crimps the Baby Food Market." *Business Week*, July 13, 1974.

"It's a Bear Market for Babies, Too." *Fortune*, December 1974, p. 139.

"The Baby Business: Can You Succeed in a Failing Market?" *Product Marketing*, April 1977.

"Why Gerber Makes Such an Inviting [Takeover] Target." *Business Week*, June 27, 1977.

Other Documents

Brief for the Assistant Attorney General in Charge of the Antitrust Division: In Support of Request by Swift & Company to Modify 1920 Consent Decree to Allow Swift to Compete in the Food for Babies Market, June 1962.
Corporate Annual Reports (of firms traced through endgame).
Corporate Interviews: three producers of baby foods, two producers of baby products, one pediatrician.

Chapter 7

The following sources provided useful information for the preparation of the chapter which analyzed the percolator coffee-maker endgame.

Periodicals

Advertising Age
Appliance
Barrons'
Home Furnishings Daily
Mart
Merchandising Week

See especially:

"Drip Cuts Department Store Perc Sales; Expected to Hold at 80% of Total." *Home Furnishings Daily*, November 5, 1975.
"Price Sells Percs Discounters Find." *Home Furnishings Daily*, November 6, 1975.
Corporate Annual Reports (of firms traced through endgame).
Corporate Interviews: four percolator coffee-maker manufacturers, three major outlets for percolator sales (New York, Chicago, Los Angeles), one former small housewares appliances sales representative.
A special acknowledgment is due to the research staff of Fairchild Publications, Inc., in New York City for their reference services and assistance in preparing this chapter.

Chapter 8

The following sources were especially useful in preparing the analysis of the cigar endgame.

Periodicals

Advertising Age
Barrons'
Business Week
Financial World
Forbes
Fortune
New York Times
Tobacco International
Wall Street Journal

The following articles were especially useful.

"A Good Five Cent Cigar: An Old Industry is Profiting from New Technology, Better Products, Growing Markets." *Barrons'*, November 11, 1963.
"Cigar Outlook Good (Maybe)." *Advertising Age*, March 30, 1964.
"Huffing and Puffing: Cigar Makers Have Increased Sales Much Faster Than Profits." *Barrons'*, May 3, 1965.
"Millions of People Just Won't Smoke Cigars." *Fortune*, September 1965.
"US Cigar Review." *Tobacco International*, November 26, 1971.
"Cigar Sales Down Again in '75; No Changes Predicted in Consumption Patterns." *Tobacco International*, January 1976.
"Hope for Cigars May Rest in Beer Sales and the Post War Baby Boom." *Tobacco International*, March 3, 1978.

Corporate Annual Reports (of the firms traced through endgame).

Corporate Interviews: Three wide-line cigarmakers, one specialized cigarmaker, tobacconist-shop proprietor, trade association.

This chapter relies heavily upon information developed by the statisticians of the Cigar Association of America, Inc., for much of the information about shipments by IRS classifications.

Chapter 9

The following sources were especially useful in preparing the analysis of the rayon and acetate endgame.

Books

Coleman, D.C. *Courtaulds: An Economic and Social History*, Volume II. New York: Oxford University Press, 1969.
Markham, Jesse W. *Competition in the Rayon Industry*. Cambridge, Mass.: Harvard University Press, 1955.

Periodicals

Advertising Age
Barrons'
Business Week
Chemical Marketing Reporter (Oil, Paint and Drug Reporter)
Chemical and Engineering News
Chemical Week
Daily News Record
Financial World
Forbes
Fortune
New York Times
Textile Journal
Textile Organon
Textile Reporter
Wall Street Journal

The following articles were particularly useful.

"Mystery: The American Viscose Company." *Fortune*, July 1937, pp. 40-47, 106.
"The U.S. Rayon Industry: After 65 Years, It's Come a Long Way from Artificial Silk." *Daily News Record*, September 18, 1975.
"The Rayon Story Retold." *Textile Industries*, July 1978.
"Shiny Disco Look Helps Acetate Fiber to Oversold Position." *Daily News Record*, August 21, 1978.
"Saga of FMC Fiber and Avtex Illustrates Management Buyouts' Risks and Rewards." *Wall Street Journal*, December 15, 1978.

Corporate Annual Reports (of firms traced through the endgame).

Corporate Interviews: seven cellulosic fibers producers, two raw-materials suppliers, and one textile producer.

A special acknowledgment is due to the research staff of the Reference Library at Fairchild Publications, Inc., New York City, for their reference services and assistance in preparing this chapter.

Chapter 10

The following sources were especially helpful in preparing the analysis of the acetylene endgame.

Books

Stobaugh, Robert. *Petrochemical Manufacturing and Marketing Guide*, vol. 2. Houston: Gulf Publishing Company, 1965.
Hahn, Alfred. *The Petrochemical Industry: Market and Economics*. New York: McGraw-Hill, 1966.

Special Studies

Stanford Research Institute studies on the economics of acetylene-versus ethylene-based hydrocarbon chemistry, including *SRI Chemical Economic Handbook*.

Periodicals

Business Week
Chemical and Engineering News
Chemical Engineering
Chemical Marketing Reporter
Chemical Week
Oil and Gas Journal

The following articles were especially useful.

"New Markets for Acetylene." *Chemical and Engineering News*. August 2, 1954, pp. 3032-3034.
"Acetylene Triple Play." *Chemical Week*, February 29, 1964, pp. 61-63.
"Acetylene Chemical Industry in America." *Chemical and Engineering News*, July 18, 1949, pp. 2062-2066.

Corporate Annual Reports (of firms traced through endgame).

Corporate Interviews: conversations with seven producers (or former producers) of acetylene.

Index

Index

About the Author

Kathryn Rudie Harrigan is an assistant professor of business and social policy at The University of Texas at Dallas. She received the D.B.A. from Harvard University and was the 1979 recipient of the General Electric Award for Outstanding Research in Strategic Management. Dr. Harrigan was selected as IBM honorary research fellow by the American Association of University Women for her research concerning declining industries. Her current research includes industry structural dynamics, strategic planning, and corporate governance.